MW01258917

# THE DEFICIT LIE

# THE DEFICIT LIE

## EXPOSING THE MYTH of the NATIONAL DEBT

Rick Boettger, Ph.D.

THE SUMMIT GROUP • FORT WORTH, TEXAS

T H E  S U M M I T  G R O U P

1227 West Magnolia, Suite 500 • Fort Worth, Texas 76104



99 98 97 96 95 94     5 4 3 2 1

Printed in the United States

Library of Congress Cataloging-in-Publication Data

Boettger, Rick, 1948-
The deficit lie: exposing the myth of the national debt/Rick Boettger
p. cm.
Includes bibliographical references and index
ISBN 1-56530-159-5
1. Debts, Public - -United States. 2. Budget deficits--United States. 3. Recessions--United States. 4. Money Supply--United States. I. Title.
HJ8101.B64 1994
336.3'4'0973--dc20     94-3644
CIP

*Jacket and book design by David Sims*

*To the memory of Gino*

*With hope for my graduating seniors*

*And in trust to my daughter*

# Contents

*Preface* .................................................................. *ix*

**PART I: The Problem and Solution in Brief**

1. Introduction:
Don't Blame the Economy—Blame the Economics .......3

2. The Problem:
Permanent Unemployment Caused by the
*Real* Deficit in the Money Supply ..................................23

3. The Solution:
Spend More and Tax Less ............................................51

**PART II: The Problem: The Old Economics of "Scarcity"**

4. The Myth of the Deficit:
Apocalypse Never ........................................................75

5. The Big Lie:
The Inflationary Obsessions of the
Economic Anorexics ....................................................85

6. The Lesser Lies:
The Bogeyman Defense—The "Cure"
Causes the Disease ....................117

7. The Power of Bad Ideas:
Butcher-Generals and Bloodletting ....................139

8. Supposed "Scarcity"
In an Age of No Scarce Resources ....................159

**PART III: The Solution: The Economics of National Abundance**

9. Real Wealth:
What It is and Where It Comes From ....................177

10. Balancing Money and Abundance:
The "Cyber-nomic" Gas Pedal on the Money Supply.197

11. Cracking the Paradox of Productivity:
Utilizing Our Real Wealth ....................245

**PART IV: The Future and How to Get There**

12. Practical Political Action:
Here's What I Want You to Do ....................277

13. Creative Spending in a Secure World ....................307

14. The National Dividend:
Your Share of America, Inc ....................335

Footnotes ....................353

Bibliography ....................373

Appendix:
A Critical Review of Other Books on the Economy ...377

Acknowledgments ....................383

Index ....................387

# Preface

Many people have spent too much time talking about and fretting over a national debt, which actually isn't there. It's a mirage, a myth, a phony creation of economists who wouldn't know real wealth if it came up and bit them where it hurts. Sad to say, this theoretical national deficit in the United States has taken on a life of its own, much like one of those horrible monsters in a fifties' B movie that exists only because of man's foolish tampering with nature, science, or some such thing.

By the time you finish this book, you will understand three major points:

1. ***The so-called "deficit" is a myth.*** What we call the "federal deficit" is an irrelevant accounting error. It did *not* cause the recession, nor does it fuel the recession. In fact, *none* of the evils blamed on this bogus "deficit" are true. Rather, the tax increases and spending cuts made to cure the deficit are exactly what *caused* the recession.
2. ***Our only problem is a shortage of cash.*** We have created a great abundance of real wealth. Nothing is scarce anymore. But we haven't printed enough money to let us work and earn

the wealth already on the shelves. The *real* deficit causing any recession is the shortage of cash we have printed compared to the wealth of goods and services we have already produced.

3. ***The solution: Spend more and tax less.*** A safe, conservative path to jobs and prosperity is to increase government spending and reduce taxes 1 percent each year, indefinitely. This will slowly reduce the true deficit in the size of the money supply, creating new jobs which in turn will allow us to use our existing real wealth and increase production.

The Great Recession will never end if we keep raising taxes and cutting spending. There is no "recovery." Miniscule improvements do not change the fact that our economy is still sick. Fortunately, a simple, common-sense approach will get the economy going again. All that stops our recovery is an ungrounded fear of the deficit. But bad ideas, even when they make no sense at all, have had disastrous effects throughout world history. The old economics solved the problem of scarcity, but now, in a time of abundance, new principles apply. The main principle is to create enough money to match our real wealth. Applying these new principles allows us to work toward a better world.

That is the substance and flow of *The Deficit Lie.* Part I describes the problem and solution briefly. Part II shows what's wrong with the old thinking, the economics of scarcities, and deficits. Part III develops the new, post-deficit economics of national abundance. Part IV tells what actions we need to take.

Breaking down this preview further, the three chapters of Part I give an overview of the book. Chapter 1 is a form of the speech I give to audiences. The critical, *trick* question is, "How have you *personally* been hurt by the deficit?" The trick is that no one has been hurt by the bogus "deficit." People are hurt by the recession, which is the opposite of the deficit. The difference between the bogus "federal deficit" and the real deficit in the money supply is illustrated by what I call the Parable of the Miracle Cancer Cure. The second half of the chapter presents the short answers I give to questions I have fielded at these speeches.

Chapter 2 describes the Great Recession and its causes. Millions of people are losing jobs, businesses are losing customers, investors are lacking decent growth or dividend opportunities, taxes are rising, people can't sell their homes, and retirement programs are in danger of obsolescence. The old guard of economists one minute offers false hopes for early recovery; the next minute, they're pinning misdirected blame on innocent scapegoats (productivity, foreign trade). But these "old-timers" caused the recession themselves, through the Federal Reserve's "Soft Landing" fiasco. If we continue to follow their prescriptions, employment and spending power will continue to spiral downward, international tensions will rise, and our domestic confidence will continue to wane. Although America will not collapse, tens of millions will continue to suffer greatly. Even the rich are far less well off than they should be.

Chapter 3 outlines the solution to our economic problems. The true deficit causing the recession is the *shortage of money* in circulation compared to the amount of real wealth we have already produced. Suppose the government had ten thousand doses of a cancer cure, but the economists printed only six thousand ration coupons. Much of the medicine—like much of our real wealth—would go to waste, expiring on the shelves: exactly what happens with unsold homes, cars, and airline seats. The false deficit is the irrelevant discrepancy between the amount of money the government thinks it should spend and the amount it actually does—whereas the true deficit is the gap between the amount of money we have (small) and the amount of real wealth that backs it up (large). The old economists would rather let real wealth go to waste than print more coupons or money to let us use it. What backs up money is not government promises or even gold, but a nation's real wealth—which we have in abundance. The government's main job is to print a currency both sound and sufficient enough to provide employment that maintains and increases that real wealth. *If we do, the "national debt" can be paid off at any time, more easily than a bank or corporation can cover its own obligations.*

The five chapters in Part II show what's wrong with the old economic thinking. Chapter 4 tries to make sense out of the nation's deficit obsession, and demonstrates how wrong the deficit fanatics are in every one of their arguments. The language they use to discuss deficits has been more hysterical than logical. Deficit mongers constantly predict apocalypses that never occur. People want fiscal responsibility, and confuse their own prudent checkbook writing with a much different animal, the economy of a nation. Calm, renowned writers have tried to explain the truth of deficits, but they have been drowned out by the rhetoric of the deficit mongers.

Chapter 5 confronts the mongers' biggest lie: their inflation obsession. In fact, deficits have no relation to inflation. Six fallacies about inflation are uncovered, and the ten real causes are described.

Chapter 6 dismisses the other spurious harms the deficit and debt supposedly cause. Most of these accusations share the flaw that the deficit mongers' "cure" is actually what causes the disease they describe. Their claims are both factually wrong and conceptually nonsensical. The real disasters in the United States, Europe, and Japan have been caused not by the deficit itself, but by the attempts like our "soft landing" to reduce the deficits, or "balanced budget."

Chapter 7 explains the human reasons behind our obsession with the false deficit. The sad fact is that nations of people and their wisest advisers have made hideous mistakes throughout history. One excellent analogy to this disaster is that caused by the British generals in World War I. Their self-destructive military strategy called for the "sacrifice" of nearly a million British soldiers by marching them into German machine guns. A second bad idea was the ancient medical practice of bloodletting, which killed millions. Bad ideas persist because: 1) they seem simple, 2) people in charge never change their minds despite any amount of evidence, 3) their followers revere leaders and numbers, and 4) we refuse to accept win-win situations. Blaming each other or the U.S.

President won't help as long as we believe in the Golden Idol of the "deficit."

Chapter 8 reviews the old economics, which studied the "allocation of scarce resources." But nothing is scarce now, not even unique collectibles. Thus, the old economics is as irrelevant as an aerodynamic propeller in outer space, outside earth's atmosphere. It also assumes other patent untruths, such as full employment, Say's Law (which says that supply generates its own demand), and high demand causes prices to rise (now they actually *fall,* as with computers). The old economics is in a sense the victim of its own success. Even before the supply-side economics came along in the 1980s, we were on our way to producing more wealth than we knew how to use. But economics has lagged behind the great and surprising advances of other sciences in the twentieth century. Stuck with their gloom-and-doom prescriptions, which can only cause—not cure—recessions, some old economists want to surrender. However, just because the wing flaps are useless doesn't mean it's impossible to steer an aircraft. Old sciences always give way to new.

The four chapters of Part III develop the new economics of national abundance. Chapter 9 focuses on the creation and distribution of real wealth, including not only goods and services, but also previously unmeasured intangibles—peace, security, human welfare, and the state of our natural environment. Money is merely a tool, a bookkeeping device. It must not be an end in itself, but a *means*—a tool used to create and distribute the real wealth for which money stands. When resources were scarce, money had to be scarce in order for the currency to remain *sound*; but now when resources are abundant, economics must refocus on maintaining a *sufficient* money supply.

Chapter 10 details how we must maintain this balance between money and real wealth. Too much money relative to the supply of real wealth means inflation; too little means recession and the waste of real wealth. The balance should be maintained *cybernetically,* the way you control the speed of your car by watching the speedometer and pressing the gas pedal. The more real wealth we create, the more money we not only can but must print to match it.

Chapter 11 offers the key prescriptions for a healthy national economy. We create real wealth by being peaceful and productive, writing good regulations and international trade agreements, enhancing our infrastructure and education, and improving human welfare and social justice. The paradox—one the old economics ignored but which *must* be overcome—is that rising productivity puts people out of work, which destroys their ability to produce anything at all. The first step in cracking this paradox is to maintain people's ability to buy our wealth until new jobs are created. Otherwise, those people who still have jobs, even the rich, will themselves inevitably suffer in their turn. The government can help private enterprise create more real wealth. In fact, the feds should be encouraged to do so by being paid partially on commission instead of only on salary. Internationally, the West will be overjoyed to have a Big Customer, and will eventually employ the economics of abundance themselves.

Finally, the three chapters in Part IV tell what actions we need to take. Chapter 12 confronts practical realities. Debate or amusement is not an end in itself. Total conversion of the deficit mongers is not necessary—shutting them up is enough. The main goal is to change voter opinion about the deficit. The electorate can change the votes of their political leaders, who presently vote to increase taxes and reduce spending only because their constituents are demanding "deficit reduction." Ending the Great Recession will be accomplished only by the democratic political process, not by wiser economic policies offered by the "econorexic experts" presently leading the country downhill.

Chapter 13 sketches the wonderful opportunities we have to create a new and vigorous nation. This can be accomplished as soon as we break the chains of our deficit obsession. The government should print one dollar to create two dollars' worth of real wealth, but not actually *do* the work itself. Private enterprise can be employed to renew the infrastructure, clean up the environment, advance our space and weather research, encourage world peace, provide health care for all, rehabilitate the addicted, and bring hope to our ghettos. Failure to change means indefinitely extending the Great Recession. We can let international tensions increase until a new nuclear threat arises. Our young people can give up on having the simple opportunity to work hard that we and our parents had.

Chapter 14 anticipates a future in which we not only have jobs, but share equitably in the profits through the "National Dividend." Ultimately, with a better understanding of money and wealth, we can go beyond them, using both as necessary means to far greater ends.

# PART I

## The Problem and Solution in Brief

# 1

# Introduction: Don't Blame the Economy — Blame the Economics

This chapter is a version of the half-hour talk I've been giving for years, including representative questions and answers.

I'm going to start by asking *you* a question. It's the most important question about the economy, because the fate of the presidency of the United States rides on your answer—if you get it right, you get to be president. If not, hasta la vista, baby. Here it is: *How have you personally been hurt by the federal deficit?* Because it's such a difficult question, you don't have to answer it until the end, after you've had some time to think about it.

Meanwhile, I'm going to explain the difference between the bogus "federal deficit" you've read about and the *real* deficit that's causing the Great Recession we're in. You'll be able to figure it out yourself if you can see through the puzzle in the following . . .

## Parable of the Miracle Cancer Cure

Imagine scientists discovered a cure for cancer in a government laboratory, then proclaimed they could produce ten thousand doses of the cure in the first year. In turn, the government decided to ask its wisest economists for help in allocating this valuable medicine. They advised printing six thousand ration coupons, each good for one cure. Suppose Congress then tackled the difficult task of deciding exactly who would get the coupons. Among the factors considered were severity of the disease, age of the person, type of cancer, quotas of recipients by race and state of residence, and "merit" of the applicants.

Of course, the nation was divided by angry debate. Nonetheless, after fast-tracking the process in order to save lives, the government established the criteria, distributed the coupons, and administered the medicine. They made only one mistake: instead of printing the six thousand coupons the economists wanted, the government foolishly printed sixty-three hundred. The economists called the coupon overprinting the great *coupon deficit*. Anyway, of the one hundred thousand Americans with terminal cancer that year, sixty-three hundred were saved by the wonderful new miracle cure.

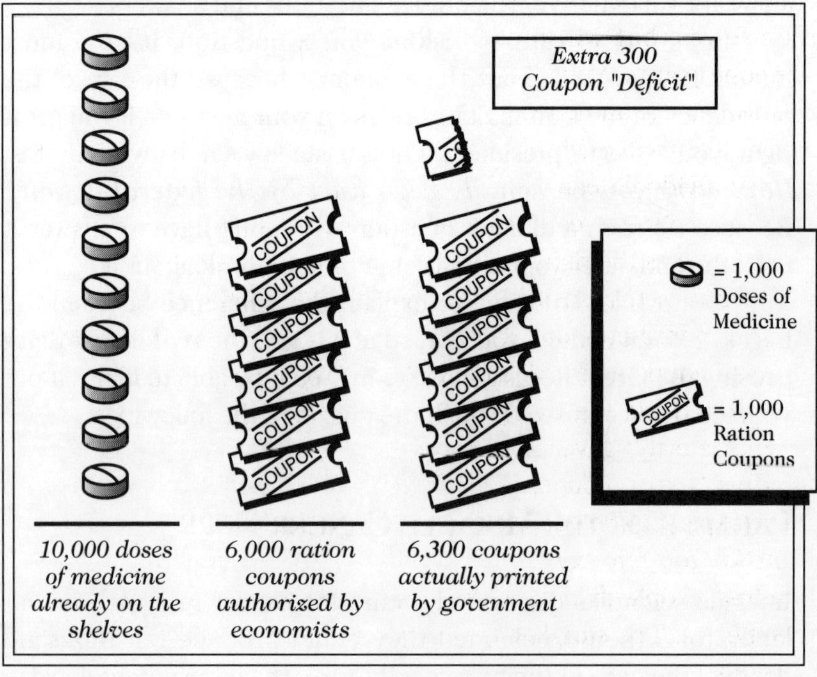


***Figure 1: Parable of the Cancer Medicine***

Notice that something went awry in this imaginary scenario, which actually is an analogy of what's really happening today with our economy. The cancer cure debate shifted from the problem of *allocation* to the problem of the great *deficit* between the number of coupons authorized and the number redeemed. As the years went on, this *deficit* kept occurring, accumulating into a huge *national debt* of coupons, a "deficit" and "debt" which were increasingly blamed for the sad deaths of cancer patients throughout the land. Even the cancer patients themselves blamed this deficit and debt for their inability to get a dose of the miracle cure. Meanwhile, unused doses continued to expire on the shelves every year, so no one bothered to open extra production facilities to make more.

So: *What's wrong with this picture?* Specifically, what would you recommend doing if you were called upon to advise the government? At this point in the talk, I pause to let people mull it over, while I show them Figure 1. The parable is just challenging enough that most people will not be able to figure out the trick themselves, but will recognize the answer immediately when someone points it out. The "someone" does not have to be me. I usually ask the audience to discuss the problem for a few minutes among themselves, in groups of three or four people. Although most individuals can't come up with the right answer on their own, most groups can. As I said, as soon as one person in the group suggests the right answer, everyone will agree.

What is the answer? The problem is not with the bogus three-hundred-coupon "deficit." The *real deficit* is thirty-seven hundred coupons, the difference between the sixty-three hundred printed and the ten thousand doses already on the shelves. The big mistake the government made was not the printing of three hundred "extra" coupons, but listening to the idiot economists in the first place. The economists made the fatal error of deciding to print *far too few* coupons. Because of their error, thirty-seven hundred people died needlessly while their medicine expired on the shelves. The simple solution to the problem is to *print more coupons.*

What does this cancer cure parable have to do with the Great Recession? Easy. First, our real miracle is not an imaginary cancer cure, but a *great abundance of real wealth* which is almost as miraculous. Think of it: is anything in short supply? To the contrary. The shelves of all our stores are overflowing. Car lots are full. More houses are for sale than people can afford to buy. Gold, airplane tickets, hotel rooms, Rolls Royces—we have shortages of *nothing*. Just as thirty-seven hundred doses of the cancer cure expired unused, we allow airline seats to fly empty, cars age on the lots, houses sit vacant, and resort hotel rooms and hospital rooms everywhere sit unoccupied. Meanwhile, people who want the "cancer cure," or, in real life, a share of our great abundance, suffer without.

*What does this cancer cure parable have to do with the Great Recession? Easy. First, our real miracle is not an imaginary cancer cure, but a great abundance of real wealth which is almost as miraculous.*

Second, the cause of the pointless waste is the same. Because of bad advice from our economists, we have not printed enough coupons—in real life, U.S. dollars. Our economists tell the government we should spend only a certain amount of money, which turns out to be far too little. The government overshoots the mark by a relatively small amount. Just as the three-hundred-coupon "deficit" is only a small fraction of the six-thousand-coupon budget (and a smaller fraction of the real wealth of ten thousand doses), our so-called "federal deficit" is only a small fraction of our budget (and a tiny fraction of the real wealth backing up the dollar).

The real deficit is the shortfall of coupons or dollars. The amount our economists call a "deficit" actually *helps* alleviate the pain of their tight-money dogma. What we have been calling a "deficit" has not caused the recession, but is a *solution* to the recession. In the parable, the bogus "deficit" should be thirteen times as big as it is in order to overcome the economists' error, and bring the number of coupons up to the number of doses of medicine. In real life, our bogus "federal deficit" should be a multiple of what it is in order to help overcome the pointless cash-flow problem our economists have cursed us with. Conversely, reducing the bogus deficit increases the real deficit of cash and helps cause the very problems the deficit hysterics cry about. "Deficit" reduction is the *disease*, not the cure.

This explanation is so obvious and simple, once you look at it the right way, you might assume that economists would understand it and be able to respond sensibly. But they have a shocking blind spot. They have *not* been "looking at it the right way."

Here's a test: Ask a friend of yours who claims to know a little bit about economics two questions. One, what does he think of our nation's real wealth? You will have to explain that real wealth is like the cancer cure medicine, not the ration coupons. The economists are so mesmerized by their creation (money or the ration coupons) that they have completely lost sight of what real wealth is. Real wealth is what we spend money to get; real wealth is what money only stands for. But the old economist will, first of all, not recognize either the existence or the importance of our great abundance of real wealth. You will have to point out the complete lack of scarcities, and he will have to scratch his head and think about it for a few seconds before agreeing. (Worse, he will think about it and remember some commodity or other—one or two out of thousands traded—that has gone up a few percent in price, as though that somehow indicated a shortage, therefore disproving the fact of our general abundance.)

Even worse than that, economists in general seem only able to describe our great abundance of real wealth as a *problem*. Our wealth of cars, steel, VCRs, computers, and everything else represents "over-production," "excess capacity," and "consumer surplus" which has been "dumped" on us. Their response to great abundance is to *get rid of it*. Thus, they have accused our great triumphs in productivity, leaner management, mechanization, and foreign trade of being the culprits in the recession. They would have regarded the thirty-seven hundred wasted doses of cancer medicine as problems of "overproduction."

*If an economist were responsible for dressing your growing child, he would shorten the kid's legs, rather than buy him longer pants.*

Back to your expert friend and the second of your two questions: Ask him how much money should be flowing through the economy. At first he'll chuckle at your naive question, because the economists have gotten themselves utterly confused as to what money is, even in their terms. They have so many versions of money, they have started giving them code numbers—"M1" is cash, "M2" includes savings, and so on through M, M1B, L, etc. They dither about, debating what goes in each category. But he'll stop chuckling when you ask whether he agrees with the monetarists that the money supply (by whatever measure) should ordinarily slowly increase a few percent per year. He'll mutter a few qualifications and yes-buts before agreeing, but he will. Then ask what basic economic principle states how large the money supply should be.

He'll start blustering. You might have thought I was unfair to make the parable's economists advise printing only six thousand coupons when ten thousand doses of medicine were already on the shelves. But our real-life economic wise men are exactly that stupid. Listen to your friend. If he ever gets around to saying that the amount of money should roughly match the amount of things for sale, *call me collect* (817-732-0329). Folks, the authorities running our economy, the folks who got Bush kicked out and who got Clinton to raise taxes, have no idea how much money we should print, other than it should be a little more than we had last year.

Thus, we have wasted real wealth, including people who want to work and are instead sitting at home or using half their skill. We converted a healthy economy into the 1990s' Great Recession by following the tight-money economists' prescription for a "soft landing." Germany and Japan followed. We've wasted our real wealth by squeezing our money supply for no reason. We asked our economists for advice, and they did us wrong.

So much for sad history. How can we fix what they have broken? Easy. *Spend more and tax less.* Don't sell even more T-bills to make up the difference between inflow from taxes and outflow for expenditures. Rather, we should follow the time-honored custom of what the economists shyly call "monetizing the debt," which in simple terms means "printing more money." The folks who brought us the Great Depression and the Great Recession will scream because the bogus "deficit" number they fear will get bigger. The economy will flourish because we will begin to reduce the real deficit—the gap between our abundant real wealth and our inadequate money supply.

The national economy needs to be run by an entirely new principle, exactly the opposite of the principles that cause recessions. Discussion of the economy is dominated by the bogeyman "federal deficit" that haunts the minds of America. People have confused the "deficit" with the *recession itself,* as proven by the trick presidential debate question. ("How have you personally been hurt by the deficit?" Keep thinking—we'll get back to it at the end of the chapter.) The deficit is an entirely imaginary beast, like the bogus "deficit" number in the parable. Just because a number can be measured doesn't prove it *means* anything. But both the politicians and the people rank the deficit as "Public Enemy No. 1." Thus they raise taxes and cut spending. Both actions cause job loss and our Great Recession.

The obsession with "deficit" reduction is a relic of the old thinking of tight-money economists as foolish as those who recommend printing only six thousand coupons in the parable. They mistakenly think we need to balance numbers with numbers and have completely lost sight of what the numbers stand for. We really need to balance the number of coupons with what the coupons stand for. We should have as much money as we have things for sale. If you have ten thousand doses, you should print ten thousand coupons. How obvious is that? Incredibly, however, our economists embrace a pathological fear of too much money, an obsession which makes them follow a different prescription: less money is better. Why? They offer a host of reasons, *all of which are wrong*. Their real reason is psychological. I call them "econo-rexics," because their hatred of money is as illogical as an anorexic's hatred of food, and just as harmful.

The old economics demands we *lower the deficit by raising taxes and cutting spending, keeping the money supply tight, no matter how many millions lose their jobs and how badly the infrastructure and society fall apart.*

*The new economics proposed here demands we create a sound but sufficient money supply, encouraging full employment through the creation of real wealth.* The key is the phrase "sound but sufficient." Too *little* money is as much of a problem as too much: we need the amount of money to balance the amount of real wealth for sale. Thus the key principle is "money/wealth balance," or "balancing money and wealth." In the parable, the ration coupon is "sound" as long as no more than ten thousand are printed. But the number of ration coupons is not "sufficient" if fewer than ten thousand are printed. Money must match real wealth. Without enough money, real wealth and real human lives are wasted.

Let's go back to the opening question. How have any of you been hurt *personally* by the "federal deficit" or "national debt"? Sorry, folks—that's the same trick question that cost George Bush the presidency. The trick is that *no one has been hurt by the so-called "federal deficit."* The number measured as the bogus deficit is the difference between income taxes and federal expenditures. So you have been hurt by the deficit only if you have been hurt by a tax that was too *low* or by the government spending *too much money on you*. Funny, but I can't find anyone who will admit to being hurt by a tax decrease or a government check in his name.

Here's how poor George got nailed. He got asked the trick question, and he stumbled around a bit, making a fool of himself, giving the pinheaded answers his advisers had coached him to give. Besides being wrong, those answers are abstractly impersonal, and the questioner jumped on him for it—"You *personally*," she interrupted, when he wandered off on the interest rates and such.

Then came the crucial moment. The moderator stepped in and made the same error our economists, Congress, and all of America have made. She mistakenly explained that the questioner, by referring to the national debt, "means more the recession, the economic problems." And that's the question Bill Clinton got to answer! He got to describe, compassionately, how people he knew in Arkansas had been hurt by higher taxes, reduced government services, bankruptcies, and lost jobs—all of which get worse the more we try to *reduce* the deficit. Which question would you prefer to answer, with the presidency on the line: How have you been hurt by the deficit? or How have you been hurt by the recession?

## QUESTIONS AND ANSWERS

### *What's wrong with the economy?*

SIMPLE. We don't have enough money. In just the last twenty years, we have earned a great fortune in *real wealth*. Real wealth is more important than money—it's all the goods and services we spend money to get. We as a nation have already earned this real wealth. How? We avoided war. We added machines. We're more productive. We allow free trade. As a result, we have a huge surplus of all the goods and services we could desire. But we have convinced ourselves we can't afford them! We have doubled the supply of real wealth, without adding anywhere near enough money to match. So we're letting that real wealth go to waste by not creating enough money to match it.

### *What do we have to do to fix it?*

SIMPLE AS WATER FLOWING DOWNHILL. The government has to print and spend more money, enough to give us the cash flow to enjoy our real wealth and produce even more. Right now, we as a nation are too cash poor to buy and enjoy the tremendous surplus abundance we have already created, much less create and buy new things. Our economic guideline should not be the so-called "federal deficit." The real bottom line is (1) a sound currency while allowing (2) useful employment in (3) wealth-creating enterprises. We can accomplish these goals in a safe, conservative fashion by raising spending 2 percent per year and cutting taxes 1 percent per year.

***But if the government prints money, won't that cause inflation?***

NO. Under Ronald Reagan, the government printed a huge amount of money, and inflation went down. Inflation is caused by too much money chasing too few goods. But now we have too many goods. Also, if printing one dollar helps create two dollars' worth of goods, the dollar you print not only creates a job and a product, it also helps *lower* inflation. Remember that food, shelter, and clothing came before money did—money was invented just to help keep score, just to make it easier to trade our real assets among ourselves. We have let our real wealth get way ahead of our measuring device. We have let the tail wag the dog, as our leaders falsely believe a low supply of money is more important than a large supply of what money stands for—real goods and services. A *false fear* of too much money is itself what reduces the real wealth that money is supposed to represent.

When I tell groups the parable about the miracle cancer cure, on rare occasions a brilliant and brave member of the audience will blurt out the right answer right away: "They need to print more coupons." I tell them that the parable's respected economists would answer them this way: "You crank! Don't even *think* of printing more. Our coupons would become 'funny money,' losing all of their value in a hyper inflation of paper."

The old economists had only recently and begrudgingly come around to the idea of using mere paper for the coupons. Real coupons, they felt in their hearts, should be made of gold. (To them, gold was more important than food, shelter, security, or happiness. They had confidently predicted worldwide financial panic when the world left the gold standard, and their faith in their Golden Idol never wavered, despite the no-show of financial apocalypse.) Without gold, the whole coupons-for-cancer-cure system stood on shaky ground, and all sorts of serious repercussions would surely occur if too many of the coupons were printed. They were also sure that six thousand were more than enough—especially since *every single one of the economists* already had access to a coupon for himself.

***I can't keep writing more checks than I can cover with my bank account—why is it any different for the government?***

THE MAIN DIFFERENCE is that you don't print and back up your own currency. The factor that should determine the number of cancer cure coupons to be printed in the above example is the amount of cancer cure medicine we have. The government should not print more coupons than cure—or more money than we have goods. But in the example and in real life, the amount of coupons and money lags far behind the amount of goods. To use your bank account metaphor, it is as though a bad accountant hadn't told you how much money was really backing up your checking account. You kept *thinking* you were overdrawn, but somehow your checks never bounced. Your personal deficit would not be the difference between your withdrawals and the wrong number the lousy accountant gave you, but the deficit between his too-low number and the real assets you had backing you up.

The government of former Yugoslavia shouldn't print more money, because the area's economy has been destroyed by war, and they no longer have any wealth to back up their money. We have been printing money to finance the deficit for ten years without inflation, because our economy has far more than enough goods to back up our dollars.

***Everybody knows, everybody agrees that the deficit and debt are actually our biggest problems, right?***

FIRST OF ALL, a great many people—perhaps *most* economists, in fact—know that "deficits" are, at best, badly measured, and are definitely *not* as bad as they are portrayed in the popular press. What everybody agrees upon is that our economy has something wrong with it. We just went through a recession we can't understand, and we want to blame someone or something. Although it makes no sense at all, the "deficit" has become the scapegoat, only because the very words "debt" and "deficit" *sound* bad, and both have gotten bigger since the boom of the eighties.

***How can you be right and basic, old-fashioned macroeconomics be wrong?***

THE WORLD HAS CHANGED, my friend. The old economics was designed to *eliminate scarcities*—which it has *succeeded* in doing. This miracle has been completely ignored in the current economic debate. Our workers, businesses, and government have accomplished great things, and deserve a *reward*, not pointless belt-tightening "sacrifice." The old economics was the science of "the allocation of scarce resources." The challenge to the new economics is the *distribution* of *abundant* resources. The science of abundance requires different principles than the science of scarcity, just as the science of flying in the vacuum of space requires different principles than flying through the atmosphere of earth.

What is most perverse is that our economic leaders have all learned the special rules that apply to economies with surpluses such as ours, and the need to create demand for the goods produced. They have all studied the monetarists' tight-money approach to impoverished Third-World economies on the one hand, and Keynes's stimulus approach to Western economies with abundant resources on the other. But they simply choose to ignore the relevant approach *in favor of the one that doesn't work!* They are like the British generals in World War I who knew about the power of machine guns to destroy attacking infantrymen, but continued to apply the old cavalry principle of "Attack with bayonets high, men!" These generals saw twenty thousand killed in one day. They ordered *insane charges* for *four years*, until 925,000 brave soldiers who trusted the wisdom of their leaders had been thrown up as targets for German bullets. Those deaths accomplished nothing. The war was won by a naval blockade and the invention of tanks.

The generals had been taught when it was right to attack and when to defend, but chose to follow the glorious path of attack, even against machine guns, even across the low ground, even through impassable mud bogs. Many outside the circle of top commanders *understood and complained about the senseless slaughter* of their countrymen, but were ignored. For four years, the top generals refused to admit the obvious impossibility of taking a machine-gun nest with waves of human flesh. Right now, our Greenspans and Perots would likewise stubbornly send more brave young Americans to make *their* "sacrifices" and "contributions"—jobs, taxes, promotions, security, the normal decent lives they deserve—while they themselves sit securely in headquarters at the rear, unaffected by the human tragedy they inflict with their budgetary and monetary policies.

***There are many good reasons to fear deficits. For example, if we just print and spend money, that's a clear prescription for inflation—as in Germany, Brazil, and today's Russia.***

I'LL EXPLAIN THIS AGAIN. Inflation is the most common fear after that of the deficit itself, so I always have to repeat this answer a dozen times before it sinks in. There is one basic cause of inflation: *Too much money chasing too few goods.* Weimar Germany caused a war which destroyed their factories. Brazil has foolish protectionist laws restricting the supply of foreign goods, and hamstrings its own businesses through corruption. Russia has the legacy of a communist system that could not put erasers on its pencils. We, on the other hand—meaning all of Western free enterprise—have been so damn *smart and hard-working* over the last twenty years that we have produced an excess of everything we need and want.

Here's a test: Try to think of a single good or service that is in short supply. Folks, *nothing* is in short supply. Not gold, not Rolls Royces, not seats on the Concorde. And we could make twice as much in a year without building a new factory if consumer demand existed. I'm *not* saying we should print banknotes by the boatload, but only enough to get the economy healthy again. People obsessed with inflation react like seriously ill anorexics confronted with a single hamburger—"But if I eat *fifty* hamburgers I'll get fat!" Our economy is seriously short of cash, but the inflation and deficit hawks insist, "If we print a boatload, we'll get inflated!" For both, their fantasized fear of an imaginary extreme stops them from taking the moderate steps necessary for their health.

***Okay, okay. I'll let it go for the moment. How about the "crowding out" theory—if the government borrows money to run up a debt, then how can our good old American businesses borrow money to build new factories and create jobs the old-fashioned way?***

YOU'RE TALKING LIKE an economist now, which means you're on thin ice. I never said I wanted the government to borrow money from anyone—the government just has to print more money, the old-fashioned way. Leave money in the banks for them to loan to businesses. You probably don't know it, but we already do finance our debt to a great extent by printing more—the government calls it "monetizing" the debt. It creates a big government bond, and then prints enough money to buy it.

To recap: the government (1) prints money, (2) pays it to itself, (3) spends it, and (4) promises to pay itself back sometime in the future. They keep this pretty much a secret, because it sounds sure to cause *inflation*, right? But it doesn't. The old economics, the science dealing with the allocation of *scarce* resources, was sure inflation would follow, but the clear and overwhelming fact is that eight years of successful supply-side expansion resulted in disinflation (lower and lower inflation). And by printing its own money, the government has left plenty in the banks, so they can make all of the loans they want. Less than 5 percent of the debt is held by commercial banks anyway, compared to the 46 percent held by U.S., state and local treasuries, and the Fed (U.S. Federal Reserve banks).

***But then why haven't businesses been borrowing and investing to make new jobs? Isn't it because interest rates are too high, due to the deficit?***

NONSENSE! What business would want to expand its production when its customers can't afford the goods already sitting on the shelves? Even if interest rates were zero, would you commit yourself to a big investment to add to our *surplus* of unaffordable goods? The story old economists tell about the relation of the "deficit" to interest rates, business investment, and good new jobs is so hilariously wrong, there's only one reason they can tell it with a straight face: nobody but other economists can understand it. The fact is that these days any business investment that does occur goes toward eliminating good jobs, by adding robots and computers. Businesses know that they can't sell more goods into a saturated market, so they intelligently work towards greater efficiency and lower prices, not expansion.

***How will our grandchildren ever pay back the crushing debts we are dumping on them?***

WHAT DEBTS? What payback? Look at history—these bogus "deficits" and so-called "debts" are never paid back—because they aren't really debts and deficits at all. In the cancer cure parable, it would be as though you were demanding "repayment" of the "excessive" coupons that were printed. Our parents supposedly incurred crippling debts spending our way *out of the Depression and winning World War II.* Have we ever paid off those debts? No. Could we if we had to? Yes. Think of a bank in good shape. It owes its depositors far more than it has in its vaults. Why don't they panic and cause a run on it? Because the bank has assets to back up its promises. So does the U.S.—and that means all of us, not just the government. Just like a company that has sold stock publicly, both our equity issues and our paper debt are backed up by the value of the buildings, accounts receivable, goodwill, security, and capital gains in general that have been accrued.

***Do you think the United States can back up the $4 trillion we "owe"?***

IF WE WERE A COMPANY, we would have been subjected to a leveraged buyout years ago, because the breakup value is far more than our capitalization and debt combined! What really backs up every dollar in the world is what you can buy with it—and the dollar buys more here than any other currency buys in its own country. To prevent people from dumping their dollar assets, all we have to do is maintain the value of the immense wealth we have already. How? By investing in our assets and *keeping our people working* to build more. The only way to cause a lack of faith in our country is to do what the economic anorexics demand—the bankrupting of America by letting it go to ruin through unemployment and excessive taxation.

In the past, we kept up the value of our assets by accruing huge "debts" that served to keep our nation strong and the value of life here the highest on earth. For example, the money our parents spent creating jobs to end the Depression and winning World War II has been a classic case of spending one dollar in order to make two dollars' worth of goods. We still ride our cars on the roads and flush our toilets through sewers made by the Works Progress Administration (WPA). We speak English instead of German on Capitol Hill because of the immensely productive investment we made in winning World War II. The only debt our grandchildren might have to pay is the one we're threatening to give them right now—*a society without jobs, with broken roads and rusted bridges, suffering widespread social unrest and global insecurity*—because we slowly but relentlessly bankrupted ourselves due to the twin delusions of "deficit" and "debt."

***This talk of the Depression and the WPA exposes you as another tax-and-spend Democrat. So who's going to "contribute" this time—the middle-class "rich," retirees on Social Security, or hard-working, risk-taking businesses?***

NO ONE. To repeat, we have to spend more and tax less. Taxation degrades the money supply, siphoning off 7 percent here (sales tax) and 31 percent there (income tax), not to mention the multiple and redundant taxes on every step of honest business dealings. A middle-class wage earner pays about 60 percent already, including wages withheld for taxes by employers, and we have just passed the widest-ranging tax increase in our history, and retroactively to boot. The problem is *not enough money,* and taxation makes the problem worse, by snipping a corner off our dollar every time it passes through someone's hands.

Since we have to create money anyway to make up the true deficit between the amount of this country's real wealth and the insufficient supply of cash we have to cover it, we can simply give that money to the government first. That's what happens anyway when we "monetize" the debt, as I described above. The only "sacrifice" I ask of anyone is that they spend a long career working at a job that uses their full measure of energy, skill, and devotion, instead of spending years in unemployment lines or demeaning temporary jobs that use only a fraction of their abilities. The only "sacrifice" I ask of people is that they work as hard as their forefathers did, and for roughly the same rewards.

### *What evidence do you have that deficit spending works?*

PLENTY. When we incurred deficits, we prospered in the 1930s, through World War II, under Kennedy, and during the mid-1980s. When we got scared of our success and squeezed the money supply for a "soft landing" in 1988, we ourselves caused our endless recession. Germany prospered despite the prophets of doom who said that making Ostmarks into deutschemarks would cause rampant inflation. It didn't. Nonetheless, their own anorexic Bundesbank followed our "soft landing" philosophy with a vengeance, plunging all of the European Community (EC) into a recession and threatening the fledgling union itself. Japan worried about its "bubble economy" bursting, and squeezed its own money supply about the same time. Of course, that itself is what burst the bubble.

On the up side, exports are booming for Britian, Sweden, and Italy, the first countries to break free of Germany's economic rigidity. Currently, the two Western countries with the highest deficit-to-GNP ratio, Canada and Italy, are outpacing their tight-money neighbors. Japan passed a $117 billion spending plan (ours for a mere $16 billion failed at the first hurdle), which helped, but they need a lot more.

***Haven't you heard that two things are inevitable: death and taxes?***

AGAIN, if you are unshakably convinced that we have to *spend less* and *tax more* in order to reduce our scary deficit, then you are in league with the economists running this country. Those of you who want to fire more people and raise taxes even higher are yourselves responsible for the inevitable poverty we are making for ourselves and our children out of the relative prosperity of the 1980s, a prosperity that should be our *legacy* and not mere *memory.* But to argue about which taxes to raise and which expenditures to cut is as pointless as arguing over which vein to open and how much blood to let out, which was the whole range of the debate for thousands of years of bloodletting. Our politicians are defining the problem in a way that makes it impossible to solve, giving you a Hobson's choice among alternatives they all can plainly see are doomed to failure, immediate and long term.

Death is inevitable, but taxes are not. First of all, understand that bad taxation provoked our fight for independence from Britain. Our country did damned well for two centuries *without income or sales taxes*. Haven't you ever wondered why some states of this union to this day have no income tax? Why many countries have no income tax or sales taxes either?

***Why should we take any chances when the indicators say that the economy is already beginning to improve? Things aren't so bad that we have to risk change.***

YOU'RE WRONG; things are bad, and they can't get better. We have just begun to fire people. Haven't you noticed that everybody is still laying off workers, and almost no one is hiring? The efficiency movement in management and manufacturing is expected to wipe out as many as twenty-five million jobs from the ninety million private sector jobs still surviving today. Professionals are becoming as much at risk as high school dropouts. The defense industry has just started its layoffs: we've lost nine hundred thousand through 1992, with another 1.9 million slated to disappear by 1997. With the ripple effect, job losses in defense alone will top five million. And do you really think that some new computer software, high definition television, or other electronic gewgaw is going to ignite a jobs explosion in this country? People who desperately want the cars and houses we *already have* can't afford them because they're unemployed.

Second, what we do have in this country is only half of what we could have. We could clean up the environment, rehabilitate many of the addicted, fly to Mars—heck, we could build a canal from the Arctic ice pack to Baja (Mexico peninsula) with the workers, scientists, engineers, and managers looking for jobs right now. Sure, this country will always be okay, even if we were ruled by Idi Amin. But it's as though we're running in the marathon with a bowling ball tied to one ankle. That bowling ball is not the deficit itself, but our unreasonable fear of the deficit. Only the scary myth of this imaginary number stops us from realizing the greater destiny we have already worked so hard to earn.

# 2

# The Problem: Permanent Unemployment Caused by the *Real* Deficit in the Money Supply

We are stuck in an endless recession. People at all levels, from CEOs to unskilled labor, from physicists to key-punchers, both American and Japanese, have lost their jobs. The jobs destroyed are the best jobs: sciences, computers, defense contractors, and manufacturing sectors. They won't come back. Business has lost too many customers, because we've cut defense and science spending, and because higher productivity allows fewer people to produce more things. Also, those who still have jobs quite rightly fear spending much, because everyone's job is at risk. Businesses are forced to invest in efficiency—which means downsizing, which means firing more workers and managers—just to survive.

Retirees and the independently wealthy have far less income from their safest investments, so they turn increasingly to the dangerous bubble in mutual funds. Social Security is under constant attack. People who counted on selling their house to help finance their retirement find they can't sell it at all, or if they do sell it's at a fraction of what they planned on a decade ago. Soon, they'll be lucky to sell at any price. Furthermore, they might be forced to sell; retirement programs admit they are in danger, with many already starting to cut back on benefits such as medical coverage. Early retirees find no decent employment in their fifties, but at least they got far greater severance packages than those who stayed—and who now find themselves threatened with outright layoffs.

Our economic leaders just don't get it. They keep writing that the recession is over—on the same page that one more major company reports another ten thousand layoffs. To our economists, recession is just a state of mind, and it must be over, because the nation has followed their economic advice. But consumer psychology—profound gloom—is now and has historically been far more accurate than the economists' arithmetic. They still use the same tools they used when predicting, for the first four years of the depression, when things in reality kept getting worse, that recovery was already underway.

*Our economic leaders just don't get it. They keep writing that the recession is over—on the same page that one more major company reports another ten thousand layoffs.*

The scapegoats for the economists' failures are in fact innocent victims of bad economic theories. Our workers are the most productive in the world. We have more education and training than our businesses can use. Our financial system is the best in the world—supposed financial "excesses" encouraged cellular phones and fiber optics. Hyperconservative regulations stopped the banks from lending. Now they will lend again, but no sane business can risk borrowing—no matter how low long-term interest rates go. Supposedly "excessive" consumption in the 1980s was an engine of growth—now we desperately need people to buy more, but they can't afford to spend the money. Communism died, and military costs are dropping precipitously. Free trade has stocked our shelves and toughened our industry. The former "culprits" have been proven heroic.

The only remaining scapegoat is the so-called national debt or federal deficit. But "curing" the false deficit is what causes the recession, so current policy will make things *worse*. As in 1931, we greet a recession by throwing fuel on its flames—raising taxes and reducing spending, costing us jobs and destroying consumer demand—in the name of "deficit" reduction. Employment and consumer demand will continue to spiral downward, heightening domestic demoralization and class strife, as well as international tensions. Welcome to 1932 all over again.

## BUDDY, CAN YOU SPARE A DIME?

Layoffs, layoffs, layoffs. The figures numb the senses. Can you remember what 1988 felt like? Yes, we had problems—but we also had jobs.[1] Yes, Reagan had only a general idea about what he was doing. But what sense does it make to blame him for our current problems? Eight years of the currently reviled supply-side economics brought us more than sixteen million new jobs; a decrease in inflation from 10 percent to 4 percent; and an average annual rise in the gross domestic product of 4 percent after the end of the Volcker recession in 1982.[2]

So the economic brain trust decided the economy was "overheated" and we had to "cool it off"—bringing it in for a "soft landing" in order to avoid a crash. The first solution to the problem of prosperity was to severely re-regulate the banks (which reduced investment and cost us jobs). Bush next bowed to his chief economic adviser, Roger Darman, and Senator George Mitchell, and raised taxes (which reduced purchasing power and cost us jobs). Meanwhile, the nation's top central banker, Greenspan, chairman of the Federal Reserve Board, had been raising interest rates (which reduced investment and consumer demand, costing us jobs).[3] And all our leaders agreed the most important economic goal was to reduce the federal deficit by raising taxes and cutting spending. What brilliant leadership! Did they outsmart the evil Reaganomics, or what?

Here are the results of the program they initiated and *which continues today*. Since 1990, we have suffered a net *loss* of full-time jobs. The mere 2 percent rise in the official unemployment figures in that time does not begin to tell the full story.[4] Millions of workers, especially the young, the old, and mothers, have simply stopped looking, taking themselves out of the labor force and out of the percentages. The jobs that are lost are the good ones, with high wages, decent benefits, and desirable working conditions. The ones created tend to be part-time and lower paid, without benefits.

In one single year of the Great Recession (early 1991 to early 1992), over *half* of our country's families had at least one work-related problem, including the following: being out of work and looking for a job for a month or more; losing a promotion or being demoted; or owning a business that lost money. These are depression-era figures, folks. A quarter of the households had pay cuts for dad or mom or both. An additional one-sixth had one or the other losing their jobs. All that's just in one year.[5]

It's not going to get better. January 1992 saw 46,136 announced layoffs; the same month of 1993 had 83,103, with plans for hundreds of thousands more. Our leaders keep estimating that growth will be three times what it turns out to be, that we'll add 130,000 jobs—but we end up adding only 13,000. As I said, you go numb from reading the same kind of huge numbers year after year, for five years running now. Americans in every category are affected, from CEOs to the unskilled, in every industry. Here's the full banquet of bad news, bite by bite.

## CEOs and Scientists

No one is immune. Within months, three of the most powerful capitalists on earth got fired—the chief executive officers of IBM, General Motors, and Westinghouse, following the messy dismissal of the CEO of American Express. No need to feel sorry for these guys—their severance packages alone, aside from retirement pay, keep them wealthy men indeed. The point is, no amount of knowledge, skill, or corporate power ensures anyone his or her job these days.

Say you spent your life as a science nerd, a lab rat, a bookworm. Always top of your class. Straight A's for a decade straight. All the best schools, concluding with a post-doctorate in physics at a major national laboratory. You are at the cutting edge of science, the product of the best scientific educational system in the history of the world. You've devoted your whole life to the most difficult and demanding intellectual challenges that exist, and you've come out on top. You are the kind of person who has something to contribute to the world, due to your state-of-the-art expertise in chemistry, astronomy, physics or math. Right?

*Wrong*. Like everyone else, you have just sent out two hundred copies of your perfect résumé, and you have no interviews. No one's hiring. The jobs aren't out there. And you won't even show up on the unemployment statistics, because you will end up teaching basic high school level science at the local junior college for three hundred dollars a week, no benefits. Honorable work, to be sure, but it wastes about ten years of your education and 90 percent of your talent.[6]

## DOCTORS, LAWYERS, AND ENGINEERS

Doctors are still safe from unemployment. Their union, the American Medical Association (AMA), still is the strongest around. But even they face a reduction in wages, due to the same kind of efficiency gains accomplished by the rest of Western industry, on top of the Clinton health plan. Other health-care professionals are already feeling the pain. Pharmaceutical salesmen are getting the ax. Office workers in doctors' offices are being "downsized" (i.e., fired). Mergers and corporate restructuring are getting rid of 20 percent of the managerial staff at hospitals. About one-fourth of the hospital capacity will be cut, taking with it many of the hospitals' three-and-a-half million workers.[7]

Say you did what it took to get a law degree from the University of Buffalo, finishing in the top 15 percent of your class, with forty-eight thousand dollars in debt you want to pay back through hard work. You've gone to the nationals in the moot-court competition, and passed the New York state bar exam on the first try with a score high enough to qualify you in two other states. You inquire for a job with two hundred prospective employers. Hooray! You won't show up on the unemployment statistics—you landed a single offer: processing workers' compensation claims, on a temporary basis. And it's not just the beginners. The top firms in the nation have cut back 5 percent in a year, frozen salaries, and extended the probationary period for partnership.[8]

All we need is more highly trained engineers to get this country rolling again, right? And isn't it a shame that our awful educational system can't train competitive engineering talent, right? Wrong again. We're not just talking about defense engineering, which will lose 127,000 of its 342,000 jobs it had in 1990 by 1995, or aerospace, or the supercollider. Even our most cutting-edge, consumer-oriented industry—electronics—lost ninety-nine thousand jobs in a year.[9] Remember all those forecasts for an increased need for engineers right about now? They were *wrong*. No matter how educated you are, no matter how well-trained, no matter how well you have kept on top of current events in your field, many of the jobs just aren't there anymore. And they're not coming back.

## MANAGERS AND TECHNICAL STAFF

A loud crash on a suburban side street in Pennsylvania brought four men out to the curb (it was only a road-paving machine, not a car accident). All were middle-aged men who had lost their jobs. None knew the others' status, though they were neighbors. When you're a forty-five-year-old man who used to make more than a hundred thousand, and you haven't worked in a year, you tend to hide out during the day. Especially when your wife has to work now, your kids are at school, and you, Mr. Former Big Shot, are home alone.[10]

These guys won't starve. Eventually, they'll sell their big home, move, and manage a 7-Eleven. The sharp résumés they conceive in their support groups won't come to anything, but the psychological support will help—crucially. Because it is hard to understand that the business world doesn't need you anymore, when for years you happily served the sixty-hour weeks necessary on the road to the top, or near-top. And don't say you got canned because you were a generalist (an MBA type) instead of a technical specialist. The bookkeeping, accounting, auditing, payroll, and billing jobs have been among the hardest hit white-collar job destruction areas.[11]

## FIRST-TIME WORKERS AND THE SEMI-RETIRED

Hello, proud parent. Your child has successfully negotiated the hurdles of adolescence, high school, and college, and now stands next to you in cap and gown for graduation pictures. The cost of education reached six figures, overall. Usually the graduate has a loan in five figures. What luck for the economy!—one more bright, eager, energetic young person to help make the world a more prosperous place. Right?

*Wrong* again. Between 1988 and 1992, the number of graduating college seniors rose eleven times as fast as the number of full-time jobs. Graduates working at jobs that don't use their college education rose to 35 percent—that is, more than one in three college educations turns out to have been a waste of time and money, from an employment standpoint.[12] Maybe they're too lazy or timid to go for the good, tough jobs. Wrong. Apple computer received eleven thousand applications for one hundred entry-level jobs and three hundred summer internships.[13] Our kids' desire to work is vivid; but the jobs just aren't there.

So then they should skip college and take the easier jobs, you say. Wrong, wrong, wrong. The unskilled jobs aren't going overseas, folks. Sears didn't move your local store to Mexico. They closed it. Retailing used to provide jobs for half of all employed teenagers and a quarter of those in their early twenties. Great efficiency gains, of the sort that keep prices down at Sam's, have permanently reduced the number of people it takes to sell you a pillow. The number of employed young people is two million below what it was in 1989.[14] The silver lining—more are lingering in college as long as they can, since we have nothing for millions of them to do once they graduate or drop out. At least our unemployed work force will be better-read and better-spoken than their Depression-era counterparts. When they can stall no longer and are forced to graduate, they can expect to spend a year looking for a job. University employment centers are swamped. In ten minutes early Friday morning, all slots for the next week are scheduled. One counselor says, "I keep a box of Kleenex for people who come in feeling like their legs have just been cut off."[15] Bob Dylan sarcastically sang, "Twenty years of schooling and they put you on the day shift." Wrong, Bob. Twenty years of schooling and they don't put you on any shift.

At least the old folks are doing okay, right? Not if they want to work. "Old" is down to a precise fifty-seven years and ten months in Germany, and we're headed towards kicking ourselves out of work that early here as well. Good thing you've got Social Security (40 percent have nothing else), because McDonald's doesn't have enough part-time work to occupy all of you. Thought you'd take that early retirement and go on to better things? Hah! In the 1980s, you could get a better job half of the time. Now, only 48 percent of workers over fifty-four can expect to find work at all. And what jobs! One fifty-six-year-old former General Motors engineer took what he could find after a two-year job search: washing cars and sweeping up at the local dealership on Saturday mornings. He won't give his name to *The Wall Street Journal* interviewer. He's ashamed.[16]

At least he got a decent early retirement package. More than 40 percent of our large companies offered packages in the last three years. More will follow, with layoffs threatened if enough don't volunteer. The size of the packages is shrinking—and not just for future retirees. Twenty-two percent will not offer health care to future retirees, and an ominous 3 percent have suspended health benefits for current retired recipients. Because of the lack of alternative employment, one-third of older Americans suffer from "job lock"—that is, they can't leave a job they want to quit, because they can't replace the benefits.[17]

## WORKING HARDER, UNDER PRESSURE

At least the people with jobs are better off, right? Only if you're the type who feels all the more triumphant and elite when the percentage of survivors is lower—although it means you are now doing the work of two people. Real wages have been effectively frozen for years, even counting the current low inflation. And who has time to enjoy the money they earn? On average, we work 164 hours more per year—that is, an additional month, compared with twenty years ago. At this rate, the average workweek will be sixty hours when the baby boomers begin to retire (those who have jobs to retire from, that is).

Many of those remaining in a restructured, re-engineered company suffer the equivalent of shell shock. They've seen the layoff bomb go off around them so many times they're ready for the next fatal explosion at any moment. How pleasant, to know that any perceived, much less real error on your part will put your name to the top of the next layoff list—great for your feelings of risk-taking and initiative, isn't it?

Are you being paranoid? No. they really are after you—your job, that is. One blue-collar car worker no longer hopes, because all of his possibilities are bad. He just spent three months on a temporary assignment thirteen hundred miles from his family. He slept in his car every night, saving rent money for his drive home every weekend. A layoff brought him home again, for a while—at a poverty-level income.[18] Now the auto industry is bringing back the third shift, returning many workers to fractured schedules, despite hundreds of vacant factories sitting empty all day long.

The workers put up with the industrial-age conditions because they see the destitution of their laid-off coworkers, sitting home or suffering an endless string of part-time, temporary, low-pay, no-benefit, no-security jobs that never become permanent. "Defiance has been replaced by an empty well of frustration," says *Business Week* (October 18, 1993, p. 76). Better any indignity on the job, than no job at all. I don't recall that credo in the Declaration of Independence, but we should add it in recognition of our new Life in These United States under the Deficit Mongers.

## NO CUSTOMERS

The reason for all layoffs is the same: perfectly good businesses, even entire industries, are losing more and more of their customers. Legitimate reasons for layoffs include the following: a decaying, inefficient industry (as in the former Soviet Union); poor or overpriced products; a lack of capital for expansion or maintenance; or declining demand for your output. None of these apply to the great majority of current layoffs (all except the direct layoffs in defense). Consider the example of Bill Jones and Carl Abbott. Bill makes cars and needs a house. Carl makes houses and needs a car. Both need and make desirable products at a fair price. But they cannot be each other's customers due to the current deficit hysteria.

And all the conditions that prevent Bill and Carl from working to build and buy each other's products are getting progressively worse. The deficit mongers demand that we cut evil government spending. We have! Federal purchases of goods and services dropped 3.3 percent in 1992, the largest decline in almost twenty years. Defense cuts were 6 percent, and other expenditures were down 1.8 percent. These cuts caused the destruction of about four hundred thousand jobs.[19] This is only the start of a trend, due to cuts in future federal employment and caps on discretionary spending: cuts in the first quarter of 1993 were 17.9 percent. Aren't you spending cutters proud of yourselves!

Due to the multiplier effects of public and private spending cuts, we can expect to lose twenty-five million of our ninety million private sector jobs.[20] And surprise! People out of work don't buy as much as people with jobs. It's not a matter of consumer confidence or psychology, how they "feel" about the economy. They just don't have the money; worse, they don't see how they're going to get much anytime soon.

The trade warriors' favorite magic bullet is export. Let's just get more competitive and sell more stuff to foreigners, they say. Yeah, right. The foreigners have the same problem we have, only worse. They are also desperate for customers. We're closer to starting trade wars with everyone than we are to opening up new markets. Everyone loves our goods, but no one thinks they can afford each other's production, no matter how low the price. The international system that tries to help trade, GATT (the General Agreement on Tariffs and Trade) has had so much trouble it's going to disband and start over. The European Community is cracking in the very year it was supposed to get together. Don't look overseas for customers when we can't even get Bill and Carl working, and buying each other's cars and houses.

Even those with jobs and a little money aren't too enthusiastic about blowing it all. Why? If you have a brain in your head, you can see by now that no one's job is safe. Taking on consumer debt to finance consumption is simply not as responsible now as it was in the 1980s, when consumer purchases fueled expansion—and created jobs.

## LET'S BUILD A FACTORY!

What the old economists hated most about the deficit was that it supposedly caused high long-term interest rates (actually, it didn't—see chapter 6). According to them, these high rates prevented businesses from borrowing money to build new factories. If only we cut the deficit, they said, rates would go down, and capitalists would run like hogs to the trough to borrow money and build new factories employing millions, all to the greater glory of their righteous economics.

Interest rates reached rock-bottom lows. Any lower, and you'd be able to borrow it and put it right back in the bank to collect higher interest than you're paying. So where's the predicted rush to build new factories? There isn't any.[21] That's about zero for fifty on predictions by the deficit mongers.

Why aren't businesses rushing to build new factories, or expand and hire new workers? Because businessmen aren't as stupid as the economists, that's why. What fool wants to expand when people can't afford to buy the products already on the shelves? The old economists shared a Santa Claus fantasy called Say's Law. It declared that supply creates its own demand. That is, if you build cars, someone will be able to buy them. Kind of like in the movie, *Field of Dreams*—"Build it, and they will come." Well, American and other Western businessmen have been building everything from houses, cars, computers, and airplanes—and building them very well, if you please—but not enough customers are coming. People want the product, all right. Alaska Airlines was voted best airline five years in a row. But being good isn't enough when people don't have the money in their pockets to be able to spend it on your product. Alaska Airlines lost $116 million in 1992-1993.

*The old economists shared a Santa Claus fantasy called Say's Law. It declared that supply creates its own demand. That is, if you build cars, someone will be able to buy them. Kind of like in the movie, Field of Dreams—"Build it, and they will come."*

By the way, those low interest rates are being used—in order to destroy more jobs, not create them. A business that wants to exist five years from now knows it will have to make things cheaper and cheaper, with fewer and fewer workers. So they invest in robots and computers, with better training for the remaining workers. You know that it takes fewer men to build an automobile due to automation. Now, even electrical engineers can manage three times as many projects as before.[22] And increased computer productivity has only begun to affect the 16.7 million back-office employees who process orders and track inventories.[23] These jobs are ideal for the computer. Computers are great workers, but they don't buy much in the local or international economy. Don't blame the computers or the companies, however. If they modernize and re-engineer, they at least will be around employing some fraction of their workers. If they don't, none of their employees or managers will have work.

## WHAT HAPPENED TO MY CDS?

So, you worked hard all your life and put money into your IRA and bought some CDs. You're not stuck in poverty, or living on Social Security alone. But what just happened? Your interest income has collapsed under anti-deficit economics. So much for the free-spending vacations you had planned, or that new car. (Bill and Carl won't be working to make any extra cars or vacation cottages for you.) Low interest rates mean you are not quite the consumer all of us wanted you to be.

Aha. You think you're too smart to get stuck with CDs at 3.5 percent interest. You got into mutual funds. Great. I wish you luck. As long as everybody keeps their money in these funds, you will be as safe as the conservative folks who trusted their money to the banks in 1926, before Federal Deposit Insurance. Those folks trusted there would be no run on the banks. Today there is no Federal Mutual Fund Insurance. Ask your broker what happens if everyone decides they want to pull their money out of their mutual funds, as people did to the banks during the depression. He or she will insist that people would do no such thing. Press the issue. Ask, "Well, humor me. Just what if..." If you can't get an answer, check with *The Economist*, *Wall Street Journal*, or *Barron's*. And good luck with your investments.[24]

## AND WHAT HAPPENED TO MY TAXES?

They've already gone up, the first retroactive federal tax increase outside of war time. And the most wide-ranging single tax increase ever.[25] Glad to see we're making history, aren't you? And they are going to go up some more, lots more, if we continue to follow the rotten advice of our deficit mongers. If you want a lower deficit, that means you want some combination of lower spending (which costs jobs) and higher taxes (which cause higher taxes as well as costing jobs). Simpletons hope the taxes will fall on someone else. These fools are like the optimists in Stalin's Russia: "Well, sure, they've thrown most of my successful neighbors into the gulag, but they won't pick on me." Some of you are glad to pay higher taxes—one just donated $16 million to the IRS for the deficit! Such noble souls remind me of the young Britishers who happily volunteered to lead the charge into the German machine guns (see chapter 7). Good for you, hero—but I feel sorry for your fellows, condemned to a similar fate by your delusions.

## MY HOME IS MY CASTLE—AND NEST EGG

You're not worried. Your house was worth two hundred fifty thousand dollars in 1986, and you've put thirty thousand dollars into it since then. So what's it worth now? No one knows. Whatever its "true" worth (a murky concept), its effective worth is exactly what you can get someone to pay for it. Think of the old philosophical puzzle: "If a tree falls in the forest and no one hears it, does it make a sound?" If your house is worth three hundred thousand dollars, but no one can afford to buy it, is it really worth that much?

Most of us don't know what our homes are worth. We only know we can't sell them. In one of my town's most desirable neighborhoods, ten homes have been on the block for more than a year. One sold at the old "market" price (which pleased everyone) to one of those young people who earned new-job wealth—he started a home nursing-care business. But noticeably in short supply are the rising-executive types who used to be the young people that bought here.

Look in your own neighborhood. Count the homes that aren't selling, and the people who will soon be considering selling and moving for retirement. Then count the people who might be expected to buy those homes. We don't have hard data for this comparison. But the kind of jobs people had in order to buy your home are exactly the kind of high-paying jobs that are now disappearing. Just count noses. To judge by the sea of "For Sale" signs all over the country, the buyers just aren't there. They've been on the sidelines so long, and not because they are waiting for a lower price; they've already lost years of better living, if that's their plan.

If they are waiting for a further crash in prices, they just might be right. If the remaining nine homeowners here decide they have to sell at any price, what would that price be? Take the amount of funds available to the top nine qualified buyers and divide by nine. I bet we're looking at half the marginal market rate, if that. Fortunately, home sellers are at least as well off as the mutual fund buyers. People by now are resigned to not being able to sell their houses, and pride prevents them from selling at the only price they can get. Still, if you really want to get anything at all, you would be better advised to sell for what you can get now, rather than later. The high-tax, low-spending economics of the deficit mongers will only drive the price of your home down further, not up.[26]

## BUT THE ECONOMISTS ARE OPTIMISTIC

The old economists desperately want to believe that the end of the recession is at hand. After all, they are the ones who got us in this mess. They recommended we raise taxes, cut spending, and squeeze the money supply with higher interest rates in their quest to slay the evil deficit. Of course they look at the tiniest flicker in any of a hundred economic indicators as the light at the end of the tunnel. At times their desperation verges on the pathetic. One indicator they love is housing starts. The following figure gave them cause to cheer:[27]

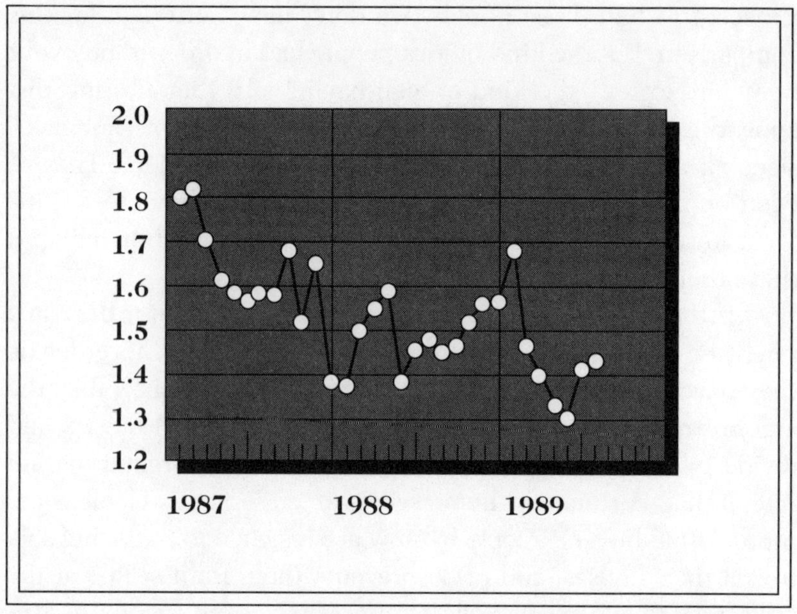


***Figure 2: The Economists Celebrate***

The tiny blip at the end evoked this response: "A slight pickup... in homebuilding in July helped chase away lingering fears that the country is slipping into a recession... 'What the numbers are telling us is that the economy certainly isn't headed into a recession.'" Of course, following the old economists' advice had also caused us by this time to start a holy crusade for deficit reduction and squeeze the money supply while severely re-regulating the banks. Let's see how accurate their optimism turned out to be by extending this graph:

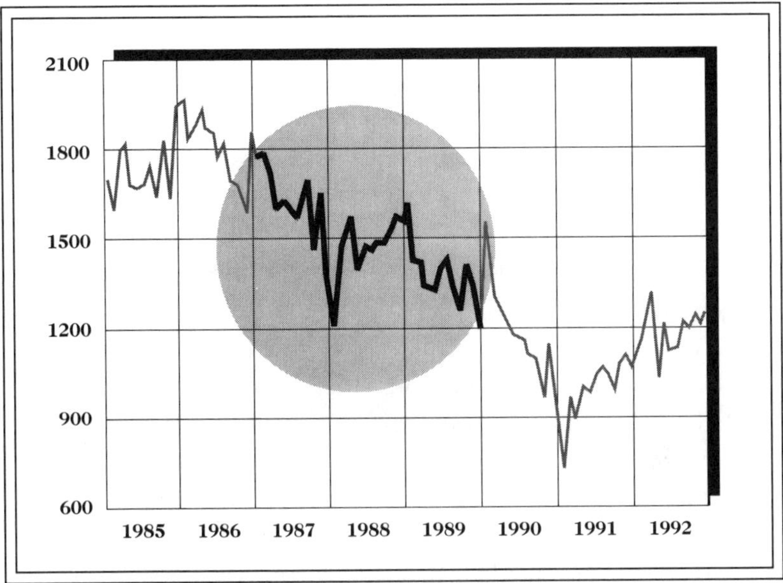


***Figure 3: The Whole Story***

The tiny blip signaled nothing. Millennialists trying to divine the end of the world from the Book of Revelation have as good a record as the old economists. Their chief forecasting tool—the index of leading indicators—jumped strongly just as the recession officially began in mid-1990. And they declared the recession to be officially over in March 1992, despite an unemployment rate of 7.3 percent that didn't even include more than a million who had given up looking and another 6.7 million part-timers who wanted full-time jobs.

They also are like the millennialists in their staunch interpretations of every worldly event as confirmation of their beliefs, no matter how many times they get their confident predictions wrong. Fortunately, the millennialists do not guide public policy. Unfortunately, the old economists do. And their refusal to admit that something is dreadfully wrong with their analysis makes it impossible for us to begin to mend the error of their ways. They are like anorexics who refuse to admit they have an eating disorder. As long as the old economists refuse to admit that their deficit hysteria has caused the recession, they can in no way help us find a cure. They wait for the rest of the world to solve problems they themselves have created. They wait for consumer confidence to grow, so people will spend freely again—consumers the economists have laid off or put in fear for their jobs. They wait for businessmen to expand their factories and hire more workers—businessmen who have lost their customers to the ax of the deficit mongers' pro-recession economics.

The recession is not a matter of psychology. Real jobs have been lost. Real customers have lost their incomes. What the economists call consumer "psychology" is actually consumer wisdom, clear-sighted business discernment, which has over the years been more accurate than the economists' sorry predictions.

Their optimism is another way the Great Recession is like The Great Depression: The Sequel. Not only were the economic leaders in the 1920s unable to forecast the depression; and not only were they unable to forecast either the declines in output or the large deflation; but also both the Harvard and Yale economic forecasting systems, as well as the top independent, Irving Fisher, remained relentlessly optimistic for two years into the depression. (As Fisher wrote in October 1931, "September should mark the low of the depression." Sound familiar?) Worse than all these mistakes of the past is how the economics profession has failed to learn from them. In their top professional journal, they review all the data used and still conclude, "The Harvard and Yale forecasters cannot be faulted for remaining optimistic after the Crash. Their continued optimism is consistent with our conclusion based on [the latest state-of-the-art whiz-bang math]…"[28] That is, the mainstream economists have learned nothing from the mistakes of the past. Just as they failed to recognize a depression even when it was upon them, the same old theories and methods, gussied up with fancier math, prevent them from recognizing an endless recession when they're in the middle of one. Or at the beginning of a permanent state of lowered expectations and wasted lives. This is where we are right now.[29]

## SCAPEGOATS AND WHIPPING BOYS

In the old days, when a community had a problem they didn't understand, they made themselves feel better by blaming innocent but convenient scapegoats—Jews, witches, heretics, neighboring countries, etc. Or they threw some more virgins in the volcano. Now, we're much more sophisticated. We throw jobs in the volcano of deficit reduction. We blame workers, managers, bankers, yuppies—or the Mexicans for working too hard and too cheaply.

Of course the old economists want to blame someone else. It's the national pastime—when you mess up, blame someone else, and sue them to boot. None of the old economists are coming clean, admitting that their deficit reduction policies have brought on the recession. The more sophisticated of their number pitifully defend their record by saying, "It's plain impossible to help or hurt the economy. The government shouldn't even try." (See chapter 8.) The rest round up the usual suspects and ladle on the guilt.

But the usual suspects are not only blameless themselves, not only are they fellow victims with us all, victims of the economists' folly, but it's the opposite—our workers, managers, financiers, and trading partners have brought us an incredible abundance of real wealth. The economists did not build the mountain of cars unloaded at our factories and into our ports. The economists did not manufacture our VCRs or help develop cellular phones and fiber optics. God knows the avalanche of foreign tourists to our shores do not line up to visit our economists. Hitler blamed an ethnic group that was not only innocent of causing Germany's mid-war blues, but who would have helped Hitler develop the A-bomb—if he'd let them stay. Sadly, the German people backed him up. But we are as guilty as those Germans of shooting ourselves in the foot if we support our old economists as they try to blame the innocent for the economists' own folly.

Chapters 9 and 11 explain at length the many sources of our country's real wealth. At this point I only want to emphasize, briefly, the destructive futility of the old economists' scapegoating.

By blaming the sources of our country's wealth, they will make the Great Recession worse, not better. They blamed our poor competitiveness; it turns out we're better than both the Japanese and Germans.[30] Bad education? Yes, in high school—but in college, we're easily best in the world.[31] Not a single industry suffers from a lack of well-trained, capable employees, so further job training won't help.[32]

Financial excesses? We fund innovation and start-ups better than anybody else in the world. In the 1980s, Milliken's junk bonds got fiber optics and cellular phones off the ground.[33] Stingy bank lending? The deficit mongers stopped our banks from lending, with excessive regulations. Now that the banks have been given a longer leash, no one wants to borrow, because they have no customers.[34] So then shame on all those awful yuppies for spending us into poverty. What hypocrisy! The same economists who perk up at a flicker of consumer optimism try to say it was that same consumer optimism that got us into trouble! What on earth, pray tell, was the harm caused by people with jobs and money buying things? Did we run out of goods? Did the shoppers sprain their ankles in a shopping frenzy? Were the producers worked into exhaustion?

Perhaps it was the spendthrift defense industry that depleted our economic strength. One famous blame-the-innocent book attributed the decline of all great powers, not just our own, to excessive military expenditures. It was published just as our own wild and crazy "Star Wars" spending helped scare the communist system into peace and freedom. Yes, defense spending is wasteful in that it creates goods that none of us can use—but what good has it done simply to fire all of the soldiers, engineers, and blue-collar defense workers? Under anti-deficit economics, we merely move them from the assembly line to the unemployment line. The "Peace Dividend" was turned into a "Peace Penalty" by dimwitted economists who didn't know how to cash the check, and lost it under the bed, just as weird old great-uncle Harry did with his Christmas bonus check every year.

The most blameless scapegoat is free trade. Look at life in these United States in the 1980s and compare it with the lifestyles and spending power of any people on earth. No one has benefited more than we have from free trade. We have the cheap cars, great VCRs, and cheap labor; the Japanese have a trade surplus, overpriced rice and everything else, tiny apartments, skinny roads, and one overworked international airport intentionally designed to keep them at home. Because anti-deficit economics stops us from re-employing our workers in the better jobs I describe in chapter 13, we risk killing our golden-egg-laying goose.

Again, haven't we learned anything from the depression? At that time, to "protect jobs" we passed Smoot-Hawley, which succeeded only in (1) costing every nation jobs; (2) reducing every nation's lifestyle; and (3) heightening international tensions to the point of World War. Blaming free trade for a loss of jobs is like blaming the postman for stopping you from taking a walk downtown every day.

## OUR PRIME SCAPEGOAT: THE BOGEYMAN

The old economists have toned down their castigation of the usual scapegoats, because they have finally had to accept that the above arguments are, on the face of it, indisputably true: The Great Recession has not been caused by poor competitiveness or education, financial excesses, the banks, yuppies, communism, defense spending, or free trade. Only those as desperate for votes as Ross Perot argue up those blind alleys. So they focus all their guns on the one remaining scapegoat, the cause of all our woe: the Bogeyman—whoops, I mean the "deficit."

Why call the deficit a bogeyman? The mission of this entire book is to explain the answer to that question at length. But the first similarity is easy to understand. Just as no child has ever really been hurt by the bogeyman, no one has actually ever been hurt by the deficit. Just because you are scared of something doesn't mean it can actually harm you. Think of it: How have you or anyone you know ever been hurt by the bogeyman? How have you or anyone you know ever been hurt by the deficit?

I guess that's a trick question. No one can answer it. Sympathize with poor President Bush—ex-President Bush. He got nailed to the wall with that one, his worst moment in the debates with Clinton and Perot. Poor Bush. He, like everyone else on earth, has *never* been hurt by the deficit or debt. He gamely tried to give the answers he'd been coached to give by his old economic advisers: interest rates, the burden to our children. All are abstractions—and dead wrong, to boot (see chapter 6). His answer sounded as though he didn't understand the problem, as though he, as a rich man, could not sympathize with the plight of the common man, a common man presumably left unemployed by the bogeyman deficit. Bush had no answer. His old economic advisers had never thought of such a question, because they, too, had no answers.

The moderator of the debate saved Clinton, whose turn was next, by stepping in after George sputtered to a halt to explain, "I think she meant more the *recession...*" Now there's a question that any challenger would love to answer. Everyone, including the rich, has been hurt by the recession. Even if you have kept a job and made lots of money, you would have made even more if not for the recession. And everyone knows friends or relatives who have suffered more directly. And that's the question Clinton got to answer. A big break for him—I wonder what he was thinking as Bush stumbled and stalled.

In my speeches I give people the same choice of questions. If they have ever been hurt by taxes that were too low or federal spending that was too high, they have been hurt by the deficit. They rack their brains, but I have not been able to find one person brave enough to admit out loud that he or she or anyone they know has suffered from paying too few taxes, or from receiving a federal grant or job. Maybe they're just shy.

The alternate question, the one Clinton got, helps those in the audience overcome their shyness. The recession means fewer jobs, higher taxes, and reduced federal and state spending. I ask if they or anyone they know has ever been hurt by one or all of those, and I'll be darned if they're not so shy anymore. The recession is not a bogeyman. It, unlike the deficit, causes real harm, harm you can see wandering jobless on the street, harm you can measure in your checkbook on April 15.

How did that scamp Perot answer the question? What a rascal! If he'd been asked how he'd been hurt by the bogeyman, he probably would have answered, "The bogeyman scared me so much that I ran and ate a bunch of cookies instead of my vegetables for dinner." His answer to the deficit version made no more sense: "(The deficit) caused me to disrupt…my business and (run for president)." But it illuminates the most dangerous threat posed by anti-deficit economics.

## IRRATIONAL FEAR OF THE BOGEYMAN

Say you get so scared of what you are sure is a bogeyman in the attic that you sprint down the stairs, fall, and break your arm. Did the bogeyman break your arm? Of course not. It was your fear of an imaginary monster which caused you to break your arm.

The same with the anti-deficit hysteria. It is not the deficit that has broken down our economy, but what our economic leaders have done to reduce the deficit. They copied the plan of the 1930 U.S. Congress, which also decided the best medicine for a depression was to reduce the deficit. That's what they did, refusing even to advance the World War I veterans their settlements a few years early in order the stimulate the demand everyone knew we needed. It took them two years and a change of presidents to admit the uselessness of that philosophy. So what have we learned? Nothing. Less than nothing. At least then they had an excuse for taking aggressive actions, although those actions were dead wrong. This time, we have already survived a giant drop in our stock market with barely a ripple in the economy. We had no economic problems that needed fixing, but the old economists, led by Alan Greenspan, made up an imaginary emergency.

They decided high growth and a large deficit must be a problem, an illness with no symptoms, but an illness nonetheless. So they applied the leeches. They headed off what they felt sure would be a "crash" by causing a "soft landing," cooling down our "overheated economy" by raising interest rates. Other Western nations did the same. All fought the deficit by causing a recession. Everyone raised taxes and reduced spending and continues to do so through years of pointless recession.

## Bleed Me Some More, Doc

Even the old economists admit that raising taxes and reducing spending costs us jobs and prolongs and deepens the recession. But they are so mesmerized by their belief in anti-deficit economics that they continue to raise taxes and reduce spending nevertheless. In this way they are worse than the old surgeons who bled their patients to death. After a week of cup-a-days, the bloodletters would increase it to a pint per day if the patient wasn't responding favorably to the best treatment the medical profession had available. These doctors at least had the excuse that they truly didn't know how harmful the slow but steady loss of blood was to their patients. Our present bloodletting economic leadership knows that leeching us with taxes, drawing off federal spending, is causing the economy to get progressively sicker—but they keep doing it anyway. That's all they were taught to do, and they are not even attempting to learn any new lessons.

What's more, their treatment, deficit reduction, "has never been so trendy as it is now," as one of them gloats.[35] Senators Warren Rudman and Paul Tsongas command the headlines and talk shows with their Concord Coalition. Senator Paul Simon leads the yearly fight for a balanced budget. A hundred of our federal legislators have taken a pledge to reduce the deficit or forego reelection.[36] And people send money to Ross Perot, which is like pressing a dollar into the hand of a wealthy executioner. Perhaps they want him to make the decapitation of their own job swift and painless, which his program threatens to do.

## A Long, Slow Spiral Downward

But the Great Recession will not end quickly and painlessly. And (the only good news), I don't predict it will end with a five-year world war, as the depression did, or with a collapse of all Western economies, as the mongers predict. Instead, we and the rest of the West will continue to cut jobs, which reduces spending, which costs more jobs, which reduces spending even more, and on and on, down and down. Those who keep their jobs also keep the tension of ever-threatening downsizings, reduced benefits, and overwork. International tensions will not lead to nuclear war. But you might have to pay more for your car or electronics, you might find fewer markets for your products, as the West sacrifices the gains from free trade, gains that took our parents' generation forty patient years to win.

At home we can continue to see the increasing demoralization of the working class, of our young high school and college graduates, families broken by endless money problems, beaten children,[37] and overworked supermoms. In our search for scapegoats we will increasingly divide ourselves along us-versus-them lines, rich against poor, young against old, native-born against immigrant, our country versus everyone else's. Sure, we all have done a great job over the last twenty years, creating an overwhelming abundance of real wealth, achieving relative peace, turning the corner on the environment, and opening our hearts and lands to a healthy diversity unprecedented in history. However, our economics has converted what should be a win-win landscape into a country of people who have already lost and those who can see what's coming, and rightly fear for their economic future.

In a way, the most dangerous Americans have the kind of attitude that I like the most, the friendliest spirit to be around. They are the optimists, the people who see the glass half full instead of half empty. As long as anyone gets a job, they feel that jobs are available for all, if only you try hard enough. As high as taxes get, the optimists appreciate the money they have left. As depressed as everyone else gets in the Great Recession, they still awaken with a smile to greet a sunny day. In World War I, they would have counted only the survivors staggering back alive from the carnage of the machine guns, and forgotten the million massacred. They would have remembered the patients who survived two weeks of bloodletting, and forgotten their own sisters who were bled to death. Most soldiers survived the war, and most patients survived the bleeding. Similarly, most of us have jobs and most of our income is not yet taxed away. We are not yet at war, nor have the ghettos erupted in riots.

## THE END OF THE WORLD IS NOT AT HAND

And most of us will, indeed, have jobs. We should get to keep about half of our income away from the tax collector. I do not predict we will go to war with the Japanese, nor will ghetto rioting become widespread. One of the many ways the deficit mongers have been wrong is in their shrill prophesies of imminent doom, as I describe in chapter 4.

Take, for example, Henry F. Figgie, Jr.'s, hilarious book, *Bankruptcy 1995*. He predicts retirees having their house bought from under them by the Japanese, Mom losing her computer job to the French, Dad losing his machine operator's job to the Germans and Mexicans, both losing their savings in a bank run, their daughter's state university closing, a stock market crash that lasts, inflation of 100 percent, and the dollar being refused in world currency markets—all by "Doomsday 1995!" The mongers should publish their folly in the supermarket tabloids next to Jeanne Dixon and the other astrologers, based on their near-perfect record of wrong predictions.

I predict that Figgie's above predictions are dead wrong. His only correct predictions are of the evil that will befall us *if we follow his advice*. He predicts higher taxes, lower property values, bridges collapsing, and reduced Social Security, pension, and unemployment benefits. These indeed will occur if we do what he recommends: raising taxes and reducing spending in order to attack the so-called "deficit."

Fortunately, we have a social safety net that will prevent the Great Recession from becoming another Great Depression. The only reason we have this safety net is because we overruled the deficit-mongering Figgies and Greenspans of the 1930s and instituted Social Security, unemployment compensation, and Federal Deposit Insurance. If we repeal them, we would be in trouble. The only one in real danger is Social Security. Leading deficit mongers brag that "all politicians" regard Social Security and Medicare entitlements to be the main cause of the deficit, and Tsongas invites a "generational war."[38] But even if the American Association of Retired Persons (AARP) lets down its guard and our retirees go back to dog food, the U.S. is too strong now to suffer collapse.

*The people of America simply want what their parents had: a chance to work and work hard for an honest living, a fair share of the incredible wealth that we as individuals and as a nation have earned with the labor of our backs, brains, hearts, and souls. Too much of that wealth sits rotting on the shelves.*

Half of us will still have good jobs or a decent income, and half of the rest will still muddle along. The tragedy of pointless un- and under-employment will hurt a minority of voters, many of whom will be brainwashed into thinking their personal disasters are their own fault, unavoidable, or somehow due to the bogeyman deficit. The majority, I predict, will suffer only higher taxes, fewer job opportunities and promotions, and lower incomes due to the deficit reduction madness. The world will not come to an end. Most World War I soldiers took their bullets and lived. Most of the bloodletters' patients rose from their sickbeds after the leeches got their pint. Our country is living with an illness that saps our strength, but which will not kill us.

Perhaps the worst loss is our vision of the normal future of our country. Realize that we have already done a great deal of very hard work, for ourselves and for the world, for business and peace, in physics and basketball, in medicine and movies. God knows, we have made mistakes, and we shall never be the philosopher kings of the world (we'll leave that to the French). Our people, our children are not asking for nirvana or ambrosia. We are not all trying to crowd into first class. The people of America simply want what their parents had: a chance to work and work hard for an honest living, a fair share of the incredible wealth that we as individuals and as a nation have earned with the labor of our backs, brains, hearts, and souls. Too much of that wealth sits rotting on the shelves. Only the deficit mongers, with flinty hearts and clouded vision, sit guarding the bars of the cage they have put us in. To push them aside and regain the wealth we have already earned, we only have to understand how wrong they are, and how easy it is to do what is right. The deficit has no clothes. All we have to do to prosper is spend more and tax less, as explained in the next chapter.

# 3

# The Solution: Spend More and Tax Less

How could such a widespread and devastating problem as the Great Recession have such a simple solution? The fact is, throughout history, terrible problems have often had simple solutions. The simple solution to the Great Recession is to stop the unnatural practice of cutting spending and raising taxes during a time of increasing employment.

Cutting spending will cause further unemployment as surely as everyone knew charging into the machine guns during World War I would kill them. We have to stop the unnatural practice of raising taxes during a time of inadequate consumer spending power. We have bled our businesses of solvent customers, drop by taxing drop, as surely as the old doctors leeched their trusting patients to death.

Stopping the charges would not instantly have won World War I. Nor would stopping the bloodletting have instantly cured all illnesses. Similarly, raising spending and lowering taxes a modest 1 percent per year will not instantly give every American a good job and every business eager customers. But it will be the first step on a steady path back to prosperity. That represents a great difference from continuing and increasing our pace in the wrong direction, a pace we have maintained since 1988. Anti-deficit economics means raising taxes and cutting spending, automatically converting prosperity into recession. Reversing their program and ending the recession is as easy as cutting taxes and raising spending, as easy as not charging the machine guns and not bleeding the sick. All that is required is grasping this and deciding that is what we want to do.

*How* to fix our economy is easy. Understanding *why* we can lower taxes and increase spending while ignoring the so-called deficit is the hard part. You have to comprehend a new economics based on the relation between money and real wealth, and why the old economics is irrelevant in an age of abundance. Dry knowledge is not enough; well-entrenched institutions ignore logic, common sense, and all evidence, because they don't want to take the blame for their mistakes. You must understand how, in practical political terms, any change can be accomplished in the face of adamant and powerful opposition (chapter 12). Only then do I conclude by envisioning the great good that can be accomplished by a re-invigorated country after the death of anti-deficit economics.

There is simply too much to absorb all at once. Thus, this book takes many single steps. The preface was a conventional synopsis of the whole story. Chapter 1 gave you sharp sound bites of parts of the argument. And here, I will attempt to give you a few intuitive images of the new economic principles. These principles are explained at greater length in Part III. Explaining why the old economics is wrong itself takes more than seventy pages. But I also don't want to spend that much time on the old, wrong approach before giving a brief explanation of the solution to the recession. To overcome this chicken-and-egg dilemma, I circle up on the goal by giving you a brief view now of the main principle of the new economics our nation needs for us to thrive in the age of abundance: the need to balance money and wealth.

## OVERVIEW

What if a cure for cancer were discovered—but we let half of the miracle medicine go to waste? Absurd as this scenario sounds, it precisely matches the cause of our Great Recession. By following a false and irrelevant measurement of a spurious "deficit," we have ignored the *true* deficit—*insufficient money* to buy the real wealth we have already created. The criminal negligence of the old economics is its failure to comprehend the need to match the nation's money supply to its supply of real wealth. The misleading metaphor that leads people astray is the family checkbook. A nation's books are different, because a nation is responsible for printing its own money. A hypothetical example of how a family's financial concerns would change drastically if it were responsible for printing and backing up its own currency demonstrates, again, that the only deficit which matters is one between the amount of currency in circulation and the amount of real wealth backing it up.

> *By following a false and irrelevant measurement of a spurious "deficit," we have ignored the true deficit—insufficient money to buy the real wealth we have already created.*

Our Great Recession is caused only by a deficit in our money supply. As proof, note how easy it would be to pay off the "national debt." In the business world, the U.S. as a corporation would have suffered a corporate buyout and been cashed in for a multitrillion-dollar profit, based on the relatively tiny size of our obligations compared to the immense value of our assets. Correcting the real deficit is easy. All we have to do is lower taxes while increasing government spending. The bogus "deficit" will rise, but the true deficit will decline—bringing us the jobs we need to use our real wealth and create even more.

## A CURE FOR CANCER, REVISITED!

For a brief moment, let's refer back to the cancer cure parable and add some variables to the equation discussed. As a reminder, some of the basic information is repeated here, but let's take it a step further and flesh it out.

We talked about the hypothetical scenario in which a cure for cancer had been discovered in a government laboratory. The lab would be able to produce enough of the cure to make *ten thousand* doses the first year. Each dose could save one person's life. Next, to prevent the price of the medicine from rising sky-high, the government asked its highest-ranking economists for help. The economists decided people could buy the cure only with special ration coupons. So they counseled us to print *six thousand* coupons good for one cure each. We then tackled the difficult task of deciding exactly who would get them. We considered the following: severity of the disease, the age of the person, the type of cancer, quotas of recipients by race and state of the union, and the "merit" of the applicants. Now, let's add some thornier criteria: we take into account income, IQ, industriousness, creativity, beauty, athletic ability, etc. The nation was divided by angry debate. Nonetheless, after rushing through the process in order to save lives, the government established the criteria, distributed the coupons, and administered the medicine. Of the one hundred thousand Americans with terminal cancer that year, *sixty-three hundred* were saved by the wonderful new miracle cure.

So what do you think of this process? If you are like 99 percent of the Americans arguing about the Great Recession, you would focus your energy on the debate of who gets the cure. You would contend that the groups you belong to (elderly, creative, Midwestern, white, etc.) be favored more and the other groups less. But I hope you, as a reader of this book are in the minority who can see the error in logic of printing ration coupons.

The troublesome minority complained that, because only sixty-three hundred coupons were printed, much of the medicine ended up expiring, unused, on the shelves of government laboratories. "We should have printed more of the…" they tried to say, but were shouted down derisively by the government economists in charge of the coupon supply.

"You cranks! Don't even *think* of printing more," those respected men said. "Our coupons would become 'funny money,' losing all of their value in a hyperinflation of paper."

In their hearts, the old economists felt real coupons should be made of gold. Without gold, they believed the whole coupons-for-cancer-cure system stood on shaky ground, and all sorts of serious repercussions would surely occur if too many of the coupons were printed. They were also sure that six thousand were more than enough—especially since *every single one of the economists already had access to a coupon for himself.*

Let's backtrack a bit more. At the end of the year, the debate took a nasty new turn. Although the government economists had authorized only six thousand coupons, the laboratories ended up redeeming *sixty-three hundred* coupons for medicine. The debate shifted from the problem of allocation to the problem of the great *deficit* between the number of coupons authorized and the number redeemed. As the years went on, this *deficit* kept occurring, accumulating into a huge national debt of coupons, a deficit and debt which were increasingly blamed for the sad deaths of cancer patients throughout the land. Even the cancer patients themselves blamed this deficit and debt for their inability to get a dose of the miracle cure. Meanwhile, unused doses continued to expire on the shelves every year, so no one bothered to open extra production facilities to make more.

## WHAT THE "FEDERAL DEFICIT" AND "NATIONAL DEBT" REALLY MEASURE

"What a foolish country," I hope you're thinking. Yes, they (the economists) are foolish—but they are doing exactly what we are doing in this country today. What we measure as the deficit and debt are as irrelevant to the economic health of the U.S. as the three-hundred coupon "deficit" in the number of ration coupons in the cancer-cure scenario above. In fact, the measurements are worse than irrelevant, because our misguided efforts to reduce these irrelevant numbers is what *causes*, not cures, the Great Recession. Figure 3 below shows the flow of money that the deficit measures:

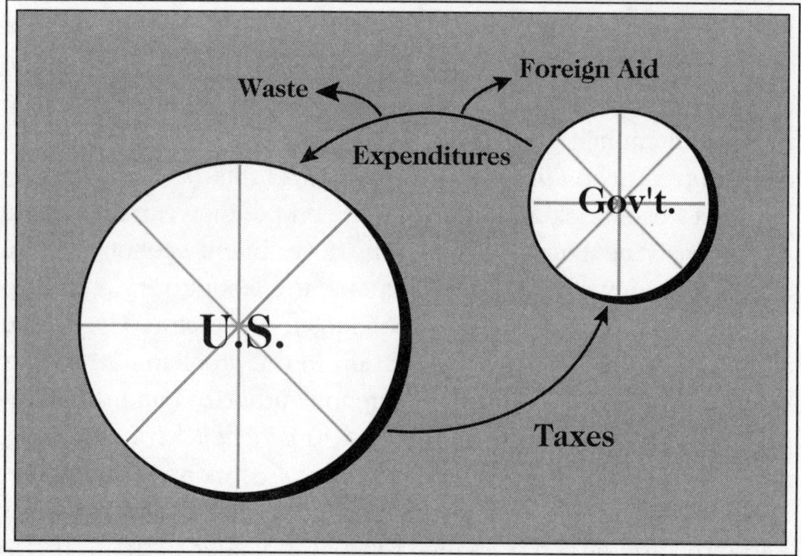


***Figure 4***

What the deficit measures is simply not important. The pie on the left represents the real wealth of the U.S. economy. The smaller pie on the right is the government. The line running from the large pie into the smaller one represents money flowing out of the U.S. economy into the government—that is, taxes. The line on top, running out of the government and back into the U.S. economy, represents government expenditures. Most of the expenditures are transfer payments, such as Social Security and Medicare, which go right back into the U.S. economy. But much of it gets spent elsewhere, say on foreign aid or government waste—those expenditures are represented by the arrows shooting off into space. (Of course, even most waste and foreign aid make their way back into the national economy.)

Thus, the only thing the deficit measures is the difference between one line and the other—the outflows from the government and the inflows of taxes. The deficit mongers authorize us to spend no more than we take in taxes. But the purpose of our national economic policy has relatively little concern with those flows. What really matters to us is the size of the large pie (the U.S.).

Let's go back to the example of the cure for cancer. What should have mattered was the amount of the medicine, not the number of coupons. The coupons, like money, exist only to utilize the real wealth that people create for each other. So who cares that the government cashed in more coupons than were authorized? That number was an irrelevant red herring, just as our so-called "debt" and "deficit" are. Just because a number exists doesn't prove it means anything.

## THE *REAL* DEFICIT

The real deficit in the cancer cure scenario is, obviously, the shortfall in the number of coupons printed by the government to be traded for the medicine. What a waste! Think of all the effort, all the education, the financing and managing of the laboratory, the inspiration and perspiration it took to make the discovery, the practical job of manufacturing the cure once it had been invented. And then an idiotic mistake by the government economists caused almost half of the medicine to go to waste. All they had to do in order to save far more lives, in order to use the wealth of medicine already on the shelves, was print more of the coupons. This scenario exactly parallels our own economic crisis. The extensive wealth we have already created sits rotting on the shelves for one reason only: we have not printed enough "coupons"; that is, *money*, for us to use it. The wealth on our shelves is not as magical as a cure for cancer, but it is life-giving and important nonetheless. With a great deal of talent and effort it already has been created, but sits there wasting away, just like the cancer medicine. It includes all the things we need, want, and are willing to pay for—goods, homes, cars, services, travel, security, safety . . . and medical care. Let's alter figure 1 on the cancer cure just a bit to look like this:

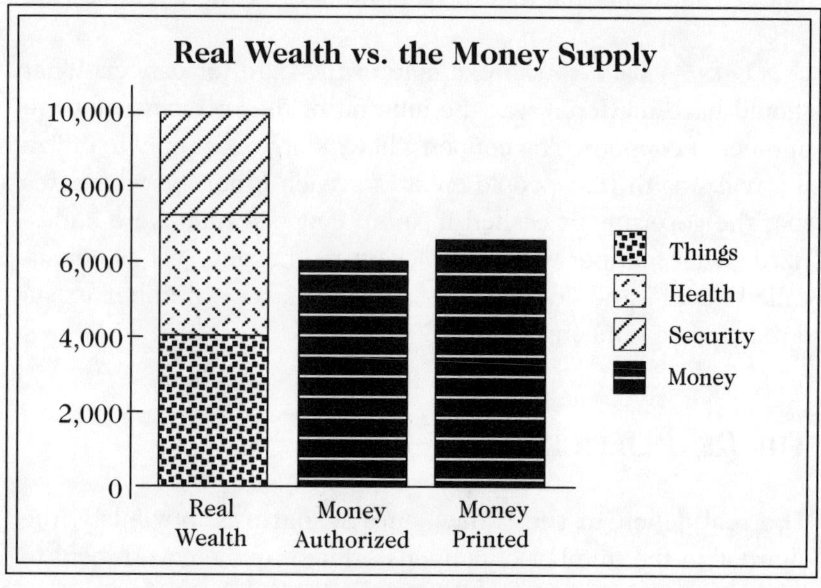


***Figure 5***

Our real wealth is all the things money can buy. Our real-life economists have mesmerized the nation into thinking less money is always better. *Any* mention of increasing the money supply causes them to foam at the mouth with dire warnings of another Weimar hyperinflation, bushels of marks, etc. The marvelous surplus of every conceivable good and service which the modern Western economies are supplying with great dexterity seems to have escaped their attention.

The parallel with the cancer cure medicine is no exaggeration. What backs up money is not and has never been gold sitting in some central reserve bank. What backs up money is what you can buy with it, just as surely as the cancer cure backed up the ration coupons. The *real* deficit, again, is the shortfall in the money supply caused by the economists. By decreeing tight money—in their hearts, you know they yearn for a return for the gold standard—they render useless the full abundance of wealth already produced. They ignore the huge gap between real wealth and our purchasing power, focusing instead on the relatively tiny and wildly irrelevant difference between the budget they would authorize (column 2) and the amount of money actually spent by the government (column 3).

Just as in the cancer cure scenario, the government in real life prints unauthorized "coupons" resulting in a false "deficit." In point of fact, this bogus "deficit" helps to reduce the *real* deficit in the money supply. As you can see, the deficit would have to be twelve times as great just to catch up with the real wealth we have already created. (The size of the columns is drawn roughly to scale: the false "deficit" is less than 5 percent of measured GNP; I estimate the money supply to be no more than 60 percent of our real wealth.)

What is miraculous about this ordinary wealth is how *much* of it we have created. Supply-side economics of the 1980s and before was, in fact, a great success—not at lowering the bogus "deficit," as its economist inventors foolishly predicted it would, but at helping us create a great abundance of goods. The miracle is that we have a shortage of *nothing*. The tragedy is that so much goes unused while so many people suffer from want of what we already have created.

How did this pointless tragedy come to pass? Why do thousands of people want for jobs, homes, cars, and medical care, while thousands of homes and hospital beds sit empty, thousands of cars sit unbought on the lots, and many thousands more are not even manufactured—while the jobless rolls threaten to claim millions of more lives? Our real wealth is being wasted for exactly the same reason the miracle medicine rotted on the laboratory shelves in the cancer cure scenario: the idiot economists did not understand the simple concept of matching the number of coupons with the amount of medicine.

## THE CRIME OF ECONOMICS

Believe it or not, contemporary economics has exactly the same blind spot. They have no basic concept of how big the money supply should be. Have you heard of "monetarism"? It's their main theory these days, but all it says about the size of the money supply is that it should be a little bit bigger than it was last year—just a *tiny* bit bigger. And they have no suggestions about *how* to make it bigger, now that their only method, lowering interest rates, has proven not to work. Worst of all, for no logical reason they still have a gut-level horror of making it at all bigger. In their hearts, they would like to see it smaller, and preferably backed up by gold.

My parody of their reaction in the cancer cure scenario is not an exaggeration. *Any* mention of printing money elicits an instinctive, irrational hysteria: "funny money" will ignite an "Argentina-style hyperinflation" and cause "thousands of traders to dump hundreds of billions of dollars" so that "interest rates will shoot up like an Apollo booster." Our government "will end up falling from power," probably in a "bloody revolution." And these quotes are from an economist who not only understands, but also *emphasizes,* that the current *decline* in the money supply has caused our recession![1]

As I said, logic and reason are not at work in their minds. They more remind me of anorexics who, even while admitting with one part of their brains that they need food to live, still react to all food as though it caused evil fat. Unfortunately, these econorexics, who react to all money as though it caused evil inflation, are in charge of our economy—as if you had an anorexic in charge of your family's meals. They can't handle the miracle of abundance. They are a science for a bygone day, a science devoted to "scarce resources," a science badly needed in Russia and Africa, but worse than useless to us now in the West.

## SKIP AHEAD, OR...

If you now understand the difference between the bogus "deficit" and the real deficit between real wealth and money, and want to hear what the old economists have to say in defense of themselves, you should skip on ahead to Part II. There I expose all their arguments against the bogus deficit for the hogwash they are. Better, if you are already persuaded the old economics is misguided and you don't want to waste any more of your own time beating a dead horse, you should skip all the way ahead to Part III. It describes in relative detail the nature of real wealth and why we need to balance that real wealth with the money that represents it. Remember, this is *your* book to read on *your* terms.

The rest of this chapter offers a second scenario, to reinforce the cancer cure example, of the need to print enough money to match one's real wealth. This second example is cast at the level of a family business and personal checkbook instead of a whole government, so some readers might find it easier to follow, or further illuminating. The chapter concludes with an answer to the easy question, "How do we pay off the 'national debt'?"

## WHAT THE DEFICIT IS NOT

The greatest obstacle to understanding our national economy is confusing it with an individual's personal finances. Deficit mongers never tire of scorning our country's supposedly spendthrift, errant ways. They say, "If I were to spend beyond my means the way our government has, I would be destitute and bankrupt. Worse, my children would be cursed with paying off the debts I had accumulated via my squandering, spendthrift ways." That is a standard attack. But the nation does not defend its borders the way an individual defends his home; the nation does not choose its allies the way individuals choose friends; and the national budget is not at all like your private bank account—unless you've got a printing press in the basement and make your own currency. If you did, your prime financial duty would be to back up all of the currency you printed with something that people find valuable.

Likewise, the duty of a nation to create a sound currency is the primary difference between national finances and your personal budgeting. You personally must earn money printed by someone else. But the U.S. does very little of its business in foreign currency. You buy and sell the things you want to people outside of your family by using that currency you did not print; however, as a nation, most of our business is done among ourselves using the currency we have ourselves created.

Think of what an immense change it would mean for the way you conducted your financial affairs if you indeed did print your own currency. Let's say, because your name is William, you decided to call your currency BillyBucks. You printed them up, and when you went to the store or gas station, you paid for your purchases with your fresh, hot-off-the-presses BillyBucks. What would allow you to get away with this? Why on earth would the grocer or cashier ever be persuaded to accept your currency?

To make your currency worth more than its novelty value, you would need something of value to back it up. In the old days, everyone thought we needed to back up all paper currencies with a single commodity everyone agreed had "real value," usually gold or something similar that could be used to make jewelry. But in practice what backs up a currency is *any form of real wealth*. A currency is fundamentally an *IOU* for the things we really want. Originally, human wants did not range much further than food, clothing, and shelter. Money exists only to make it easier for us to exchange the things we really want amongst ourselves. (In chapter 10, the origin and nature of money are discussed at length.)

Let's say the most valuable asset you own is a high-rent downtown office building you inherited. If, for whatever reason, you wanted to print BillyBucks to run your affairs, you could denominate each one as worth a rental of one square foot for one month in your building. Imagine what a complete difference this would make in the way you conducted your finances! What would matter most was that your BillyBucks retained their value—that people would continue to want to accept them. This is the primary principle of a sound currency, and applies as precisely to our national economy as it does to BillyBucks. Of course, the point of this BillyBucks example is to illustrate the fundamental principles of our national economy, so please draw parallels at any stage of the following explanation.

## THE VALUE OF BILLYBUCKS

So what do you have to do to keep BillyBucks valuable? People have to want to rent your building. Thus your first order of business is to keep up the building—if you inherited one in good shape, don't let it get run down or behind the times. People will not want a BillyBuck that only allows them into an office they would not care to rent. So you should spend some of your BillyBucks on maintaining and improving the building. If you print and spend one hundred BillyBucks to replace the carpeting, that expenditure can have an effective value of two hundred BillyBucks if it makes more people want to rent from you—which makes them need to earn your BillyBucks, either directly from you or from someone else who has earned a BillyBuck from you.

## INFLATED BILLYBUCKS

You cannot print more BillyBucks than you have room in your building to back them up. The instinct of economists trained to focus on scarce resources would always be to put this consideration at the top of a list—a list for many of them that has only this single, tunnel-vision entry. If you had a million square feet, but started printing 1.5 million BillyBucks per month, you would cause classical inflation—too many BillyBucks chasing too few square feet. You and the people who used BillyBucks could handle this excess in two ways.

Like the communists, you could maintain prices but make people wait on a list for your offices, just as they waited seventeen years for a car in Russia. The currency retains its absolute value, but loses its desirability, because you cannot spend it for what it is supposedly worth. The second way is too allow a free market in rents to bid up the price of your office space to absorb the BillyBucks you've printed. Then people will realize a BillyBuck is no longer worth a square foot, and the smart ones will demand more BillyBucks for their goods and services than they did before.

For the old economists, the previous paragraph is the whole story. Print fewer BillyBucks, they say. End of discussion. But note the critical condition that triggers inflation—printing more BillyBucks than you have square feet to back them up. That is, the building would have to be full—you need a shortage of what you use to back up BillyBucks in order for inflation to threaten. If your building has empty offices, you can indeed print more BillyBucks than you have been printing. The U.S. has no shortage of the wealth we use to back up our dollars. In fact, you can buy more for your dollar in the U.S. than you can for other people's currency in their countries. *Nothing is in short supply.*[2] That is why we have had inflation go down while the "debt" was quadrupling.

## TOO *FEW* BILLYBUCKS

If you had whole empty floors of your building backing up your BillyBucks, you would be a fool not to print more. Consider how foolish it would be to obsessively keep printing too few BillyBucks if you had unused wealth (empty offices) and members of your family in want. You could buy your spouse a car, but you let him or her take the bus. You did not send your daughter to college, but let her sit around the house. You never printed up some

BillyBucks to take a vacation. Worst of all, you skimped on the repairs and renovations needed to keep up the property.

Compare that fiscal policy—keeping the printing of BillyBucks as low as possible—to the strategy of your downtown neighbor. While your building has entire floors empty, he has printed so much of his currency that his building is 95 percent full. With his currency he has purchased a better home and car than yours, his children are all at private schools, and he takes his family to the Riviera. He also has completely refurbished his building, adding the wiring for easy computer networking as well as remodeling the interior. Last year he added an underground parking garage, so he can build an additional building where the parking lot used to be. Now, despite the much greater amount of currency he has printed compared with you, his currency is in more demand than yours at the same time he and his people are living a far better life than you are.

As you sit and look at your miserable family and contemplate your empty floors of offices, I hope you take immense self-satisfaction in having fewer BillyBucks in circulation than your competitor has.

## A Twin Deficit of BillyBucks

The real deficit would be printing up too few BillyBucks to keep your building occupied. What a waste if half of your building were empty because your economic advisers told you not to print and spend more BillyBucks than you printed last year. It would be a waste like that in the miracle cancer cure example; printing too few coupons allowed much of the medicine to expire, unused, on the shelves. And that is the waste we have inflicted on ourselves in the Great Recession. Immense wealth we have already created sits empty or unused, because our economic advisers dread printing enough to let us take advantage of what we have already earned.

We have to stretch our imaginations to figure out a BillyBucks deficit that parallels the bogus deficit terrorizing our country. Say you hired someone to manage the finances of your building. You gave him a certain number of BillyBucks each month, and expected him to spend no more than that. Behind your back, however, he snuck into your basement and printed more. He then spent these extra, unauthorized BillyBucks. When you discovered his crime, you counted the extra amount he printed as your "budget deficit." But how would this so-called "deficit" matter, as long as the currency was still sound? How would these extra BillyBucks hurt, if every one printed could still be exchanged for space in your office building?

Your manager might have been printing BillyBucks in order to finance a combination of "infrastructure" and "welfare" payments—that is, he printed extra BillyBucks to pay for the maintenance of the heat pump and for a detox program for your younger son. While he was paying for these, you ran a bogus "deficit," in that you printed more BillyBucks than you took in as rent those months. But what difference does that arbitrary "deficit" make, as long as you had plenty of office space to cover the obligations your manager incurred when he printed the extra or "deficit"-causing BillyBucks?

Go back to the cancer cure scenario. What did it matter that the government let an extra three hundred coupons be printed every year? They already had much more medicine—real wealth—than coupons in the first place. All the bogus "deficit" of coupons did was *save lives*. The bogus "deficit" of BillyBucks would finance a better life for your family and an improved property. And the bogus U.S. federal "deficit" has financed social and infrastructure improvements that have only helped our country, not harmed it.

## THE GOVERNMENT'S MAIN JOB: MAINTAINING A SOUND AND SUFFICIENT CURRENCY

The same reasoning applies to the U.S. deficit. Our government, in effect, manages our "building"—the government controls much of the wealth of our nation, even though private citizens own most of it. The minimum estimate I have found of U.S. wealth is $18 trillion—compared to a "debt" of $4 trillion. The guiding principle for our government, just as for the manager you hired to take care of your building and who printed extra BillyBucks, is to maintain a sound but *sufficient* currency. We have a sound currency. Inflation has died, even while Reagan was printing hundreds of billions of dollars to finance Star Wars and tax reduction. But we still do not have a *sufficient* currency. We still don't have enough money in our hands to buy the wealth we ourselves have produced.

*Inflation has died, even while Reagan was printing hundreds of billions of dollars to finance Star Wars and tax reduction. But we still do not have a sufficient currency. We still don't have enough money in our hands to buy the wealth we ourselves have produced.*

The U.S. has so much unused capacity right now, it is as though we're renting out only half of the building we inherited. People who want to work sit at home unemployed. Modern factories are shuttered. Others are employed at jobs that use only half of their capabilities. Many factories operate at a fraction of their capabilities. Other factories exist as the ideas of entrepreneurs who could build them tomorrow if the demand existed.

Consider what would happen if your building manager were subjected to the equivalent of a balanced budget amendment. Strict laws prevented him from sneaking into the basement to print more BillyBucks for maintenance and your son's drug treatment program. *Great*. Instead of four empty floors in your building (unused capacity), you have five empty floors (even more unused capacity). The BillyBuck is still worth the same. However, you will pay the price in the long run. The poor maintenance of the building will lead to a breakdown of confidence in your tenants in the value of renting there. Letting your son stay on drugs has long-term implications for the health of your enterprise in the future.

The parallels for the situation in our country are obvious. We have a great deal of unused capacity. The budget cuts we are contemplating threaten the health of the infrastructure we have inherited. Drug treatment programs turn away thousands due to underfunding. Meanwhile, the dollar is still the world standard, used as the unofficial reserve currency—in effect, serving much of the world as gold used to.[3] Meanwhile, our unjustly maligned currency buys more for us in this country than any other currency buys for its people in theirs.[4]

## PRINTING MONEY PROTECTS AND INCREASES THE VALUE OF OUR ASSETS

The point of the BillyBucks example is to show how printing more money is necessary to *protect* and *increase* the value of our nation's assets. What matters when you print money is not how much you issue this month compared to how much you collected, but how much you have printed compared with what you have to back it up. If a refusal to print money causes you to let valuable assets go unused, or, worse, deteriorate, you have been penny-wise and pound-foolish. That is the state we are in as a nation today. By letting our infrastructure deteriorate, we are in the equivalent position of destroying our inheritance.

## HOW CAN WE PAY OFF THE NATIONAL DEBT?

The short answer is that the U.S., like a major corporation, will not and ought not ever pay off its debt. However, that answer is unsatisfying even for people who are themselves always carrying a mortgage and car loan. A different approach to this question which you have not heard before is to look at the debt question as it would arise if the U.S. were, again, a giant corporation. If it were, we would see that our national debt was too *small*—compared to the worth of the American Enterprises, Inc., our equity and debt obligations are so tiny that the Carl Acahns and T. Boone Pickenses of this world would long ago have grabbed a piece of the action. If the U.S. were a publicly traded corporation, with assets of $18 trillion and obligations of only $4 trillion, it would have been subjected to a hostile takeover, if necessary, by corporate mergers-and-acquisition (M-and-A) raiders!

Why? For the same reason M-and-A raiders went after R. J. Reynolds and dozens of other multibillion-dollar companies. Those companies were far more sound business investments than the stock and bond markets gave them credit for being. Thus it was cheaper to buy them out at a large premium over their market value—by taking on huge debt obligations of "junk bonds"—and selling the pieces of the corporation for billion-dollar profits. The only difference with the U.S. would be that the raiders would enjoy *trillion*-dollar profits. Our much-criticized country has so little debt and is capitalized so far below its worth, that they would make a fortune by selling it off in pieces. To protect ourselves from such a takeover, we would have had to take on great amounts of *additional* debt in order to make ourselves a less attractive target, as well as adding "poison pills" to our portfolio of assets. As it is, the entire national debt is only a fraction of our net worth.

The $18 trillion estimate is an extremely conservative measure, incorporating only those forms of already measured wealth that economists love best, and ignoring the greater sums described in chapter 9. A newer and better measure, the "national income and product account," or NIPA, is the best the old economists can do for now, although it still only measures wealth that already has a price on its head. Even the conservative estimate credits the U.S. with making more than $6 trillion in 1993.[5] Let's make this personal. It's as though you had an income of sixty thousand dollars a year and a total debt—including everything acquired over the years, such as college loans, home mortgage, car loans, medical costs, and credit card debt—of only forty thousand dollars in all. (A few years ago, "your share of the national debt" was being touted as seven thousand dollars—at the same time per capita NIPA was around twenty thousand dollars.) So how horrified should you be about your "demon deficit," the "malignant force" that "condemns your children"?

*You are actually in great shape—as is our country.* A mortgage alone can normally be four times annual income, whereas all our debts combined are less than one year's income. Your real danger would be in letting your property run down and lose its value, or letting your earning skills deteriorate because you have been spooked by scary tales of your imminent "bankruptcy"—so spooked that you fail to repair the roof, ignore your car's red oil-warning light, cancel your health checkup, drop your computer class, and pull your kids out of college. Sure, you'll have lower debt—but a permanently damaged net worth as well.

## So How do We Fix the Real Deficit?

Fixing the deficits in the cancer cure and BillyBucks examples was easy. Print more ration coupons for the cancer medicine, at least up to the amount of medicine already waiting on the shelves. Print enough BillyBucks to fill up the building every month.

Knowing exactly how much money the U.S. should print is more complex, as is the question of exactly how to print and distribute the money. But the basic idea is just as simple. We already have a great abundance of real wealth, sitting wasted on the shelves as sure as the hypothetical cancer cure sat unused, as surely as floor after floor in your hypothetical building sat empty. The main point is to print *more*, and get them into circulation in any way we can.

I explain in chapter 6 how our government already prints money and pays it to themselves, calling it "monetizing the [bogus] debt." We have been doing it for generations with good effect, but not good enough. To increase the amount of the debt we monetize, we only need to spend more and tax less. I explain that we do not sell more government bonds at ever-higher interest rates. We do not add more "interest payments" to our already onerous tax burden.

The most interesting challenge is tackled in chapter 14, which puts forth a number of examples of ways to get new money into circulation. In the BillyBucks example, you could maintain your building, educate your daughter, and cure your son's addiction. This country can do that and more, on a massive scale. We already have all the real wealth created in the past and present—the infrastructure, utilities, homes, food, cars, VCRs and computers, the airline tickets. When we begin to fix the true deficit, we can begin to create ever more of the real wealth of the future. Only our misplaced fear of the bogus "deficit" holds us back.

# PART II

# The Problem: The Old Economics of "Scarcity"

# 4

# The Myth of the Deficit: Apocalypse Never

This country's seemingly insurmountable problems could be easily fixed by spending more and taxing less. All that holds us back is the pervasive myth of the deficit. This chapter demonstrates how false and harmful that myth has been. As with all myths, the language used is more hysterical than logical—for example, the deficit is "the malignant growth" that "dooms our children." Like end-of-the-world preachers, deficit-mongers constantly predict catastrophes that never occur. Calm voices that have looked at the facts are ignored.

The myth plays off of our gut fears and emotions, no matter how unreasonable those fears may be. Every specific evil imputed to the deficit turns out to be wrong: inflation, crowding out, high interest rates, international panic, and the supposed "burden to our children." Instead, history shows that following the deficit mongers' advice *causes* the very problems we need to avoid. Cortez did not destroy the Aztec civilization; rather, it was the myths the Aztecs believed, and which the Aztec people followed to their deaths, that protected Cortez's small force in its swath of destruction.

## SHRILL VOICES

In place of facts, the deficit mongers use a hysterical vocabulary of scare tactics. The deficit is a "malignant force" that "guarantees tremendous social, cultural, political and economic upheavals." It is "the Strangelove economics that condemns our children" to "fiscal oblivion." The "demon deficit" is "Public Enemy No. 1" with a "tight stranglehold on fiscal policy." "The evil twins, the humongous federal budget deficit and debt" are an "economic crime" leading to the "bankrupting of America." A billboard in New York constantly keeps score of the national debt ("Your family share: $56,168"), and congressional candidates take a solemn pledge to forego re-election if they can't cut the deficit in half. Anyone using the facts to question their views is a "Dr. Feelgood" whose "addiction to debt" makes him a "wacko" who's likely to believe in the "Tooth Fairy."[1]

## THE END OF THE WORLD IS AT HAND!

The deficit mongers remind me of religious apocalyptists. One sect alone has confidently predicted the end of the world in 1918, 1925, and 1975. Despite these frequent "resets, the movement continues to grow by leaps and bounds."[2] Similarly, the deficit mongers have predicted disaster from deficit spending in the 1930s, the 1960s, and in 1981—in fact, the quote above about deficits "guaranteeing tremendous social, cultural, political and economic upheaval" is from the Inaugural Address of Ronald Reagan, who then tripled our deficit while bringing relative prosperity to the land. In 1984 one warned that "If $150 billion is not cut by 1987, the present recovery in both the U.S. and the rest of the world will come to an untimely end."[3] Of course, that much was *added* to the deficit, and the recovery had accelerated.

But do the religious apocalyptists let their continuing failures get them down? No. Numerous studies show the different sects *reaffirming* their faith in the leaders who made such bold and clearly disproven claims. Failure only inspires them to redouble their efforts to gain additional converts. Similarly, today's deficit mongers—e.g., Henry Figgie—confidently predict a currency collapse, widespread bank failures, cuts in Social Security benefits, and hyperinflation—all by 1995!

## VOICES OF REASON, UNHEARD

Meanwhile, calm and respected voices have stood fast against the flood of rhetoric and attempted to show the errors of fact and logic surrounding the deficit. Two Roberts, Eisner and Heilbroner, have led the way for decades. These gentlemen are definitely *not* wild-eyed radicals or "Dr. Feelgoods." Robert Eisner was the 1988 President of the American Economic Association, the old economists' primary professional group. Robert Heilbroner wrote one of the best-selling economics books of all time, *The Worldly Philosophers*, and has lectured at more than a hundred universities. Milton Friedman won a Nobel Prize for his early work, which advocated unlimited deficit spending in the service of economic growth,[4] and which affixed blame for the depression on our squeezing the money supply. He backslid into a fanciful monetarism, but still comes to his senses occasionally, describing the federal and trade deficits as "twin delusions," even a "blessing."[5]

Nobel laureates Robert Solow and James Tobin have long tried to downplay our obsession with the deficit in favor of encouraging economic growth. Increasing numbers of economic columnists such as Paul Craig Roberts have begun to question the old economists' conventional wisdom—even in hard-core deficit-think publications such as the *Economist*, the *Wall Street Journal*, and *Business Week*.

## CALM DISPASSION VERSUS GUT FEARS

Why are these prominent people and their ideas such a quiet background noise in the present deficit debate? Calm reasoning rarely wins arguments against shrill rhetoric that plays off our deep-set, gut fears. On one side of the debate, the deficit mongers prophesy imminent doom for us and sure disaster for our children. On the other side, the two Roberts say that deficits are not as bad as you think, and aren't properly measured. The deficit mongers play off the image of the overdrawn personal checkbook, with the implication that the country has spent far more than it has earned. The two Roberts say that other considerations are more important—like employment, consumption, and economic growth—and we have to tolerate some level of deficit.

*The deficit apologists have not offered an alternative vision, a reason for taxing less, spending more, and letting the accounting error known as the "national debt" keep rising as it always has.*

The reasonable arguments are *too* calm. When you hear one side say, "The deficit is terrible—really terrible!" and the other side counter with, "Well, it's not as bad as all that," you are left with the impression that something is indeed *wrong*, and it is only a question of *how* wrong it is. The current arguments in favor of the deficit have not gone far enough in showing how completely wrong the deficit mongers are. The deficit apologists have not offered an alternative vision, a reason for taxing less, spending more, and letting the accounting error known as the "national debt" keep rising as it always has.

This book offers a clear alternative vision. I am not merely saying the deficit is "not so bad." Rather, I am saying that the numbers we call the deficit have *no* bad effects, and in fact should be much *larger* than they are. This analysis is based on the principle of balancing money and real wealth; that is, real wealth is more important than money, and we must print enough money to match the wealth we have created. The *true* deficit is the *shortfall in our money supply* as compared with our real wealth.

The theory of balancing money and wealth is the core of the book, and is presented at length in Part III. I would just as soon ignore the old economics and get on with the new. However, the deficit hysteria so dominates the nation's economic thinking that I can't just brush it off. Almost everyone believes the old ideas—just as everyone once believed in bloodletting. It's very hard to believe two opposite things at once. So people must first see how the old ideas are wrong, before they can open their minds to a new explanation. Because the old ideas *are* so glaringly wrong in every particular, this task is not difficult. Unfortunately, covering so many particulars takes a long time.

## NATIONAL DEFICITS ARE *NOT* LIKE YOUR PERSONAL CHECKBOOK

The old economists do not explicitly make their most insidious claim about the deficit, because they know it is so wrong. But they allow the vague image of the family checkbook to underlie our thinking and even their own. Get this straight: As I said before, your checkbook is not like the government's, because *you do not print your own money.* You earn and spend money printed and controlled by the U.S. government. You have to back up your expenditures with your earnings in someone else's currency.

For the government of any nation that prints its own money, the story is completely different. *Technically*, all that backs up a nation's money is more of its own money. That is to say, all you can get for a ten-dollar bill from the U.S. treasury is two fivers—and the same with deutschmarks at the Bundesbank. *Theoretically*, all that backs up money is other money, whether coins, different denominations, or a pile of gold supposedly buried somewhere.

In practice, *what backs up a nation's money is what you can buy with it.* What makes the dollar worth anything is that you can buy stuff with it—almost anything in the world. We take it for granted; but think how hard it would be to set up such a system by yourself. Even a world superpower couldn't get it right. The Soviets had a super-sound ruble system by the standards of the old economists, but you could buy almost nothing with a ruble—not good food, or a car, or a vacation—and certainly not a house. Yet their national books seemed to be perfectly balanced, as did Romania's under Ceaucescu.

For you to print up your own money as the government does, imagine what you would have to go through in a dollar-less society. Grant for the sake of argument that you did have a lot of real wealth to back up your private currency. In the BillyBucks example, I used commercial property as the real wealth, but imagine you had oil, wheat, expertise in tax accounting, etc. What you had, many people wanted. Instead of always bartering your good or service directly in exchange for other people's goods, you gave them an IOU payable to the bearer on demand. *You* control the number of your IOUs in circulation. So: exactly *what* do you have to do in order to be fiscally responsible?

Each IOU you print up and hand out is like a check, if you want to use the checkbook analogy. What would constitute a deposit? The deposits are what back up the "checks" (IOUs) you write. And in your dollar-free society what backs up your checks is the good or service you supply. Each barrel of oil or head of cattle you produce allows you to write out more IOUs for cattle or oil, obviously. A real deficit would occur if you wrote out more IOUs than you had cattle. If you were as financially obtuse as the deficit mongers, you might use some other pair of numbers and call their difference a "deficit." For example, say you wrote one thousand IOUs last year, but only nine hundred fifty were redeemed. You could call this fifty IOU difference a "deficit," if you wished, and cut way back on your printing until the "deficit" were "made up." If you were as stupid as the deficit mongers, you would ignore the fact that you had fifteen hundred head of cattle backing up your one thousand IOUs in the first place. Because of the bogus fifty IOU "deficit," you would cut back on feed, new pasture land, a course on new stock techniques, better antibiotics, etc. What would be the result? If you cut back enough on spending because of your fear of this bogus deficit, you could cause a real problem to develop. Your cattle would begin to die. The number you produced would fall off. Then, indeed, you would not be able to print and spend as many IOUs as you had previously been able to. But it would not have been the fault of the bogus "deficit." It would have been the fault of foolish economic reasoning.

## METAPHOR OF THE BAD FINANCIAL ADVISER

The crux of the problem with using the "federal deficit" to measure the state of the nation's economic health is that the numbers employed ignore much of our most important national income. Look at the cancer cure example once again. Say the reason the economists said to print only six thousand ration coupons was that they did not understand how much of the medicine had actually been produced. Perhaps they only recognized the medicine produced by private industry, and ignored the four thousand doses that had been produced in government labs.

Right now our economists only recognize government "income" as that collected from private citizens and businesses as taxes and fees. They have no concept of the government having created any wealth itself. But the wealth the government adds, just like the additional four thousand doses of the cancer cure, is as real as that produced by private industry. Understand that a government that avoids world war for fifty years has in effect created a great deal more wealth than its ancestor governments that held a worldwide destructive orgy every twenty years or so. Also, allowing free trade puts more real wealth in the hands of our citizens, it being a kind of foreign aid *for* Americans—if only we would understand and value it properly. Ultimately, the "deficit" is irrelevant, but the number itself could be used in a figurative way to measure previously unmeasured wealth. The point is, our national accounting figures now ignore much of our most important wealth.

Thus, the national ledger would be like your family checkbook, only if your family checkbook failed to include much of your most important income. Perhaps you have hired a very bad financial consultant to take care of your affairs, and you trust his estimates of how much you can spend. But he has a very narrow, rigid view of income, and refuses to credit you with the dividends you get from the family inheritance or the royalties you earn on your patents. He only credits you with your salary. Subsequently, he tells you that you only have half of the money each month that you really have. You stay in a small house, drive an old car, cut out vacations, and decide not to send your daughter to college. Even living this poorly, you spend more than he says you should, so over the years you have built up a huge negative balance on your checking account, according to his figures.

Each year it gets larger. Actually, you are not quite sure why this negative balance hasn't caused some problems at the bank—your checks never bounce, nobody hauls you to bankruptcy court—but you feel awful about it. So every month you, your family, and your financial consultant promise to cut out more "wasteful expenditures," like fixing the leaking roof, or to increase your income, by sending your daughter out to work at McDonald's. You survive, but life is not as good as it should be.

Our political and economic leadership has been like the dimwitted financial adviser above. Our national "income" recognizes only one source: taxes, the parallel to the family financial adviser's recognizing only salary as a source of income. And we recognize only a single way to increase our national income, raising taxes, no matter how painful and fruitless that becomes, like sending one's daughter to work at McDonald's. The point is, this nation has already accrued a huge amount of "inheritance dividends," which are the accrued gains of our forefathers' under-rewarded sweat and toil. We have already earned "royalty income," which is the surplus value of laws and inventions that have been worth a thousand times what the people who came up with them were ever paid. (The nature of this surplus wealth is explained in chapter 9.) The reason that the "bank" tolerates a years-long, increasing "negative balance" is that *the money is already in the bank*—but your foolish financial adviser wasn't smart enough to tell you about it. Similarly, the additional three hundred doses (indeed, four thousand doses) of the cancer medicine were already on the shelves, and the addle-brained economists didn't recognize them.

How foolish to fear this seemingly huge national debt, supposedly getting bigger every year! People still believe the government's addle-headed financial advisers, although we suffer none of the disasters they keep threatening us with. The government's checks aren't bouncing. Germany is not foreclosing on the capital. Japan is not hauling us into bankruptcy court. Of course, our economists know that the "deficit" they measure must be a terrible thing, so they make up a description of the evils it causes. You should be suspicious of such a preposterously huge number when it has such an invisible impact, especially when the effects of trying to *reduce* the number are great and immediate. The fact is, the "deficit" number has no effect because, like the calculations of the simple-minded financial adviser described above, the "deficit" calculations are just plain wrong.

# 5

# The Big Lie: The Inflationary Obsessions of the Economic Anorexics

The case against the federal "deficit" is based on such bald-faced inaccuracies that I think it is only fair to call them *lies*. What the mongers say is simply not true, and they know it. At my talks I pass out a one-page list of their arguments, in case someone in the audience wants to argue, but forgot exactly what it was those mongers were saying. Sad to say, I can't get anyone to make any of those arguments against me in public—and do you know why? Because they know they'll be made fools of in front of their friends if they try to uphold the mongers' ridiculous assertions. The deficit does *not* cause inflation, crowding out, or high long-term interest rates. Germany and Japan will *not* panic if we lower our taxes. Our children will *not* have to pay back an astronomical principal or make crushing interest payments. No one has a moral burden from the deficit, except the deficit mongers themselves.

The mongers' arguments are wrong in both of the ways an argument can be wrong: factually and logically. First, what they say doesn't agree with the facts. They have constantly predicted, "If the deficit goes up, such-and-such (e.g., inflation) also will go up." And they have constantly been wrong. The deficit has gone up, and inflation or whatever has gone *down*. In fact, they usually have it backwards: such-and-such has gone up when the deficit has gone *down*. Second, the reason their predictions don't come true is that their arguments don't make *sense*. The following pages in this chapter marshal the facts that contradict the mongers and explain the absurd flaws in their reasoning.

## THE BIG LIE: "INFLATION!"

This is the big one. As stated in chapter 1, I expect to have to explain inflation a dozen times before it sinks in. The deficit mongers don't bother to explain it at all. Check out the *Economist* or the *Wall Street Journal*. According to them, financing a deficit by printing money causes inflation to rise which causes interest rates to rise, the bond market to fall, and the stock market to rise. They bother to discuss only the interest rates, stocks, and bonds—to them the first part, inflation, is as obvious as gravity or "the sky is up." They have been thoroughly indoctrinated with "monetarism," which states that "inflation is always and everywhere a monetary phenomenon."[1] They expect you to share their dogma, so what's to discuss or explain? Why waste time thinking or looking at the facts?

The next few pages will do the work the old economists haven't bothered doing. I will first cover six of the fallacies about inflation, and then explain ten other factors that really do cause inflation, besides the size of the money supply. No single factor causes inflation. It takes a combination. As I will explain, inflation can go down while the money supply goes up. It has happened before and it will happen again, if we understand the other ten *real* causes, and play our cards right. The old economists, blinded by their simple-minded dogma, don't care. They let their fallacies pass unexamined.

## INFLATION FALLACY NO. 1:
### *"If the government prints more money, mine will be worth less."*

The secret fear that dominates many people's attitude towards printing money is that if more money is printed, the money they already have will be less valuable. This simple fear could perhaps be traced to their early experiences with hard-to-get baseball cards or marbles, or their first learning that gold is valuable because the supply of it is limited. They try to explain inflation to me like this: "Say you have a set number of bushels of corn and money so that each bushel costs a dollar. But if you then print 10 percent more money, the price of each bushel will rise to $1.10." Yes, but only if you presume the supply of goods *does not increase*—which is presuming the *opposite* of the facts in the real world. Their laws of economics may apply to Mars or the old communist economies where shortages are the norm—but not to our world, where surpluses are everywhere. But they insist on presuming an imaginary condition, because only then does their reasoning apply—a reasoning appropriate to a harsh world of shortages that must be fought over.

Thus they view the economy as a win-lose game: even if society at large would gain a great deal from printing more money, the relative status they already have would nosedive. In dark moments I fear that many of those in charge of our economic policies actually do take pleasure in the suffering of others, to judge by the results of what they have done and want to continue doing. In that case, nothing any of us says about the common good will change their minds. And they have created a self-fulfilling prosperity. By squeezing the money supply, they can indeed create unnecessary shortages out of plenty, and the harsh struggles of man against man will arise again.

But if they pay any attention to the historical facts, they have to admit that printing money no longer has any relation to inflation in the West.[2] Their old, simple theory has been stood on its head. Why? As I explain in the next chapter, the old economics was based on the allocation of *scarce* resources. We are now in the age of *abundant* resources.[3] Many of the rules have therefore changed. For example, the old law relating prices to demand said that increased demand for something made its price go *up*. But nowadays, we wait for increased demand (for computers or HDTV—High Definition TV) to bring the price *down*. Likewise with inflation. In the age of abundance, printing one dollar in order to create two dollars' worth of real wealth is actually *anti*-inflationary.

That is exactly what happened in the 1980s. Through hard work, we have seen an explosion in the creation of real wealth. Only a too-small money supply has held us back from enjoying our hard-earned real wealth and creating even more. In the Reagan years the money supply *grew* much faster than before, even while inflation kept going *down*. The old economists had been sure that printing so much money to pay for the "deficit" would cause high inflation, hurting them personally. But even one of their most hard-core leaders, the author of *Day of Reckoning*, has had to admit: "Monetary growth has simply been irrelevant."[4] In fact, the main effect it had was making the people with money even richer relative to the poor.

The evidence is overwhelming. In the U.S., we financed a run-up in the deficit from one to three trillion dollars while bringing inflation down.[5] Furthermore, during that time we saw the purchasing power of the U.S. dollar increase, in terms of what we can buy with it compared with what you can buy in other countries with their own currency. (This measure, called Purchasing Power Parity (PPP), compares how much you pay for a Big Mac or a two-bedroom apartment in different countries.) Japan saw an explosion of monetary growth with very low inflation. West Germany created $37 billion worth of deutschemarks in a single day to exchange for worthless East German ostmarks. Despite endless predictions of inflationary disaster, they had less than 3 percent inflation plus high economic growth that year. Thereafter they reversed course, using tight-money policies to cause both higher inflation, and, incredibly, negative growth—an actual decrease in their gross domestic product from the year before.

How could this be? Why were the inflation alarmists wrong? The old economists forgot an even older principle: Inflation is caused by too much money chasing too few goods. Current mainstream thinking among the old economists takes the preposterous position that an "increase in the quantity of money is the one and only important cause of inflation."[6] Which brings us to:

## INFLATION FALLACY NO. 2:
***"The only cause of inflation is too much money."***

Their purist proportion is as absurd as saying that, "The one and only cause of being overweight is eating too much," and ignoring the effects of exercise, smoking, and heredity. The inflation of the 1970s was a puzzling surprise for them, because the obvious shortage of oil should not have had any effect on inflation, according to their calculations. It took a great deal of soul-searching for some of them to admit that a sudden "supply shock"—that is, a reduction in the supply of a good—could cause its price to go up.

But that lesson was so dimly learned that they cannot apply its moral to the current situation. That is, if an undersupply of goods (such as oil) can cause prices and inflation to go *up*, then an oversupply of goods will cause prices to go *down*. And that's exactly what we have—*a great abundance of goods.* How can you have inflation if a slowly increasing supply of money is chasing a rapidly exploding supply of goods? Those who can indeed realize that we have a great abundance of goods tend to treat abundance as a *problem*—they call it "overcapacity"—which must be treated by decreasing our ability to make real wealth. They are obsessed beyond reason with squeezing the money supply—so obsessed that they would remedy the imbalance between too little money chasing a great many goods by *destroying the goods* rather than increasing the money supply. I will not presume to psychoanalyze these people, but read on about "economic anorexics" and "inflation alarmists."

## INFLATION FALLACY NO. 3:
### *"It's everywhere, it's everywhere."*

People see inflation even when prices are going *down*. This odd phenomenon has no definite explanation, but I suspect it is related to the tendency to remember criticism better than we remember praise. If people go to the supermarket and buy twenty items with unchanged prices, five items costing less than the month before, and two items costing more, all they will complain about to their friends are the two items costing more.[7] Complaining about rising prices is a comforting ritual, like knocking the weatherman. It occurs whether prices are rising or not. People chat about *lower* prices as rarely as they credit the weatherman with an accurate forecast.

The fact is, inflation is dead in Western economies. The best measures we have say it's between 2 percent and 4 percent, and those measures are biased upward about 2 percent (refer to the Consumer Price Index in chapter 10). A paradox is that while consumers always notice more inflation than is there, they are starting to wait to buy things because they have learned to expect prices to *drop*. And they are right to do so. Prices are falling everywhere. Credit Wal-Mart with bringing us lower prices on regular consumer goods, as they have applied information technology to providing us with what we want more efficiently. Beer, cigarettes, and diapers are cheaper. Commodities across the board have stagnated or gone south in price. Luxury collectibles have declined as well, because even the rich are beginning to worry about their next million. Artistic photographs, exotic sports cars, and rare coins have crashed. Hotels can't raise their rates even to keep up with low inflation. A power glut keeps electric bills down. A permanent oil glut, unimaginable ten years ago, keeps gasoline prices lower than they were at that time. Even the most reviled expense, the evil health care, is yielding to price pressures.

The picture is so clear that even the magazines editorially dominated by inflation alarmists and deficit mongers have admitted, repeatedly, that "inflation is at bay." "The cold wind of the economy is putting prices on ice." We don't have to fear "the ghosts of inflation past." "Inflation is about as real as Spielberg's dinosaurs." The headlines scream what should be good news day after day.

Unfortunately, overwhelming evidence never sinks into the inflation alarmists and the deficit mongers. The people guiding our economic policy still regard it as their mission, above all, to guard against an already vanquished enemy—inflation—while we are being ravaged by immediate and far greater dangers: unemployment, crippling taxes, a decaying infrastructure, social unrest, and international tensions. Alan Greenspan looks at the facts and still says, "We must be especially vigilant not to be mesmerized by the current tranquillity of the inflationary environment." He then sadly concludes he will have to raise interest rates again, recession or no, inflation or no. No matter what the facts, he just *knows* that inflation is the illness and tight money is its only cure.

*The people guiding our economic policy still regard it as their mission, above all, to guard against an already vanquished enemy—inflation—while we are being ravaged by immediate and far greater dangers: unemployment, crippling taxes, a decaying infrastructure, social unrest, and international tensions.*

I call people like him, Wayne Angell (for years one of the most extreme tight-money members of the Fed's Board of Governors) and Helmut Schlesinger (of Germany's Bundesbank) "economic anorexics," or "econo-rexics." Their numbers are legion. The single goal of regular anorexics is to be thin—in their eyes, any weight gain is ugly. The single goal of the econo-rexics is low inflation—in their accounts, all money is easy and disgusting. Anorexics are convinced food causes the ultimate evil, fat, so they eat as little as possible, and purge themselves afterwards. Econo-rexics are convinced money causes the ultimate evil, inflation, so they want to create as little as possible, and raise interest rates afterwards. Anorexics are willing to pay the price for eating by riding the stationary bike for two hours after a single chocolate chip cookie. Econo-rexics are willing to lay off a few million more people, or add a dozen extra taxes here and there, as the necessary price to pay for printing the evil money they despise and fear. Anorexics let their bodies run down, eating less and exercising more, until they die. Econo-rexics let their countries' industries and workers run down, spending less and taxing more, until endless recession leads to who knows what. Both are pathologically convinced that their austerity is righteous and proper, even beautiful, despite the sure evidence of their deteriorating conditions. They even interpret their declining health as evidence for even greater rigor—eating less, taxing more, exercising harder, spending less—and die with smiles on their faces, knowing they did the right thing until the very end. Here's the comparison in a table:

| ■ *Food Anorexics* | | ■ *Economic Anorexics* |
|---|---|---|
| All food causes fat | ► | All money causes inflation |
| Eat as little as possible | ► | Print as little as possible |
| Purge afterwards | ► | Raise interst rates afterwards |
| Starve yourself | ► | Lay off millions |
| Do exhausting exercise | ► | Pay high taxes |
| Let body run down, die | ► | Let economy run down, have a recession |
| Gaunt is beautiful! | ► | Recessions are healthy! |
| I'm getting sick—better eat even less | ► | Recession's getting worse—better squeeze money supply |
| I'm dying, but I've done the right thing | ► | The recession is permanent, but we've done the right thing |

How can this craziness, this sickness, persist? Because what both kinds of "rexics" do is, *in the proper measure*, very healthy indeed. Extreme gluttony can cause obesity, and runaway printing presses can cause hyperinflation. Some exercise is of course healthy. Even unemployment is healthy, if the alternative is communist-style make-work jobs in decrepit industries which are protected from bankruptcy. We might even admire the anorexics' rigorous austerity, knowing how hard it is to eat less and exercise more—they are amazing champions of the diet and workout wars.

What transforms the rexics' germ of a good idea from health-giving to death-dealing is their simplistic extremism. All food is dangerous to an anorexic. All money is dangerous to an econo-rexic. The anorexic begrudgingly allows, say, eight hundred calories a day, the amount appropriate for a small child. The econo-rexics begrudge us a slow but steady increase in the money supply, appropriate for an economic weakling, not a country with huge potentialities opened up by peace and international trade. The concept of *in*sufficiency, of food or of money, is beyond their comprehension—neither can conceive of any circumstance requiring more fuel. Neither will admit any proof of the failure of their philosophy. The main difference is that anorexics suffer a private tragedy—none are in charge of the eating habits of a nation. Sadly, the econo-rexics dominate the Fed and our entire economy. We are letting the inmates run not only the asylum, but city hall and the Capitol.

## INFLATION FALLACY NO. 4:
### *"Any inflation is bad inflation."*

I too hate and fear inflation. The main measure of our nation's economic health will be the inflation rate, as I explain in chapter 7. But the new economics does not advocate economic anorexia, that is, *zero inflation at any price.* The second half of that opening phrase is "and *sufficient* currency." Note that the human body eats more and gains weight—call it "inflate" if you must—when it is growing, when it is getting bigger and stronger as it develops into adulthood. For the same reason, our nation's currency will have to grow or *expand*—not "inflate"—to keep up with our gains in real wealth.

The goal of "maintaining a sound and sufficient currency" is to encourage "full employment of our human and natural resources in the creation of real wealth." Therefore, the "soundness" of the currency—or low inflation—must be constantly balanced with the need to print enough of it to encourage employment and the creation of real wealth. Unlike the anorexic, I advocate risking a few extra calories now and then, in order to make sure I eat enough to stay healthy. The old economics failed in its impossible and pointless challenge: balancing the budget. The challenge of the new economics will be balancing the needs for soundness and sufficiency in our currency supply. Having a sufficient currency requires that we find the boundary between too much and too little.

This boundary line of inflation may be anywhere between 2 percent and 5 percent. How can 5 percent inflation be healthy? Consider this possibility. What if 5 percent inflation guaranteed you a 7 percent pay raise every year, whereas 3 percent inflation meant your income would go up only 2 percent each year? And, say, zero inflation resulted in widespread unemployment, wage reductions, crime, and international tensions? Which would you prefer? I know that some people, for reasons of theology or simplicity perhaps, would prefer zero inflation at any price. But the likelihood is that some inflation is like oil in a car. It is not fuel, but without it the engine will not run. Chapter 10 treats this at length as "the cybernetic adjustment of the money supply."

## INFLATION FALLACY NO. 5:
### *"We still do have inflation."*

What makes us think we have any inflation at all, anyway? A single measure dominates discussion: the Consumer Price Index, or CPI. This index measures the changes in prices of an immense basket of goods, from housing and electricity to food and TVs, taking into consideration how our use of different items changes over the years. The index is fairly sophisticated, and a great deal of intelligent labor has gone into its development and use.

Unfortunately, the CPI is strictly limited in what it can say about the soundness, much less sufficiency, of our currency. The people who make the index are careful to point out its limitations. Most importantly, it is not a cost of living index. It does not say how strong the dollar is. It does not tell whether you have to work more for a loaf of bread or new car now compared with ten years ago.

The most important limitation is that the CPI cannot measure the cost of items that don't sell, even at a reduced cost, because no one can afford to buy them. Most important is real property. Can you remember when buying a home was an *investment*, which you reasonably expected to profit by? Now houses sit unpurchased for years, even at prices below their cost. Commercial real estate, completely unmeasured by the CPI, has lost half of its value in large areas of the country. In many ways, we are unable to realize or measure actual reductions in prices when the currency shortage has gotten so bad that no one can afford to buy, even at fire-sale rates. People also refuse to sell at a loss, because they hope that prices will rise before they die, and they won't ever have to admit they took a loss. We do not measure the strength of currency in terms of how many options we have at a certain price—six years ago, you might have found one home you liked at the one-hundred-thousand-dollar level in an area. Now you'll find dozens.

Our indices are not set up to be able to measure what was thought inconceivable—deflation. We could not conceive that the dollar would actually increase its purchasing power. But now you have more options and higher quality, if only you are able to get the dollars in the first place. The old economists have to admit we are in "disinflationary" times, though they would choke before they could utter the word "deflation." I would say that real inflation is close to zero, and our currency is deflating further as the recession drags on and on. However, deflation cannot be effectively examined because of the way the data are presently gathered.[8]

## INFLATION FALLACY NO. 6:
### ***"Growth and jobs cause inflation."***

This is the most insidious and destructive lie about inflation. Our top economists have gotten really desperate. They can read the data—inflation is dead. Even the CPI is holding steady. They have cast about in all directions trying to find some numbers, any numbers at all, to confirm their deep-held presumptions that inflation is imminent, but can't find any—producer prices, commodities, anything. So they have convinced themselves that the truest underlying cause of inflation is a *growing, healthy economy*. They fear a drop in unemployment. They fear tiny rises in economic growth. Both, they are sure, inevitably lead to inflation. Of course, the evidence does not support them—from 1983 for six years unemployment dropped, growth rose, and inflation *declined*. So they look at a still stranger proxy for actual inflation: their own "expectations" about future inflation, which they read in the bond market.

The bond market is composed of people whose sole reason for working is to see inflation everywhere. Asking them if they see inflation is like asking a fundamentalist preacher if he sees any signs of sin around. They don't even follow their own rules, proudly admitting, "Bond people are perverse."[9] The *Economist* predicted one week that if the Fed tightens, the bond markets will be happy. The Fed tightens. The bond market crashed. So the *Economist* responded that people who are "perplexed…display an imperfect knowledge of economics."[10] *Business Week*'s response was better: "Earth to the bond market: What planet are you on?" (April 18, 1994, p. 29). In a later editorial they went further: "Remember the 'limits to growth' crowd in the 1970s? They're back. But instead of concerned liberals worrying about running out of resources (boy, were they wrong!), we now have jittery bond traders worrying about the economy running out of capacity. Like Chicken Little warning that the sky is falling, these worrywarts are scared silly by growth and run around squawking, 'Inflation! Inflation! Inflation!'" (May 16, 1994, p. 130). This would be funny except for the fact that these idiots are running *our* economy, and they're doing their best to run it into the ground.

## INFLATION, PART II: THE REAL CAUSES

Remember the general, indisputable cause of all inflation: *too much money chasing too few goods*. The old economists do not understand their own maxims. They look only at the first three words. I will explain the meaning of the last three: what causes "too few goods." The goal should be to maintain a *balance*.

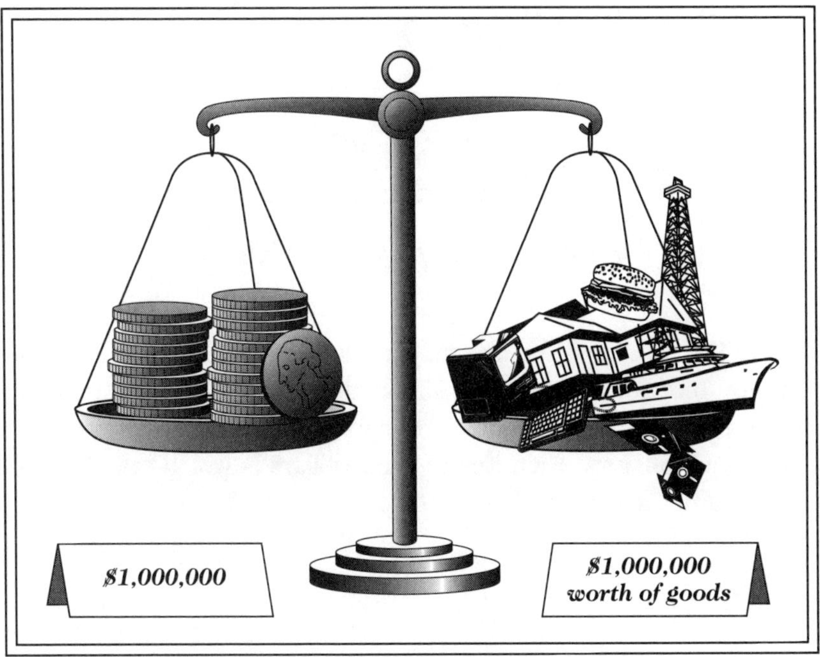


***Figure 6: A Good Balance***

Figure 6 shows the right balance of money and goods. On the left is a million dollars. On the right is a million dollars' worth of real wealth: houses, cars, airplane tickets, and oil. So one dollar buys one dollar's worth of goods.

***Figure 7: Inflation Hawks' Nightmare***

Figure 7 shows the inflation hawks' nightmare. The supply of money has doubled to two million dollars. It takes two dollars, then, to buy the same amount of goods you could buy before for only one dollar. So each one of their dollars is worth only half as much, and they feel robbed.

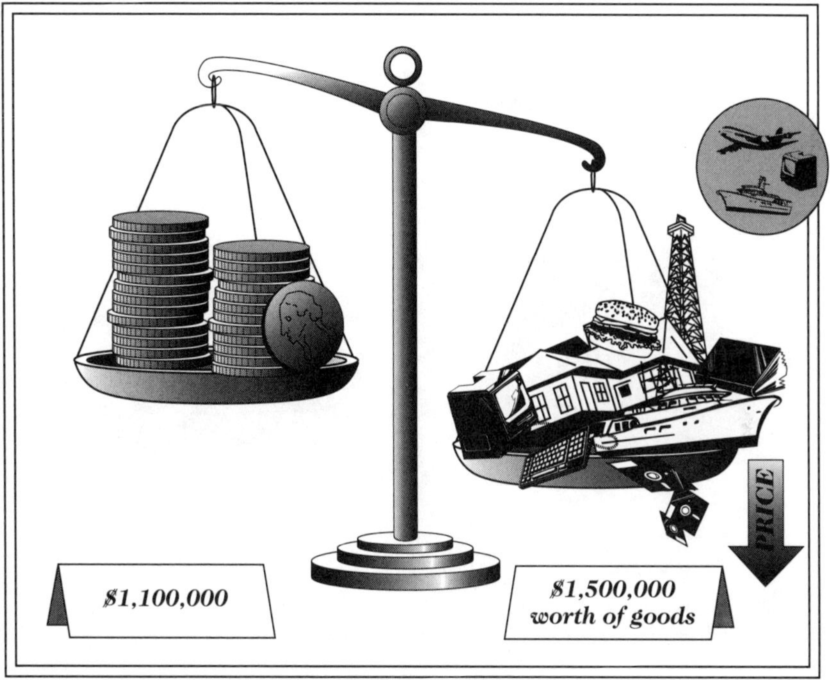


***Figure 8: The Recession***

Figure 8 shows the recession. The inflation hawks and econo-rexics are in charge of the economy, and they have no intention of allowing figure 8 to take place on their watch. To keep up the value of their dollars, they have tightly controlled the size of the money supply, allowing it to increase only a careful 10 percent in five years. They feel great about themselves. But they have ignored what has happened on the right side of the balance. The supply of goods has gone up by *50* percent, not 10 percent, in that time. Not only has inflation stopped, but many prices have gone down. If you are lucky enough to have a dollar, you can buy anything in the world with it. For many reasons, however, prices do not go down as fast as the money supply does. Therefore, many of the goods are never bought, as in the example of the unused cancer medicine. Worse, the dim circle of goods to the right of the balance represents goods and services that could have been made, but never were. Why make more goods when people can't afford to buy the goods already on the shelves?

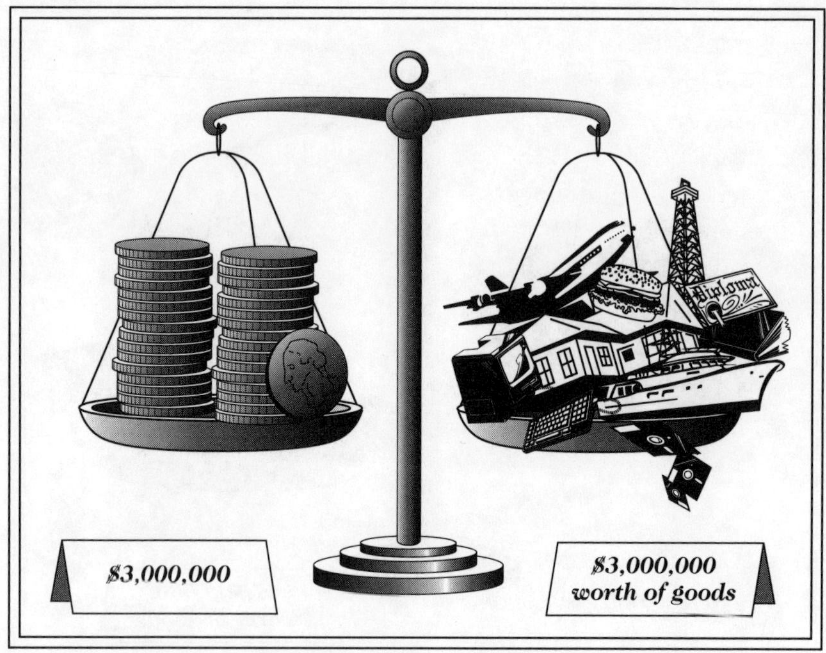


***Figure 9: A Better Balance***

Figure 9 shows the solution to the recession. The wonderful new fact of life for Western economies is not a miracle cancer cure, but a huge abundance of goods and services. Remember, despite all of the predictions in the 1970s that various scarcities would overtake a greedy world, we have shortages of *nothing*—not food, cars, houses, airplane seats, hotel or hospital rooms, gold, jewels, Rolls Royces, great art, university classes, basketball teams, you name it. The cornucopia of goods we have and could make with factories on the ground and workers already trained is bulging. Say, for the sake of illustration, that we now have $3 million worth of goods.

All that the new economics recommends, in a nutshell, is that the amount of money on the left end of the balance be raised to $3 million to match the $3 million worth of goods on the other end. Thus, one dollar will still buy one dollar's worth of goods.

Because there are three times as many of each, people will be more prosperous—even if there were twice as many people.

You might think the above story too simple to bother telling, but it covers twice as much ground as the economics presently running our country. Believe it or not, the old economists absurdly assert, "The one and only important cause of inflation is an excessive increase in the quantity of money." That is the idea which won Milton Friedman and a half-dozen others their Nobel prizes. It is as though they cut off the right side of figures 6-9 entirely, and looked at only the left side of the balance.

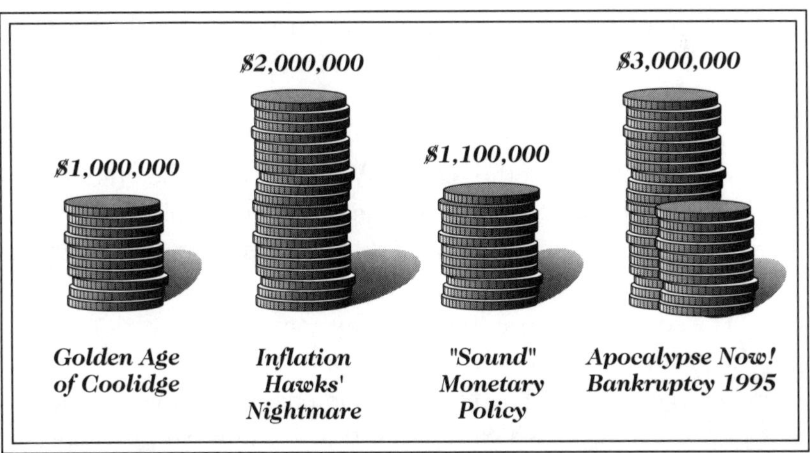


***Figure 10: "Inflation is a purely monetary phenomenon."***

Just as health is affected by a wide variety of causes (e.g., exercise, smoking, germs, and heredity), so inflation—and the lack of inflation—are the result of a host of causes. But do the people running our economy ever mention the other half of the equation? No. Check the policy statements of our economic leaders, as reported in their official documents, *The Wall Street Journal*, or the *Economist*. Absolutely not a word about the supply of goods—not a word.

Instead, the next word after "increase in the money supply" will be "hyperinflation." Whenever the old economists hear any words having to do with printing or creating money, the word "inflation" blurts out of their mouths faster than your knee jumps when the doctor pops it with his little hammer. "Money equals inflation" is as deep as their thinking gets. As one interested person wrote after reading an early galley of chapter 1: "By definition, printing more money creates inflation…Anyone holding currency is diminished." But the largest money printings in history, in real terms, were during the Reagan era here and in Germany when ostmarks became deutschemarks. The fact that these caused no inflation—despite all of the economists' dire warnings—seems to make no difference to them. They all act as though they were scared by a fifty-million-mark Weimar Republic note at an impressionable age, as Figgie was.[11] But perhaps this imperviousness to reason is due instead to simple ignorance of any alternative sources of inflation. Their single-cause theory may be due to their never having been exposed to the various other causes. When they see the other causes, they might understand that inflation is not as simple as they had thought. Thus the first purpose of this long discursion on inflation is, hopefully, the education and salvation of lost economic souls.

The second purpose here is to lay some groundwork for Part III, the positive plan for our new economic future. The real causes of inflation are a complete blueprint for a bad economy in general, not just inflation. As we go through this list, however, it becomes clear that the U.S. economy has done a great job of avoiding these root causes of both inflation and poverty. The only thing we have done wrong is not on the list: we have not printed enough money. But we have earned our low inflation, and we would be enjoying the further fruits of our nation's hard work and talent, if only we would get beyond our obsession with the deficit. Tragically, the deficit obsession is presently causing us to commit the very sins we have successfully avoided for so long—excessive taxation, trade wars, new regulations, etc. A resurgence of these economic sins will cause the very inflation we could avoid if only we printed more money. Thus, the following list simultaneously describes what causes inflation and what we as a nation have done so well to avoid over the last twenty years.

## REAL CAUSE OF INFLATION NO. 1:
### *War and Defense*

The most vivid cause of "too few goods" is war. War destroys goods in every way. The former Yugoslavia is a perfect case study in destruction. Homes, buildings, and personal property are directly destroyed by bombs and fire. The factories that would make more goods cannot do so. The people who would work in the factories are either dead or manning the barricades. Any economic activity and service that does occur is overwhelmingly oriented towards the production of a good that has no value except for the tragic condition of war: the killing of supposed enemies. Great energy is put into this ignoble, but seemingly necessary end, at a great expense to all other production.

Defense is less inflationary than war, but has many of the same features. Defense production differs from virtually every other type of production in that its best use is no use at all. We recognize that our nation exists only because we never have had to launch the terror bottled up in our nuclear ICBMs. But it is impossible to see the invisible losses, the "too few goods" resulting from taking two generations of our best and brightest and focusing their efforts on inventing, manufacturing, and staffing trillions of dollars' worth of "shadow wealth," wealth that had a potential use, but whose potential was never realized. To put it another way: You are likely to be aware of the benefits of Boeing's extraordinary development of the 747. But how many of you have ever ridden in an F-16, or a Stealth Bomber? The military aircraft took far more of our real wealth—people and factories—to develop than did the 747, but added no value to our lives.

"No value!" you say. "That's nonsense! The money we spent on those ICBMs kept the Soviets from sending their own bombs over to destroy us. The value of our ICBMs is the value of all of America that remains standing because of our military vigilance." If that's what you say, *you're right*. In chapter 11, I explain the huge value of avoiding war. We did it for forty years with nuclear bombs and large NATO land forces. Let us pray that the next forty years continue to be like the last five. That is, we are substituting peaceful relations with the Russians for nuclear bombs and giant standing armies.

What does this mean to the economy? It means we've doubled our savings. Avoiding war, even at the cost of expensive armies and weapons, helps keep up the "supply of goods" at a lower cost than did the cost of war itself. Because we've attained peaceful relations with our mortal enemies, we can avoid war with far fewer weapons and soldiers than before. Thus we maintain the supply of goods at an even lower cost. Avoiding war is anti-inflationary. Avoiding costly armies is even more anti-inflationary. Paul Kennedy makes the point in his *The Decline of Nations* that superpowers are weakened by the cost of their militaries. We have now greatly reduced that cost.

## REAL CAUSE OF INFLATION NO. 2: *Natural disasters*

An earthquake in Los Angeles destroys factories that produce goods. A hurricane in Florida crosses certain towns off vacationers' lists for a few seasons, reducing tourism. Midwestern droughts and floods reduce the nation's harvest by 10 percent. We have less control over the items in this category than we do over the other sources of inflation, but whatever effect we have is generally getting better. We earthquake-proof new buildings and old. We restrict some construction near the oceans. We have a slightly better sandbag technology than we had a century ago. Of course, our efforts to protect ourselves from floods and hurricanes have been shamefully primitive, and it would be easy to do better (see chapter 14). But at least we have not made the effects of natural disasters appreciably worse in the last twenty years.

A perverse effect of the old economics is that we can expect natural disasters, like wars, to stimulate our economies. What an absurd paradox! The 1993 floods in the Midwest accomplished what common sense would not allow: the federal government was forced to print billions of dollars to spend on the cleanup. This occurred just a couple of months after both houses voted down a modest stimulus spending program, due to the shrieks of the deficit mongers. Everybody realizes that a good war or nice calamity causes the government to spend money, put people to work, and get the economy going again. If you are stuck in this perverse rut of thinking because of an overdose of the old economics, why can't you just pretend we had a war or earthquake, without our actually having to go through one? We could then enjoy not only the spending stimulus, but the still-living soldiers and the still-standing factories as well.

## REAL CAUSE OF INFLATION NO. 3:
***Supply Shocks***

If all the farmers in this country decided not to sell their wheat and corn this year, what do you think would happen to the price of wheat and corn? This was an easy question for the monetarists, whose answer was, "Who cares about the supply of wheat and corn! Tell me about the size of the money supply, and I'll tell you about price increases." I trust by now you are smarter than the economists running our country, and you can draw figure 11 by yourself:

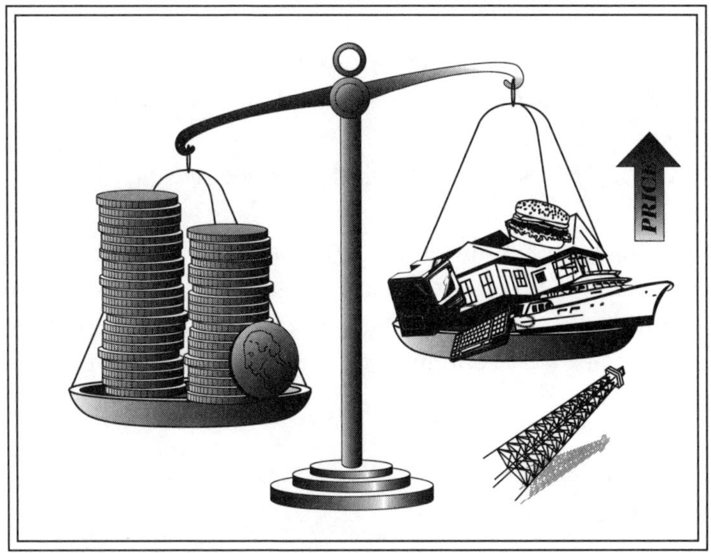


***Figure 11: The Oil Supply Shocks***

When the money supply stays the same, but the supply of goods gets smaller, the price of the remaining goods rises. When one million dollars is chasing a half million dollars' worth of goods, the cost of each dollar's worth of goods rises to two dollars. A good thing our farmers aren't that mean—and well-organized. But once upon a time a large group of suppliers was, and accomplished the most fearful U.S. inflation in our memories. Remember OPEC? That's the Organization of Petroleum Exporting Countries, including the Arabs and a few others like Nigeria and Venezuela. In the 1970s, everyone knew about OPEC's every move as we waited in long lines for gasoline, the price of which doubled and doubled again.

The OPEC cartel succeeded in controlling the production of oil by its member states. The supply of a vital good was kept down, in effect making the bag of goods on the right side of the balance smaller. The money supply was increasing more slowly in the 1970s than it did in the 1980s. But in which decade did inflation rise to well over 10 percent, and in which decade did it fall back down below 4 percent? The old economists have had a rough time with this evidence. It took them until the mid 1980s to admit that the oil supply shock may indeed have had something to do with the 1970s inflation. This may seem obvious to anyone who understands the principle of inflation being caused by "too much money chasing too few goods," but it's a real stretch of the imagination for a monetarist.

After a little soul-searching, the monetarists still believe their gospel that "Inflation is always and everywhere a monetary phenomenon." The oil supply shock was a one-time anomaly, they feel, that has no bearing on the overall correctness of their theory. Check the references.[12] And remember that these people are the professional experts running our economy and "educating" our children.

## REAL CAUSE OF INFLATION NO. 4:
### *Protectionism*

One obvious way to keep your country's supply of goods down is to stop goods from entering at the border. Imagine that your friends and neighbors wanted to give your family lots of gifts, vacuum-clean your rugs, and sell you things you need below their own cost. You, however, wouldn't let those goods in the front door. Idiot countries like Albania, Romania, and, to a lesser extent, Brazil and Argentina, "protected" their citizens by barring imports with every trick in the book, including the execution of "smugglers." The most extreme (e.g., Cuba) even barred outright monetary gifts from relatives overseas.

Imagine the cost and quality of cars in this country if we had kept out Japanese and European cars the way the Albanians did. Think what a TV would cost and how badly it would flicker if we'd barred Asian electronics. And we wouldn't even have invented the VCR, because our local boys wasted their hundred million on trying to make a phonograph-record version of a video player. (Yes, it had to rotate a thousand times per minute, which was sure rough on the tiny diamond stylus.)

The argument for protectionism is the same argument as that for barring bulldozers. Foreign goods and big machines take jobs like assembly-line manufacturing and ditch digging away from American workers. These jobs are lost, it is true. And we do suffer as a nation if we do not re-employ those displaced workers, finding them better jobs that add even more to the common wealth. Chapter 11 explains how to accomplish such job creation.

At this point, I want you to understand that free trade *reduces* the threat of inflation by *expanding* the supply of goods. One more time: The...cause...of...inflation...is too much money chasing too few goods. Protectionism reduces the supply of goods. Over the last fifty years we have done an amazing job of maintaining and increasing free trade, helping earn our low inflation. Resistance occurs because we have failed to invent new and better jobs for the displaced workers. Those unfortunate people have done nothing wrong and have every right to complain. But under the new economics, we shall have the pleasant task of saying "Thank You" to our international neighbors for "dumping" their high-quality products on our shores, while simultaneously taking our workers off of the assembly lines they hate and putting them in the far better jobs described in chapter 14.

## REAL CAUSE OF INFLATION NO. 5:
### *Enslaved Enterprise*

An undisputed talent of free enterprise is its ability to increase the supply of goods. Consumer goods and services sprout like weeds if only you let them. Human beings seem to love making things and selling them to each other, if only they're allowed. Inflation is hard to achieve if you let people create the huge supply of goods and services they want. Unfortunately, wrong lessons from the past lead sensible and well-meaning people to cut off the supply of goods by stopping their fellow citizens from making things. Such obstructionism adds to inflation. Why does this occur?

Many people resent free enterprise business activity for both good reasons and bad. Whole countries made free enterprise illegal for a century, under communism. Private enterprise was intrinsically bad, they thought, so they outlawed it. Instead, the people, as a collective, ostensibly ran all business production through the scientific process of central planning. Central planning is the opposite of free enterprise. It was a disaster.

I spent a semester as a Fulbright professor in Moscow in 1992. What central planning had done to the Russians was both tragic and hilarious. The Workers' Paradise gave its workers junk as a reward for their suffering labor. If free enterprise sprouts like weeds, the vision of central planning is to keep pouring gasoline on the ground. The purpose of government under central planning was to *stop* business whenever it threatened to make useful and desirable goods and services for the citizens. The best job a communist can envision is being able to stop business from occurring. The bureaucracies were staffed with twenty layers of pompous obstructionists demanding kowtows, bribes, and endless patience.

Looking at the immense, forty-story Ministry of Foreign Trade, I observed that the best thing Russia could do for foreign trade was to retire every person in that ministry to a dacha on the Black Sea. Eliminate their former "jobs" completely. Foreign trade would multiply without the ministry whose main function was to obstruct foreign trade at every turn. (A side benefit would be opening up precious living space for Muscovites, since the Soviets were also unable to create even college-dorm-quality housing.)

A deep-set bias against free enterprise by many elites in this country also leads to restraining every business with a governing bureaucracy. Many people, especially in the government, have the same attitude toward business that they have towards their eight-year-old: everything not required is forbidden, because otherwise mischief is inevitable. This bias supported two opposite delusions: the first was that letting a business get too big was dangerous, because it would set high prices. The second completely contradicted the reasoning of the first. The second delusion was that the government itself had to support certain large businesses through strict regulation, so the government would itself *set* high prices. When business sets high prices, that's bad. When government sets high prices, that's good. History shows that the truth is exactly the opposite.

*Many people, especially in the government, have the same attitude toward business that they have towards their eight-year-old: everything not required is forbidden, because otherwise mischief is inevitable.*

In the 1970s we stopped prosecuting IBM on antitrust grounds, and we deregulated the airlines. The old fear was that large businesses would charge exorbitant prices once they drove out competition. Federal prosecutors now admit that fear is far-fetched and groundless; in point of historical fact, every company that tries to kill its competition with a price war only ends up hurting *itself*. Meanwhile, it gives its customers great deals.[13]

The evidence on deregulation overwhelmingly supports its benefits to the consumer, though our surviving socialists still argue in a losing cause. The success of supply-side economics was based on two obvious economic truisms: (1) economies of scale, supplied by large businesses, provide better value for the consumer dollar (let innovation come from the small start-ups), and (2) the government hurts the consumer when it tries to help by setting prices on anything from airplane tickets to milk products.

To be sure, business doesn't want and shouldn't have a completely lawless economic battlefield. Chapter 11 explains the difference between regulations that destroy real wealth and those that help create it. It also discusses how to balance the conflicting demands of drafting adequate but restrained legislation for business enterprise.

The point is, in the last twenty years we have already made great strides in letting business perform its humble task of providing consumers with the goods and services they want. Whatever our failings may be, every other large nation is worse. We have cut off inflation by simply letting business provide a great many goods.

## REAL CAUSE OF INFLATION NO. 6:
### *Taxes*

Taxes might be the main cause of inflation in the Western nations at the present time. They cause inflation at the cash register by adding a sales tax to the final price. They add to the price before it reaches the cash register via value-added taxes or taxes on business that increase manufacturing costs. Taxes can stop people from opening or expanding a business, thus preventing a growth in supply that would lower prices.

The CPI (consumer price index) measures the effects of prices that make it to the cash register, directly or indirectly. But the CPI does not measure the effect of higher income taxes. Income taxes affect inflation in two ways. First, they take money out of the hands of consumers, reducing demand. These days, reduced demand is likely to lead to lower economies of scale and thus keep prices high. Second, the CPI admittedly does not even try to measure the cost of living. Remember that the CPI is only the best existing measure we have, a substitute for what we would really like to measure: How much do you have to work to earn a certain amount of goods? If prices went up 5 percent while your salary went up 10 percent you would be better off. Similarly, if prices went down 2 percent, but your salary stayed the same and your income tax went up 5 percent, the effect would be worse than inflation.

Deficit-think constantly forces tax increases on us—tax hikes that *cause* the very harm they are supposed to cure. We rail against taxes before we even take into account their effect on inflation. We raised taxes in 1929 to head off the Depression, which only made things worse. We reduced taxes in the 1980s, helping our relative boom to occur. Following the deficit-think advice of the old economists, we raised taxes in 1990, helping trigger the recession. Again, give credit to what we did in the 1980s for helping reduce inflation.

## REAL CAUSE OF INFLATION NO. 7:
### *Featherbedding Unions and Country-Club Management*

It's not the twenty-dollar-an-hour blue-collar wages and multimillion-dollar CEO pay packages that are the problem. The problems are, first, that lazy *unions* can reduce the supply of goods with featherbedding rules that restrict the efficiency of the workplace. In the height of union power in the 1950s, trains were famous for having coal men riding the diesel engines, and factories required three people to change a light bulb—one to take off the cover, one to unscrew and replace the bulb, and a third to sweep up the dust. Thus, more people make fewer goods.

Second, slovenly *management* hurts by refusing to keep up with changes, running the company for the immediate comfort of the CEO and his buddies rather than for the health of the organization. Some of America's biggest corporations were its softest. U.S. Steel always hired and promoted from within its closed community, missing the boat on new technology until they were a decade behind. Our auto makers had to be legislatively forced by the government to do the right thing on gasoline mileage—the greatest shame a free enterprise corporation can admit to.

Why are high wages or exorbitant CEO packages less inflationary than bad work practices? As long as neither are automatically indexed to increase every year, and the company makes enough goods to keep its prices competitive, the money paid workers or management is merely shifted from one pocket to another. The amount of money chasing the goods is not affected. Instead of going to the stockholders, it goes to the workers or management. Of course, if price competition does not exist, and the company has to raise prices to pay itself, inflation goes up. But that's a big "if." With deregulation and free trade, a company that raises salaries by raising prices finds itself out of business. But if, like Coca Cola and Walt Disney, they are able to pay themselves well while keeping the customers coming, they are doing their job. Henry Ford was able to double his factory workers' salaries up to the famous five-dollar day without inflation, because at that double wage they were making four times as many cars as workers had made before. Doubled wages combined with quadrupled output results in deflation, not inflation, remember.

## REAL CAUSE OF INFLATION NO. 8:
### *Wage, Price, and Benefit Indexing*

Do you know what causes feedback between a microphone and a public address system? A small noise picked up by the mike is amplified by the PA, making a louder noise picked up by the mike. This louder noise gets amplified even more, and so on. This spiraling process happens within a second because of the high speed of sound.

Wage and price indexing leads to the same out-of-control amplification of inflation—fortunately, not as fast as the speed of sound. One of the major causes of inflation in the 1970s was that the oil supply shock was amplified by incorrect indexing agreements we had in place at the time. Too many wages and especially government benefits were indexed to rise automatically as the CPI went up. Social Security and government pensions, in particular, really amplified the effect due to an innocent agreement to round up fractional percentage point increases.

The great hyperinflations are invariably accompanied by automatically indexed increases in wages and benefits. This indexing creates a feedback loop magnifying the real source of any imbalance between "too much money chasing too few goods." Even now, with too many goods being chased by not enough money, we could artificially instigate inflation by indexing, say, at double the rate of our minuscule inflation.

Indexing should be outlawed. I abhor restrictive laws in general, so I do not say this lightly. The socially benign point of indexing is to make sure the recipients of wages and pensions do not lose out due to price rises. But the CPI does not claim to measure the welfare of the people who receive money. If we cared about the recipients' cost of living, we might measure that, but the cost of living is different from the cost of a basket of goods. Raising too many incomes indiscriminately means that much of the increase goes to people whose cost of living may have even gone *down* in the interim, not up. People who need the money ought to compete for the real increases they need or deserve, if any. If they don't holler, they don't need it as badly as the loudest screamers do. Also, the real cause of a problem with the cost of living is more likely to be increased taxes or import restrictions rather than inadequate wages and pensions. Indexing tends to take the heat off the government for the real changes that need to be made.

Indexing is the most insidious source of inflation, because it makes no attempt whatsoever to balance an increase in the supply of goods with the increase in the supply of money that indexing requires. Note that the amount of the money is not the issue. The program I advocate would create much more money than indexing at current CPI levels would imply. But under the principles of the new economics, the money would be spent so as to encourage the creation of real wealth, not just add to consumer demand. Indexing adds to demand without addressing supply or the issue of equitable and efficient distribution.

## REAL CAUSE OF INFLATION NO. 9:
### *Third-Party Payers*

You're bringing in your car for some repairs. Think how your attitude changes depending on whether you or your insurance company is paying. The same at the hospital. CAT scans at one thousand dollars each are just fine when your insurance is paying, but you'd pause to reflect if you had to write a check for each one. In fact, we often don't even ask the charges when third-party insurance is paying. Compare that attitude to our normal shopping. A gas station charging just a few cents more than the one down the road loses most of its customers. People watch grocery prices with painstaking care.

The best, most effective inflation fighters are informed consumers spending their own money. Expenses rise when you "give" people whatever they want regardless of cost. Insurance blurs the line between what you pay and what you get by making you cover other people's illnesses as well as your own. Once you have paid, it makes sense to grab as much as you can get. But when everybody follows this reasoning, everyone ends up overpaying. Unfortunately, just as health-care costs are coming under control even while research is booming, we threaten to raise costs while inhibiting advances. If you want to control costs and encourage research, give people money and let them decide themselves how to spend it. Don't set costs and then let people have as much as they can get from the approved list. Shades of Mother Russia.

## REAL CAUSE OF INFLATION NO. 10:
### *Panic Psychology*

If people go crazy and start to pay outlandish prices for items, inflation could occur even if we decided to destroy money instead of printing more. A combination of panic, folly, and greed led people to pay $850 for gold, $60 million for a painting, and hundreds of millions for a golf course. Realize that your town's local billionaire could clean out the grocery stores all by himself, perhaps forcing you to pay ten dollars for a loaf of the bread he had monopolized. Tomorrow, all of the world's billionaires might get together in a secret cabal to buy up all of the cheap cars and double their prices.

These are not silly scenarios. People really did pay far more for gold than any conceivable appraisal of its real value would warrant. Rare paintings, like gold, have lost half of their value, but are still grossly overpriced. And our last inflation was not caused by any real shortage of oil; the supply shock was artificially induced by the last successful cartel, OPEC.

Panic psychology can create an artificial shortage of goods in the midst of plenty in two ways. First, large numbers of people can refuse to sell what they have. Alternatively, they could buy up everything on the market whether they need it or not. OPEC members agreed among each other not to sell the oil they had readily available.

The Russian people suffer from chronic shortages and inflation in part because they ravenously buy and hoard all the food they can find, even if that means filling up a whole room with it and letting it spoil. The world had plenty of gold for all of its industrial and jewelry uses at five hundred dollars an ounce, but the owners of the gold refused to sell at that price for a few magic weeks in 1980. And remember when we were all culling through our change to find the older silver variety, which then got melted down?

In this country, unlike in Russia, a panic inflation of the prices of useful goods is inconceivable. Your local billionaire did not get rich by following any hare-brained schemes to corner the market on anything—in fact, two local fellows, the Hunt brothers, *lost* their fortunes when they tried to corner silver. But the threat of the Golden Idol will not go away. The Fed seriously entertains plans to keep gold in a basket of items it will use to determine our monetary policy.[14] The gold bugs are distinguished by an uninterrupted string of wildly incorrect predictions based on their favorite fetish, but they will not go away. Their numbers have reached a critical mass of "greater fools," so occasionally they make money off of each other. Incredibly, some greater fools made money by buying gold at seven hundred fifty dollars an ounce—because they sold it to the *greatest* fools in the chain at eight hundred fifty dollars. The permanent attraction of panic psychology is that, in a fools' market, people who are half foolish and buy gold at six hundred dollars or Old Master artworks at $10 million, and then sell before the crash, make more money than do the prudent souls who understood from the start that the high prices were ridiculous. Panic buyers who respond to bull markets win just often enough to keep coming back to lose more and more, like poor players in a tough poker game

A sad fact about democracy and freedom is that if enough of us panic and start to act stupid, bad things will happen. Nations have decided to kill millions of their own people, or start suicidal wars. In this country, if the deficit mongers in effect cried "Fire!" in a crowded theater loudly enough, they might induce an inflationary panic. If everybody decides to believe inflation will occur, they could create a self-fulfilling prophecy. Like those who predicted gold would reach eight hundred fifty dollars, they would be right for a while. But like the people who predicted gold and oil would go even higher and stay there, their prophesies, built on illusions, will inevitably prove as foolish as such predictions have been in the past.

# 6

# The Lesser Lies: The Bogeyman Defense—The "Cure" Causes the Disease

The remaining deficit lies share a common flaw. For each lie, the mongers say that their bogus "deficit" is causing a Problem X which needs Cure Y. In fact, Problem X they have brought on themselves out of a false fear; Cure Y ends up causing the *real* Problem Z, which is our endless Great Recession.

Earlier I wrote that the deficit was like the bogeyman, in that people who were afraid of it couldn't say exactly how they or anyone they knew had been personally hurt by one. The deficit mongers are like kids who hurt their arm jumping out of bed when scared by a sudden noise they think is the bogeyman. Problem X was an imaginary attack by the bogeyman. Cure Y was jumping out of bed. *Real* Problem Z was their bruised arm. They blame their injury on the bogeyman, but it is only their fear of an imaginary demon that caused the injury they brought on themselves.

Ross Perot used the bogeyman defense to great effect in the presidential debates. He had first crack at the killer question that ruined George Bush: "How have *you personally* been hurt by the deficit?" Ross answered that he was so scared of the deficit that he decided he had to run for president to save the nation from it.

Running for president *hurt* him, he said, because it took him away from making further billions running his business.

This great-sounding answer fooled the audience, but it's just an adult version of the bogeyman defense. "Ross, why did you skip school today?" "Well, Mom, the bogeyman kept me up. I had to watch TV all night to keep him out of the bedroom. So now I'm too tired to go to school." But in truth it was not the bogeyman that made Perot tired, nor the deficit that made Perot run. It was a delusionary *fear* of the two bogeymen, not the bogeymen themselves. The same fear-of-the-bogeyman fallacy applies to the crowding out, interest rate, paying interest, and burden-to-our-children arguments.

## DEFICIT LIE NO. 2: "CROWDING OUT"

The "crowding out" theory states that the government borrows so much money to finance its debts that there's not enough left for the private sector. Then, when your local tycoon goes down to the bank to borrow money to expand his business and hire your sister-in-law, the bank is out of money. The bank spent its deposits on super-secure treasury bonds, leaving your tycoon "crowded out" and unable to lead this country to economic greatness.

This argument is wrong on two counts. First, it is not a lack of money that stops the bank from loaning money to businessmen. Businessmen are failing to invest for a wide range of good reasons, as explained below under *Deficit Lie No. 4: Long-Term Interest Rates*. But insofar as the banks are concerned, Draconian laws prohibit their making normal loans they can afford to make. Because we went overboard in deregulating the savings and loans, we went overboard in re-regulating our financial institutions. In order to prevent any more bad loans, the new regulations succeed in choking off good ones. Businesses with perfect records of repayment and excellent balance sheets find their lines of credit revoked because of some ill-judged footnote in a new nationwide bank regulation.[1] It's as though you first let your three-year-old run in the street for a few weeks, and then corrected your over-permissiveness by locking him in the closet for a month.

Second, any lack of funds in the financial markets is not due to the deficit itself, but rather to our deficit-related *fears*. The deficit does not make us borrow money on the open market. We can print it—as we already do, when we "monetize the debt." "Monetizing" is one of three ways the government gets the money that backs up your Social Security or any other check. The main source of funds is taxes or other money, such as Social Security payments, that has already been collected. The second source is treasury bonds the government prints and sells to selected buyers. When you read that "Treasury bills are at an all-time low" they are referring to these bonds. "Crowding out" refers to the money that is spent on these treasury bills—the idea is that the institutions that buy treasury bills would otherwise lend money to private businesses to expand and create more jobs.

But the third way the government honors that check is by printing money. They do not do it in a straightforward fashion. Rather, they print a bond they then buy themselves. In order to cover their tracks, they do not buy precisely that bond, but they purchase an equivalent issue of their own bonds already on the market. To complete the charade, they pay themselves the same interest they have to pay outside sources! (See *Deficit Lie No. 3: "Interest on the Debt."*) More than 25 percent of our national debt is owed *by* the government *to* the government. So *if* "crowding out" were indeed a problem, which in fact it is not, it is a problem we have made for ourselves. We have proved over the decades that we can monetize when we want *without inflation*, so it is only unfounded fears that make us raise cash on the open market in the first place.

## DEFICIT LIE NO. 3: "INTEREST ON THE DEBT"

The deficit mongers cry that the interest alone on our debt is eating us alive, ballooning out of control, devouring over 10 percent of our tax dollars. Again, it is not the deficit itself, but our anxious over-reaction to it that hurts us. As described just above, we pay interest only because we *choose* to pay interest. One-fourth of that interest the government pays to itself—switching the money from one pocket to another. The interest we pay on almost all of the rest goes back to American taxpayers, who hold almost all of the bonds that finance the deficit. And if we only decided to, we can print money without charging any interest on it at all.

You have not heard this argument from the deficit mongers as much lately as in the past, because they too can see how preposterous it is. But a certain number of people have an acute aversion to paying interest—a gut issue for them similar to the Islamic ban on interest, or the biblical injunctions against usury. But you have to remember that it is possible to make money by paying interest. If you pay 10 percent interest on a loan, but use that money to earn a 20 percent profit, you are making money. Most businesses carry loans on this principle, even after they are able to pay them off.

Even on a purely consumer purchase, not an "investment" in profits, you can get more value by paying interest. Say you have the choice between waiting two years to save up the money for a good stereo, or you can get it now and pay 10 percent interest for two years. Realize that the 10 percent interest has added two years to the amount of time you can enjoy your purchase. If you owned it for 10 years, 20 percent of the value (i.e., two years of the ten) would have been purchased with 10 percent of the money you paid (i.e., the interest rate).

Government debt can likewise be used to create more value than it costs. Chapter 11 details the kinds of investments that more than repay the interest we choose to pay to finance them.

## DEFICIT LIE NO. 4: "LONG-TERM INTEREST RATES"

The fantasy of "hypersensitive" long-term interest rates is the most fanciful and enduring of the deficit mongers' gripes. It is a four-part story which is wrong in each of its compounded claims. The only reason the deficit mongers keep telling it is that it is complicated—so complicated that it *sounds* smart, and most people don't take the time and energy to follow it.

The story says:

1) The bond market is sure that deficits cause inflation.
   (*Wrong*: Deficits do not cause inflation, and the bond markets know they don't.)
2) Therefore, interest rates go up when deficits rise.
   (*Wrong*: For twenty years, interest rates and deficits have gone in *opposite* directions 76 percent of the time.)[2]
3) When interest rates go down, business will borrow and invest.
   (*Wrong*: In a dead economy, businesses know it is suicidal to expand their output when people can't buy what is already on the shelves.)
4) When businesses borrow, they hire more workers, who then produce more and spend their salaries to stimulate the economy the natural way.
   (*Wrong*: These days, prudent businesses borrow in order to automate and fire people. They have to, in order to keep costs down enough to survive through an endless recession.)

What a convoluted fable! How can they believe it? Perhaps it satisfies a desire for an orderly (albeit Rube Goldberg-like) universe in which one mathematical lever pushes another all the way down the line to free-market prosperity. While they may find it a comforting and mathematically interesting story, it has no relation to events in the real world. The long-term interest rates have just hit their all-time low, despite our assuring ourselves of deficits in excess of $200 billion per year through the millennium. Despite record-low rates, businesses refuse to invest by hiring more workers.

Have these old economists ever run a business? They should realize that interest rates are only one factor in an investment decision.[3] Many investments don't require loans at all. Ongoing investment can be funded by current cash flow. Much investment is funded by accrued income—but now, due to the recession, companies with large positive balances are buying back their stocks and paper rather than invest.[4] And a *zero* interest rate is not low enough if you cannot see the future customers who will repay your investment.

*Businesses are smarter than the economists. They do not run, like Pavlov's dog, down to the bank when they hear the interest rates drop. When we print enough money to buy the real wealth we have already created, and then begin to buy more, business will get the idea.*

Interest rates don't matter to a business as much as *customers*. In a cash-starved economy, it is foolish to invest. Businesses are smarter than the economists. They do not run, like Pavlov's dog, down to the bank when they hear the interest rates drop. When we print enough money to buy the real wealth we have already created, and then begin to buy more, business will get the idea. If business jumps for anyone, it's for their potential customers. When they have enough customers, the interest rates don't matter. When they have customers in a growing economy, business will pay 10 percent to expand and make 15 percent profits, as they have done in the past. Interest rate hikes can cause recessions, to be sure. But the reason rates rise is that the Fed raises them on purpose, for the express purpose of causing recessions.

## DEFICIT LIE NO. 5: "INTERNATIONAL MARKETS WILL PANIC"

You don't hear this one much anymore. Before the Western economies inflicted the wonderful fiscal restraint upon themselves that plunged us all into recession, the fiscal moralists preached a kind of peer pressure among each other. Instead of

"Johnny does his homework and gets good grades," they said, "Germany and Japan have low deficits, and they're now richer than we are." Worse, they said, "If Germany and Japan think we're becoming monetary bad boys, they will somehow take all of our or their or someone's money away from us, and boy, will we be sorry." No scenario for a panic was ever made explicit—the closest Figgie would come was that the dollar would be driven lower.

Now, of course, Japan and Germany are suffering from their economists as badly as we have suffered from ours. Everyone is fighting to have the lowest-valued currency, in a fool's game to export more to the others. Instead of preaching fiscal "responsibility" to each other, we're all trying to get the others to spend, spend, spend! One *Wall Street Journal* headline says, "Clinton Endorses Decade of Greed in Japan" (December 3, 1993, A14). The only possible panic might arise from the multiple slow-burning trade wars and international tensions becoming similar to those in the 1930s. We'd all love one nation to get the ball rolling towards prosperity by printing enough money to buy the great wealth we have produced, help everyone's economies grow, and put one hundred million workers around the world back to work again.

## DEFICIT LIE NO. 6: "THE BURDEN TO OUR CHILDREN"

The hokiest lie of them all. It reeks with guilt (for us) and martyrdom (for our children). The dim idea behind this one is the image of a spendthrift, drunken, gambling Dad who dies with his markers out. The bank forecloses on the house, and the kids still have to pay half of their earnings to the mob's juice men for the rest of their days. Dad spent, but the kids pay—to the tune of twelve thousand dollars for every man, woman and child in the country.

Dry your eyes. This schmaltz could not be further from the truth. First of all, our children will not pay back the debt. They don't have to. We did not pay back our parents' debts, incurred during the depression and World War II. Second, our kids would only be paying back the debt to themselves. Remember, we owe more than 88 percent of the "debt" to *ourselves*. Our children all owe each other the money, if you want to look at it that way—another version of switching the money from one pocket to another. But in point of fact, no one person's child owes anyone any money.

Ah, but you say, although they don't exactly owe anybody any money, they will have to pay taxes to keep up the interest payments on the debt, and so forth. *No*, they don't. See Lie No. 3 above. If the next generation also cannot see through The Deficit Lie, well, yes, they will suffer the consequences. Their suffering will not be due to the debt, however. In the Reagan years and during World War II, no one suffered from past debts. If they suffer, it will be due to their own self-destructive actions taken due to fear of the debt, not the debt itself.

And what if we really did have to pay off the debt? You're asking me to tell a science fiction story. Here goes. If the U.S. were a corporation with a large load of debt, they could pay it off either through their cash flow or by divesting themselves of their assets. The country's cash flow is great. We make more money every year than we owe—which compares to making more every year than you owe on the mortgage of your house. And our asset value is a minimum of $18 trillion. What this country owns is a high multiple of its debt. While the deficit hysterics are crying "Bankruptcy!" they are being thrown out of court. You cannot declare bankruptcy if your debts are ten thousand dollars and your assets are worth a million.

In fact, if we were a corporation, we would be so *lightly* leveraged, compared to our real worth, that a corporate raider would have picked us off years ago. Were it possible to buy this country for the value of its liabilities, raiders could have offered two dollars on the dollar, paid off all the "debt," broken us up, sold the pieces, and made a multitrillion-dollar windfall profit.

The value of our country is immeasurable. What we are leaving our children is, in effect, a multimillion-dollar estate with a puny second mortgage that we took out in order to add a game room, and a one-month credit card balance. If the kids are bums and quit work, sure, they'll have trouble. But they'll work as hard as we did, if we only let them, and they'll end up adding to the estate. The real burden we may put upon them is the accrued "sacrifices" we have made in the cause of "deficit reduction"—an estate fallen into disrepair, surrounded by desperate neighbors, in a world where widespread unemployment is passively accepted as normal.

## DEFICIT LIE NO. 7: "THE MORAL PROBLEM"

One sincere but misguided man I know has stopped arguing with me about the above "technical issues," as he calls them. But he won't change his attitude towards the deficit. (Why not? See the next chapter.) So he tries a different tack:

> The debt is not irrelevant or something that can be ignored. It is symptomatic of many of the excesses that this country has indulged in over the last thirty or forty years. If nothing else, it is representative of a moral problem. It represents mismanagement, self-indulgence, misplaced priorities, and an unwillingness to discipline ourselves. For these reasons, I think it is dangerous not to hold ourselves accountable.

This attack is dangerously wrong in every particular. First, what *excesses, self-indulgence,* and *mismanagement* are you talking about? I see us working excessively hard, "indulging" ourselves in the greatest technical, medical, scientific, and political advances in the history of the world, and managing our business and political fortunes so well that we remain the envy of the world, and its only remaining superpower.

Yes, those of us lucky enough to have jobs own more things now than people did forty years ago. We also are healthier and better educated, and we work harder, longer, and smarter than did people in the 1950s.[5] Nothing we presently enjoy has been given to us. In fact, America has given to the rest of the world the green revolution, most medical and scientific advances, and relative stability in far greater measure than we've received in return. VCRs are nice, yes. But even that would not be in our homes had we not led the way in encouraging world trade. Imagine if the world had followed the Japanese mercantile model—all nations would be their own little islands unto themselves, like the old Albania.

*What we've got we've earned.* But the deficit mongers disregard that unarguable fact, point only to their favorite number, and say the "debt" we have "incurred" proves we did everything wrong. The fact is, we did most everything *right*, but don't know how to measure the worth of the wealth we have created. Look at our "excesses" and "self-indulgence." We have too many nice homes. (We built them ourselves.) We have far more big new buildings downtown than we can fill with businesses (Guess who built them?). Tens of millions of people can now fly who couldn't afford to in 1950 (Who builds and flies the planes?). In the 1950s we ate out once a month, and your average city had one ethnic restaurant—Chinese. Who developed and staffs the huge variety of restaurants we now dine at an average of twice a week? We "indulged" ourselves in an extravagant moon walk, I suppose. And think of all the money we wasted on our nuclear defense and NATO! Think how nice our balance sheet would look if we'd ceded space and Western Europe to the Communists.

As a business professor, I find the charge of "mismanagement" particularly galling. Put a 1950s company in the current competitive environment and they wouldn't make it through the year. We have steadily increased worker productivity, and now lead the world again. Our management is lean and mean to the point of exhaustion. We have incorporated the best of foreign management techniques, especially Japan's remarkably demanding Just-In-Time or *kanban* system. Our versatile corporate financing allows us rapid innovation and risk-taking which the rest of the world finds impossible to duplicate.[6] Our top managers in the 1950s often didn't even have college degrees. Now most top managers have one, and an MBA as well. Their education includes high literacy in a demanding device that didn't even exist a generation ago, the computer. People love to take potshots at the MBA, but people have voted with their feet in this country and abroad, making it the most desired and acquired graduate degree of all time. And remember that it was in the 1950s, before the age of the MBA, that we sat back and lost the manufacturing advantages we had over the devastated Axis powers. It was the soft-working, uneducated managers of those days, and their union counterparts, who lost our lead. We regained it after the wave of MBAs took over in the 1970s. Meanwhile, universities around the world race to develop their own MBA programs, because thousands of their best students desert their homelands in order to come here and learn business.

*The charge that we have been "unwilling to discipline ourselves" is nonsense. Tell it to the union members whose increased productivity has been gained through more demanding work rules, lower real wages, and reduced benefits.*

The charge that we have been "unwilling to discipline ourselves" is nonsense. Tell it to the union members whose increased productivity has been gained through more demanding work rules, lower real wages, and reduced benefits. Tell it to the remaining managers in a merged organization, who work an extra five hours a week for less money. Tell it to the poor, whose job opportunities have gone down even faster than their welfare benefits. Tell it to our fail-safe military and political leaders, who chose a wonderful time to skip the usual world war we used to have every generation—because this one might have ended the human race. Tell it to our patient foreign trade negotiators, who have struggled for forty years to put our drugs in world markets and Japanese electronics in our living rooms. If anything, we are too disciplined. Out of excessive respect for the sad lessons of Vietnam, we got out of Iraq within a hundred hours after the end of the ground war, leaving Saddam Hussein and an elusive nuclear bomb program behind.

The *real* moral problem is the injustice and waste caused by the deficit mongers, not by the deficit itself. Bill and Carl sit at home, building neither cars nor houses, while their families fall apart. The fifty-eight-year-old expert engineer who helped us win the Gulf War has been fired from the defense industry, and he paints bathrooms in our neighborhood till his back aches. Finding employment for our ghetto citizens is given up on as hopeless. Our MBA students finish six or seven years of a no-fun college education only to wind up selling fast food.

The deficit mongers call for "sacrifice." Their form of "sacrifice" means highly trained, eager people sitting at home wondering why nobody will hire them. To them, "sacrifice" means taking the money out of the hands of people who have worked hard to earn it, taxing away their ability to consume our plentiful goods and thus employ the people who want to work to produce even more. The deficit mongers' "sacrifice" means nothing more than *waste*, pure and simple—the waste of our earned real wealth, the waste of people's lives, the waste of the spirit and future of our nation. In 1917, people like our current veteran, respected deficit mongers—from the comfort of their armchairs—called for further "sacrifice" by the soldiers in the trenches. And unsympathetically clucked their tongues when those brave boys continued to die in hopeless charges against the machine guns

## DEFICIT REDUCTION IS THE *ILLNESS*, NOT THE CURE

If the deficit mongers were mere academic writers, it wouldn't matter how wrong they were. Unfortunately, we have put the deficit hawks in charge of the monetary henhouse, and they have wrought great destruction in economies everywhere. These econo-rexics and their inflation obsessions have caused recessions and depressions over the decades and around the world. With ample opportunity to test their dogmatic theories, they have been greeted with resounding failure again and again. And do they repent? No—they promise rather to redouble their efforts. Following are four examples of deficit *reduction* causing a recession or worse: (1) the Great Depression, (2) our own "soft landing," (3) the Bundesbank's continuing ruination of the European money supply, and (4) Japan's pricking of its "bubble economy."

## THE GREAT DEPRESSION

Most people think the depression was caused by the stock market crash of 1929. Wrong. It was caused by what we did *after* the crash. Between 1929 and 1932, our leaders shrank the money supply by *one-third*—that is, we destroyed a third of our nation's cash. To make things worse, in 1932 both the Democrats and Republicans decided that deficit reduction was the nation's greatest need, and passed the largest tax increase in our history. Why? Conventional economic thinking then, as now, wrongly blamed the depression on the "excesses" of the previous decade. The depression was an act of God, they thought, to punish us for extravagance. We needed more thrift, they thought. And the confidence of the nation would only be restored by balancing the federal budget. Overseas, Europe and Japan suffered as they followed our example (less so in Japan) and lost our business, because we could no longer afford to buy their products. Then the world compounded everybody's mistakes by escalating a trade war. Sound familiar?

How then did we ever get out of the depression? Fortunately, one leading economist at that time, Marriner Eccles, was smarter than the rest. He had been raised Mormon in a tough, skinflint, Utah banking family. As late as 1925 he followed the conventional econo-rexic wisdom, writing, "Progress comes only through toil, economy, and thrift." But he had learned his banking on the job, by observing the real world, instead of by studying economic theory in the university. Thus he was able to see how the real world had stopped obeying the rules he had followed in his youth, and he was able to change his mind. By 1932, he realized that too much thrift was the *problem*, and we needed rather to *spend more* instead:

> We have been preaching the negative [i.e., the *wrong*] doctrine...Our depression was not brought about as a

> result of extravagance. The difficulty is that we were not sufficiently extravagant as a nation. We did not consume what we were able to produce.[7]

The financial establishment listened with a mixture of skepticism, belief, and hostility. Fortunately, FDR discarded the establishment's plan and followed Eccles's: unemployment relief, public works, farm mortgage refinancing, tax reform, bank guarantees, and passage of laws on child labor, the minimum wage, and old-age pensions. Eccles was named a governor of the Fed and then chairman. Ironically, the Federal Reserve Building in Washington, D.C., is named in his honor—the same building where Alan Greenspan now sits and dishonors Eccles's memory. Greenspan, Warren Rudman, and Paul Simon would be more in sympathy with the opposition to Eccles's plan. One U.S. representative, John Taber, vilified the Social Security Act of 1935 as follows:

> Never in the history of the world has any measure been brought in here so insidiously designed as to prevent business recovery, to enslave workers, and to prevent any possibility of the employers providing work for the people.

Today, we have Greenspan instead of Eccles, and Clinton instead of FDR. Thus, the John Tabers of Congress rule the economy.

## Greenspan's Recession: The "Soft Landing" of 1989

Life was not perfect in 1988. People died, divorced, and got fired. But we had experienced a decade of high growth, low inflation, and expanding employment. We had even survived a five-hundred-point stock market crash without a ripple in the economy. You could read headlines in the *Wall Street Journal* such as, "Morning of Prosperity in America. Own Data Misled Stagnation Prophets. The Poor are Trickling Upward" (November 3, 1988, A18). Things were going so well that our leading economic anorexics just knew in their hearts that something had to be wrong. Reagan had tripled the national debt. We "owed" half a trillion for the savings and loan bailout. For such blasphemous excesses, they thought, we deserved to suffer, not prosper. So they intentionally created our endless recession.

First, the conservative Fed, under Alan Greenspan, decided to forestall an imaginary collapse by causing a "soft landing." They would cool down our supposedly overheated economy by raising interest rates—squeezing the nation's money supply—on top of the tax increase. The result is described in chapter 2—our endless no-growth recession. The Fed is like an anesthetist who can knock people out, but can't wake them up again. They can raise interest rates all by themselves, which squeezes the money supply and cracks the economy, but years of lowering rates cannot put Humpty Dumpty back together again. Even the old economists are beginning to admit how "peculiar" it is to regard people like Volcker and Greenspan as *heroes*, since the Federal Reserve has itself caused every credit crunch since World War II. Nobel winner James Buchanan marvels that the public never blames the Fed for its failures. Paul McCracken, a former Chairman of the Council of Economic Advisers, says that Greenspan's actions have been the worst since 1931.

Second, the Democrats persuaded Bush's adviser Darman to dishonor the "No new taxes" pledge. We raised taxes. Why? To fight the demon "deficit," of course.

Bad things have happened to the U.S., but they haven't, in general, been all our fault. The world wars started in Europe. The inflations of 1974 and 1979 were caused by the OPEC cartel's raising the price of oil. AIDS seems to have originated in Africa. But this recession is all *our fault*. We not only caused it, but our leaders, especially Alan Greenspan and Wayne Angell, did it with the full consciousness of what they were doing. What makes their actions all the harder to understand is that they refused to apply everything we learned from the Depression.

What lessons they did apply from the Depression worked perfectly. In 1987, they avoided the "liquidity crisis" that helped turn the stock market crash of 1929 into a general depression. A liquidity crisis simply means there isn't enough money. In our October stock market crashes of 1987 and 1989, the Fed acted properly, pumping money into the system and sending clear signals that it would spend as much as needed. They printed money, averted disaster, and earned lots of praise. Why, then, didn't they learn the rest of the lesson? Why did they raise interest rates? Why do they preach against "deficits" and call for higher taxes, imitating the criminals of 1930?

I have no sensible explanation for their inability to face obvious facts. Even after four years of recession, they absolutely refuse to admit the possibility of any error in their tight-money approach to life. Greenspan says he would make every single policy decision exactly the same way if he had it to do over again. Angell is worse; he would put us back on the gold standard. And they are doing it again. With continuing and chronic high unemployment, and growth forecast at less than 3 percent, they are raising interest rates on top of the 1993 tax increase. See the next chapter, which examines the sad history of world leaders' tendency to massacre their own followers without a shred of either common sense or remorse.

## THE BUNDESBANK'S RECESSION: "THE COST OF REUNIFICATION"

If we Americans can be stubbornly penny-pinching to our own detriment, the Germans can be twice as bad. And they *have* been, causing not only their own recession but Europe's, causing the breakdown of the European Monetary Unit and threatening the health of the European community as a whole.

Some people can't stand prosperity. West Germany suddenly found themselves in possession of a new country, their formerly communist eastern third. They didn't want all their poor relations to rush over the border to the West. So, in one momentous, brilliant stroke, they created $37 billion in a single day by exchanging ostmarks for deutschemarks. That year, 1990, the Germans spent over $100 billion on the East. By the old theories of inflation ("everywhere a monetary phenomenon"), bad things were supposed to happen. Wrong. They didn't. Germany enjoyed high growth with low inflation and low unemployment, while stabilizing the powder keg of Eastern Europe.

Unfortunately, their old economists came to the rescue. They could not comprehend that acquiring East Germany was like suddenly owning the house next door. They had gained real wealth. Of course, short-term expenses had to be dealt with, but overall they had just enjoyed a huge capital gain. But the Bundesbank and the rest of their economic leadership didn't see it that way. Following the U.S. example, they dogmatically assumed that their economic "extravagance" and "lack of discipline" *had* to cause disaster. So, like us, they caused a disaster themselves.

They raised interests rates and taxes in a brave fight against illusory inflation and the demon deficit. They succeeded in causing all of the obviously predictable disasters and a few surprises as well. Unemployment went up. Growth declined so much that the vaunted German economy actually shrank in 1993. Taxes are higher. Large companies like BMW are sending their manufacturing abroad for the first time. Even Germany's greatest strength—its middle-sized companies—are caught between high taxes and high interest rates, and are suffering even worse than is the rest of the economy.

Everybody complained, inside Germany and out, but the Bundesbank under Helmut Schlesinger ("Germany's Alan Greenspan") was stalwart, keeping interest rates up no matter what the cost. Thus Germany, considered most responsible for maintaining monetary stability in the European Community, ironically caused the destruction of the European Monetary System through their own perversity.[8] Other countries tried valiantly, but could not keep up with Germany's high rates. With Germany offering 7 percent, the other members had to keep rates high. Otherwise, they would suffer a loss of capital for investments, or watch speculators bet on when their currency would crack.

Efforts were heroic: At one point in September 1992, Sweden's Riksbank raised the cost of borrowing from the central bank to *500* percent. France spent $50 billion in foreign reserves buying up their own currency in an effort to keep it as overvalued as the deutschemark—but the franc succumbed anyway. Even after the monetary union broke down, Belgium raised rates to 25 percent, despite 13.5 percent unemployment, in a vain effort to remain in lockstep with Germany.

The smart countries gave up early. Britain bailed out of the monetary union first. They lowered interest rates, kept inflation low, and are the only major European country expected to have any economic growth in 1993. Sweden and Italy turned the corner faster than countries that stuck with Germany, like France and the Benelux group.[9] France is even considering capital controls, stepping back to the past, imitating the communist and African regimes.

## JAPAN'S RECESSION: PRICKING "THE BUBBLE ECONOMY"

In 1989, Japan was making some headway in buying the world. They owned prize properties in Hawaii, Pebble Beach, Australia, and pretty much anywhere they wished. Unemployment was negligible, business was expanding as ever, and they were even beginning to improve their miserable standard of life.[10]

Unfortunately, their economists came to the rescue. For years the economists had been forecasting, without success, the collapse of a "Bubble Economy" based on speculation. Despite negligible inflation, they felt sure that the rise in price of stocks and Tokyo real estate would somehow start affecting the price of eggs and rice. When it didn't, they decided to follow the lead of their brilliant role models in the U.S. and Germany. Yasushi Mieno, Japan's "Paul Volcker," had their central bank raise interest rates from 2.5 percent to 6 percent in a single year.[11] This would put their house in order, they knew.

They succeeded in trashing their economy as badly as their U.S. and German brothers did.[12] The money supply shrank. Shares on the stock market lost half their value. Real estate collapsed. Banks teetered on the edge, and lending slowed to a dead stop. Some major companies canceled the implicit contract of lifetime employment, and others gave senior employees "look-out-the-window" jobs until they quit in shame. Unemployment is still low, but the jobs available are declining in number and desirability.

The Japanese have tried harder than we or the Germans have, but so far they have not done enough. They put Yasushi back in his cage, lowering rates to 2.5 percent again. While our Congress was rejecting a measly $16 billion stimulus package, Japan's government approved one for $117 billion—even during the middle of a constitutional corruption crisis that caused the first-ever loss for their ruling Liberal Democratic Party. They spent $39 billion on their infrastructure, loaned $21 billion to business, put $20 billion into local projects, and $16 billion into housing.

Japan handled the Great Depression better than we did. The wise policies of their finance minister at that time, Korekiyo Takahashi, allowed Japan to escape relatively unscathed.[13] They got off of the gold standard (much to the chagrin of their own old economists), reduced interest rates, and used runaway deficit spending in order to create demand. It worked then. It's working again, when they do it, but they've stopped doing enough.

## FURTHER CASUALTIES OF DEFICIT REDUCTION: PEACE, FREE TRADE, ETC.

The purely economic pain caused by the deficit mongers is bad enough. We lose jobs and destroy our real wealth. Beyond that looms a series of international disasters linked to deficit reduction. Most important is peace. For forty years we and the Soviets lived with the daily threat of Mutually Assured Destruction. We paid trillions of dollars to counter that threat. Now, we could spend 1 percent of that amount to keep communism in the grave.

No better money could be printed than that which would assure our children's peaceful lives. Instead, we watch Russian free enterprise swing in the breeze, balanced between a return to Stalinism and a move ahead to markets and democracy. Instead, we agonize about the "deficit."

It has taken fifty years to construct the international web of free trade through GATT and long-term trust relations with our international trading partners. Europe has been working for two decades to build better bonds within its own community. The Bundesbank's death grip on its anti-deficit and anti-inflationary obsessions have set them back, perhaps irreparably. No Western nation wants to take on the role of customer, fearing its bogeyman deficit, so trade war rumbles grow louder. Free trade hangs in the balance. The newly developing countries of Eastern Europe and Africa want to sell us their goods. We set up barriers, to keep down our "deficits," of course. This is the reward we give them for trying out democracy—who cares about peace and prosperity, with the Golden Idol of the deficit shining above all other considerations.

The infrastructure, our ghettos, renewable energy, the environment, our substance-addicted citizens, health care, our educational system, defense against terrorism—all are secondary to our obsession with the deficit. We can improve all of these real concerns, or we can serve the cause of a will-o'-the-wisp number, chasing a bogeyman over the cliff to our deaths. This sounds like an easy choice to me, but we have never done so much to make this decision the wrong way. In 1993, our Congress, bowing to the will of its president and people, voted *against* a modest spending increase and voted *for* widespread, retroactive new taxes. All in the cause of deficit reduction.

## WHEN WILL THEY EVER LEARN...?

The facts reported here are pretty straightforward. You would think the failures of deficit reduction around the world and throughout history, you would think the incredible achievement of abundance might enter the consciousness of our economic leaders—but they don't. The deficit mongers don't think they need to even bother disputing the merits of their dogma. No matter that raising taxes and cutting spending have caused major ills and will cause more. No matter that increasing deficits and loosening up the money supply causes recovery. They look at the same facts I have described and ignore them all.

Don't wait for your leaders to change. They won't. Alan Greenspan will go to his grave comfortable in the knowledge that he never made a mistake in his management of the economy. Such is the way of the world. You might find it hard to believe that so many supposedly respectable and responsible people could be so stubbornly and tragically wrong. In the next chapter, I show that world leaders often have led their people to destruction, in the face of all common sense and evidence. Only when the people demand change, and vote in new leadership, will recovery begin.

# 7

# The Power of Bad Ideas: Butcher-Generals and Bloodletting

How can our leadership have been so wrong? If we respect our country and its institutions, we might have trouble believing that the people we have appointed to improve the economy could themselves be the *cause* of all our economic troubles. I sympathize with your skepticism. How could so many politicians, all their silver-haired economic advisers, be so wrong, and this book be correct? How could the solution to such a grand problem as the recession be as easy as "spend more and tax less"? You might categorically refuse to believe in your heart that so many top leaders could err so badly, and the solution could be so simple—no matter how well I answer the questions in your brain.

Believe it, folks. No law of nature ensures that world leaders know what they are doing. The sad message of this chapter is that leaders have been wrong so often in human history that tragic error is more the norm than the exception. Heads of state such as Pol Pot (Cambodia), Joseph Stalin (Soviet Union), and Adolf Hitler (Nazi Germany) almost destroyed their countries, purging and executing millions of their own citizens. Scientific, religious, and academic leaders have been just as wrong in their own fields. Even worse is the authorities' record at changing their minds in the face of devastating evidence against them. They *never* admit they are wrong. Only when they die of old age or they are thrown out of power can their bankrupt policies be changed. Societies that waited for change from above suffered and died. We, the people, have to demand it ourselves.

Our paralyzing fear of the deficit is, in essence, a bad idea, a corrupt and misleading theory. Bad ideas litter history. This chapter explains two that best mirror the deficit hysteria in the widespread destruction they caused. The first is the bad military idea to charge into machine guns, which killed nine hundred thousand British soldiers and millions of French and Germans in World War I. The second is bloodletting, a bad medical idea that killed billions throughout recorded history.

Bad ideas persist, despite the destruction they cause, for many reasons. First, they seem simple to understand, even while they put the blame in the wrong direction—as though blaming a bogeyman. Second, the people in charge never change their minds and admit they are wrong. Third, we have an excessive reverence for complicated numbers explained to us by men with coats and ties and impressive titles. Fourth, we treat life like sports—for me to win, somebody else has to lose. As a result, the rich scorn the poor while the poor resent the rich. Right now we find it easier to keep blaming and changing our presidents than changing our ideas. However, no president can succeed as long as the electorate believes in today's Golden Idol—the deficit—and demands more human sacrifices.

## LEADERS MAKE HIDEOUS MISTAKES

History is full of examples of leaders destroying their own people by following bad ideas. The Aztecs, invincible for centuries, allowed the dictates of their pagan beliefs to hamstring their defenders so badly that a handful of invaders captured Montezuma and enslaved the population. Strong men, warriors committed to fight to the death, were rendered utterly impotent by a metaphor that told them to lay down their arms before the white-skinned "Sun god." Similarly, the South African Xhosa followed the prophecy of a sixteen-year-old girl, who told them to kill all their farm animals and burn their own fields—this sacrifice would somehow drive the invading white men from their land. (It didn't. The Xhosa starved themselves and had to surrender.) The Shakers allowed their entire religious order to wither and die by banning sex even for the purpose of procreation. Certain Arab and African women encourage their own daughters to be "circumcised." Hitler's Nazi dream, Stalin's Marxist theories, and Mao Tse-tung's "cultural revolution" decimated their own countries.

This chapter will focus on examples much closer to home, examples of tragic folly that affected most of the West: World War I military strategy and the universal medical practice of bloodletting.

## THE BRITISH BUTCHERS OF WORLD WAR I

The most inexcusable example of horrible leadership I have found is that of the British generals in World War I.[1] They sent nearly a million of their young men marching to their deaths before German machine guns. They lived through the Boer War when machine guns were introduced, and personally understood the power of the new weapon to massacre infantrymen. On one day at the Battle of the Somme, July 1, 1916, twenty thousand British soldiers died. A German biographer wrote:

> Dense masses of infantry, line after line, came into sight on the ridge...offering such a target as had never been seen before. Never had the machine-gunners such straightforward work to do nor done it so effectively. They traversed to and fro along the [British] ranks unceasingly. [Our] men stood...and fired exultantly into the mass of [British] advancing across the open grassland. The effect was devastating and they could be seen falling in hundreds. The English made five consecutive attempts to

> press on past the wood, but finally, weakened by their terrible losses, they were forced to give in.

A thousand-man battalion was wiped out by only two German machine-gun posts. By the end of the war, 925,000 British soldiers were dead. The war was won *not* by infantry charging into German defensive posts, but by a naval blockade of German goods and the threat of newly invented allied tanks.

## THE GENERALS WERE TAUGHT TWO STRATEGIES; THEY CHOSE THE SUICIDAL ONE

How could four years of pointless carnage have been tolerated and allowed to continue? The British generals had been educated about the value of defense, but repeatedly ordered thousands of their innocent young countrymen into hopeless attacks, through mud and barbed wire, into the barrels of machine guns. They had witnessed the devastating effect of this new weapon in the Boer War; but they ignored it. In Sandhurst they had read von Clausewitz on the value of the defensive position; but they nonetheless attacked. They had read in detail about the value of the high ground; but they pressed suicidal attacks through lowland bogs against bunkered hills.

Why? Because they had begun their careers in the horse calvary. Instead of taking von Clausewitz to heart, they embraced the spirit of their 1907 Calvary Training Manual: "It must be accepted as a principle that the rifle, effective as it is, cannot replace the effect produced by the speed of the horse, the magnetism of the charge, and the terror of cold steel." The main British butcher, General Douglas Haig, went further: "Success in battle depends mainly on moral [sic] and a determination to conquer." Unfortunately, they, like our current economic leaders, followed a simple-minded, out-of-date, and tragically incorrect idea instead of facing the simple facts.

The effect of thousands of soldiers marching into the German machine gun nests was not "terror"; the Germans were instead merely amazed as they went about the cold work of slaughtering the innocents. The morale, determination, and even suicidal bravery of the hundreds of thousands of British soldiers could not overcome the idiocy of their commanders. The British generals were blind to the failure of their simplistic thesis. They blamed lower level officers and the dead men themselves.

The same thing is happening today. Our economic leaders have two strategies available to them: Keynes and monetarism. The one they follow, monetarism, says to cut jobs and raise taxes like cavalrymen leading a charge against terrible inflation. Never mind that the world has changed. Just as the machine gun changed the reality of war, the fact that we have earned a great abundance of goods has changed the nature of economics. Our leaders nonetheless refuse to believe their eyes, that jobs are being lost without replacement, that inflation is not a threat. Yes, they can read the reports in the *Wall Street Journal* but, like the British generals, they refuse to let what it means sink into their made-up minds. Rather, they call for even further charges, more brave "sacrifice," more "contributions" of economic blood from the very people they have already put out of work.

## BLAME THE VICTIMS, HONOR THE CRIMINALS

What is most insulting is that they implicitly blame their own victims for the plight of the economy. For two decades they have blamed the American union worker for excessive pay, for poor education, for low productivity. But in that time the unions have died, wages have shrunk, and our productivity has become the highest in the world. Just as the bravest sacrifices of the British soldiers didn't help when they were following a suicidal strategy, the Herculean efforts of our businessmen and workers come to nothing when our economic leaders have decided to sacrifice American jobs to the Golden Idol of "monetarism," to the bad idea of a tight money supply. Or they blame the politicians for not lowering spending and raising taxes even more—when that corrupt strategy is what brought us the recession in the first place.

No butcher-generals were punished—rather, they received honors. Haig's proud statue still towers above Victoria Square. Are the people who engineered our so-called "soft landing" in 1988, which changed the Reagan boom into the Bush recession, apologizing for their folly? Are they in disgrace for the pointless harm they have done? No! Alan Greenspan is still in charge of the Federal Reserve. Not one economic adviser on Bush's team has admitted that anything he said or did was wrong in the slightest. Nobel Laureate James Buchanan is amazed that the American people revere people like Greenspan and his predecessor, Paul Volcker, despite the harm they have done to the economy.

## Bloodletting Surgeons

The most common medical remedy throughout human history has been bloodletting. For thousands of years, up to and including this century, it was as commonplace as taking two aspirin and going to bed is today. It had absolutely no beneficial effects. It killed billions.

Because "plethora" (too much blood) was thought to be the cause of virtually every ill, people would have a vein opened or a leech applied for almost anything—the flu, skin diseases, a headache, even a broken arm. And this was not a casual, isolated intervention. A good patient would see his surgeon every day for two weeks, losing a half-pint every time. He also would endure what they called "heroic purgation"—taking a strong emetic every day, causing him to retch till he was empty. Needless to say, if you were in an already weakened condition, these "remedies" would kill you.

The simple idea that gave birth to these fatal remedies was the pimple or boil. Lancing a boil hurts sharply for a second, getting rid of diseased pus. Then you instantly feel some relief, and the infection heals more quickly than if you had not lanced it. It seemed elementary (my dear Watson) that if the whole body were sick, "lancing" it would get rid of the "diseased pus" and you would begin to heal. Doctors and their patients never questioned this metaphor, just as we do not challenge the presumed parallel between our national debt and an individual's overdrawn checkbook. Physicians were sure the blood of a sick person was bad, so they imagined all sorts of "bad blood" conditions: a crust, a "brownish turmoil." They wrote whole libraries detailing how to analyze patients based on the appearance of their blood, whole libraries of complete balderdash. They waged debates for centuries over whether to lance near the wound or away from it, and which kinds of leeches were best—debates which were utterly irrelevant. The benefits of draining blood are absolutely imaginary, and the benefits of leeches are so rare that it makes the newspapers when a single obscure use is discovered.

*Our deficit mongers are obsessed with the evil deficit number. They analyze which "government expenditures" are worst, which taxes are best, and whether to lance here or leech there. But the benefits of draining money from the economy are entirely imaginary.*

Similarly, whole books are written on the evils of the national debt. Instead of "bad blood," our deficit mongers are obsessed with the evil deficit number. They analyze which "government expenditures" are worst, which taxes are best, and whether to lance here or leech there. But the benefits of draining money from the economy are entirely imaginary. The bloodletters never tested whether their treatments worked. They followed their dogmatic beliefs, and scorned those who did not accept their time-honored, traditional wisdom.

The bloodletters at least had the excuse of not having the basic scientific method as a part of their training or world view. In its essence, the scientific method says you have to see if the facts match your pet theory. Instead of merely saying your pet theory is true, you have to see if its predictions match what actually happens. If the bloodletters had ever once randomly divided a group of one hundred patients into two groups, bled one group for the standard two weeks while neglecting the other, they could have seen the folly of their bloodletting theory. One physician proposed such a test in the 1600s, but was ignored. Finally, in the 1800s, Pierre Louis ran conclusive tests showing the harm caused by bloodletting, but "failed to cause the typical physician to change his methods…many believed that Louis's attempt to evaluate the efficacy of bloodletting was a rash, reckless rejection of the wisdom of the ages…Some argued that Louis's data actually proved that venesection was ineffective when performed too conservatively…Advocates of bloodletting argued that more patients were lost through timidity than loss of blood."[2]

Our economic bloodletters, however, are just as guilty. They have been carefully trained in the scientific method. But they refuse to acknowledge the facts, even when others have gathered them. Who cares if it keeps killing the patients, they say—give me my knife and let me at that vein! And if squeezing the money supply this much is harming the economy, that actually proves we need to raise taxes and cut spending even more.

How much harm did the bloodletters cause? George Washington was bled to death because he had a badly constricted sore throat. The youngest of his three surgeons wanted to try a tracheotomy, but the two senior surgeons would not approve such a radical approach. Instead, they stayed with safe, conservative bleeding and purging. Near the end, George begged for no such further "treatments," but they continued to torment him with blisters and cantharides to bring as much blood as they could to the surface. Afterwards, one almost regretted their butchery:

> Had we taken no blood from him, [he might be] alive now. But we were governed by the best light we had [conveniently forgetting the pleas of the young surgeon whom they overruled]; we thought we were right, and so we are justified.[3]

It is conjectured that Napoleon Bonaparte's chief surgeon, a "heroic" bloodletter, killed more of Napoleon's troops than were killed in battle. And calculating the amount of senseless carnage caused by bloodletting is much harder than counting the dead British soldiers sacrificed to the German machine guns. Rarely did the loss of a single pint of blood directly kill a patient. It always made things worse, but the direct effects were impossible to see in a single patient. The murders only accumulated statistically. Similarly, any single American has trouble pinning his own unemployment on any single raise in the Fed's interest rates, any single tax raise, or any particular cut in government spending. The endless layoffs and destroyed lives accumulate statistically.

## WHY DO WE PUT UP WITH THIS?

Why do we let ourselves be ravaged by an imaginary economic bogeyman? What makes us passive accomplices, like the brave soldiers and stoic bleeders? Most of our education throughout our lives trains us to respect and learn from authority. Not once in our twenty years of schooling is it correct to stand up and say, "I'm sorry, teacher, but I think you are completely wrong." Of course, our teachers and elders are overwhelmingly correct, at least compared to the uninformed and barbaric natural knowledge we have as untutored youngsters. In general, it is necessary and effective to rely upon the accumulated and sifted wisdom of the ages, learning from instead of fighting with our parents and other moral and educational leaders.

But the dangerous side effect of learning to bow to the wisdom of authorities is that we too passively accept their errors. Their error now is believing the national economy is like a family checkbook. We have a quasi-religious respect for hard economic numbers, perhaps engendered in seventh grade when we either got math anxiety or overcame it. And we presently let a set of botched numbers like the "national debt" or "deficit" guide our economy, despite their clear disconnection from any real-world effects. As Montezuma's men—on his order—did not fight, so does our trained work force sit idly behind empty factories, while millions yearn for the goods these people could produce. As the Aztec soldiers humbly respected their robed priests' advice to not fight Cortez, to accept passive death, our work force humbly follows the gray-haired academic call to passively sacrifice their jobs and taxes. People these days may have no special devotion to white-robed priests, but they instead give the same blind and trusting allegiance to suit-and-tie Ph.D.s whose record on the current economy matches the Aztec priests' in war and the British Generals' on the fields of France.

## THE PHILOSOPHY OF BAD-TASTING MEDICINE

So many people, leaders and regular Americans alike, seem willing to give up their jobs and pay high taxes. There must be a psychological component driving their twisted logic. As with all psychology, I'm just guessing here. But many of us are raised to believe some or all of the following: The worse a medicine tastes, the better it is for you. Pain builds character. No pain, no gain. *Guilty pleasure* should be one word. You should not expect to enjoy your work. If it tastes good, it's bad for you. Life is hard, and then you die.

You know what I mean. For all our talk of 1980s' self-indulgence and the hippie excesses of the 1960s, our culture still has strong Calvinistic, Puritan, Protestant, almost ascetic roots. Millions run and work out. Millions restrict their favorite high-cholesterol foods for thirty years in order to increase their life expectancy by one month. While Japanese and European college students enjoy four years of "summer camp" and smoke-filled cafes, we accept many years of impoverished sixty-hour weeks on the way to our own engineering, medical, business, and law degrees. We assume that "successful" people work late and on weekends.

So it is no wonder that Warren Rudman's severe demeanor, his General-Haig-like face appeals directly to our guilty consciences. All our lives, senior tough guys like him have been telling us to knuckle down and pay the price now for success in the future. When those tough guys knew what they were talking about, their grim advice was right. Youthful laziness might have let us stay home watching TV when we needed to spend the night at the library or chem lab. However, now the old tough guys do *not* know what they are talking about. Their anti-deficit advice demands that millions of Americans who *want* to work hard should instead do what we were tempted to do as students—stay home and watch TV while collecting unemployment checks.

Watch Rudman and Tsongas. I can see faces like theirs grimly advising more attacks into the machine guns. I can hear them telling me to be tough enough to take another week of bleeding and heroic purgation. I watch them lead millions of our innocent and earnest young people to lives of waste and needless privation. And too many of us, especially those of us who, like Rudman and Tsongas themselves, do not have to share in the suffering, hear a persistent, callous voice whispering in our souls, "Suffering is the just lot of humankind...don't be a baby...pay high taxes...give up your job...give up your life...Why? 'Cause I said so."

Folks, be honest with yourselves. If that kind of mean inner spirit turns you on when you watch the deficit mongers give their speeches, nothing I say will change your mind. Return this book and try to get your money back.

## FOR ME TO WIN, YOU GOTTA' LOSE

Suffering for the sake of suffering is one sick, self-defeating bad idea. Another is the idea of life as a football game: If you win, that means I lose. I suspect this fallacy pervades Western thinking even more than the fallacy of bad-tasting medicine. From childhood on, we are indoctrinated with competitive sports, grade curves, and hierarchical pyramids in which fewer and fewer make it up the rungs of the employment ladder. When are we ever taught, by example, that a rising tide raises all boats? That the success of a fellow student helps you out as well? That business collusion is outlawed as an "antitrust violation" because cooperation is such a powerful force? One clear, never-taught fact of modern liberal capitalism is that both rich and poor have improved their lot, mutually and severally, over the last century.

This deep-seated metaphor of life as a competition is so strong that I sometimes despair of overcoming it with any amount of argument. People at my speeches will understand that our nation's abundance of wealth already exists, waiting on the shelves, and we only have to distribute it to all in order to create even more. They will understand that money that starts out in the hands of the poor inevitably ends up in the pockets of the rich. They will understand that rich and poor, young and old alike suffer from insufficient cash flowing through the economy. But then their ingrained win-lose view of life stops them cold when they see that I am not only on their side, I seem to be on the other guy's side as well. The rich folks in the audience blanch at the thought of being taken in by some guy (me) who is advocating putting lots of money in the hands of the poor. The liberals, unemployed, and poor folks gag at my saying, "I love rich folks! I *want* them to end up with the money that trickles and flows up into their pockets."

## Class Prejudice and the Politics of Envy

Again, look into your own hearts. Mere logic and reason is not enough to change the workings of the world from wrong to right. There was nothing logical about charging into machine guns. Bleeding sick people to death made no sense. Killing the best farmers in Stalin's Ukraine and the smartest teachers in Mao's China was idiotic on the face of it. And today in the West, squeezing the money supply with high taxes and low spending, causing people to idly sit at home while goods rot on the shelves, *makes no logical sense*. But if the voters of this country prefer to cast common sense and self-interest aside in favor of following their lowest, gut-level hatreds and emotions, no one's book or argument will matter a bit.

Say I tried to make the following deal with a poor ghetto resident and a rich merchant. I would print up one thousand dollars and give it to the poor person on the single condition that he spend it at the store of the rich merchant. I personally know poor and rich people who would *refuse* to spend and accept the one thousand dollars under these conditions. No matter what I would say about the legitimate source of the one thousand dollars, etc., no matter that they would both clearly benefit, no matter what they said to try to make some sense out of their gut-level distaste for such a deal with each other, it simply comes down to class prejudice by the rich and the politics of envy by the poor. Some rich people want poor people to stay poor, and damn their own profit margins. Some poor people want the rich brought down a peg even more than they want themselves brought up a peg. Admit it—you know people like this, even if you are not one yourself.

Russians are world champs at this kind of thinking. Marxism-enshrined class warfare fits right into their psyches. The classic joke describing the self-destructive nature of Russian envy has a genie being evoked by a Britisher, a Frenchman, and a Russian. He grants them each one wish. The Englishman wants a grand estate like his neighbor the duke, with lands and servants. The Frenchman wants a chateau like his rich neighbor's, with vineyards and a beach on the sea. The Russian says, "My neighbor just got a new goat. I want you to kill it." To this day, what most inhibits perestroika is a widespread envy that makes the citizens more interested in seeing their partners fail rather than helping themselves succeed.

## YOU WANT ENEMIES? OK, I'LL GIVE YOU ENEMIES

The fact is, we do have real enemies in our fight against the Great Recession. But they are not in the lineup of the usual cast of suspects. The enemy is not the greedy rich or lazy poor, the irresponsible young or untaxed old, liberal Democrats or conservative

Republicans; it's not the Communists, Japanese, Germans, or Mexicans; it's not labor and it's not management. It's not the number-crunching financiers or blood-sucking attorneys. It's not even politicians as a class. If we waste our energy attacking each other, all fellow victims of the same recession that afflicts us all, we will never begin to defend ourselves against our true enemies, the people who caused the recession and who are continuing to do everything in their power to make it worse.

Who are they? I have named them before. I will continue to attack them throughout this book and in every public and private speech I give. They are the *deficit mongers*, the eminent silver-haired economic "experts" who preach a corrupt gospel. "Raise taxes, cut spending, and raise the Fed's interest rate!" they righteously cry, and many of their deluded supporters cheer. Some examplars are Alan Greenspan, Wayne Angell, Warren Rudman, Paul Simon, Paul Tsongas, Phil Gramm, Henry Figgie, Jr., and James Davidson. Add the guy at the barbershop and your loud-mouthed uncle.

These well-respected, self-righteous opinion leaders are morally and intellectually responsible for the recession. They are to blame for the following and more:

- millions of un- and under-employed Americans
- empty houses when honest families live in their cars
- businessmen with good ideas and no customers
- international tensions
- the evaporation of chances for a permanent conversion of communism
- the decline of modern scientific exploration
- much of the crime and despair in our ghettos
- the addicts who have no rehabilitation programs open to them
- children stuck in day care whose mothers have to work but who would love to stay with their babies
- children who do not even have day care but come home alone to an empty house every day
- low retirement incomes and underfunded pension plans

Our misguided economic "leaders" are as respected and powerful as the eminent British generals were who ordered hundreds of thousands of men to certain and futile death. They are as responsible as the respected physicians who confidently counseled still more bloodletting and killed their trusting patients. They are as responsible as Hitler was for massacring millions of his own citizens and sending millions more to death in a vicious war. As responsible as Mao and his henchmen were for the Cultural Revolution which ruined tens of millions of lives. As responsible as Pol Pot for his own version of responsible economic redevelopment via austerity.

Folks, I am not exaggerating the intensity of my feelings towards the deficit mongers. You do not have to be a genocidal dictator to cause pointless suffering on a national scale. The generals and physicians were trained, senior professionals in their fields, motivated by a sincere desire to do what all of their peers thought was the right thing. Following the highest professional standards is just fine when the standards are correct. But when the standards are wrong, then you end up killing people—or, these days, firing them. As your soldiers are massacred, as your patients die, as your fellow Americans are laid off by the millions, you are comforted by the fact that your fellow generals, physicians, and economists at the old boys' club all continue to respect you for doing the right thing.

And this is what makes me mad. These leaders care for their standing in their professional community, not for the millions of lives their decisions ruin. Worse, they profit, and profit highly, from the misery they cause. That's why I use the term "monger." "Whoremonger" is an old term for those who pimped in the slums. They profited off others' tragedy, a tragedy they helped cause, by selling a sadly soiled bill of goods. So is it with the deficit mongers. For their own profit, they sell a corrupt economic bill of goods, one that ruins lives the mongers don't give a damn about.

Many mongers are deficit opportunists, using alarm to line their own pockets. Warren Rudman, writing for the Concord Coalition in a mailing I've received three times, pleads: "...if we work together and we all do our part we can avert disaster. But it is more important that we all get fully involved." How do we "work together" and get "fully involved?" The next sentence puts the touch on: "Please try to send your Charter Membership dues back, twenty-five dollars if possible, when you accept membership in this historic effort."

James Dale Davidson (*The Great Reckoning*) uses the old skyrocketing-debt graph to predict not only a debt-caused recession, but "the coming end of the world." After vividly imagining a lawless, garbage-strewn suburb, he offers a way out: "Somebody Will Still Be Rich. Will It Be You?" Guess exactly how you can protect yourself: "Fortunately, you won't be one of the people stuck in the decaying neighborhood I described—if you heed my warnings and read my newsletter, *Strategic Investment* (see page 115...). It does not direct you to your local library to find Davidson's life-saving advice. No. You get an order blank (actually, four of them) for a "No-risk introductory subscription offer (*for new subscribers only*)" for fifty-nine dollars for twelve issues.

One enterprising fellow doesn't bother to write his own scare story. He just quotes the biggest screamers from Figgie's *Bankruptcy 1995* to set up his own pitch: "I wanted to give my readers an answer to relieve the anxiety they faced from this awesome problem that I don't think is going to get solved." Of course, he had just spent two pages causing that anxiety to the best of his ability. How can you then "relieve the anxiety"? Send him 149 dollars for his "Investing Made EZ" course.

## A Mind at Rest Tends to Remain at Rest

Nothing is harder to change than someone's mind. Decades of education, we presume, teaches us what is right. We are never taught to question the authorities. Were you ever once in all your years at school taught about the British generals, bloodletting physicians, or any other respected professional group who were just plain wrong? The next step would then be to teach you how to begin to make independent judgments of right and wrong. But step one is never taken. The only people in world history who have ever been wrong have been the *other* guys, usually the enemy, such as the Communists, Nazis, racists, Confederates, etc. Heaven forfend, not *us*. In fact, political leaders who change their minds based on new information (Former President Jimmy Carter and former California Governor Jerry Brown, for example) are derided for inconsistency or a lack of "principles" (read: lack of pig-headedness).

It takes energy for a body at rest to be knocked out of its orbit. Think how much easier it is to follow the herd of lemmings, keep blaming the deficit, keep hollering at scapegoats—easier than it is to read this book and understand a different explanation. On top of inertia is the standard human fear of trying something new. Sadly, many people are proud of having *never* changed their minds. No number of facts will budge them an inch. But that doesn't mean that those of us who can and do change our minds should just give up. Change *is* possible and has occurred regularly throughout human history. It is not accomplished by changing minds that are already made up, which invariably includes all of the professional experts in any field.

The best-known study of change is Thomas Kuhn's *The Structure of Scientific Revolutions*. From before Copernicus to the present, change in the way we see the world has never occurred by getting the people in charge to say, "Gee, sorry—I guess we've been wrong all our lives." Change is accomplished by the non-professionals, the young, the people who are not as professionally committed to maintaining the status quo as the "experts" are. These people—the readers of this book—can look at the issues with an open mind. You are free to choose a new, a better way of doing things—whether it be defense over attacking the machine guns, sanitation over bloodletting, or balancing money and wealth over econo-rexia.

Unfortunately, Kuhn reveals that change is not accomplished until the old "experts" relinquish their power—which they only do when they *die of old age*. They retain their preconceptions and their power until death. Their ideas die with them, because the next generation chooses not to imitate their folly. But we can't wait that long with the economy, and we don't have to. As I said before, if I had to rely on the old boys' club of economists to admit that they have ruined millions of innocent lives, I never would have bothered to write this book. The academic economists of the old school will continue to write learned treatises on irrelevant trivia to each other as though this book and the Great Recession didn't exist.

This book is not written *for* them, but *against* them. These ideas are written expressly for the real macroeconomic decision-makers in this country: the voters. We don't have to wait for the economists. We don't have to give a damn what Alan Greenspan thinks or when he raises rates. Every voter can influence our representatives in Washington. Bill by bill, we can choose to tax less and spend more, and to hell with the "deficit," to hell with the bankrupt economics of the deficit mongers. Thomas Kuhn's world of science had no democracies. We have one. Let's use it.

## A Golden Idol Receiving Innocent Sacrifices

This is the most dismal of the three images I use in this book to describe deficit economics, in addition to that of the deficit mongers and econo-rexics. In various primitive societies people would sacrifice their goods and even their virgin daughters to a Golden Idol they invested with magical powers. They just knew that if they sacrificed, if they hurt themselves on behalf of this Idol, the Idol would somehow make things better for them all. Wise priests of the Golden Idol spurred them on, assuring them that more, ever more sacrifice would make them ever richer, that the happier the Golden Idol, the more the Idol would shower wealth back upon them. They wanted goods, lambs, and healthy children. They sacrificed their goods, lambs, and healthy children. The Golden Idol never gave them a thing.

We want jobs and low taxes. Our "priests of the high deficit" have convinced this country to reduce employment and pay high taxes in order to *increase* employment and pay *lower* taxes. Some poor suckers swallowed their line so badly they offered up their own daughters to the knife. Does that sound inconceivable? They have soul brothers today. This year the Treasury received a $12 million check from a "patron" to help reduce the public debt![4] Think of all the good that could have been accomplished with that kind of money. Now try to imagine a *single effect of any sort* that will occur because of his demented largesse. He might just as well have thrown it in a bonfire. In World War I, he might have led his platoon in a volunteer suicide mission against the guns, losing ninety-five of one hundred men, himself included, to capture thirty yards of land that would be lost again the next day.

We have been in the grip of an idea with the strength and intuitive appeal—to those raised in its spell—as strong as that of Marxist socialism. But even the Marxists have learned from history, admitted they were wrong, and changed. We have the simple idea of a national economy with a budget balanced as though it were a family checkbook. The Marxists had the idea of a national economy as a small business run by a single smart businessman. But they eventually found that the more they concentrated decision-making for a giant economy at the center, the worse their economy became. They couldn't even use their great resources to make simple goods.

*We have been in the grip of an idea with the strength and intuitive appeal—to those raised in its spell—as strong as that of Marxist socialism. But even the Marxists have learned from history, admitted they were wrong, and changed.*

We let the exact opposite condition become a problem. Our relatively *laissez faire,* free-market system has made a great abundance of goods—even in nations like Japan and Hong Kong with few natural resources. At the same time, we let the goods rot on the shelves, unable to be purchased by the very people who make them and who want to make more. Are we as smart and adaptable as the ex-communists? Can we change, or are we more like the pagan idolaters and their Golden Idols?

## THE GOLD STANDARD

I use the term "golden" advisedly. A prime tenet of faith for the old economics was that the yellow metal was the very symbol *and* substance of wealth, well-being, and sound doctrine. They believed in the Gold Standard as the ancient pagans believed in their Golden Idol. Like the pagan idolaters, the old economists prophesied that world monetary systems would fall into anarchy and ruin when we abandoned their holy Gold Standard. They were wrong. The West prospered as never before, once released from its chains of gold. Chapter 10 will explain the role of gold as a primitive form of money. But first, chapter 8 details the other fatal mistakes and misunderstandings of the old economics.

# 8

# Supposed "Scarcity" in an Age of No Scarce Resources

The old science of economics was designed from the ground up to deal with a condition that no longer applies: scarcity. The most popular textbook defines it as, "the study of how to employ scarce resources." I will *not* attempt to teach you the old economics. The point of this chapter is to explain why the old economics is *wrong*, so I will discuss the old economics only in order to criticize it. You are welcome to check any standard economics text, either to better understand the old economics or to judge whether I am representing its arguments fairly.

The point of criticizing the old economics is to discredit it badly enough that you will be open to the new approach presented in Part III. The old approach is based on a false assumption, "scarcity," which is as relevant to the modern economy as air is to space travel. Nothing is scarce anymore. Other irrelevant assumptions are that money is bad, everyone has a job, everything manufactured will be purchased, and higher demand causes prices to rise.

But now, economies of scale and international competition have overcome both scarcity and monopoly power, so now both antitrust laws and government regulation are unnecessary. By failing to adapt to the times, the dismal, gloom-and-doom science has lagged far behind all other sciences in the twentieth century. Stuck with nineteenth century math, it has proven useless at either forecasting the future or explaining the present. Some current practitioners, having endlessly failed, want everyone else, too, to give up on trying to fix the economy. But economics is more important than ever. The old version still applies to scarcity-plagued nations in Eastern Europe and Africa. And a new science of economics is ready to carry on now that the old has reached its limits and lost its way.

## WHY CRITICIZE THE OLD ECONOMICS?

Why bother to use any time discussing the old economics only to dismiss it? Alternatively, why not simply present the new approach? Because my analysis of the national budget is new and not just a modification of existing economic theory, it is necessary to do more than add on to what you already know. Rather, the mission of this book is to get you to change your mind, to alter your preconceptions of how our national economy operates. In the literature of organizational change, we speak of "unfreezing" people's minds as the first step toward accomplishing change. People will not hear a new approach if they are consciously and unconsciously wedded to the old way of understanding and doing things.

Thus, the fallacies of the old economics of scarcity have to be highlighted and explained—not to correct them, but to open your thinking to the new concepts necessary in our changed world. Usually science advances by small steps in the same direction. Sometimes, however, a great many small steps lead one into a completely different realm of understanding, in which the old laws do not apply, and a completely new approach must be taken.

## LIKE WINGS IN AIRLESS SPACE...

The science of aerodynamics explains how a vessel obtains lift and guides itself through the air. But when a vessel that successfully follows those laws finally rises out of the atmosphere, different laws take effect. Wings will not lift it farther, nor will the rudder turn it. A purely aerodynamic scientist trying to explain the vessel's flight will say that there is no sense to its motion anymore, that it is futile to try to guide its flight.

Similarly, economists limited to the old way of thinking find that the flows and levers they thought would guide the economy no longer work. For example, Charles Morris writes that it is impossible to manage the economy. He sadly notes that all of the old rules and laws have inexplicable effects or no effects at all. He concludes that the best we can do is not even *try* to be clever, and that our presidents ought simply to follow their instincts.[1] Paul Krugman writes a whole book that tells, he admits, "... a not particularly edifying story....What happened to the magic economy [of the 1980s]?...Let me cut to the chase: the real answer is *we don't know*."[2]

But we can do much better than that. Our scientists have not had much trouble understanding how to navigate in airless, weightless space, once they understood how different the new environment was. In many ways, navigation in space is easier than through air and gravity. In space you can propel your vessel only by pushing it in one direction or another—fine steering by ailerons and stabilizers is useless. Flying by jet propulsion in space is quite similar to flying by jet through the atmosphere, with the exception that earthly jets push air through their engines, while spacecraft must generate their exhaust without any input. Propellers are useless and wings are only for show, but at least the principle of jet propulsion applies in both environments.

Similarly, the economics of abundance is easier in many ways than the economics of scarcity. The broad principle of propulsion replaces the fine tuning of ailerons and rudders. But the absolutely first step is to understand what is different—as different as the absence of an atmosphere is to aerodynamics—and why that difference makes the old science irrelevant in the new environment.

## FALSE ASSUMPTION NO. 1:
### *Resources are scarce*

The fundamental problem the old science of economics was designed to tackle was "the allocation of scarce resources." But nothing is scarce anymore. Aerodynamics was "the science of flying through the atmosphere." When you escape the atmosphere, aerodynamics no longer applies. We have escaped "scarcity." That is why the old economics no longer applies.

We already take the most remarkable development of our generation, abundance, for granted. We can make everything we need. Food. Clothing. Housing. Services such as air travel. Counseling and therapy. Not everyone who wants one can have a house or airplane ride right this moment, but that's not due to scarcity. Only our bad economics prevents us from enjoying the wealth we have already created and which exists in abundance.

Abundant wealth should be a shocking development. As recently as 1972, a famous Massachusetts Institute of Technology (MIT) study commissioned by The Club of Rome persuasively demonstrated that the world's physical resources would be exhausted within a few decades—that is, around *now*. Their powerful arguments convinced a generation, especially after OPEC put that generation waiting in line to buy gas. But the MIT doomsayers turned out to have been completely wrong. Oil prices fell, and the supply has been called a glut for a decade, with OPEC powerless to capitalize on their cartel. Gold, the classical scarce commodity, has fallen to half of its highest price and stayed there for fifteen years, while money supplies have quadrupled. The green revolution has left even India with food surpluses. When people starve as in Somalia and the Sudan, the culprit is civil war, not scarce resources.

Think for yourself. What is scarce these days? Not Rolls Royces, not houses, not even seats on the Concorde. People might not be able to buy what they want because they can't afford it, but the people who design, manufacture, and market goods and services have full shelves and could probably double their production in one year without training anyone new or building a new factory.[3] Even scarce collectibles have plummeted in price in the age of abundance—modern art, old masters, jewelry, coins and stamps, baseball trading cards, fancy plates. Because we can make so many beautiful versions of anything, collectors have gone bankrupt trying to keep up the prices of any particular collectible. Again, one major point of this book is that real wealth exists in abundance. The only scarcity we suffer is not a "resource" at all. The only thing in short supply these days is *money*—money we need in order to buy the abundant real wealth we have already created.

## FALSE ASSUMPTION NO. 2:
***Money is bad***

Our problem is not a failure to create real wealth. Our problem is that we have not created enough money to match the real wealth which money is supposed to represent. Why have we not created enough money? The old economics is obsessed beyond all reason with prices and inflation. Understand that I, too, am as concerned with the value of money as they are—the very first guiding principle of the new economics of abundance is maintaining a *sound currency*. But for an economics founded on the no-longer-applicable condition of "scarce resources," the principle of *sound* currency was superseded by the principle of "the less currency the better." They did not understand the simple relations explained in chapter 5. Five figures showed how the *balance* between the supply of money and goods affected inflation. As simple as those figures are, the old economists' figures are simpler still. They ignore the supply side of the balance. As they say, "Inflation is a purely monetary phenomenon." Thus they need only two figures:

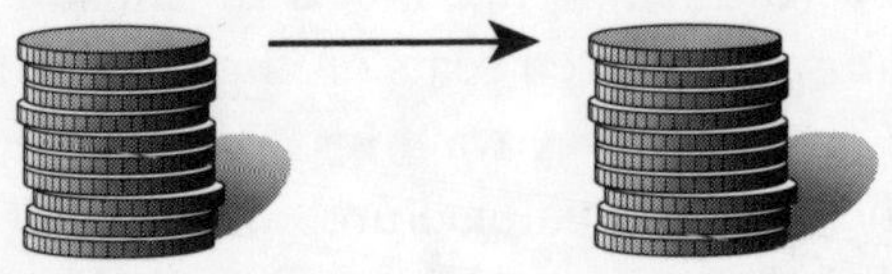

The stack of money has stayed the same size. Thus there is no inflation.

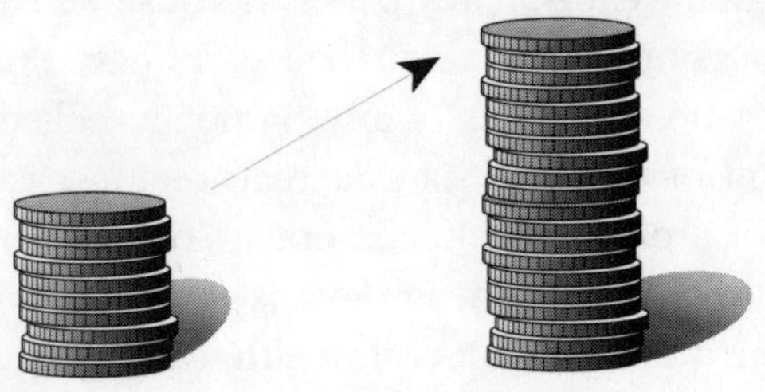

If the stack of money gets bigger, there *is* inflation.
End of story, to them.

How did they go so wrong? I do not understand. The most widely read popular text, *Money*, has gone through thirty printings in the last fifteen years. It states very clearly the principle that to me seems obvious, and which is the cornerstone of the principles I discuss in chapter 4. Ritter and Silber understand the answer to the question of "How *much* money should there be?":

> *We should have enough money that we can buy all the goods and services the economy is able to produce.* (page 10)

A straightforward statement, and I've heard no one disagree with the abstract *principle*. Milton Friedman agrees, saying that the number of dollars you have isn't important:

> *I believe that on reflection you will agree that what really matters is your real cash balances—what the nominal balances will buy.*[4]

That's it—the essential concept of balancing money and real wealth. Were they to elaborate on this central principle, I wouldn't have had to write chapter 10. But instead they drop the ball. That's all they say. They have no understanding of the implications of that statement under current conditions—that is, when the economy is able to produce an incredible abundance of goods and services. The undeniable implication is that we need to create more money. But the old economists are physically incapable of saying the three words, "Print more money."

If you want a laugh, watch me press the question to an old economist in a debate. In the cancer cure scenario, we have ten thousand doses of medicine, but only sixty-three hundred coupons. The simple answer to the dilemma is "Print more coupons." In Ritter and Silber's terms:

> *We should have enough [coupons] so that we can buy all the [doses of medicine] the economy is able to produce.*

In Friedman's terms:

> *...What really matters is [the number of doses of medicine]—what the [number of coupons] will buy.*

But an old economist cannot get those three words, "Print more coupons," out of his throat without gagging. He will stutter and beat around the bush, he will stand on his head discussing tangential issues, but will not be able to state the obvious. He can see where I am leading him. And an old economist feels sure he will go straight to hell if he ever utters the blasphemous words, "Let's print more money!"

For a while the followers of Keynes could, but they have been shouted down. Keynes understood a very important part of the story I have to tell: People need to have enough money to buy what they can produce. He advocated printing more money as a temporary corrective to a recession. The young Milton Friedman agreed with him, suggesting only that the government drop money from helicopters rather than hiding bottles full of cash where enterprising boys might find them, as Keynes whimsically proposed. But the old Milton got confused. He declared that if you doubled the supply of money, but also doubled wages and prices, unemployment would stay the same. All that would change was the "unit of account"—that is, what used to be called one dollar now would be called two dollars—thereby proving the "neutrality of money." Economists by the hundreds of thousands have fallen for the elder Milton's fabulous oversight. His imagination overlooked the most important thing to double, *the supply of real wealth*. During a decade of huge "deficits" and money printings, prices and wages have stabilized. What has greatly increased is our supply of real wealth. And real wealth is what really counts, despite its being utterly ignored by the old economists. Due to their single-minded obsession with the unit of account, money, they have neglected what money accounts for—the supply of real wealth.

Instead of studying the implications of the need for a balance between money and goods, the old economists spend *their* lives studying the Byzantine workings of our banking system. Read them and stay awake if you can. Our fractional reserve system (which does *not* create money, despite what they say) and system of Federal Reserve Banks is a Rube-Goldberg-type machine whose only virtue is that it works well enough to not bother changing it. *No one* would ever consider building a system like ours from scratch, but it has been adequately cobbled together over the decades. It is amusingly baroque and *recherche*, but it is not the problem. Because the "independent" Fed always obeys Congress' request to increase the "National Debt," our democracy still has the power it needs to fiscally correct what the monetarists will not do: "Print more coupons." In his younger days, Friedman could say it: "Government expenditures would be financed entirely by tax revenues or the creation of money...and the government would commit itself to retiring, through the issuance of new money, a predetermined amount of the public debt annually."[5] Ah, Milton, where did ye go wrong?

## FALSE ASSUMPTION NO. 3:
### *Everyone has a job*

The old economic universe suffered both scarce resources and an imminent shortage of labor. Thus, the second main assumption of the old macroeconomics is the phrase, "...under conditions of full employment." But we have widespread unemployment that is getting worse, as detailed in chapter 2. To guide our economy according to principles based on such irrelevant assumptions is, again, like guiding our spaceship with a rudder based on the condition of flying through an atmosphere. To be sure, in an atmosphere the rudder works as it is supposed to. And the old economics was correct to keep a tight money supply when resources were scarce and everyone was already busy working. If resources and people are already all being used, then printing more money only makes everything more expensive. (People who work get paid more, so they come out even, but it is a crazy way to live—and harmful to those on a fixed income.) But when resources are *not* scarce, and well-trained people are *begging* for work, then a shortage of money is what keeps the resources unused and the people unemployed. Tight money changes from a virtue to a curse, the source of the problem instead of its cure.

## FALSE ASSUMPTION NO. 4:
### *Supply creates demand*

When resources and people are scarce and fully employed, then many other basic principles of the old economics do indeed apply. For example, Say's Law states that supply creates its own demand. That is, all the cars that are built will find customers to buy them. True enough under conditions of scarcity; with the slightest attention to customer demand, markets of goods would clear. But under conditions of abundance, great supply exists without enough demand to use it up. Our modern productive capacity has outstripped our ability to consume, due to our inability to understand the new mechanics of the money supply that apply.

## FALSE ASSUMPTION NO. 5:
### *Increased Demand Raises Prices*

Another fundamental insight of the old economics of scarcity is the Law of Supply and Demand. You might remember the famous curves drawn in those Edgeworth boxes you learned to love if you took Econ 101. Among other points, they demonstrated how an increased demand for something caused its price to go up. But in the age of abundance, this "law" is wrong more often than it is right. For very good reasons more demand for something generally causes the price to *fall*, not rise. From the time mass production gained prominence on Henry Ford's assembly line, prices of individual items have tended to fall as mass quantities of them are produced. Cars, color TVs, computers, faxes—the new law is so reliable that we now count on it. When HDTVs are introduced, we know they will at first be so expensive that only people who don't care about prices will buy them. Then, when a high demand is established, the price will fall. Note that the cause of a high price is not just newness; when a new product turns out *not* to have a high demand, such as digital audio tape or the audio diskman, the prices stay high until the item disappears.

## SUPPLY-SIDE ECONOMICS AND ECONOMIES OF SCALE

Why does more demand cause lower prices? Our efficient businessmen and productive workers know how to use economies of scale to make things more cheaply when we need more of them. Supply-side economics, a relatively advanced development of the old economics, helped the recent acceleration of large-scale economic efficiency. Later in this book, the sources of our wealth will be fully described, but at this point it is appropriate to give credit to the last positive achievement of the old economics. The insight of supply-side economics was to let normal business become just a little bit more free. Under conditions of scarcity, big government did, unfortunately, have to put a paternal hand on free enterprise in order to protect consumers as well as workers from greedy exploitation. Under conditions of scarcity, a trust or monopoly's power to drive out competitors and then raise prices did occur in the nineteenth century. Business was regarded as the exploiter and enemy of the people, and thus needed to be tightly restrained in many important areas. Our antitrust laws in particular exercised a strong influence against the excesses of business.

But in the 1970s we began to see that strict regulation and antitrust were hurting consumers and workers, rather than helping them. What happened? In brief, international free trade opened up even the largest industries, such as automobiles, to competition. The decades without destructive wars freed enough capital from the age-old task of rebuilding destroyed factories. That capital was then free, around the world, to finance the construction of new car factories. Widespread technical and managerial expertise and an ever-more-educated citizenry meant potential businesspeople stood ready to punish those greedy manufacturers who tried to charge too much. When they did, new entrepreneurs would jump in and make a competitive, less expensive product. With free competition, ready financing, and widespread talent arrayed against bad ol' big business, it became less of a threat. In fact, we began to see that some businesses needed to be larger in order to stand up to our biggest overseas competitors. We could begin to relax the enforcement of our antitrust laws. A watershed decision was the dismissal of the decades-long antitrust suit against IBM.

Second, we tested the theory that businesses such as airlines did not need the strict, price-by-price regulation we imposed on our utilities. We freed them and trucking. Meanwhile, businesses like microcomputers grew rapidly where regulations did not exist to stop them. (Even businesses' self-imposed regulations, such as Apple's using a different operating system, have given way to more competitive "open systems.") Never-regulated businesses such as retail expanded with new technologies and business smarts. Now, brand-new competitors like Wal-Mart have overtaken national institutions like Sears.

The national policy of standing back and giving business more of a free hand was not at all an obvious choice. Remember that the main economic competitor to *laissez-faire* capitalism for a hundred years was communist central control. In China and the USSR, virtually every economic transaction was under the strict control of the state. European middle-of-the-roaders were influenced almost equally by free market and market socialism principles. And we began deregulating industries and defusing antitrust *before* communism gave up. Our politicians were smarter than our economists, thank God.

## "THE DISMAL SCIENCE" CANNOT KEEP UP WITH THE TWENTIETH CENTURY

Unfortunately, the practical insights of deregulation and supply-side economics were not matched by theoretical developments in the academic science of economics. Compared with most other sciences in academia, economics has done little of note in this century.

Consider developments in other fields. Physics went from Isaac Newton to Albert Einstein, developing remarkably counter-intuitive propositions ranging from the energy within the atom to the plasticity of space-time itself. Medicine advanced from blood-letting to heart replacements. Snake oil has been superseded by bioengineered miracle drugs. We've gone from Edison's light bulb to bubble memory, from a scratchy radio to satellite dishes. Popular transportation has advanced from the horse and buggy to the automobile. Air travel began—then, before we knew it, we were on the moon. The mechanical calculator became a tiny, powerful computer. From the basic telephone we now have cellular phones and fax. The visual arts, dance, literature, and music have exploded with more innovations in this century than in the previous twenty (whether you like all the new stuff or not, give the artists credit for remarkable creativity). Psychology was first conceived as a formal practice. Our managers have gone from the initial understanding of bureaucracy and time-and-motion studies to Just-In-Time and Total Quality Management, while surviving the efficiency demands of lean-and-mean downsizing.

Meanwhile, economics has earned the title of the "dismal science" for two dismal reasons. First, economists admit they cannot predict, much less control, anyone's economy. If economists launched bombs, they would not be able to tell you where the bombs would land or whether they would explode. Corporations have largely disbanded their large economic forecasting departments due to their uselessness. During the depression, the two top economic forecasters, Harvard and Yale, spent years forecasting the imminent end of the depression even as it continued to get worse. (These forecasts were defended as *sound economics* in their top journal as late as 1988!)

*Economists still use the math of the nineteenth century. It is as much fun for them as Nintendo is for youngsters, and about equally as useful for the challenges of the modern age of abundance.*

The second reason economics is called the dismal science is its incessant doom-and-gloom message. Against all evidence, "sound" economics advises us to raise taxes and lower spending—a sure prescription for further joblessness and misery. Economic counsel is virtually synonymous with a call for sacrifice, belt-tightening, and paying the price. I fear a Calvinistic asceticism is more at the heart of the science and its practitioners than is common sense and an appreciation of historical facts.

Economists still use the math of the nineteenth century. It is as much fun for them as Nintendo is for youngsters, and about equally as useful for the challenges of the modern age of abundance. They wield nineteenth-century math with devilish dexterity and professional relish.[6] However, the crystal-clear equations are based on assumptions, such as full employment, that are just plain wrong. They even presume every firm and worker responds as quickly as the Fed does to the old economists' grand multivariate equations of expansion and contraction, obediently lowering wages and prices due to everyone's "rational expectations." And the equations themselves, the very "equal" signs, fail to comprehend the prime discovery of twentieth century mathematics—Goedel's Theorem. I discuss at length the implications of the Goedelian insight for the economics of the nation-state in my technical book, but here it is sufficient to say that Kurt Goedel proved that closed analytical systems are a vain wish, even in purely mathematical terms. Of course, in the real world such desires for clean-cut equations lead to not only wrong but completely misleading conclusions.

## THE OLD ECONOMISTS GIVE UP

Charles Morris carries the despair of the old economics to its logical conclusion: "Managing the economy is a sham," he asserts.[7] The national economy is not "computable" via the old economics. Worse, he says, the large effects that economic policy does have cannot be even generally predicted by its current practitioners: "Eliminating the budget deficit in four years, for example, might create a nasty recession or a runaway boom—economists, as always, disagree." He concludes that the president ought therefore not even try to manage the economy. What our leaders should do, instead, is a bit vague: "Presidents should trust their instincts over models... [Clinton should] appeal to citizens to do the right thing—to endure some pain..." I have never read such a sad conclusion by a practitioner of any other science.

As noted above, Paul Krugman, the "most celebrated economist of his generation" according to *The Economist*,[8] admits the "unedifying message...that *we don't know* what happened to the magic economy [from the late 1940s to 1972] is not a very satisfying answer." He's happy to see the "serious economists" (that is, professors like himself) devote themselves to "technical theories that best allow a clever but not very original young man to demonstrate his cleverness" and gain tenure. The original thinkers Krugman dismisses as mere "policy entrepreneurs."

Original thinking or practical problem solving has no place in the world of "serious economists."[9]

## BUT THE SCIENCE OF ECONOMICS MUST NOT JUST GIVE UP

Giving up is the easy way out. After all I have said in criticism of the old economics, I will now say that economics is at present the most important of the sciences. Why? All the advances of the modern age are undercut, even rendered impotent, if we do not know how to use what we have created. Factories sit idle. Trained people can't work. Research labs are closed. Our resources remain merely potential, sadly wasted, until our economics can help us use the abundance we have in our hands.

Note how successful the old economics was at solving the problem it set for itself—the allocation of scarce resources. Even now, the old science is desperately needed in those countries suffering scarcities—the former Eastern Bloc and Africa. They need the prescriptions of an old science for countries living in the economic dark ages—*they* need to spend less and tax more, among other actions, because their currency is *not* backed up by real wealth. Their economic system, Marxist central planning, proved a failure compared with our old economics. They looked at the facts of their situation, and realized they had to stop blaming their people and instead lay the fault where it was due—upon their economic philosophy itself. Where their central planning failed, our old economics of scarcity will succeed. *They* are not giving up, but are laboring mightily to change, a change which is surely the greatest ever attempted by a country of its own free will in modern times.

Likewise, our economics must not just give up, as Morris and Krugman do, whining that our national economy is past influence or understanding. The fact is that we *can* guide our economy—we have done it through our disastrous "soft landing" programs, for example. Because one confused and outmoded approach doesn't work here anymore does not mean that all economics is helpless. It is as though doctors, admitting that bloodletting didn't work, counseled against all other medical theory or intervention, because their own false theories proved helpless.

The old economics was successful, by analogy, in getting us up out of the atmosphere and gravity's pull. We are now above the harsh scarcities which the old economics figured out how to allocate. In the world of science, few engineers who spent their lives working on winged aircraft changed into space engineers. Sadly, many present-day economists will not adapt their way of thinking to the completely new environment and principles that guide the economics of abundance. But the fact that their science no longer works should not stop us from developing an approach that will guide us successfully to where we want to go.

Finally, we must see that our metaphor for economic growth is sick, when we can show how destroying a town in war and rebuilding it would create great economic growth and prosperity, but are unable to show how to capitalize on a miraculous peace. I am showing how keeping the town alive and healthy creates wealth, at least relative to humans' historical standard of periodic self-destruction, and this wealth can be increased by going on to create more and better environments. Unfortunately, thousands of politicians held in thrall by as many eminent economists will lead us to ruin if we, the people, do not overrule them according to our democratic right and duty. The war with these defenders of a failed faith will not be easy. But it must be fought, and it must be won, as much for our children's sake as our own.

# PART III

## The Solution: The Economics of National Abundance

# 9

## Real Wealth: What It is and Where It Comes From

An economic system designed to deal with the presence of *abundant* resources works differently from an economics which assumes resources are "scarce." Part III, starting here, develops the new economical approach necessary to deal with abundance. You have already been introduced to the *main idea* of this section:

- Real wealth (the cancer cure medicine itself) must be matched by the amount of money in circulation (the number of ration coupons printed).
- The two additional questions Part III answers are:
  1. How do we decide *how much* money to print?
  2. How do we get it into circulation?

Real wealth is not money—rather, real wealth is everything we spend money to get. Money is merely a bookkeeping device. It helps us exchange, increase, and measure our wealth more easily. However, if we mistakenly let money become more important than real wealth, a money shortage will end up destroying wealth. For money to be an accurate and useful scorekeeping device, we must create the right amount of it—neither too much nor too little.

An imbalance between money and real wealth is the fundamental cause of economic misery. When money is created faster than real wealth, inflation results. And when money is printed too slowly to match a rapid creation of real wealth, a recession or depression is the result. The key principle is balancing money and real wealth. If this principle is ignored, a tragic paradox occurs: the admirable policies that cause an increase in real wealth will also cause permanent unemployment, creating needless misery and smothering our ability to enjoy greater gains.

Thus, the *first* economic task of government is to create a currency that is *sound* (low inflation) but *sufficient* (no recessions). We attain this balance by printing money up to but not beyond the point where inflation occurs. The more wealth we create to back up our money, the more we can print—and enjoy. Thus, the *second* economic task of government is to encourage *full employment* of our nation's human and physical resources towards the *further creation of real wealth*. We create wealth by avoiding war, being productive, developing our infrastructure, writing fair laws, educating our children and ourselves, protecting our environment, and inventing new and better ways to do things.

Once wealth is created, the next economic task of government is to encourage its allocation. Because the efficiencies of free enterprise allow a small number of the best producers to create a great deal of wealth, employment inevitably shrinks, and demand withers, unless the means to use that wealth is distributed widely. Making sure that enough money starts off in the hands of the poor will allow even greater gains to end up in the pockets of the rich. Government can be paid according to its own success, in effect earning a "commission" as opposed to taking a "salary" through taxation. Our international competitors will benefit as well, whether they emulate our policies or not. Just as we have historically benefited from full-money and full-employment policies, we will again enjoy great advantages compared with other nations, and they will follow our lead.

## WHAT IS "REAL WEALTH"?

Another trick question! Mention wealth, and most people immediately think of money. *But real wealth is not money*; much more important than money is what we spend the money for. We do not eat money—we use money to buy food. We do not wear garments fashioned of greenbacks—we buy our clothes. We do not live in homes made of gold—we use gold to buy a house.

The fallacy of regarding money as more important than the things money buys is the fatal affliction of the old economists. What they like most about money is that it is a nice, simple, real number. It's easy to add and subtract and put into seemingly scientific equations. In fact, the very question of wealth embarrasses the old economists. They are most comfortable talking about the price of a bushel of corn, which has a simple number attached to it, a number which changes pretty much the way their equations say it should.

But talk to them about the value of "war" or "security," and they have to turn away. For a science that can describe minute changes in the price of a bushel of corn does not even *try* to place a value on any aspect of human welfare. "We can leave some things to psychologists and sociologists," says even their best and most inclusive analysis.[1] By their standards you might value "look[ing] at an attractive police uniform" or watching "a military parade." But the real value our police and army provide, a family's security or world peace, "are better viewed as provided to protect [the buildings and people who make]… the goods…." These "goods" are the "final output," and that is all the wealth they care to measure. To the old economists, surplus corn warehoused in silos is more valuable than all of the lives saved by avoiding a war. Check their equations.[2] Their reasoning is that human life itself has economic value only insofar as more surplus corn is harvested, so by measuring the corn, you implicitly measure the value of winning peace.

And that's what happened to our peace dividend—the old economists got our check in the mail and threw it away, because they didn't know how to cash it. Because they are unable to place an *exact* value on human life and happiness, as you can on a bushel of corn, the old economists don't even try to give it any value at all. They blithely dismiss those who do.[3] The only conceptual leap necessary to understand the economics of abundance is that *intangibles such as peace, health, happiness, and freedom have a value worth considering, even if we cannot measure that value precisely.*

One way to estimate the value of things, like peace, that we do not buy, is to ask how much we *would be willing to pay* if we could, indeed, buy them. Peace is relatively easy to value by this method—after all, we in fact did choose to pay hundreds of millions of dollars each year to stave off the Soviet nuclear threat. Peace is real wealth—it is something we were willing to spend hard cash on, lots of it, for decades. We now enjoy a comparable level of safety for free, as it were, due to the death of international communism.

*Peace is relatively easy to value by this method—after all, we in fact did choose to pay hundreds of millions of dollars each year to stave off the Soviet nuclear threat. Peace is real wealth—it is something we were willing to spend hard cash on, lots of it, for decades.*

Also, consider the security of your home. You pay for it in a number of ways. Locks, bars on the windows, and alarms are only the most obvious. You probably pay much more than that for the safety of the neighborhood you live in. "Quality of the neighborhood" is one of the most important considerations in buying a home, and surely one of the most expensive. It incorporates a number of intangibles—security, prestige, friendliness, weather, zoning laws—that vary immensely in value from one location to the next. We pay for them every day. The old economists say they are worthless, and have based their bankrupt analyses on such nonsensical premises.

## THE NATURE AND SOURCES OF REAL WEALTH

A full catalogue of every manifestation of real wealth would take more than a book to describe. It would include not only everything we do pay for, like food, but everything we *would* pay for if we had to, like air and happiness. The point of this section is to expand your awareness of what does matter, so you can appreciate what we already have—and what we may *lose* if we continue to follow the deficit mongers' program.

For each of the following categories of real wealth, think of their value in terms of *how much you would pay* for them if you had to or could. I also will briefly describe how each category of wealth is created or encouraged. Keep in mind what you do to provide yourself with each form of wealth, and what your government does as well. The next chapter will elaborate on how much money we need to match our real wealth, and what the government can and should do to maintain and increase the wealth we hold in common.

**1. Natural wealth.**

The air we breathe, the land we walk on, the water we drink. We tend to take these for granted because they are virtually free. But after a couple of minutes without air, for example, we would be willing to pay every cent we owned for it; fortunately, the situation doesn't come up that often. You might complain about your water bill, but the amount you really need, that to drink, costs you just pennies a month. Land may be expensive to "own"—as if we mortals ever "own" something that was here a billion years before us and will survive us by a billion more—but we also take for granted our access to vast stretches of public land.

Consider water for a moment. At this moment, millions of people still *die* of drought. Hundreds of millions more spend a large part of their day walking miles to get water. We benefit from pipes and pumps in this country that have been paid for a thousand times over in the safety, health, and convenience they provide, compared with how much we actually paid the inventors, financiers, and workmen who put them in the ground for us. We have a permanent *surplus wealth* from the water pump and pipe they installed.

Look at it from the perspective of one individual. For forty years, he could spend two hours a day walking four miles back and forth to get his family's water. Or he could spend one week installing a pump and pipe to bring that water to him. The difference between the amount of time he spent earning and installing that pipe compared with the decades of walking for water is the surplus wealth the pipe earns him. Better, his children benefit even more. They only have to maintain the pipe their father installed.

In real life, we benefit from an enormous amount of work done in the past which we now take for granted. The pipe is in the ground. The factories are up and running. The value of the water we drink is just as high whether we walk two hours to fetch it or simply turn on the tap. Its cost is just a tiny fraction of its value. The royalties we have paid to inventors, the wages we've paid to the workers are only a small fraction of the value of the work done through the ages, from water and sewage down through the fiber-optic information highways. What is called the "deficit" and "debt" is actually a crude proxy measure of the invisible, unmeasured accumulation of surplus wealth that our ancestors earned for us. That number is huge and should be even bigger—just as the "deficit" of three hundred coupons in the cancer cure example should have been thousands of coupons greater.

Perhaps we can best appreciate the value of our natural wealth when it begins to be taken from us or degraded. The communist systems of eastern Europe poured millions of tons of pollutants into the air their citizens breathed. Smog in U.S. cities is declining, but still a health threat. Much of the third world still uses the same water for drinking and sewage, leading to constant illness and death; in the Nile delta, most people suffer from the water-borne bilharziasis parasite and die in their forties. Land may be taken from us in a number of ways. It might be laid waste, as in Africa, by a combination of natural and man-made catastrophes such as drought and over-grazing. Feudal lords or their modern counterparts might lay claim to vast stretches of the best land as their private preserves. Modern governments, with the best of intentions, might protect the ecological purity of a park so rigorously that human beings aren't even allowed to look or visit.

Natural wealth is a variable. People and countries can have more of it or less, in part depending on how they handle what they have. We can ruin our air through pollution, or we can make laws that keep it clean. (Even smarter would be to locate cities away from inversion layers.) The same for water—and, as I propose in chapter 13, even the drought/flood cycle could be tamed if we thought about it for ten minutes.

Land is trickier. The laws we make regarding land require trade-offs. Some people would keep the land pristine by banishing human contact entirely, while millions of our ghetto residents spend their lives in concrete wastelands. The other extreme would allow "owners" of land to dump toxic waste on it. Our common interest lies in encouraging human use that does not degrade the gifts we have inherited. Note that a substantial portion of our natural real wealth results from the guarded access we allow to foreigners. Despite the strict limitations we already place on what an "owner" can do to property in the U.S., we are still far more liberal than nations which do not allow foreigners to "own" title to their land at all.

**2. The wealth of life itself.**

This may sound fuzzy, but it is as real and more important than a bushel of corn. The very "right to life" itself was not exclusively an abortion issue for most of recorded history. Rather, capricious kings and barbarous neighbors tortured and killed the innocent to an extent that makes our own ghetto violence look quaintly benign by comparison. Hitler, Stalin, Mao, Pol Pot, etc., showed in this century that the nation-state may decide to outlaw life itself for a large number of its best citizens. Freedom from arbitrary death does vary among nations, and is not to be taken lightly.

Freedom of the spirit is a fuzzier kind of wealth, I'll grant. But a visit to the communist regimes shows that, for too many, the demise of totalitarianism came too late in their personal lives to do them any good. Like the bird who remains in its cage after the door is opened, these people have given up too much of their spirit compromising with communism to be able to take flight now. The freedom and ability to think and feel for oneself, the freedom of intellectual and artistic expression, the freedom not only to survive but to live the variety and intensity of life you choose to live rather than what has been forced upon you—all these vary among nations as well as among the people within nations.

A remarkable source of human wealth is the diverse groups of like-minded people who define for themselves what's good and bad. Church groups, the horsy set, and Hell's Angels all create their own systems of self-esteem for their members. You don't have to have a lot of money or be an advancing junior executive for a Fortune 500 firm to "be someone" in America. Life is not a simple contest in one dimension where we all have a score that determines how successful we are. You might have a job you hate and which gets no respect, but you do not have to allow that job identity to define and limit your life. By freely choosing the one group out of the thousands in this country—Rotarians, hobbyists of all stripes, bridge players, conspiracy theorists, political activists, amateur athlete, etc.—which you are best at or which you best enjoy doing, you can construct for yourself one of the prime rewards of life: respect from your like-minded peers. In that way, people can overcome the so-called "social limits to growth," which says only the boss can enjoy pride of place in the social order.[4]

But even freedom of the spirit has an economic component. In rare cases, yes, money can act as a golden cage. But far more often, people suffer from the chains of poverty and underemployment, from the lack of time and money to go back to school or write their book, than suffer from the excessive demands of too much work and too little time. The laws and national economic policy have a great deal to do with offering citizens the opportunity to do with their own spirits as they wish. I would include in this category not only religious freedom but the right to better oneself and one's children through education and merit.

**3. Stuff.**

I think I should list the things people commonly think of as wealth at this point so you don't lose the thread of continuity between "regular" wealth and the different forms I am attempting to explain. Yes, a new car and the title to a house in the suburbs are also forms of wealth. Include in this category airplane trips and movies, clothes and restaurants—in fact, include everything the old economists can measure as part of our gross national product.

But even in the form of wealth that is easiest to measure, the old economics falls down. Wealth is not only the fish you just caught, hanging on the end of your line. Wealth is the stock of fish still in the lake beneath you. Right now, for all of the cars, houses, and plane rides we already have, we have an unmeasured amount of unrealized wealth waiting to be caught, which we may never catch due to bad economic policy. The old economists ascribe value to a bushel of harvested corn that no one will eat, but give no value to a factory ready to make cars that thousands would want to buy, if only those potential customers had jobs and an income to afford them. Remember that some countries, like Russia, not only lack the cars themselves, but also lack the ability to make them. Our invisible wealth in "stuff" includes the desirable products and services people would love to make if only their customers could buy them.

Where does "stuff" come from, and why do some nations have more than others? Since prehistoric days, people have supplemented the things they make for themselves by trading for what other people make. People are really good at making things for themselves and others. If the state does not get in people's way, an abundance of things is a natural consequence of free enterprise (but do not forget the value of laws that govern the trade-off, for example, between abundant energy and air pollution). Under free enterprise, consumer goods sprout like weeds; it takes a perverse system like communism to keep pouring poison on the ground, stopping the weeds from blossoming; or the corruption of tinpot dictatorships like those currently ruining Africa. But a part of America's wealth has long been that our system is better even than Japan's or Europe's at getting things from one person to another—which includes not only manufacturing, but also marketing and development.

The old economists, even while measuring their specialty—*things*—forget that the things themselves are more important than the numbers they use for measurement. Decades of so-called "trade deficits" have given us the cars and VCRs the Japanese have been kind enough to manufacture for us. The Japanese' foolish protectionist, neo-mercantilist laws puff up their old economists' favorite numbers while sending their real wealth overseas. While laughing at us, they have made themselves the self-appointed coolies of the world, working themselves to death while denying themselves the real wealth their hard-earned greenbacks could buy if only they allowed themselves to use them. For two decades we have collected cars and VCRs at lower cost than the Japanese charge themselves. Meanwhile, we allow them to build us our biggest hotels downtown, which they sell at a loss after ten years. We keep the cars, electronics, and hotels; they end up with some IOUs, which we shall be all too happy to cash in. But a whole generation of Japanese workers have sacrificed their own wealth in order to supply us with a better lifestyle than they have allowed themselves—and that lifestyle includes every other type of wealth listed here, as well as "stuff."[5] People work, but their country's economic policy can help them or hinder them from enjoying the wealth people strive to earn.

**4. Security.**

The nation helps us, in varying degrees, to be free from war and crime. In my opinion, the greatest and most obvious failure of the old economics is that it did not even attempt to value peace and security. According to the old economics, the only value of avoiding war was already measured by the number of widgets coming out of the factories not destroyed by bombs, built by the hands of men not killed by enemy bullets. The horror of war, according to the old economists, has nothing to do with wealth or the national economy.

What nonsense. Yes, a soldier lost money during four years of war, but how many counted that as the primary sacrifice of their lives on the front lines? Think instead how much people will pay to avoid a war. In the past, foolhardy boys might have thought of war as a kind of game they wanted to enter and win. But now everyone recognizes that the horrors of destruction for the individual and the nation make even a successful war an orgy of terror and loss. The only "gain" is that losing the war, on the ground or by not daring to fight, might be even worse. But even wars we avoided losing, such as Korea and, to some extent, Vietnam, offered us dubious gains at best. And our most recent successful war, the Gulf War, left us no better off than we would have been had we been able to convince Saddam Hussein not to invade Kuwait in the first place.

Thus the avoidance of World War III with the Soviet Union was a glorious economic as well as political triumph for both sides. All forms of wealth catalogued here were saved: natural (think of nuclear winter), human (life itself, in the billions), things (factories as well as the cars already built), and even further security (society would have broken down after the holocaust). Given human history, world war has been the expectable norm for millennia. To Western credit, we have managed to keep progressing despite our once-a-generation idiotic war. Many of us took eventual nuclear attack for granted as we crouched under our school desks in bomb drills. But now our great triumph in avoiding the Big One has allowed our generation the opportunity to realize a great leap forward in real wealth, unmatched by any generation in human history. Only an outmoded economics, based on "scarcity" and hobbled by its worship of money over wealth, stops us from consolidating an amazing and hard-earned triumph.

A less cataclysmic but more pervasive security we may have or lose is from robbery and murder. If you have ever been mugged, you know the cost is more than the amount of money in your wallet. If your child was murdered by a mugger or drunk driver, you know the loss was more than the cost of his or her funeral. An individual and a society is wealthier to the degree that it has less crime. Give Japan and Europe credit for being far ahead of us on this metric, especially as German tourists keep getting killed in their formerly favorite hot spot, Florida. Two murders might translate into a reduction in income to Florida of tens of millions of dollars in canceled tourist revenues, a number even the old economists can understand.

But the losses from crime go deeper than the loss of income or goods. When you choose a neighborhood or town in which to live, you are likely to pay a premium for a relatively safe area far in excess of the cost of the goods you would have to replace due to robbery. Safety is a value in itself. People in safe neighborhoods or safe nations enjoy a level of wealth valuable in its own right. Thus, any money spent to reduce crime is not money lost, but a case of spending one dollar to create or save two dollars' worth of wealth. Printing a dollar to spend in the ghettos or to ferret out white collar crime is *anti*-inflationary when it saves or encourages the creation of two dollars' worth of real wealth. Saving those dollars and enduring the crime is the sort of false economy and "sacrifice" urged upon us by the deficit mongers.

**5. Social bonds—brotherly love.**

Societies in which people "love thy neighbor as thyself" are categorically wealthier than those in which beggar-thy-neighbor policies predominate. I'm talking about more than the fuzzy bonds of friendship, as important as those are to us social creatures. A hard-core, bottom-line influence on everybody's wealth is the way people get along. A catastrophe like that in Bosnia, as extreme as it is, is all too common, and is expected to occur again and again in Eurasia and Africa in the future. Just three years ago the people of Yugoslavia led fairly comfortable middle-class lives complete with compact disks and nice restaurants, to say nothing of indoor plumbing. But now a set of disastrous social attitudes has these same people risking death by machine gun just to gather firewood and drinking water.

Human beings can make each other rich or destroy each other's lives, depending on the social and economic compacts they have made with each other. The Yugoslavian calamity is only the most extreme example of a mutually destructive way of thinking that pervades civilization. That way of thinking looks at all of life as though it were a sport or war: that is, if you win, I lose. Greed is not what brings people down; rather, a type of greed that says "I cannot succeed unless you fail" is what causes people to compete until both lose.

*The U.S. Constitution is worth a fortune to us, enshrining our right to "life, liberty, and the pursuit of happiness." Imagine how much we would agree to pay to have such a constitution, if the alternative were that which guides Yugoslavia.*

One basis for the real wealth of America is simply our avoiding the worst excesses of this sort of zero-sum thinking. Communism took seriously Marx's view of life as a "class struggle"—that rich and poor are inevitably at each other's throats, and for the poor to prosper, they have to destroy their rich opponents in armed struggle. As history demonstrated, no one impoverished the masses, both physically and morally, worse than their own dictatorship, free of the financiers and entrepreneurs they murdered. Now, African tribalism threatens to bring a whole continent back to a state worse than colonial. And in the Balkans, we witness age-old animosities, gladly embraced by leaders and commoners alike, destroying a civil society within two years.

The West is only too close to the days of its own religious inquisitions and world wars. But we have made an honest effort to incorporate at least the shape of diversity, if not all of the substance, into our civic legends. The U.S. Constitution is worth a fortune to us, enshrining our right to "life, liberty, and the pursuit of happiness." Imagine how much we would agree to pay to have such a constitution, if the alternative were that which guides Yugoslavia. In business, many managers really do respect the human rights and capabilities of their employees. The employees' unions have accomplished what they could through the necessary decades of confrontation. Now their cooperation with management is a major reason they are the most productive workers on earth. We have begun to add women and minorities to our wealth of human capital, and we are the stronger for it.

But now the politics of the deficit threatens to bring us back to the dark age of us versus them, of rich versus poor, of your entitlement is my tax. The deficit mongers would set retiree against taxpayer, employee against manager, and the U.S. against all our trade partners. The politics of cooperation is the most delicate achievement of any society, and never perfectly attained. But it is as real as friendship, with all of the "fuzzy" values as well as hard-core bottom line benefits. Countries in which people work together are richer than those in which civil war, corruption, or constant "class struggle" makes everyone's neighbors his first and worst enemies.

**6. Health and welfare.**

Supposedly we are suffering a "health crisis" in the United States, requiring a massive, complicated restructuring of our health system. Health crisis? What crisis? Are we short of doctors and nurses? *No.* We have a glut of hospital beds, and are in fact closing hospitals as this industry, too, "downsizes" on its way to "lean and mean." I guess the "crisis" means we are running out of life-saving drugs—but of course we aren't. And technologies like magnetic resonance imaging, laser surgery, and laparoscopy advance the science of health care monthly.

The only "crisis" is one we make for ourselves when we say that doctors and nurses should stand idle, hospital beds lie empty, drugs and technology sit on the shelves, while sick or injured human beings die in their midst. The only crisis is like the crisis the World War I generals made for their own troops, running them into certain death. Now we convince ourselves we can't afford to utilize the wealth we have already accumulated, letting caregivers idly sit while their hopeful patients suffer and die. That is the crisis—an economic system that regards *incorrect measures of the money supply* as more important than real wealth and even life itself. A real health crisis would be the Black Death or radiation poisoning from nuclear war. A real health crisis was any hospital just a hundred years ago, before the need for antiseptic cleanliness was understood. A health crisis for thousands of years was the bad idea of bloodletting.

Related to health is common human welfare. A nation's social and economic policies can help or hinder its citizens from enjoying the normal human joys of family and personal fulfillment. Current economic policy is forcing many men to hide in their homes for a year sending out résumés, dishonored in their own eyes (and secretly, guiltily, in the eyes of their families). Meanwhile, many women endure that side of equality that allows them to work outside of the home during years in which they would prefer to be spending more time with their children. This is a direct outcome planned by the deficit mongers—downsizing the kinds of jobs that allow a single wage earner to support a family, and generating masses of low-paying, no-benefit jobs that allow us to "compete" down to third-world standards.

The callous heartlessness of the deficit mongers towards the welfare of their fellow citizens is what bothers me more than anything else. It is one thing to take money out of people's hands through pointless and excessive taxation, and deny us use of the goods rotting on the shelves. But even worse is declaring an entire generation expendable, unneeded in the work force, sacrificed to the Golden Idol of deficit reduction. The deficit mongers cannot deny that the sure and certain consequence of raising taxes and cutting spending is to fire a lot of dads while sending a lot of moms to work longer hours in convenience stores.

Again, part of being a wealthy society is allowing its citizens to fulfill the personal and social roles *we have raised them to think* were theirs to fill. What good is it if the deficit idol is satisfied by tidy, irrelevant numbers—if, as a result, our citizens live diminished lives, bereft of a sense of worth and purpose? The deficit mongers care more for the quality of their anal-retentive and irrelevant bookkeeping than they do for the quality of human life, of your life. Outside of their vague pronouncements, always wrong, of imminent catastrophe, have you ever heard them describe a single human being who was ever helped by deficit reduction? *Not one person* has ever been helped by the mongers' shrill prescriptions. People by the hundreds of millions have only been *hurt*, as they are being hurt now. And the deficit mongers don't care.

**7. Gold and silver…**

are *not* real wealth. Remember, you don't eat gold, or wear it against the elements, or live under a golden roof. Gold has some marginal and negligible value as a conductive metal and pretty bauble, with many substitutes for both functions. Gold is only mere money, and you must understand that money is not real wealth—real wealth is what you spend money to *get*. What backs up money is real wealth, the things you want to *buy*—not gold, which is merely another form of money. Using gold to back up money is like using old poker chips to back up new ones. The old economists, because of their obsession with numbers, reflexively compare our money to gold, or to other countries' money—but this is nothing but a big shell game, a game of musical chairs. What truly matters is what the money can buy, not what it's worth in terms of other money. And gold is nothing but an old-fashioned form of money.

How strange and perverse that so many people are still entranced by the yellow metal. Order a brochure from one of the gold bugs who advertise constantly in your financial pages. They write as though from another planet about the great and enduring value of what they call "tangibles"—gold, silver, gems, etc. Against all evidence and common sense, they are permanently optimistic that a renewed worldwide passion for their own fetish is right around the corner. Gold bugs are soul mates of those who revere the horse and buggy as the best form of transportation, like the

Amish. The difference is that the Amish have no influence on our nation's transportation choices, whereas the closet gold bugs in the Fed (e.g., Wayne Angell) have had a powerful negative influence on our nation's economic health.

Why was gold ever wealth in the first place? Life was tough in the old days, in the ancient millennia when gold first earned its good rep. There wasn't much real wealth, back then. No good restaurants—no restaurants at all, in fact. Not too many resorts or cruise ships. Hard to get an airline upgrade. Nomadic types never rented an apartment, much less bought a house. Cable TV—no. And no bank accounts, charge cards, or automatic teller machines. In a dreary world, after you watched enough sunsets, about the prettiest thing you could buy was that soft yellow metal.

But now we have vastly more real wealth. Just as in the old days a covered wagon was the best ride you could hitch across the country, in the old days gold was the most exciting thing you could buy. But nowadays there is not much call for covered wagons. And gold is pretty useless as well. The only current demand for it is by the old-fashioned types who themselves live in the past, or have only recently been liberated from it. When the Arabs first cashed in on their oil reserves they purchased hoards of the yellow metal, but rapidly outgrew that adolescent infatuation—especially after Iraq stole the gold Kuwaitis had hoarded.[6] The newly rich Chinese are described by the gold bugs as great lovers of gold, but the Chinese are proving to be even faster learners than the Arabs. As it turns out, they want only a small amount for their baubles, and that only at three hundred fifty dollars an ounce or less. And I suspect the Eastern Europeans might skip the gold stage completely when some of them get rich after communism. Think of your own friends who revere gold. Not your local financial whizzes, I'll wager.

But scratch a deficit monger or inflation hawk and you'll see yellow underneath. What they like most about gold, and a return to the gold standard, is that gold is in a permanently limited supply, and they've already got some. Their obsession with a "sound" currency goes no further than a certainty that life is a zero-sum game—an austere and severely limited I-win-you-lose situation. Gold fills the bill perfectly at keeping us in the chains that deficit reduction would lock tightly around us all. The "social limits to growth" that our most Calvinistic social theorists love are perfectly enforced by gold. Gold limits rather than allows human growth.

What backs up our currency is better than gold. It is the wealth, power, stability, and talent of the wealthiest, most stable, and surely the most powerful nation in the history of the earth. The gold bugs could not care less about our real wealth. They would prefer we find a secret room in Fort Knox containing a cube of gold twenty meters on a side. Imagine it had been hidden there by the gold bugs for the same reason DeBeers hoards its diamonds—to keep prices up by not flooding the market. By the simple-minded accounting of the old economics, this cube would eliminate the deficit, and all of our economic problems would be gone! They wouldn't care if ten nations threatened us with nuclear war, or if we had communist-level productivity, or our doctors and scientists were the worst in the world, or our land were so polluted and the roads so decrepit that no one wanted to buy property here, or new laws rescinded the Bill of Rights and banned new private enterprises. They would see only the block of yellow metal and cry, "Hooray for the US of A! All of our problems are solved!"

**8. Ancient traditions and our national religion.**

Of course, these are not forms of *American* wealth. Due to our brief history and our heritage of diversity, we in the U.S. value tradition less than Africans do and religious conformity less than Moslems do. I mention these values in order to point out that real wealth is, of course, not the same for every individual, and also varies among nations as a whole. People in other countries are quite willing to spend their money to maintain tradition or religious unity, and a willingness to spend money on anything is the criterion that makes it real wealth. Thus nations must have different currencies, because the wealth backing them up varies according to what they perceive to be real wealth. Foreign currency exchange rates only relate measures of wealth held in common esteem among nations.

## THE DEFICIT MONGERS AND REAL WEALTH

What do the deficit mongers say about real wealth? Nothing. I have spent so much time on the preceding outline of real wealth because this concept is their primary blind spot. The deficit debate focuses on *numbers* with no attempt to relate those numbers to reality. In fact, our economic poobahs snicker at the mere thought of trying to value "peace"—in fact, they snicker at the attempt to measure anything that is not already on their list. Meanwhile, the economics profession bemoans the poor quality of the statistics they collect.[7] Their numbers are losing relevance, they admit—but they won't go so far as try to come up with any new bases for their numbers.

They don't get it that food, housing, and human welfare are real. Money is a number, a mere score-keeping device. The deficit mongers have no more concern for your real wealth than an anorexic has for his health. The anorexic cares only about the weight shown on the scale, and takes it as a given that the lower this number, the better. Even as he starves himself to death, as his kidneys fail, as he collapses while trying to walk, the only health criterion he believes in is that simple number on the scale. He does not even conceive of any other measures of health, having encapsulated all of his faith in that single number.

Similarly, the deficit mongers take it for granted that the so-called deficit is the critical measure of our economic well-being. Check their writings for any mention of the concepts of real wealth I have described above. The concept of real wealth is as alien to them as the concept of real health is to the anorexic. Fortunately, the anorexics are not in charge of our nation's diet. Unfortunately, the econo-rexics are in charge of our nation's money supply.

# 10

# Balancing Money and Abundance: The "Cyber-nomic" Gas Pedal on the Money Supply

Think back to before recorded history. What do you think came first: food, clothing, and shelter—or money? Of course, the human condition requires food, clothing, and shelter. The human condition does not require money. A human or group that has real wealth does not even need other humans, for trade or any other purpose.

However, humans have often existed on the bare edge of survival, and more people will live if those with extra food and no clothes trade with other people who have extra clothes and no food. Trade or barter may predate language as the first fundamentally human activity. Primitive barter continues today, especially in the presence of a ruined money supply. Russia under communism was a barter society. The ruble by itself was useless for buying goods—it was mainly used for balancing the books of the state enterprises. Note that communism allowed no budget deficits and had zero inflation. At the same time, people were impoverished, because this technically "sound" money couldn't buy anything. Vodka was more useful than rubles in getting your plumbing fixed, and you had to pass out cigarettes to get a proper injection at the hospital.

Carrying around your bushels of corn or your bottles of vodka is less convenient than using bits of metal or colored paper—or plastic cards, as at present. Anything can be used as money—not only gold or paper, but shells and bits of rope. What makes money valuable is nothing intrinsic to the medium, not even scarcity. The only thing that makes money valuable is that enough people agree among themselves that their money can be exchanged for something they want. Enough people may be as few as two—if you have ever sent a card with coupons offering your Mom "Dishwashing for a week" or "No arguing about going to bed," you have created your own little money supply. All that makes the coupons valuable is that both of you take them seriously.

The same with that old standby, gold. All that made gold worth eight hundred fifty dollars an ounce was a brief period of belief that it was worth that much. All that makes it worth three hundred fifty dollars an ounce now is the teetering beliefs of an ever-smaller proportion of the populace. People used to put "jewels" in the same magic category of real "tangible" worth, precious enough to steal and smuggle into an exotic land as your fortune. But any woman who has tried to sell her diamonds knows that their diminishing, non-liquid value is just barely propped up by the DeBeers cartel, an arrangement that is almost sure to collapse as South Africa evolves and the undisciplined Eastern European countries dump their hoards. The value of diamonds in this country rests completely upon the talent of the advertising agencies writing those beautiful ads for diamond anniversary gifts. The only way diamonds will retain any value beyond that of the next generation of zircons is if enough sentimentalists continue to believe in the mystique of a rock that can be so closely copied that only experts can tell the difference between "real" ones and imitation. The same with old master art work. As stores of value, so-called tangibles are all relics of the past.

But back to our bushels of corn and rustic clothing. The original money, lost in the unrecorded past, might have been a conveniently small item of real value, like salt or flints or needles. While corn and skins might be traded directly, the person who makes houses can't package up his wares for exchange, or may earn so much with a single item that the equivalent in food would spoil before he could use it. Thus the provider of a large good or service would prefer to be paid in a smaller, more convenient store of value, like salt, that he could use over a longer period of time, or trade with third parties.

The problem with using real wealth as money is that you tend to use it up. Salt is eaten. The needle dulls. And without enough money, trade and commerce dry up and stop. So an essentially useless, non-degradable substitute for real wealth gradually gained wider use—gold and its like. The essential attraction of gold was not its real value, but rather its artificiality—with almost no use, it wouldn't get used up. None was lost, and as more was discovered, the money supply would continue to grow.

The growth in the supply of gold was a lucky break for humanity over two millennia. If the uselessness of gold was its initial attraction, its steady growth in volume is what gave it legs. The closest the old monetarists came to understanding the nature of money is their appreciation of the need for the supply of it to grow. Unfortunately, their understanding of growth is pretty dim, and lags far behind their much greater love of monetary scarcity. But they pay lip service to the concept of steady growth in the money supply, similar to that the world enjoyed under gold for millennia just by luck.

But exactly why should the money supply grow, and by how much? No one ever planned the increase in the supply of gold—it happened due to random searches by anyone who cared to seek it over thousands of years. The question of why or how much the supply should increase never came up. The increase just happened. Now, the old monetarists have no more than the vague idea that the increase should be slow but steady.

But a principle exists, a remarkably simple principle, one which seems as obvious to me as gravity. The supply of money should equal the supply of real wealth available for sale. People with a harvest of a thousand bushels of corn to sell one year need money worth a thousand bushels in their economy. If they enjoy a harvest of two thousand bushels the next year, their economy needs to have twice as much money. That is the fundamental principle of *balancing money and wealth.* On the salt standard, if people ate too much salt one year and had discovered no new salt licks, hopeful customers for the corn would be unable to buy it. The corn growers might have all of the clothing and other goods they needed for the time being, so, because of the salt shortage, their excess harvest might be allowed to rot unless they just gave it away. A lack of money leads directly to a destruction of real wealth. And the lucky corn growers might suffer as much as their disappointed customers. Let's say the next year a drought destroys their crop. Now they not only can't buy goods from other people, but they may themselves starve. Had enough salt existed during the year of the good harvest, they could have used it in lean times to save themselves.

As simple as this principle is, it goes beyond the meager substance of the old economics. Of course, like any other simple principle—for example, gravity—the details can get complicated. But the old economics has all of the complicated details (M1-3, P*, velocity, the tautological MV=PQ, etc.—read a standard textbook if you're curious about all these concepts; it would take me forty pages to do justice explaining all this) without any clear principles. The old economics of "scarcity" does not know how to deal with a bumper harvest. Due to a shortage of salt, gold, or, at present, money, relative to the size of the bumper crop, they let the harvest rot in the fields. Their underlying theory of the money supply goes no further than "slow but steady," which, like communism, holds society back to a mediocre rate of accomplishment. A bumper crop of wealth is wasted if the bookkeeping device, money, is not capable of matching what it is supposed to stand for. The old economic thinking accuses us of being out of money, of being bankrupt in the midst of real wealth. Their self-fulfilling theories of "scarcity" have made us cash poor in the midst of an incredible abundance, an abundance we have worked so hard to earn.

Yes, I say we need to print more money. Wait—read that sentence again. Did I just say we should print money by the boatload? *No*. Did I say we should use the Weimar Republic as our model of the money supply? *No*. The economic anorexics react to the word "money" the way regular anorexics react to the word "food." For anorexics, food equals fat; for the econo-rexics, money equals inflation. But in fact, the alternative to starvation for an anorexic is *not* obesity; the alternative to a cash-poor, deflationary economy is *not* "hyperinflation." Of course, a really sick anorexic on a binge-purge regimen might overreact and eat himself into obesity. He might correct one error with another. But that does not mean eating is the problem, but rather overeating. Similarly, when I say we need to print more money, I mean we have to print a certain limited amount of it.

*The U.S. has been an incredibly well-managed nation over the last two decades, full of dynamic, talented "employees." We have earned our bonuses. Unfortunately, our national equivalent of the corporate finance department has kept our profits off the books.*

How much should we print? The principle goal is to balance money and wealth. The more wealth we have, the more money we can and *must* print to balance it. A community with more corn, clothing, and houses can *and must* print more money than a community with less real wealth. In our modern economy, a nation acquiring more real wealth, as described above, can and must print more money than it had before it earned its new real wealth. This long, aforementioned explanation regarding the nature of real wealth is offered to make clear that we, as a nation—due to the best efforts of everyone we know—*already have earned* a great fortune in real wealth. The tremendous, quantum-level gains in international security, productivity, management efficiency, and free trade by themselves demand an increase in the money supply. The old theories cannot recognize an obvious fact of business life: just as bad management can bankrupt a company within a year, a few great management decisions by a dynamic, talented company can bring windfall profits and bonuses for all.

The U.S. has been an incredibly well-managed nation over the last two decades, full of dynamic, talented "employees." We have *earned* our bonuses. Unfortunately, our national equivalent of the corporate finance department has kept our profits off the books. They tell us that, despite our great success and prosperity, we have no money for bonuses. And it's all our fault. We have in some strange fashion all done something terribly wrong, for which unnamed sins we shall have to pay back our salaries, accept wage reductions, work longer hours, and lay off great numbers of well-trained workers. And our nation's finance department can't explain how these Draconian "sacrifices" are going to help.

The only way to realize the gains we have made in the last two decades is to increase our money supply by spending more and taxing less. Because we already have earned more than enough real wealth to back up the currency we need to print, we will activate our well-earned "bonuses," using the real wealth already on the shelves. Then we can create even more. And we can do this without causing inflation, just as the anorexic can eat a much healthier and richer diet without becoming obese.

How can we avoid inflation? Simple. We print money only up to the point of causing inflation. Allow me to repeat the statement of economic principles that I propose for the national economy: We must create a *sound* and *sufficient* currency, encouraging *full employment* of our human and natural resources towards the *creation of real wealth*. The first critical criterion is that the currency be *sound*, even before sufficiency is mentioned. The soundness of a currency can be measured in a number of ways, and I suggest we use the harshest, most conservative test: our money should be sound on *all* measures.

The fundamental task of all measures of monetary soundness is to determine how well a currency can be used to buy all of the forms of real wealth described above. That is, *can we use our U.S. dollar to buy what we want?* The yes/no answer to this question is easy: right now, you can buy anything you want, fairly cheaply, if you are fortunate enough to have money to spend. In the age of abundance, we have all of the cars, houses, airplane rides, resorts, hospital rooms, and movies anyone can possibly use. But measuring this most important quality of a currency is tricky. It is not exactly what we measure as inflation—remember that *the USSR had no inflation for decades, but you couldn't buy anything with the ruble.* In New York, thousands of apartments are cheap, due to rent control, but you can't actually rent one at the cheap rate. And inflation differs from foreign currency exchange rates. Yes, a cup of coffee might cost five dollars in Tokyo, but how often are any of us buying coffee in Japan? Meanwhile, a VCR might cost less in Houston than it does in Yokohama, where it was made—even for a Japanese paying in yen.

The best measure of this most important but numerically elusive quality is "Purchasing Power Parity (PPP)." PPP attempts to measure how well a currency allows its owners to purchase a wide range of real wealth, similar to what I describe earlier—that is, will your currency allow you to buy the things you want to buy? It's based on the idea that a dollar should buy the same amount everywhere. For example, a Big Mac is the same everywhere (even in Moscow). So why would it cost $1.03, $2.30, or $3.96 in different places? If you go to Switzerland, change your dollars to Swiss francs, and buy a burger, you have to pay $3.96 worth of Swiss francs. You can have two reactions: (1) "Oh, no! The dollar is weak. Time to fire a million people and squeeze the money supply!" or (2) "Those poor Swiss. They have to pay $3.96 for a Big Mac *every* time, not just when on vacation. It costs us only $2.30 in the U.S. What a bad deal for them and a good deal for me."

Perhaps the Swiss get paid more, but, in effect, they pay a highly inflated rate for a Big Mac because of what the old economists call the "strength" of their tight money. How highly inflated? On average, the Europeans and Japanese pay 40 percent more for things of comparable value. ("Big MacCurrencies. Our Big Mac Index Confirms that the Dollar is Undervalued Against Other Currencies," *Economist*, April 9, 1994, p. 88) And they sure don't earn that much more—some earn even less. They recognize the dollar's strength. In fact, the rest of the world believes the dollar is "as good as gold." They—not we—have made the U.S. dollar the international reserve currency. That means when nations square their accounts, they use the dollar—exactly as they used to use gold, when it was the international standard. It's as if the world had replaced gold with another element—call it "dollarium," atomic number 79 1/2 (the chemical name for gold is "aurium," atomic number 79). And good news! *All* of the dollarium mines are in the U.S.

A measure about halfway between PPP and inflation is the cost of living. The Consumer Price Index (CPI), which measures inflation, pretends you will buy exactly the same goods from one year to the next; a Cost Of Living (COL) index, on the other hand, takes into account your switching from beef to chicken if the price of one goes up and the other goes down. More importantly, the cost of living will include tax increases and other government fees.

What if you had to endure a rise in your tax rate from 28 percent to 41 percent in order to keep inflation below 2 percent? Or what if your Social Security had to be cut by a third? The CPI would look great—but your disposable income would be demolished, and you might have to cut back on your fixed costs as well. The best version of the cost of living tries to measure how much you have to work in order to maintain the same standard of living. For example, imagine that prices and taxes stayed the same, but your wages went down 20 percent (or you lost your substantial health benefits), so you had to work fifty hours a week instead of forty. In that case, your cost of living, as measured by your work, would have gone up by 25 percent. This extremely important number is entirely ignored by the Consumer Price Index of inflation.

Finally, inflation is an important measure, despite all its faults and shortcomings. The army of people who have worked for decades on the CPI are no fools. They carefully track changes in price of a "basket of goods" which they update every ten years or so in order to reflect changing consumer tastes. They offer a sea of numbers describing different urban areas and consumer groups. Their basket has three hundred sixty-four items ranging from "chicken parts" to funeral expenses, weighted according to how much of each is actually purchased—that is, food and gasoline price changes count more than do refrigerators, because appliances last so long. They determine these prices by sending their "trained representatives to twenty-one thousand establishments [for prices] and sixty thousand housing units [to see how much is used]."[1]

They try hard. Their sea of numbers is based upon lots of other numbers and man-centuries' worth of surveys. Unfortunately, the Consumer Price Index of inflation is significantly biased upward for at least three reasons. First, the CPI's main purpose over the years has been to "escalate income payments." The tens of millions of people whose wages or federal benefits are indexed to inflation see their checks get bigger every time the CPI goes up. Can you ever imagine a CPI wage *decrease*? The history and heritage of the agency is to ferret out not the existence but the magnitude of the price increases they assume to exist. Thus they make many little decisions the wrong way. For example, if you buy exactly the same Reebok shoes at Wal-Mart for 10 percent less than you would have paid at Sears, the CPI people say the shoes are a different item entirely, only because they were purchased from a different category of store.[2]

Second, the most severe deflation of all is not measured. When money is so scarce that you can't sell something at all—your house, for example—the CPI takes no notice of the fact. Remember that the essential feature of a sound currency is that you can use it to buy the things you want, that you can exchange it for real wealth. If you couldn't use your money to buy houses (as it was in the USSR), the money was flawed, no matter what a whole collection of indices might have said. The reverse applies when a currency is deflating, when a currency is too strong for its own good. When you cannot exchange real wealth for your local money—when thousands can't sell their houses—that means the money is the opposite of weak or unsound. That means the money supply is too small to do its job—there is insufficient money around to let people exchange their goods and services with each other.

The CPI cannot measure this sort of deflation, when people can't sell their homes or goods and services at all. Airline ticket prices have gone down after deregulation, but prices are even lower than they seem, when you take into account all the empty seats flying around every day. Each seat represents a perfectly good and fairly priced service, a service that thousands would like to use, but which cannot be used because of insufficient money in the system. Why don't prices go down, the way the price of corn goes down on the little graph you studied the first week of Econ 101?

Again, somebody should have written a book about this but they didn't—deflation is a politically incorrect topic in economics circles. Two main reasons: First, if you lower the price of airline tickets to the point at which you can sell all of your seats, you lose what is now the "premium price"—the price the seat is really worth, in terms of your own costs—from the customers who can indeed afford the fair price. The airlines presently do a very sophisticated job of selling identical seats for different prices, but they can only go so far. If you have to lower the price of four-hundred-dollar seats to one hundred dollars in order to sell 95 percent of the seats instead of 60 percent, you end up taking in less money overall. The problem is not the price of the seats; the problem is that consumers cannot afford to buy a seat for the price it is worth. For five years in a row, Alaska Airlines had been the top-rated U.S. airline. They lost $116 million. Other businesses have been acclaimed for their "excellence" or won the Baldridge Award and done even worse.

The second reason prices don't go down is that people can refuse to sell at a certain inadequate price, just as they can refuse to buy at a price they consider too high. Homes are the best example. People who pay $150,000 for a home often refuse to sell it for $100,000, even when that is all anyone who wants it can afford to pay. You might say this is merely psychological on their part, their not wanting to take a loss.[3] To some extent that's true. After a generation of steadily rising home prices, a generation of regarding your home as a way to increase your wealth, it has been a life-changing shock to think that you might have *lost* money on what you counted on as a sure investment.[4] Maybe you did in fact buy in at too high a price, paying more than the home was worth. But others have bought homes at very fair prices and not only kept them up but improved them. Their $150,000 home really is worth a lot more than the meager going rate of $100,000.

Selling prices are based on two factors: the intrinsic worth of what you are selling, and what your potential purchasers have in their pockets. Houses fail to sell *not* because they are worth less than their asking price, but because hundreds of thousands of people who would love to have the money to buy those houses need jobs. They need decent jobs in order to work and earn the money to buy those houses—but they *do not have decent jobs*. Houses don't sell for the simple reason that we have squeezed the amount of money in the system. The CPI has no conceptual, much less practical, way of measuring this sort of deflation. The best they have been able to do is ask homeowners what homes like theirs rent for, a measure so flawed I will not take the time to discuss it—again, I ask someone to write a book on deflation.

The third reason prices won't go down is fixed costs. Enough people won't work for free, for example. Commodity prices keep dropping, but will not become as free as air. Markets will clear below the manufacturing cost only once, at the going-out-of-business sale.

The simple aspiration of this chapter so far is to explain the concept of real wealth and show the relationship between real wealth and our money supply. I have had to take so much time to do so because the old economics doesn't offer much help. Look at any introductory finance or economics text. Their discussion of money will move within a couple of pages to a narrow range of MV=PQ type of equations. Read what they mean. All they do is relate one kind of money to another. What is money? They'll say in a sentence it is a "medium of exchange," let it go at that, and then spend a chapter discussing (in equations) why people would rather save money than hold bonds or whatever. Where does money come from? Well, from the bank, you fool! And what if you don't have any, and need to earn some? Well, get a job, you bum! And if the only job you can get pays minimum wage or commission only, that proves it—you're not worth any more.

This level of intellectually and morally bankrupt reasoning has been blindly guiding our nation's economy. Now they admit their failure. They admit that the monetary and macroeconomic principles they have believed in simply don't work. So do they offer or seek a single new idea, an even slightly different approach to take? No. The current tack is to say that, since the old economics doesn't work, it is therefore *impossible* to influence the economy of a nation—the president shouldn't even bother to try! Their response to failure is not only to give up themselves, but to discourage anyone else from trying. The last thing anyone in the profession of the old economics would do is question their first principles and come up with any new ideas. The conceit of their profession, as with every other in the ivory halls, is that everything they learned in order to get their Ph.D. was engraved-in-stone Truth. Part of the deal was that they would never be allowed to (much less *have* to) question those Truths once they had their secure and respectable places doing "research" in their universities.

So if we want to fix the economy, we shall have to do it ourselves. Don't count on them to help us, any more than you could have counted on the bloodletting doctors to figure out the errors of their ways or the British generals to admit the butchery they were guilty of committing. If this chapter begins to seem long or tedious, remember you are not reading the latest Tom Clancy novel. You are absorbing the fundamental principles of a new economics. I could have put it entirely in equations, if you think that would have made it look more pedantic and respectable (as I do in the academic version of this book). But it would then have had less substance and been impossible to read, so I didn't see the point.

To repeat: I have simply wanted to establish that real wealth is not money, it is the things we spend money in order to get. Money is a mere bookkeeping device that should keep up with the supply of real wealth. We monitor the relation between the size of the money supply and the amount of real wealth we have by checking purchasing power parity, the cost of living, and the consumer price index of inflation. The guiding principle about the *soundness* of our money is that we can use it to buy the things we want—that is, that our money can be exchanged for the real wealth we have already created.

## CYBERNETICS, OR THE GAS PEDAL ON THE MONEY SUPPLY

Did you read the part where I said we have to print trillions of dollars, banknotes by the truckload, imitating the Ukraine and the Weimar Republic? Well, I *didn't*. The inflation hawks cannot hear the words "print money" without adding "out of control" and "hyperinflation!" to the process—which says more about their own psychological problems than it says about the new economics. In fact, the only way I agree with the monetarist school of the old economics is in advocating a gradual, incremental change in the money supply.

The best example is the way you drive a car. The amount of gasoline you feed the engine determines how fast the car goes. If you want to go fifty-five miles per hour, you do not ask the computer to figure out how much gas per second you need. Rather, you get in the car and start driving. From a dead stop, you press on the accelerator. At first you may press hard, but as you approach fifty-five miles per hour your foot backs off, but not completely. At fifty-five, your foot is pretty steady, but you're ready to apply the breaks on downhills and the accelerator on uphills.

You have just *cybernetically* adjusted the flow of gasoline. "Cybernetics" means governing a flow of something based on feedback information you get from results of the flow. Using your foot on the accelerator, you govern the flow of gasoline into the engine based on feedback information you see on the car's speedometer. Similarly, your house thermostat governs the flow of oil or electricity into your furnace based on the air temperature it measures. The important measure for your car is *speed* and for your house is *temperature*.

We govern the amount of money we print based on feedback we receive about the relevant measure of the money supply: *can we use it to buy real wealth?* If the measures discussed above—PPP, the cost of living, and inflation—begin to rise, it means we are going "too fast," and we need to ease off on the accelerator. Then we will print less money. But when we have low inflation, strong PPP, and a low cost of living, as now, while enduring high unemployment and unused stores full of real wealth, we are going "too slow," and we need to press down on the accelerator. So we should print more money, by spending more and taxing less.

A visual metaphor of the cybernetic adjustment process is the "balance" figures used in chapter 5 to explain inflation. The third figure in that chapter showed the Great Recession:

***The Great Recession***

To achieve a balance between money and real wealth, you do *not* attempt to calculate the monetary value of all the available wealth on the right side of the balance, and then print up all of the necessary money at once. Too risky. It's better and easier to add increments of money to the left side of the scale until it eases into proper balance. By following the principle of printing one dollar to create two dollars' worth of goods, *both* sides of the scale can increase:

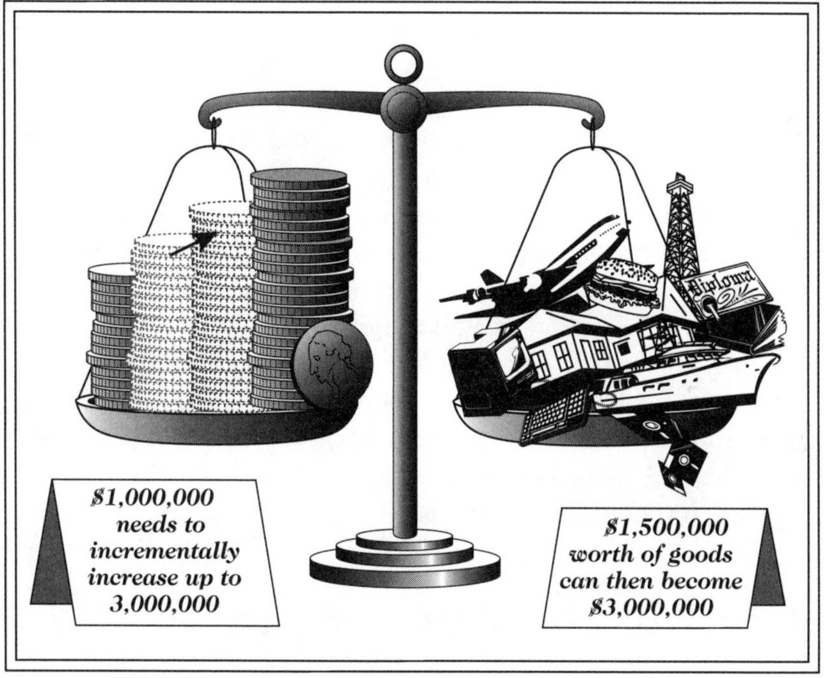


***Balancing out the Scale***

As simple and straightforward as cybernetics is (the only complicated part is the name), it is beyond the imagination of the old economics. If an old economist were offered the problem of bringing your car up to speed, he would try to make an equation to calculate how much gasoline you needed in order to go fifty-five miles an hour. He would measure the weight of the car, the engine's horsepower, the octane rating of the gasoline, the aerodynamics of the car and the wind on the road, the frictional interface between the road and the wheels, and on and on. Only then would he let you take the wheel.

And his calculations would be hilariously wrong. He would make some sensible simplifying assumptions. For example, he might use the average wind speed instead of trying to recalculate the effects of every change in wind speed and direction. But he would also have to make some ridiculously incorrect assumptions, to remain in the spirit of the old economics. In the calculations they use to misguide our economy, they assume "scarce resources" and "full employment," even though no resources are scarce and our work force is severely underemployed. The parallel for your car would be assuming third gear was fourth gear, and thus driving much too slowly—even though the economists had measured the gears, they didn't want to go through the trouble of changing their calculations. The old economists know "full employment" does not exist, but they can't be bothered to devise new equations. The assumption for your car parallel to "scarce resources," which is completely counter to the facts, would be like mistaking the brake for the accelerator and vice versa. This might sound stupid, folks, but "stupid" is exactly the way these people have been running our economy.

## TOO LITTLE IS WORSE THAN TOO MUCH

If you so fear exceeding the fifty-five-miles-per-hour speed limit on the freeway that you drive only twenty, you shall not only take forever to get where you're going, you risk being rear-ended by a semi. If you so fear overheating your house that you keep the furnace turned off, your family might freeze. The old economists so fear inflation that they completely discount the risks of having too little money in the system. The single measure they obsess over—inflation—is lower than they would ever have guessed it would be, and they still refuse to turn up the heat. Even an anorexic will recognize that his weight has gone down, and perhaps allow himself a carrot. Our econo-rexics won't even go that far.

To be fair, I must admit that the monetarist branch does understand the concept of cybernetics. They fantasize that they can control the pace of our economy with the magic lever of the Fed's interest rate. Their fairy tale is that when the Fed lowers rates, gleeful businessmen will rush out and borrow money to build new factories and hire more workers. Hooray for the private sector—who needs the government! Of course, it doesn't work that way—what idiot will expand into a low-demand recession?

The monetarists are correct that their magic lever has some effect on the economy. Raising the interest rates can indeed cause a recession, as they did during the "Soft Landing" that crashed us into the current Great Recession. High interest rates can act like a brake, even in the best of times. Combine them with the Mitchell-Darman tax hike, and Voila!—we're heading for the worst of times. But the sad news is that interest rates only work in one direction: they can make things worse, but they can't put Humpty Dumpty back together again. The monetarists are like a six-year-old with a watch. He knew just how to take it apart (the hammer helped), but now he's staring glumly at the parts. To go back to the car metaphor, the monetarists are trying to speed up the car again by pulling *up* on the brake. That helps only in the sense that it stops hurting. The monetarists have their brake, but have no clue where to find the accelerator. They call it "trying to push with a string."

In the nation's economy, what is the parallel threat to freezing our family or being rear-ended? You are living in it—and the temperature is still going down. An economy which does not have enough money to cover its real wealth destroys that wealth. Houses sitting empty, cars unbought on the lot, empty airline seats—all are wealth we have already created but which has been rendered as useless as if it had been blown up by terrorists. Worse, we are burning the seed corn, folks. Keeping people unemployed now is guaranteeing us less wealth in the future. Not only is the growing army of the unemployed *not* making more wealth now, they are not buying the wealth produced by those fortunates who still have jobs. The people with jobs today will not have them tomorrow if, due to unemployment, fewer and fewer consumers can buy any goods at all. And the unemployed are not only unable to make current wealth, they are clearly not helping to develop and build the factories and services of the future. They are not developing the skills or accumulating the sweat-equity and capital that we count on to drive the next generation of entrepreneurs.

A dark shadow dims our light. I feel a chill. Check the rear-view mirror—a huge semi might be blocking the sun.

## CREATING REAL WEALTH

Human beings are quite good at creating and exchanging the things they want. They can be stopped by disease (Third World sewage), war (one per generation until now), laws outlawing business (communism), too much money (Weimar Republic, the Ukraine), and too little money (the U.S., Germany, and Japan since 1989). Our government has a tremendous influence on how much wealth we can create and use among ourselves.

Ultimately, people create wealth. But the government can help or hinder us. The reason we have such an abundance of real wealth is that the people have been industrious and the government has been relatively helpful. This is the last phase in what I propose to be the government's economic mission: to create a sound and sufficient currency, encouraging full employment in the *creation of real wealth*. Much of the following material will mirror the discussion of the true causes of inflation in chapter 5, The Big Lie. Inflation is caused by *too much money chasing too few goods*, so if you can avoid having "too few goods," you avert inflation. Thus the discussion in chapter 5 was phrased in terms of avoiding certain errors, such as war. This chapter discusses the same principles in terms of positive, wealth-creating activities which the government can help encourage.

The reason we have a huge abundance of real wealth now is that we have done a great job over the last twenty years. In most cases, we need only to keep doing what we have already been accomplishing—accomplishments the deficit mongers would destroy on behalf of their Golden Idol. Free enterprise is remarkably creative and energetic in overcoming mild governmental obstructions to the creation of human wealth. Witness the supply-side accomplishments of the 1980s, which, building on the gains of the past, has abolished scarcities of anything. It was accomplished not by grand government programs, but simply by reducing regulation and taxes. Left to its own devices and undeterred by war, the private sector in the West will create wealth faster than the old economists will create the money we need to match it. Here's how we have created so much real wealth, and what we should do in order to continue to create more.

## PRESERVE PEACE/AVOID WAR

Of course, the benefits in lives saved and culture retained from avoiding war go far beyond the economic. But peace is the first and greatest stimulus to a nation's economy. Living human beings and buildings that have not been bombed are great producers of wealth. The clearest signal that the old economics is sick is its placid acceptance of the perverse fact that another good war would, in fact, stimulate the economy, according to their rules. Only in the cause of building weapons to destroy other people and their wealth, and to rebuild our own ruined nation, would our economic masters unloosen the monetary purse strings that strangle us.

But in an economy based on the principle of money/wealth equivalence, peace is its own reward. The Peace Dividend that the old economists have been unable to cash is already in the bank, in my plan. *The economic value of peace is the economic value of all of the people and things that would have been destroyed by war.* If that seems incalculable, an alternative way to understand this value is to place it equal to how much we have been willing to pay to assure the peace. For decades we have been willing to pay hundreds of billions of dollars every year in order to stave off the Soviets. Thus, peace, even just the narrow version of the superpowers' Mutually Assured Destruction, is worth hundreds of billions of dollars per year.

The demise of international communism means that peace is almost free. To be precise, the most expensive form of peace is much, much cheaper than it used to be. But just because something we used to pay a lot for becomes free does not mean it loses all of its value. If you won a free car, would you consider its value to be nil? If you inherited a house for free, would you list its value as zero? Of course not. Along the same lines of reasoning, if it was worth a few hundred billion each year to keep the Soviet nuclear warheads out of Omaha, we in effect have received a few-hundred-billion-dollar windfall profit, due to the virtual disappearance of the Soviet nuclear threat. According to the old economics, we simply fire all of the people who worked so hard to win the cold war. We then fire all of the people who ran the stores selling our cold war heroes their goods. Then we declare their homes unsalable. Then we fire the auto workers and home builders who would have made cars and homes for the next generation of cold warriors, had communism stayed the course. And we wait in vain for the magical "private sector" to somehow re-employ all of these people while we are raising taxes and cutting spending.

If we simply take the hundreds of billions and stop spending it, these people will never find jobs again. According to the principle of balancing money and wealth, we must continue to match the wealth we have created—peace—with enough currency to cover it. This means we may continue to fund the peace effort, to the tune of hundreds of billions of dollars per year. Even better, we get to spend the money in new and even better ways than before. We needed to spend ten million on an intercontinental ballistic missile (ICBM) that could destroy Moscow, but just sat in its silo for twenty years. For the same ten million, we might now buy ten Russian missiles that presently sit in their silos, still aimed at New York and Des Moines. Or we might invest in helping convert one of their bomb factories into a tractor works or space rocket factory—they are literally begging us to help them with defense conversions they cannot afford on their own. Yes, those millions will initially start off in the hands of Russians—but the multiplier effect of defense spending will be the same as it was when we paid our own people to build ICBMs, about two to one. That is, those dollars, like every other dollar ever printed, will find its way back into our economy, spent eventually on American goods and services, helping to employ American workers.

## BEING PRODUCTIVE

"Productivity" is a broad concept. This chapter covers, specifically, private sector productivity, which is broad enough in itself. Increased productivity lets us make more and better real wealth. Think of our primitive citizen growing corn. He becomes more productive when (1) he works harder; (2) he works smarter; (3) his society has accumulated farming wisdom; (4) someone invents a better seed corn; (5) someone helps him buy the new seed corn. The other topics in this chapter discuss other influences on his corn crop, like war, the irrigation system (infrastructure), a law against corn growing (regulation), the size of farms (economies of scale), and competition from farmers in the other valley (free trade).

We *are* richly productive in this country because we have steadily been working smarter with better systems and more good inventions nurtured by an excellent financial system. The private sector has *earned* its real wealth, and we only have to continue doing what has already made us wealthy—and disregard the demands of the deficit mongers who would have us tear down the very structures that have made us strong.

I will come back to the "work harder" point at the end. "Work smarter" includes everything from simple plowing to Just-In-Time management. The old ways were rarely the best. For example, for thousands of years masons built walls by lifting each brick up from a pile dumped on the ground. In 1912 a college graduate thought to put the bricks on a table that would rise to the level of the wall as the mason built it up. That simple idea and invention, the adjustable table, put about 30 percent more of the mason's effort into building the wall instead of lifting bricks. Today, United Parcel Service and McDonald's have time-and-motion studies down to a run-of-the-mill art which we take for granted. Check out any management text if you'd like to appreciate the details of the Japanese "just in time" (JIT) manufacturing technique. In brief, we used to warehouse tons of inventory in order to make sure we had it on hand when it was needed on the assembly line. Now, we order it to be shipped directly from the manufacturer to its precise bin on the assembly line mere hours or even minutes before it is used. As late as the 1960s, people never believed they could work that smart, under that much pressure, hour after hour—and get the job done more reliably and cheaply than before.

The individual farmer might be smart, but his intelligence is magnified by the accumulated wisdom of his forebears. So also is modern business. Everyone understands the adage, "Give a man a fish, and you feed him for a day. Give him a fishing hook, and teach him to fish, and you feed him for the rest of his life." Modern life benefits from thousands of years of fishhooks and teaching. But the old economics can count only the fish, and ignores the wealth we create through knowledge.

This wealth is immense. We are the beneficiaries of thousands of inventions which continue to pay off long after the inventors stop receiving royalties. From the ancient invention of the water pipe, through indoor plumbing and, now, over-the-counter hydrocortisone, we all continue to reap the benefits of our forebears' ingenuity. We receive far more in benefits than we ever gave them in royalties or salary. The excess I call "the surplus value of wisdom," or *surplus wealth*, with a wink at Karl Marx. He maintained that the capitalists grew fat by exploiting the poor workers, who received only a fraction of the value of their labors. I say we all gain far more from the surplus value of inventions accumulated through the ages.

So we work smarter because our forebears have taught us how to farm and have developed wonderful varieties of seed corn. The evidence is all around us, not just in corn—we possess all the abundant wealth we could desire. Nothing is scarce anymore. We cannot forget the necessary contributions of the moneylenders, who are often as vilified now as they were in biblical times. If you have ever had an idea for a new business, you appreciate how futile your best efforts are without capital. You can't start until you can find someone to put up the money to back you. A new seed corn might allow you to grow a thousand dollars more corn, but if you don't have the hundred dollars to buy the seed, and no one will lend it to you, the invention is useless to us all.

*This wealth is immense. We are the beneficiaries of thousands of inventions which continue to pay off long after the inventors stop receiving royalties. From the ancient invention of the water pipe, through indoor plumbing and, now, over-the-counter hydrocortisone, we all continue to reap the benefits of our forebears' ingenuity.*

But our financial system is the best in the world, relied on by the rest of civilization to lead the way in developing new and better ways to do things. Yes, our financial wizards spend a lot of time and energy chasing their own tails, but the bottom line is that more money finds its way into venture capital for start-ups of new firms here than anywhere else. The finance people lose more often than they win, but we all make enough money on the new seed corn they back, so their share of the profits gets them to keep taking chances on the next innovative idea.[5]

Talking about how we "work hard" makes me angry and, at the same time, sad. The deficit mongers have it in their heads that *we* are somehow at fault for the economic pain *they* have caused, and one innocent scapegoat is the supposedly lazy American worker or bad manager. I say we work harder now than we did in the 1950s. Union featherbedding rules have broken down. Time-and-motion gains make us rich, but they strain the workers—try chatting with an airlines reservations person, or spend five minutes watching the kids at McDonald's. And Just-In-Time (JIT) is harrowing to learn. Upstairs in the corner offices people have been "leaned and meaned" until they do the work of two for less money. Compare a modern manager's workday to that of his three-martini counterpart in the 1950s. And I shouldn't demean our 1950s' efforts—we were working plenty hard enough then; it's just we're working even harder and smarter now, without getting any credit for it.[6] The thought that anyone would sneer at the effort put forth by the workers and managers in this country makes me mad.

Of course, there are a lot of lazy bums sitting at home doing nothing, right? Of course there are—because our economic generals have fired millions in the noble cause of deficit reduction. That's what makes me sad. *People can't work hard if we fire them and destroy their jobs.* The deficit mongers know and openly admit that their catastrophic plan to raise taxes and reduce spending, in reverence to their Golden Idol, will cost hundreds of thousands of jobs beyond those we have already lost. But, like the British generals who knew the German machine guns at the Sommes would massacre tens of thousands of their own sons, our economic generals plow straight ahead against all common sense and without human compassion. Yes, some men at war might have to die. Yes, some workers in a free economy have to lose their jobs. But a wholesale massacre, of lives as in World War I and of jobs in the Great Recession of the 1990s, is pointless and unforgivable. The greatest source of all human wealth is the activity of human beings. Any philosophy, religion, or economic system that decrees that human beings should sit useless by the millions in sacrifice to some vague and irrelevant number is an intellectually bankrupt and immoral system. I have a job. But I am angry and sad that so many millions are un- or under-employed, and you should be, too.

To increase our wealth, we need to keep increasing our productivity. But there is no point in increasing the productivity of the remaining workers 10 percent if we are firing 20 percent of their brothers at the same time. The second clause of the economic guidelines I propose is: We must create a sound and sufficient currency, *encouraging full employment* toward the creation of real wealth. "Encouraging full employment" does not mean make-work boondoggles or immense government bureaucracies writing reports for each other. It also does not mean more jobs doing what we are already doing quite well, thank you—that is, car factories, farms, or even computer software firms. That real wealth we already have, and it would be foolish to print money only in order to fill the grain silos with cars and floppies on top of the silly corn already there. This country needs a lot that is not now presently being provided. We have an infrastructure that is falling apart, an environment we should clean up and improve, millions who need drug and alcohol rehabilitation, and a space program that is decaying. Meanwhile, we have tens of thousands of construction workers, environmental scientists and workers, psychologists, and physicists unemployed or running at quarter speed. The jobs of the future will be created and filled by the people reading this book. I suggest some jobs in chapter 13, but the hard work will be done by the people of this nation. Do you have any doubt they are up to the task, once we give them the chance?

## GOOD GOVERNMENT RULES AND REGULATIONS

...is *not* a contradiction in terms. Understand that when I blame our economic generals for the great harm they have wrought in the land, that I am not making a blanket indictment of our government as a whole. We must not condemn the many for the sins of a few. In point of fact, our government has done a great job over the last generation, when it has not been led astray by the deficit mongers. The greatest accomplishments have been peace and free trade. Thousands of smaller accomplishments have added up in the form of regulations that are a little better than they used to be, not as bad as they might have been, and definitely better than most of our Western competitors have endured.

It might sound shocking, but our government actually can create wealth for us all, at least as effectively as do lawyers, accountants, and even farmers. The government is as good at creating value as is any other business, when it does the right thing by its people.

A classic example of how government makes money for us all is the public-goods situation called "The Tragedy of the Commons." Not so long ago, villages had a square of common ground among the houses which all would share. At a certain size of village and common, the lawn would support the feeding of one cow per family. This cow would provide the dairy products for that family. But if each family were allowed to do exactly what they wanted for themselves, it would be in each family's individual self-interest to let a second cow graze the common. The "tragedy" that ensues is that with every family following its own self-interest and grazing two cows, the common would be overgrazed, the grass would die, and soon no one would be able to graze even a single cow on the now-dead commons.

A prime purpose of government is to prevent such needless tragedies. When the people of the village recognize the problem, they can democratically act as a whole to make and enforce a rule allowing each family to graze only a single cow on the common. The value of government in this case could reasonably be as high as the entire value of all the cows grazing the common, because, without government, no cows would be grazing. The point of most good environmental regulation is to prevent similar tragedies, in which individuals make money by exploiting a common good like air or water at an excessive cost to society as a whole.

In the village, people might recognize the contribution made by government to the common good, and, if the government were personified as a single governing individual, choose to give him a portion of their dairy products as payment for a clear service rendered. That payment is the equivalent of taxation, and could also be used for the other similar public goods that government supplies. Police and military forces create value by stopping individuals within the community or groups outside the community from stealing the villagers' honestly created goods. Thus they deserve a share of the value they help preserve, value which would not be there but for their efforts. As much as I hate taxes, I would be happy to pay a dollar this year for a service that would increase my income two dollars next year. Instead, we have just imposed a four-cent-per-gallon gasoline tax earmarked for "deficit reduction." We might as well *burn the money* for all the good this tax will do us.

## EXAMPLES OF GOOD AND BAD REGULATION

Good regulations are often extremely difficult to write. They involve a trade-off between safety and effectiveness, as with new drugs, or fairness and red tape, as with procurement contracts. But difficult does not mean impossible. The choices that have to be made have better and worse answers, and the following represents my opinion on a number of illustrative issues.

Good regulations make a level playing field, allowing honest businessmen to compete for customers; bad regulations let nepotism or graft guide the awarding of contracts. The absence of effective laws against crime, as in Russia, allows their Mafia to drive out honest businessmen and entire areas of enterprise.

> ***Good:*** Drug regulations that assure us our drugs are reasonably safe, or at least warn us what specific dangers they pose. Good regulations prevent snake-oil salesmen from making untrue, laudatory claims for dubious products.
>
> ***Bad:*** Drug regulations so foolishly stringent that they ban a drug that would save ten thousand lives, because the side effects of the drug would kill one hundred. Bad regulations go beyond informing us of the side effects of

the drug, to forbidding us from making our own judgment of the risks involved. Bad regulations would keep aspirin off the market, if it had been discovered today, and delay others so long that research into new drugs is effectively discouraged.[7]

***Good:*** Building codes that mean your house and home won't crumble as an apartment building in Thailand recently did.[8]
***Bad:*** A sea of regulations that differ in every state, preventing builders from competing nationally or offering economies of scale on building components. A general danger of many regulations is that they sound like they are trying to safeguard the consumer, but they are actually designed to prevent any competition with the bureaucrat's brother-in-law.

***Good:*** Some safeguards against smuggling.
***Bad:*** Paperwork as an end in itself, as it was under communism. The East German border guards required six separate documents when I returned from a one-day trip to bring my grandfather's ashes back to his ancestral property. It took me fifteen minutes to find one of them, which they found extremely distressing—I was put in the "bad people's line"—and my car was closely examined by a sniffing dog and a mirror. I suffered only this brief taste of pointless government harassment; those poor people were stuck there permanently, devoting endless man-millennia to inspecting each other's papers. Such persnickety over-inspection is not only a morally taxing invasion of privacy, and a tremendous waste of time, but it inhibits the flow of production and trade. Because of the new European Community free-trade laws, an inspection post on the Spanish border closed. Truck drivers used to wait three days at that post to clear customs. Spain employed ten people there to do

no more than collect reams of forms they filed and forgot, meanwhile keeping real wealth out of the country and raising the prices of those goods allowed in.

***Good:*** Loose oversight by an agency committed to helping provide safe, high-quality service for American consumers, like the Civil Aviation Commission after deregulation.
***Bad:*** Federal regulatory agencies committed to micromanaging prices and processes instead of encouraging honest competition, like the Civil Aviation Commission before deregulation. The history of price- and service-setting regulation shows they hurt consumers and protect big, lazy businesses which have to do nothing except follow arcane but exact government regulations, no matter how stupid they might be. Consumers lose, unless the mere sight of business in chains is worth the higher prices they pay and worse service they receive.

***Good:*** Enforcement of fair competition in the awarding of government contracts.
***Bad:*** Allowing so many appeals for contracts awarded that, for example, choosing a new computer system for the air traffic controllers has dragged on for five years beyond the first award.

***Good:*** Environmental laws that discourage the burning of fossil fuels that release carbon dioxide, when responsible scientists show that "the greenhouse effect" from these gases is causing dangerous global warning.
***Bad:*** Environmental extremism that would ban cars entirely, using spurious "global warming" and "greenhouse effect" propaganda long after even more responsible scientists have demonstrated that global warming is a myth, and we are more likely to be heading slowly towards another ice age, if anything.

***Good:*** Laws that prevent crime while safeguarding the rights of the accused.
***Bad:*** Laws that encourage crime by safeguarding the income of a legal industry dedicated to "due process" overkill and endless expensive appeals.
***Worse:*** Use of the racketeering laws specifically designed to get the Mafia, to chase everyone from politicians to abortion protestors.
***Worst:*** The renegade "drug warriors" and the Bureau of Alcohol, Tobacco, and Firearms (ATF) maniacs who break into innocent people's houses and kill them, based on entrapment or bad tips from unreliable informants.
***Unbelievable:*** The "zero tolerance" laws that allow the government to confiscate your one-airplane business without a hearing if one of your passengers has drugs in his suitcase.

***Good:*** Financial reporting laws that help us collect fair taxes from foreign corporations, so they don't gain a special advantage over U.S. corporations in our own country.
***Bad:*** Such poorly designed, catchall reporting forms that the IRS estimates that a firm doing a minuscule business overseas will have to waste *eighty hours* filling out IRS forms on the matter. This is more time than the firm spent conducting the business. The lesson? Don't try to compete overseas.

## Promote Free Trade

Preventing war and writing good laws can be hard. Encouraging free trade should be easy, and is just as helpful for creating real wealth. One of the many perverse outcomes of the deficit-reduction siege mentality is the possible wilting of the North American

Free Trade Agreement (NAFTA). Just as Hoover's deficit mongers created the Smoot-Hawley tariffs which prolonged the depression and contributed to the start of World War II, the current deficit mongers like Ross Perot aspire to be the Hoovers of the 1990s by torpedoing NAFTA.

People against free trade don't appreciate the concept of real wealth. Remember that real wealth is what you spend money to get, not the money itself. People complain about free trade when it is at its best—that is, when other countries are sending us their real wealth for us to use. Think of it. The Japanese send us cars and electronics. The Chinese send us clothes. The Europeans send us wine and other luxury items. The poor countries want to send us food and their modest crafts. Arabia sends us oil. They send us vast amounts of real wealth. All they want us to send them is some of the money we print up.

What a deal! Building cars and making clothes is some of the worst work in the world. And foreigners want to do it for us! It is as though your new neighbors offered to mow the lawn, clean your garage, and shovel the snow off your walk all winter. All you had to give them was your private currency. And, as in the BillyBucks scenario in chapter 3, you have plenty of office space available, or whatever you are offering to back up your currency. At the same time, your neighbors are happy to accept your currency and buy the goods you have backing it up.

Such is the situation with foreign trade. When the U.S. is kind enough to allow the rest of the world to send us their wealth, all they ask for is our dollars in return. We print 'em, and the rest of the world loves them. And what is the very worst thing they can do with all of the dollars we send them? They can use them to buy things from us. That is the *worst* they can do. And is there anything up for sale which we wish they wouldn't buy? Of course not—we only allow them to buy the things we want to sell. The holders of BillyBucks don't have the right to take over the office building; if you printed a currency to pay your neighbor who shovels your snow, I presume you wouldn't let him use that currency to move into your living room (unless you could build a better living room elsewhere while you were relieved of shoveling snow).

So the rest of the world wants to contribute their goods and services to the large pie of real wealth we share amongst ourselves. In return, they get dollars backed up by that large pie of real wealth. At a later date, they might decide to redeem their dollars for a share of that wealth—but only what we want to share, and we get to change our minds if we want to. Once we have the cars, VCRs, and Nikes, they have assumed all of the risk. We could repudiate our currency tomorrow, as the Russians keep doing, and everyone but us would be left holding the bag.

Actually, the rest of the world hasn't even tried to redeem their dollars. They seem to prefer hoarding our paper IOUs rather than buying the real wealth for which they stand. The amount they are kind enough to hold back is what we call our "trade deficit," another illusory deficit number that was all the rage ten years ago.

And they are the bigger fools for it. Look at what the Japanese have done for thirty years. They have imposed a harsh, austere regime of self-denial upon themselves far more stringent than that which MacArthur imposed upon them as penance for World War II. To help prevent the kind of madness that led them to attack Pearl Harbor, we imposed some of our democratic and capitalistic structures. But the Japanese thereafter went much further. Look what they did to themselves.

If we had been really bitter right after World War II, we might have told the Japanese: "Adapting some of our democratic ways to your own feudal culture isn't enough. We want you to work like slaves to provide for our every whim. And we don't want you to send us junk or pretty baubles, like the Russian *Matroshki* dolls. We want you to send us the stuff we like best—for example, cars. We're the best in the world at building cars. You have to learn how to build cars better and cheaper than ours. And televisions. They're too touchy, too much trouble. We want you to build us our TVs. And if anyone invents a tape recorder for TVs, we want you to build us millions of those, too.

"And by the way, you have to sell us all this stuff *cheaper than you sell it to your own people.* We want a VCR or Canon camera to be cheaper in New York than in Tokyo. You send us the cars, TVs, VCRs, cameras and all, and we'll give you some of the dollars we print up. If you don't want to spend them on our stuff, that's alright—by holding onto our dollars and not spending them, you help us keep down our inflation.

"If you are too stupid to spend the dollars you earn on increasing your own country's wealth and standard of living, we have a great plan on how you can use all of those dollars. First, you can loan them back to us, buying our stocks and bonds just like anyone else. And if you're real good, we'll let you build the biggest, best hotel in our downtown cities. If the hotel makes a profit, we'll share it with you. If it loses money, tough luck! Thanks for the dollars back![9] In fact, you are free to buy a bunch of other worthless or overpriced U.S. properties, as long as you promise to buy high and sell low—it fits with your follow-the-leader culture to always wait for a market top in real estate or the stock market, before you dare to invest.

"So we end up with the cars, VCRs, TVs, electronic gizmos, and big hotels. You end up with the repair bill for Rockefeller Center and a bunch of IOUs gathering dust. Meanwhile your own people live in small apartments, drive on overcrowded roads, can't get out of Narita Airport to visit the world, grow old without Social Security, pay quadruple for everything at the supermarket, and work like slaves until you drop. Thank you for making yourselves the Self-Appointed Coolies of the World."

Imagine if we had had the gall to place demands like that upon the poor Japanese. It would have made the Versailles Treaty seem like a mere slap on the wrist. But the Japanese, following their neo-mercantilist, managed-trade approach to life, imposed this austerity upon themselves. Like our deficit mongers, they either confuse or prefer money—anyone's money—to real wealth. In effect, they have been kind or foolish enough to spread real wealth around the world at their own expense. I would hate to be a fifty-five-year-old Japanese salaryman visiting the home or homes of his American counterpart, and comparing his standard of living to our own. How could he not be depressed or envious? One Japan-watcher says that's why the Japanese bureaucracy refuses to build another international airport, which they have badly needed for two decades: they don't want their citizens to go abroad and see what they have been missing.[10]

But right now, who is complaining about this scenario? *We are*. They did the extra work, and we got the extra rewards. If the numbers look funny, that's only because the same old economists who gave us the "national debt" have given us the "trade deficit." Both numbers are giant accounting errors, misconceived and meaningless, of interest only to those misguided souls who care more for bad math than they care for real wealth.

## FREE TRADE AND THE HARD-WORKING NEIGHBOR

Consider again the scenario of the hard-working neighbor. Say that for two years he works like a dog doing all of the menial mechanical tasks at your house. You keep printing up your currency for him, and he keeps taking it home and hiding it under the bed. Meanwhile, you have some time on your hands, time not spent shoveling snow or cleaning the basement. You could take a course at the local college and learn computer skills. You could landscape the front yard. You might just relax, or write short stories that everyone in the neighborhood likes to read. Your neighbor has not learned computer skills. His own property is much less desirable than yours, and would not command much interest on the real estate market. He is definitely not relaxed, and his artistic efforts are of interest only to the members of his immediate family. Basically, he's got an aching back and a pile of your paper under his bed. You wonder when, if ever, he'd like to cash some in. Perhaps you'll let him build a shed on a corner of your land for his yard implements—*you'll* decide where. Or you'll let him chop down one of your trees for firewood—*you'll* decide which tree. The parallels between this scenario and the nation's relations with our friendly neighbor, Japan, are clear enough that I invite you to draw them yourselves.

But, you might object, what if we don't take computer classes or write short stories? What if, while our neighbor mows the lawn, we just sit around moping, wishing we had something to do? Well, that would be a problem. If we used someone else's gift of real wealth as an excuse to *sit around and do nothing except feel sorry for ourselves*, that would be pretty wasteful and stupid. The people against NAFTA presume that low-level, undesirable factory jobs sucked south will leave the former U.S. workers sitting home morosely unemployed. And that is our choice to make. We may choose to let a demented monetary system convert the great gifts of peace and free trade into the "sacrifices" of higher taxes and unemployment, as the deficit mongers would have us do. Or we can use the freedom we have been given to create new and even better wealth.

Free trade only costs American jobs if we as a nation are too stupid to re-employ those workers relieved from menial jobs which other nations want to do. Our workers must not be idled—sitting home is both a waste of our country's human wealth and demoralizing for the human beings afflicted. What we must do is put our now-freed workers to work creating even more real wealth than they did before.

*Our workers must not be idled—sitting home is both a waste of our country's human wealth and demoralizing for the human beings afflicted. What we must do is put our now-freed workers to work creating even more real wealth than they did before.*

How? Imagine this challenge of re-employment in the example of the hard-working neighbor. He is doing many of the menial tasks. What can you do with your own time to take even more advantage of the situation? You can work longer hours at your main job. You can further your education. You can do more sophisticated work on your property so as to improve its market value. You might join a blockwatch committee, contributing to the safety of the entire neighborhood. You might tinker around in your basement laboratory, trying to find a cure for cancer.

Only if you had some sort of demented monetary fixation would you sit and do nothing. If you only worked when you paid yourself your own IOUs, and you had given all the IOUs you felt you could print to the hard-working neighbor, then you might sit around morosely doing nothing, bemoaning the lack of IOUs which was keeping you idle. Sound stupid? That is exactly the plan of the deficit mongers and NAFTA bashers. Our "idled" workers are already well-trained and ready to go to work on a multitude of projects that would create real wealth, such as those proposed in chapter 13 of this book. All we have to do is use the motivating power of money to get them to work again. Only the illusion that money is more important than real wealth prevents us from creating enough money to match the real wealth we have created, real wealth that has been increased greatly by our international neighbors. Only a bankrupt economic theory has taken a great gift and turned it into a curse. The old economics can put people to work for war but not for peace, and it can convert gifts from foreigners into poverty for Americans.

## IMPROVE OUR INFRASTRUCTURE

Remember back in the good old days, when you could sell your home for what it was worth, when the people who wanted to buy your home had jobs and could afford to pay a fair price? Then, you could increase your personal wealth by improving the quality of your property. You could protect and increase the value of your home by fixing the foundation, keeping out termites and dry rot, improving drainage, adding siding, fixing the roof, replacing old pipes with copper, rewiring up to modern standards, adding a rec room, etc. Outside your own property, you might work for neighborhood standards of safety, style, and substance so as to make the entire neighborhood where you live a more desirable and valuable place to live. The list of what you could do is limited only by your imagination and industry.

Similarly, working on our country's infrastructure adds to our real wealth, making us richer by improving the value of what ultimately backs up our nation's money supply. There are many ways for a nation or an individual to become wealthy. One person may work with his hands at an hourly wage, never resting and saving his paycheck, as Japan does. Others may work with their minds as scientists or managers, or with their musical or artistic skills, which is more what we do in the world of nations. Everyone who owns property can improve or leverage their earned wealth by protecting and increasing the value of what they already own. Perhaps the greatest portion of our national wealth, the ultimate source of the soundness of the dollar, is that we have the best house in the best neighborhood on earth. Part of that wealth is due to our laws and language, but a substantial portion is due to the tangible value we have on and in the ground.

The infrastructure includes but is not limited to what you commonly think of when you hear the term: water, electricity, telephone, sewage and garbage disposal, irrigation, flood control, roads, waterways, and cable TV. This technical infrastructure is now being rapidly enhanced in order to keep up with the information age, so we are adding satellites, fiber optics and digital capability in other forms as well. All of these apply to the value of your home as well as to the nation. Imagine the variations in the value of a home depending on the presence or absence of any of those basic services.

But our common infrastructure also includes the non-technological niceties that add value to our homes as well. A home downwind from a petrochemical plant is less valuable than a similar home upwind, and a nation with polluted air is less wealthy than one with clean air. Property in the flood plain is less valuable than that on the high ground, and a nation at the mercy of rainstorms—or hurricanes and earthquakes—is less wealthy than one which has better secured its citizens from natural disasters. (We should be ashamed that our main defense against rainstorms in

Iowa is the humble *sandbag*—with ten billion dollars of property and crop damage at stake, and with other sections of country suffering punishing droughts, we do not bother with techniques used in *ancient Mesopotamia*. See the suggestions in chapter 13.)

A home overlooking a golf course or the sea is more valuable than one that does not. A beautiful country is wealthier than one devoted to Miracle Mile architecture and public housing high-rises. We lag far behind the European countries such as Italy and Switzerland, which have capitalized greatly on protecting the centuries-old beauty of their architecture and landscapes. Many Italian cities forbid you from changing the exterior of your home at all—thus these cities seem frozen in time, like museum pieces. Inside, homes are modern and efficient, with copper pipes, etc. But everyone gets to enjoy the common "infrastructure" of an Italian hill town that still looks like an Italian hill town. Beauty varies among homes and among countries, making them more or less wealthy, and we can choose to make our country more or less attractive. The attractiveness of a country has a direct bearing upon its income from tourism—and tourism has recently become the number one industry in the world.

## EDUCATION AND TALENT

Much of what I say in this chapter might seem so obvious you might wonder why I am even bothering to write it. After all, everyone knows education, science, and the arts are important for society. But in the age of deficit-think, nothing is obvious. We have shown that we will subordinate everything in our society to the cause of the Golden Idol—that is, toward "deficit reduction." The debate has been *which* services to cut, *which* taxes to raise.

Although we have worked to surround ourselves with abundance, we act as though it didn't exist. The deficit debate ignores the fact and importance of maintaining and improving the wealth of our nation, neglecting even the education of our children. What is obviously good is disregarded. Just as the Aztecs ignored the fact of their own massacre at the hands of Cortez in service to their own destructive Bad Idea, we continue to sacrifice our own obvious best interests in the idiots' crusade for deficit reduction. Wealth and employment have not been a part of the debate, except to vote against them: the measly $16 billion spending package was voted down, but the retroactive tax bill was passed. Raising taxes and cutting spending accomplishes none of the wealth-building activities discussed here. Instead, what the deficit mongers insist we do only ends up destroying our real wealth.

Reducing the deficit causes us to waste and destroy the wealth we have invested in our own and our children's educations. We have already paid the price to acquire more education than the deficit mongers will allow us to use. In their feeble attempts to fob off the blame for their own failed policies, they inanely advise the country to get itself better educated and more competitive. What nonsense—Ph.D.'s in physics are being hung out to dry, along with every other college major at any level. Add ten years of successful experience and they're still getting laid off. The tight-money, no-growth jobs the deficit mongers can bring us don't even require a high school degree, unless that is what fast food is able to demand these days. (One out of every fourteen jobs created in the recession has been at a single retailer: *Wal-Mart*.[11])

In a post-deficit world, we will be able to use the wealth of education this nation has. Yes, our public schooling before college may be second-rate compared with other nations' and compared with what it could be, but the nation has been worrying about and working on it incessantly. Vouchers and school choice or some other program we haven't thought of yet might increase our real wealth in education—if we decide that education is more important than the deficit. We must hesitate before giving up on public education, I think. In world history, a country's wealth has been associated with its maintaining a tension between tradition and innovation. A common education for all or most citizens combines a common tradition with a diversity of students, which ideally allows us to develop skills for cooperation and innovation that strongly undergird our special function in the world. (As uncooperative and hidebound as we are after our education, everyone else is worse.)

But regardless of how good or bad our pre-college education is, our universities are clearly the best in the world,[12] and our graduates the best educated by any measure. We have more people getting more and higher degrees, but what good does it do us if we tell them to sit at home, or under-employ them after all their work? At present, 20 percent of college *graduates* have jobs that do not require a college education, and that proportion is expected to increase to 30 percent by 1995.[13] What will we tell our children?

And our blue-collar workers have more talent than they are allowed to use. The days of the 1950s, when U.S. companies had to hire whomever they could get, skilled or not, are over. Try to think of a single American industry complaining about a lack of trained workers. Our managers have twice as much post-secondary education as their fathers' generation had, and they keep getting more. Our well-educated workers and managers get a large measure of the credit for producing the abundant goods and services it was their job to produce. They are so good at it, we need fewer and fewer of them, so we fire many and make the rest work harder. Congratulations, workers!

It is a cliché to complain about needing more science education, but what is the point when even our best science graduates aren't allowed to do what they have spent a lifetime preparing themselves to do? We already have an army of scientists yearning to devote their lives to discovering and developing the inventions of the future, but we are cutting research and development for industry, killing space exploration, and in general relying on a skeleton crew to work on the next century. We need these people preparing us for future wealth as well as against future disasters. But we are treating our intellectual wealth much the same way we are treating our cars, homes, and factories—letting them sit unused on the shelves, convinced that we can't afford to use them.

Perhaps the most enjoyable form of wealth we have is our talent in the fine arts, entertainment, and sports. For some of you, your first reaction will be that a poem or movie is not wealth but rather a waste of wealth, mere frivolity distracting us from the real work of growing corn. But remember that the principle criterion defining real wealth is that people spend money to get it. And people spend more money on recreation and entertainment than they do on food, cars, medical care, or any other single category. Even poetry is enjoying a widespread renaissance, as people spend money not so much to read it but to attend workshops and write their own. More jobs have been created in recreation and entertainment than in any other category in 1993, overtaking health care.[14]

The arts are certainly a higher-order form of wealth than a bushel of corn, but so were cotton shirts, carriages, and indoor plumbing. Not every form of wealth makes other wealth, of course. Even corn exists to be eaten. Similarly, a fine novel or ballet performance is an end in itself, more valuable than gold. They are in fact what kings and sheiks alike have spent their gold to get. In an austere, impoverished society, using all its resources in a hard scrabble for food and shelter, there was neither time nor money to send the daughter to ballet lessons and the son to basketball camp. It is the earmark of wealthier societies to be able to afford riches such as these, surely as much as it is to be able to afford a storehouse of extra calories or a two-car garage.

Also, for you bottom-liners, the arts are a part of the next age of profit. We still make money in the old ways, through agriculture and industry, but the formerly second and third worlds are increasingly able to do those tasks for us. We are now in the information age, and the primary types of information traded are the arts, entertainment, and sports. We definitely lead the world in the last two, and I leave it to the fine arts cognoscente to claim or deny our place in their realm.

## HUMAN WELFARE AND SOCIAL JUSTICE

Health and welfare are wealth as certainly as food and shelter. We are willing to bankrupt ourselves to maintain our health, as witnessed by our elderly on their deathbeds. Yet seemingly civilized societies like the golden age Greeks, who were wealthy in the arts and culture, took poor care of their health. Worse, they never questioned the social injustice of the system of slavery that supported their literary and cultural elites.

We wouldn't be that stupid, would we? But we are! As I write we are confronting a "health crisis." What crisis? Are we short of doctors? Nurses? Hospital rooms? Medicine? Scalpels and CAT scanners? Of course not. We have all of the real wealth we need to serve the health needs of our people, insofar as money or wealth can help people's health. So then what is the "crisis"? The crisis, again, is caused by deficit-think. Our obsession with money forces us to disregard the wealth of doctors, hospitals, medicines, and technology we possess in abundance—and let them sit idle because we have not printed enough money to utilize what we ourselves have created.

We have a relatively healthy populace and we have all of the real wealth we need to make ourselves even healthier. We could be providing prenatal care for all infants. We can guarantee basic medical care for every person in this country. Remember that money does not treat your ills. Trained people in hospitals who apply our medical science are what treat your ills, and we have an abundance of those. We can choose to squeeze the money supply as we have, thereby smothering this portion of our wealth.

The Clinton health plan will not only continue to keep the money supply tight, but will tax more money away from our businesses, ultimately putting even more people out of work and making us less competitive overseas. (Large American businesses already pay more for their employees' health care than they make in profits.)

Health is a public good. Spending one dollar on health to make two dollars' worth of wealth is easy, especially when used on preventive medicine and non-technical forms of health. The deficit mongers would rather see their favorite number shrink than save the lives of children and the quality of life of their fellow citizens. They care as much for your and my health as the primitive priests cared for the health of the maidens they threw into the volcano.

"Social justice" might strike some of you as a namby-pamby, bleeding-heart-liberal sort of wealth. But try living without it. Throughout history, societies with rigid and authoritative hierarchies and a gulf between the leaders and the people tend to stick in a rut, becoming relatively poor compared to their neighbors, until they die out or become a backwater. Ancient Greece was golden only for a small percentage of the very elite—the average quality of life of the largely enslaved populace was below that of Europe's in the middle ages. Rome fell due to its own conformism and unwillingness to utilize the talent of its citizens. What triggered a great growth of wealth not only for the common people but for the nations of Europe at the end of the middle ages was the letting go by the landlords of their serfs to just a small degree—they let the serfs keep a portion of their own crops. The common people had some incentive to improve the efficiency and quality of their labors, and they did.[15]

*Health is a public good…the deficit mongers would rather see their favorite number shrink than save the lives of children and the quality of life of their fellow citizens. They care as much for your and my health as the primitive priests cared for the health of the maidens they threw into the volcano.*

Meanwhile, the leadership of the most advanced people until that time, China and Islam, decided that they liked things just the way they were, and banned innovation. The Chinese dismantled their large boats just as Europe began the age of exploration. The Islamic mullahs decided that what they already knew was the absolute apogee of all knowledge, and any new knowledge would be only a corruption of their own ultimate wisdom. Their word for "innovation" in general carried the same negative connotation as did the English for "heresy" in religion.[16]

As I granted above, these peoples were wealthy on the metrics of tradition and homogeneity of faith. That is their choice, and many of them seem to continue to be quite happy with it. These people's complacency certainly serves the wishes of their rulers well. For it is the rulers of a land who tend towards a conservative stasis of wealth, who persecute and kill those inventors and free thinkers who struggle to innovate. The ones in charge eliminate the innovators who struggle to improve the common lot by making the whole society wealthier. Why? Because the rulers already have all the wealth they want, and have no need to risk any change, because any change could hardly help them and might, indeed, hurt. Unfortunately, many people, and even societies (e.g., the Russians) care more for being better off than their neighbors than they care for their absolute level of wealth. That is, many people, if given the choice between (A) both you and your neighbor get ten thousand dollars, or (B) you lose five thousand dollars and your neighbor loses twenty thousand dollars, they perversely choose B.[17]

Unfortunately, our economic leadership is dismantling the framework of small business and social supports for the non-rich in this country. Ask a small businessman seeking a loan. Ask someone in the army of unemployed. The old economics will barely provide these people with sub-minimum-wage jobs, paying the wage which "clears" the labor market. This slave wage is all these people are worth, according to the old economics. The old theory cannot comprehend the need to mobilize and activate the full range of our human wealth toward the creation of further gains for us all.

But perhaps they can understand the dark side, the threat posed by the unemployed. What would you do if society offered you *no chance* to work and earn the normal wealth advertised on television and billboards around town, things like a house and a respectable job, things implicitly understood to be the normal lot of a citizen in a civilized country? An increasing proportion of our society is being given no chance to legitimately earn what society teaches them is a normal life. Perhaps *you* would go quietly into penury and shame. Many do, living quiet lives of modest desperation in our ghettos and depressed rural communities. Others do not. Their best chance, perhaps their only realistic chance for the good life, is through crime.

I am not soft on crime, nor do I think we should return criminals back to the street to perpetrate more crimes. But right now we are creating an ever-widening criminal class. The hard numbers of the old economics promise only to disemploy an increasing proportion of our populace. At the same time, the obvious and visible wealth at our command is dangled before millions who have no chance to earn it legitimately. When MBAs and computer scientists are out of work, what is the point of finishing your ghetto high school degree? What payoff, what rewards does society offer our ghetto survivors and rural poor for keeping a clean nose and playing it straight?

Very little—basically a chance to stay out of jail. Our approach to welfare support offers a perverse system of disincentives—punishing Dad for moving in with the family, punishing Mom or Dad for working to supplement their meager welfare transfer payment. I'm tired of hearing people who grew up with guaranteed opportunities saying, "I'm tired of hearing these criminals blaming everything on their so-called lack of opportunities." Whether you are tired of hearing it or not, it expresses a truth that won't go away. Put yourself at age fourteen into the social milieu of our underclass, and honestly imagine how you might have evaluated your options at that time—and what criminal actions you might have taken that would have defined your life forever. Our public attitude of control and punishment is still on the level the Greeks maintained toward their slaves—no opportunity to improve their lot within the system, and harsh punishment for breaking the rules.

I bet we spend more money punishing people for breaking the law than it would cost to keep them from wanting to break it. Add it up. Prisons, courts, judges, lawyers, prosecutors, police, security guards, burglar bars, and the handgun in the bedroom. We treat crime like a disease allowed to fester until it demands expensive, intensive-care treatment. Preventive treatment would be both healthier and cheaper. A society with less crime is richer than a society driven by social inequality to the point where large numbers of its citizens are only controlled by negative sanctions like guns and prisons. Spending one dollar to prevent crime—consider it a "bribe" to poor people if you must—to save two dollars on police and prisons is another easy and benign way to create real wealth. In chapter 13 I offer a few suggestions as to how to spend money in the ghetto. But the deficit mongers hear only the word "spend," and lead us and our children further toward a society of unequal opportunity and strife.

## SUMMARY: WHAT IS REAL WEALTH, AND WHY HAVE I SPENT SO MUCH TIME TELLING YOU ABOUT IT?

Real wealth is more important than money or gold—it is what you use money or gold to get. You spend money to win or avoid war, build a factory, pass a law, buy a VCR, string telephone wire, send your kids to school, go to the movies, cure your ills, and keep the burglars out. We already have a great abundance of real wealth. We need more money to match it. Without a balance between the amount of wealth we have and the size of our money supply, we destroy the wealth we already have, and prevent ourselves from creating more.

The deficit debate ignores real wealth. The old economists take an off-the-shelf number like Gross Domestic Product to be the end of the story. By deifying monetary numbers and ignoring what the numbers stand for, their bankrupt economic plan will destroy real wealth in favor of changing an irrelevant number. Such priorities are ridiculously wasteful. In order to maintain and increase the abundance and prosperity our society can provide its citizens, we must first understand that wealth is not a number. The old economics confuses the mere number with the wealth it is supposed to stand for, and thereby aims away from our true goals. Thus, the mongers' perverse goal of deficit reduction leads directly to the destruction of every sort of wealth described in this chapter. And the deficit mongers either ignore or blithely accept the destructive effects of their actions on real wealth, just as the Aztec priests accepted the destruction of their society in the cause of honoring their own false gods. To the fatal end, they said, "Trust us. Continue to sacrifice. This is the right way." So said the old doctors as they bled you to death. So said the British generals directing their young men into the machine guns. So say our economic leaders telling us to tax more and spend less on behalf of the deficit. To such leaders the real and obvious destruction, death, and, now, unemployment mean nothing compared to the pointless fulfillment of their misconceived notions.

# 11

# Cracking the Paradox of Productivity: Utilizing Our Real Wealth

Once wealth is created, the next economic task of government is to encourage its allocation. Because the efficiencies of free enterprise allow a small number of the best producers to create a great deal of wealth, employment inevitably shrinks, and demand withers, unless the means to enjoy that wealth is distributed widely. Making sure that enough money starts off in the hands of the poor will allow even greater gains to end up in the pockets of the rich.

## The Paradox of Productivity

Progress has a good side and a bad side. The *joy* of progress is that our corn grower can, by getting smarter and using a better type of seed, make twice as much corn with the same amount of effort. Having more corn for less effort can be good in a number of ways. Fewer in his family will starve in the coming winter. He gets to eat more. He can feed a farm animal and kill it to eat the meat. Extra corn can be traded for clothing or tools. He might have more free time in which to do other work on the farm or on behalf of the community, or learn a new skill. He might have a few more minutes or hours to lie in the sun, skipping a few furrows because he doesn't really need to plow them, or spend some time with his family.

The pain of progress is that "free" wealth, either from winning the lottery or increasing productivity, *can* cause trouble. Some problems are due to flaws of character, which I will not discuss in this book: the corn grower's family eats themselves into obesity, he becomes flabby from too much idleness, or, worse, starts a war due to having too much time on his hands. The main problem with productivity grows out of a normal *strength* of character: if he can make twice as much corn with the same effort, he will *use* the same effort and, indeed, make twice as much corn. Instead of all ten corn growers in the community enjoying half-days off to learn new skills or relax, five will continue to work full time—and five will be out of work completely.

Ideally, the five who are best at and who most like corn growing would stay with it, while the other five find something else to do. The other five might even end up doing work better suited to them and more lucrative, such as building houses or raising horses. In that case, society benefits from the increased productivity of the corn growers by having more houses and horses. This happy story does in fact describe the course of history—over the long run. Every single "luxury" we enjoy above the level of raw food and primitive shelter we owe to the natural concentration of work upon the most efficient producers, and the eventual re-employment of displaced workers on new, previously un-imagined projects. This loss of jobs and creation of new ones is called "creative destruction."

Unfortunately, I had to say "eventually" and "over the long run." New productive activities—new jobs—are rarely waiting for the five corn growers who just became part of the 50 percent no longer needed. Even if they had ten years' warning that half of the corn growers were going to be laid off, they probably held onto their profession until the bitter end. People who have devoted their lives to learning all of the depths and intricacies of a mature profession, whether it is farming or teaching Greek, hate to change. People begin a profession with the implicit understanding that they will be able to keep doing it as long as they do it well. Such was certainly the case for most of recorded history, and is even the case for most of the technical professions today. Our belief that *seniority* justifies higher pay and benefits is sustained by the assumption that the longer you work at a job, the better you become at it, and therefore the more you deserve for doing it. Until the most recent generation, in fact, people who changed jobs too quickly, even *within* the same profession, were looked at askance; people who changed *professions* were regarded as unstable, and thus unfit for employment in any serious profession.

Change is hard for society, and, in the past, society has even discouraged individuals from retooling themselves. Change is especially hard when you have nothing new to become. During the ten years our corn growers were warned that half their number would be fired forever, no one was begging them to come work in their livery or construction businesses. The pure paradox of productivity and progress is that not *until* the corn growers become more productive does the slack become available to create the next stage of wealth. Progress is so uncertain that no one can take for granted the corn growers' gains until they have already been accomplished. Not until then do half of the corn-growers become redundant. The glory of unfettered free enterprise is that people, left to their own devices, will produce more and more wealth more and more efficiently. The shame of free enterprise is that the faster the change and improvement occur, the more the people themselves suffer the pain of "dislocation" and "readjustment."

Let us pause to reflect on how much pain and familial tragedy are hidden behind these dry words, "dislocation" and "readjustment." One day you are able to provide food, shelter, and a place in society for your family. The next day you can't. Under primitive conditions this meant starvation and death. The best you can hope for is support from others and living under reduced circumstances, until and if you are able to attain another position.

And it is not only the unemployed corn growers who have a problem. The local weaver used to trade her cloth with them for corn. Before the great productivity boom, she had ten customers able to purchase her cloth. After the boom, she has only five customers. Those five do not double their purchases. So the weaver can sell only about half as much cloth, and receives only half as much corn. She might have to see her entire family malnourished, or see one of her children starve to death. Certainly, anything she does to improve her own productivity is missing the point—she already makes more than she can sell, because her formerly willing customers can't afford what she already has waiting on the shelves. (Does any of this sound familiar?)

Thus the interests of both the corn growers *and their customers* would be to *stop* progress. Throughout history, farsighted labor *and management* have frequently conspired to do exactly that. In 1579, the city council of Danzig feared a newly invented "ribbon" loom that threatened industrial upheaval, and secretly drowned the inventor.[1] It was reinvented twenty-five years later, over stiff resistance, in the Netherlands, as the Dutch loom. Tailors outlawed pressed pinheads in 1397. In 1299, Florentine bankers were forbidden to use Arabic numerals. In the sixteenth century, French printers revolted against labor-saving innovations in presses.

## CRACKING THE CONTRADICTION

How, then, has any progress in productivity been allowed to occur? The secret is in keeping the unemployed workers going until the new jobs have been invented. If productivity causes a crash in the demand for its own production, it is self-defeating. Thus, the first requirement for cashing in on progress is to make sure that newly unemployed workers still have an income as long as they are unemployed. In old-style boom times, only a few weeks might be enough for a worker to find a new position. If change is slow, and only one corn grower per year was rendered unnecessary because productivity was barely increasing at all, unemployment would naturally become re-employment, and the domino effect on the weaver would not be so important.

However, the new boom times are different. Productivity has increased so rapidly that the private sector cannot possibly create new jobs anywhere near quickly enough to replace the jobs we don't need anymore. Remember, these are indeed boom times in the creation of real wealth. Imagine that the primitive village had achieved three wondrous successes in a single year. First, the science of corn growing leapt forward (like our own factory, management, and worker productivity increases). Second, the village chief's son married the daughter of the chief of the neighboring village, so the ten men employed as guardians of the borders between the formerly warring villages had nothing to do (like our defense industry workers and engineers). Third, the village two ridges down had suddenly developed a great clothing and cheap firewood business after having been destitute and near starvation for a generation (like Germany and Japan).

The primitive village rarely if ever experienced such a boom in new wealth. Historically, change has occurred slowly or not at all. For example, the fellahin of the Nile delta farmed exactly the same way for three thousand years—*one hundred fifty generations*—without inventing a single productivity increase or suffering "unemployment." Before the Aswan Dam was completed, two fellahin farmers could have changed places across three millennia and both would have fit right in. The last twenty years for us in the West have brought change and new wealth which we don't understand. The simple fact of our superabundance of every possible good has not sunk in yet.

## What Do We Have to Do to Keep and Increase Our Wealth?

As described above, if we do not maintain purchasing power in the hands of the five corn growers who lost their jobs, their poverty will ripple throughout the entire economy. That is exactly what is happening to Western economies now. Unemployed defense workers are not buying cars, and are selling their homes in greater numbers and at lower prices. As a consequence, General Motors fires tens of thousands of workers, and you cannot sell your own home.

The immediate solution is to extend unemployment benefits. The length of time people receive these benefits should depend on how badly the economy needs new workers. In times of high employment, the benefits should be short-term. But when we have, through our own efforts, made millions of workers at all levels unnecessary for the tasks they formerly performed, we must as a matter of regular policy make sure they still have spending money in their hands. This is not altruism; if they don't have money to spend, the rest of the economy will fall down with them. Giving the unemployed money to do nothing does not create new wealth, of course—but it prevents the wealth we already have from withering away.

*The immediate solution is to extend unemployment benefits. The length of time people receive these benefits should depend on how badly the economy needs new workers.*

I am only advocating what we already do. The normal course of social and economic progress is to give more and more people money to make nothing. Remember that in primitive times a person would work from childhood until he died or became too feeble to move—men in the fields or factories, women as virtual slaves in homes lacking the labor-saving devices we presently take for granted. But now, the proportion of years we spend working is a fraction of what it used to be. We now spend the first twenty years in school, not ten. We live for ten to twenty years after retirement instead of working until we drop. We have a forty-hour instead of ninety-hour work week. Imagine housework without the washer/dryer, vacuum cleaner, and microwave.

Note the narrow role I assign the government. Government simply sends out the checks, just as it does with Social Security.

We let Social Security recipients spend their checks however they wish, responsibly or irresponsibly. The natural flaw of government spending is to create a bureaucracy to tell people exactly how they ought to spend their money. Welfare and public housing are the wrong way. Social Security is the right way. Just send the checks and get out of the way.

## The *Worst* Way to Give Away Money

The biggest mistake is to give money to products instead of to people. Instead of giving the money to the redundant corn grower, the government pays money for extra corn by keeping the price at a certain level no matter how much is grown. The effect is just as we have seen for two generations: corn prices remain higher than they should be, and we have silos of useless, rotting corn. Let us count the ways this is stupid. First, prices stay high. Second, the extra corn growers will never even try to change jobs. Third, further efficiency becomes less urgent, stifling the next generation of changes—as with bovine growth hormone. Fourth, trade wars start because, to keep prices high, cheaper corn from other countries is banned, as in France. Fifth, we pile up stocks of permanently worthless stuff instead of encouraging the creation of wealth people actually want to buy.

Our nation's milk price support system is crazier than anything dreamed up in seventy years of Soviet communism. Everyone knows and admits it, and it still persists.[2] We subsidize tobacco even while spending millions teaching people not to smoke. (At the same time, we throw marijuana sellers into prison for thirty years, although their drug is certainly less addictive and probably less harmful than the tobacco our government subsidizes.) The system is crazy, but we keep doing it. Why? Two reasons: First, people getting these permanent subsidies think they might starve if the subsidies stop, because they have no assurance the government would send checks to people as reliably as it sends checks to bushels of corn. Second, even when the government does in fact try to send checks directly to the farmers instead of to the corn, the farmers themselves scream the loudest. France has tried to give permanent subsidies to the noisy French farmers to simply maintain their farms as farms, but the farmers reject this form of compensation. The French government realizes the farm subsidies keep prices high, and, worse, threaten world trade agreements and the development of the European Community, but can't talk the farmers into accepting checks to remain farmers.[3]

And why won't they accept these checks? For exactly the same reason many old-thinking taxpayers don't want to *send* them checks: they feel it is wrong to pay or be paid for doing nothing. Our Protestant work ethic says it is better to pay for work that is useless and even harmful than it is to give money to people just because they are people. The farmers themselves accept this old-style Puritanism/Calvinism (call it whatever you want, you know what I'm talking about) as much as anyone else does. It would destroy their self-esteem to accept checks just for waking up and walking the fields every day, or even for working hard at improving the countryside they own. Their self-esteem requires they grow corn and receive a "fair" price for it, as their families for generations have done. They don't know whose corn goes into the surplus silo, after all, so they can presume theirs is actually being eaten. Consumers don't notice negative events like the failure of prices to go down, so they don't scream. And the effect of a trade war, or reduced international trade, seems too remote from the corn price subsidy for people to tie them together in the public debate.

It might seem to be another paradox, but the facts are indisputable: it is better to pay people to do nothing than it is to pay them to make unneeded corn by keeping the prices too high. How on earth can it ever be economically efficient to pay people to do nothing, you might ask. The fact is, we already do pay people to remain unemployed *indefinitely*. We arbitrarily say all people aged sixty-five become as unnecessary as the five redundant corn growers, and put them on permanent unemployment. We call it their retirement income. But it is the same thing as permanent unemployment. People's self-esteem doesn't suffer as much, because they feel they have earned it. But they have not earned it any more than those on unemployment have. Both have been paid less while they were employed because money was put into a common fund, which is then disbursed to qualified contributors when necessary. One fund is unemployment insurance, the other fund is Social Security. Neither the recipients nor their friends question whether the receipts match the contributions to either fund.

The way we handle our permanent "structural" unemployment should be modeled on the way we handle retirement and Social Security. In primitive times no one "retired"—they worked until they dropped dead or became so enfeebled they were unable to work. This probably occurred around age fifty-five for those who hadn't already succumbed to injury or disease. From that ancient reality we have constructed the current fiction that people today become unable to work around the same age. We all know this is a silly fiction, because these days relatively little work requires physical strength, and people might be at the top of their skills in a knowledge occupation at sixty-five. Even physical abilities might not have declined significantly.

The real reason we have people retire at sixty-five is because we don't need them to keep working, any more than we need the five redundant corn growers. Productivity advances and the accrual of common goods like roads and sewers over the years have allowed us all to spend less and less of our lives working, and more and more time going to school, on vacation, and retired. This is not sloth, no more than it would be considered sloth to have finished all of your chores by 3:00 P.M. so you could go fishing. By working smarter and more efficiently as a people, avoiding war, allowing peaceful trade, and following the other methods of creating wealth I have described, we have *earned* our time off. And to pay for our community college classes, vacations, and retirement adventures, we have devised ways to keep spending money in our hands while we are not working. This spending money allows us to keep the economy working fluidly.

To explain what I mean by working "fluidly," inspect what happens if society stops giving money to people who become unemployed due to increases in productivity. Say the five redundant corn growers get no money. Not only do they not buy cloth, they cannot buy corn from the remaining growers. Thus the village needs less corn, and does not need all five of the remaining corn growers. One or two of them are rendered redundant, despite their being highly efficient, state-of-the-art farmers. When they are fired, the economy similarly shrinks, and even the most efficient and productive of the remaining workers are threatened, due to the spiraling decrease in the number of remaining customers. As you can see, that is exactly what is happening throughout the Western economies today.

Selling a desirable product at a good price due to efficient manufacturing and service is absolutely no guarantee against imminent bankruptcy. We tend to blame the laid-off corn growers for not somehow having done better; as long as one corn grower still has a job, we blame the other nine for not measuring up. But the abundance around us proves that our problem is not the fault of the producers. We will all be firing ourselves in an implosion of wastefulness if we do not give ourselves the ability to buy our own wealth. And all we have to do in order to gain that ability is to print and distribute more money.

## WHO GETS HOW MUCH FOR HOW LONG?

The principles are clear enough. People who lose their jobs because society no longer needs their services should get enough money to keep buying goods until the economy does again need their labor. The old economists would go crazy trying to figure out exactly how to define who is no longer needed, how much they should receive, and what constitutes a new need for their labor. Fortunately, the principle of cybernetically adjusting the money supply provides a lot of leeway on all counts.

The safest and most conservative feature of the economic system I am outlining in this book is that it requires no radical changes in what we do, only in how we understand what we are doing. For unemployment compensation in particular, I recommend we offer more of it for longer. On average, we pay 50 percent of wages for six months. The Netherlands pays 70 percent for three years, and other European countries range between the Dutch and us.

Unfortunately, current unemployment benefits support only those workers hurt by the recent effects of a wealth explosion that has gone on for twenty years. The unemployment statistics mask the millions of workers who have lost jobs since 1960, who have given up looking, or are working at a fraction of their desire and ability to work. I am talking about the people who would be excellent farmers and factory workers if we needed farmers and factory workers. These people now constitute our urban and rural poor, and we have largely forgotten them. We don't need them to make cars or houses, but they would sure like to buy them. Up to our ability to afford it, we should seek to put purchasing power back into their hands as well.

But that might involve forty million people, you object. Remember, I am not proposing we start sending large checks to everyone tomorrow. The essence of cybernetic adjustment is to keep a light touch on the pedal instead of flooring it to hear the tires screech. We need to print and distribute money *up to the point of inflation,* more specifically up to the point of decreased PPP, increased cost of living, and rising inflation, as described in chapter 10. The goal is to increase the *sufficiency* of our currency while retaining its soundness.

## I'M ALREADY RICH. WHAT'S IN IT FOR ME?

You'll stay rich, and get richer. Your kids will be able to keep up with you instead of falling into the class of unemployed, as they are now. These days, nobody is so rich and secure that they don't have to worry about what the deficit mongers are going to do to them. CEOs are getting fired every week. Six-figure middle managers are becoming extinct, as information-age data bypasses them on its way from the cash register to the corner office. And even the people who really thought they had it made, living the high life on the interest from their CDs, find their income cut in half when it's time to roll their CDs over. If you think you've outsmarted the banks by rolling over into a nice mutual fund that seems to be paying what you used to get on your fully secured CD, you should worry that (1) your mutual funds are not secured; and (2) the mutual funds would have to sell at severe losses if too many investors tried to cash in at once. Present-day investors buying mutual funds are like people in 1927 putting their money into the unsecured banks just before the run on bank deposits brought them all down.

Similarly, no one is so rich that they wouldn't get twice as rich under the plan proposed in this book. "But," you say, "*I'm* not going to lose my job—I own the company. So the government isn't going to be sending me any checks. And I haven't found it yet, but I'm sure you've got it written somewhere in here that you'll have to raise the taxes on me or my business to pay for all this." You're right that the government isn't going to be sending you the checks directly. I'm saying to put the money in the hands of the poor. But where do you think this money is going to end up? People buy your products, rich man. A simple law of capitalism is: *Money that starts in the hands of the poor inevitably winds up in the pockets of the*—all together, class—*rich*. You won't find anybody to argue against that statement.

So you'll make your money the way you have before, by providing a product or service, only you'll have a lot more business than under the tight-money, pro-scarcity, high-sacrifice policies of the deficit mongers. If you just want to argue, or make me give you the obvious answer, you might persist with, "But I don't sell anything to poor people. I construct million-dollar homes or sell fancy financial instruments that poor people never heard of." You mean your customers are already rich, like yourself. You know, however, that not all of them are making *their* money exclusively off the rich, as you are. The people who buy big houses might pay with the money they earn from selling little houses—or they used to, when people could afford little houses. You know that most rich people get rich by selling to the masses. Money distributed to the masses will work its way up to the rich, you can count on that.

And higher taxes? *Wrong*. You can thumb this book to death and fill me with sodium pentothal—there is no hidden agenda for taxation in the post-deficit economics. We need to tax less. Economics in the age of abundance is not a zero-sum, win-lose game, in which one group's gain is another group's loss.

The worst moral sickness of the deficit mongers is their message of suffering and sacrifice—that economy is a negative-sum *lose-lose* game. Their program combines job losses for the poor (due to reduced spending) with income losses for the rich (due to increased taxes). Their program has already raised your taxes, while not increasing your revenues a bit. I am not playing with mirrors. The wealth is all around us. We need only recognize and capitalize upon that wealth by printing and distributing enough money to give hope to the poor and unemployed, make the rich even richer, and avoid wasting the great accomplishments of the last fifty years.

## WITH LOWER TAXES, WHO PAYS THE GOVERNMENT?

Right now we have absolutely no concept of how to pay the government. The question almost doesn't make sense, as if I'd asked, "How high is up?" The government takes some of our money in taxes, transfers most of it back to us, and spends the rest on the army, a few roads, and salaries for their own gigantic bureaucracies. Although the collection and splitting up of all this money is the prime activity of government, there are no guiding principles of how to go about it. Lacking any fundamental principles, we start every year's budget with last year's. Then we argue like banshees about who is going to get a little bit more or less this year than last.

Folks, this is embarrassingly primitive. Businesses run in this fashion went bankrupt or got bought out years ago. Of course, not all of government is like a business—the Supreme Court and the army have no private enterprise counterparts, for example. But much of government does in fact address the normal business concerns of *managing tasks in a cost-effective way so as to add value*, value in the sense of goods and services that people want so much they would pay for them if they had to.

The italicized portion of that last sentence constitutes a modest "mission statement," a normal part of a business strategy plan. Once a business has at least a vague idea of what they are trying to accomplish, then they can go about doing it. Every business at some point steps back and asks what they are doing that is a waste of time and money, and what are they neglecting to do that would support their mission. Instead of assuming that everything the company is doing now it should do forever, and anything it is not doing it should never do, you step back and try to look at everything with an open mind. What helps and what doesn't? In accounting terms, it's called "zero-based budgeting." It's the opposite of last-year-based budgeting. Instead of starting with the assumption that next year's budget will be approximately what this year's was, you start with the assumption that your task or division doesn't get a cent. Then you have to justify why you should get any money at all, and how much.

No government on earth would let itself be subject to such normal business standards, because they would have to basically put themselves out of business. In Russia, I can't think of a single part of the government, besides the natural gas and pipeline monopoly, that adds value to their society. In this country, perhaps 85 percent of the bureaucracies would get the ax. As successive presidencies have proved, however, cutting even 2 percent is impossible. Thus we must have no illusions that applying normal business standards to our government is even remotely conceivable within our lifetimes.

Then why am I bringing the matter up? To provide a frame of reference for what we *can* practically accomplish. This book does not address the great moral and legal issues of government, such as the Supreme Court. But the economic goals of government should be broadly similar to the economic goals of its citizens—roughly, to add value, to protect and create real wealth, as described in chapter 9.

## CAN WE DO BETTER THAN JUST PRINTING MONEY AND GIVING IT AWAY?

We have discussed the need to keep money in the hands of people who became unemployed due to productivity increases. The main economic job of government is to print enough money to match the real wealth people have created. That is the main message of this book, and the primary insight the deficit mongers lack. And we can do even better. While the government is printing and distributing this money, we can apply the simple business principle of trying to add value, to create even more real wealth with the additional currency. Remember that it is *not necessary* for the new money to create new wealth. Why not? Because the new money is necessary to match and recognize the wealth that has *already* been created. The ideal is to have wealth create money, which then creates more wealth and so on, in a spiral of prosperity. The alternative the deficit mongers propose is the opposite: a deflationary spiral inward, a permanent monetary squeeze in which too little currency degrades wealth, which causes less money causing less wealth and so on down to the pointless withering of our nation.

It is not easy to spend money to help create, as opposed to match and consolidate wealth the private sector has already created. Note that much of the money the government spends takes great pains to *prevent* the creation of more real wealth. Both Social Security and welfare punish their recipients for working, a preposterous thing to do. Welfare demands that families be split up, a near-criminal disincentive.

Many large government bureaucracies end up spending large sums of money only to destroy real wealth. The most vivid example I've encountered personally was the Russian Ministry of Foreign Trade, which supported the academy where I taught as a Fulbrighter in Moscow. The ministry filled one of Stalin's "seven ugly sister" giant wedding-cake buildings, forty stories of men whose mission in life was to sign documents saying "No!" to foreign trade, or refuse to sign documents saying "Yes." My question, "Does a single person in the whole ministry actually help foreign trade?" made no sense to them—as though you asked someone working for our Child Protective Services, "Who do you have assigned to molest children?"

The ministry exists to block foreign trade at every turn. Any foreign trade that took place in the Gorbachev years happened despite the ministry, not because of it. The dream job for a Russian college graduate is an office and title which forces people to get your signature if they want to do actual, useful work. Your greatest pleasure is saying "No!" Your second greatest pleasure is being driven around in Zhil limousines, wined and dined by naive but good-hearted foreigners who misunderstand your function, and think you can *help* them do business in Russia. Only after a year do they realize they dumped fifty thousand to two hundred thousand dollars dating a tease. In addition to the graft these bureaucrats earned on their own, the Russian government paid them well, by their standards. However, the Russian nation would have been much better off if they'd put every one of the thousands working in the ministry in retirement at full pay in nice dachas on the Black Sea. Then the nation would have actually been able to *do* more foreign trade, and valuable apartment space would have been opened up at a desirable Moscow address.

A second visible example was the Spanish customs office I mentioned before. Ten people were paid to hold up the trucks for three days, filing forms never again read, stopping wealth from being driven into their country and making that which got through more expensive to buy. The point of the new European free trade laws (or initiatives like NAFTA) is to close such offices.

A sad fact is that too many, perhaps most, government bureaucracies care much more about protecting their own existence than they care about the mission they were designed to perform, even when that mission was a good one.

An example of a wealth-creating foreign trade bureaucrat is easy to describe, but hard to find on the ground. We desperately need more U.S. commercial attachés in the formerly communist countries. We as a nation can benefit by gathering information, making contacts, and lobbying these governments on behalf of all of the American companies trying to do business in these new, rapidly changing economies. As it is, the few people we have in places like Russia and Kazakhstan are so overwhelmed answering our phone requests that they have little time for their main jobs—gathering info, making contacts, and lobbying the policy-making bodies on our behalf. Spending one dollar on this kind of bureaucrat can not only enhance the chance of sustaining peace within these volatile regions, but lead to more than ten dollars of new American wealth down the road.

*We as a nation can benefit by gathering information, making contacts, and lobbying these governments on behalf of all of the American companies trying to do business in these new, rapidly changing economies.*

## Create and Share the Wealth

Again, the central idea of this book is that a nation which creates more real wealth can and must create enough money to match it. If we work harder, smarter, and more peacefully to create more things, we should be allowed to use the things we have created—and we only need to print more money in order to be able to do so. We have worked for it, and we deserve it.

A corollary is that the same principle applies to the government as it does to the people. First, the more wealth the government helps us to create, the more money they get to authorize to keep up with that wealth. Second, the more wealth they help us create, the *more money they get to keep themselves*.

The first just restates the theme of the book. The principle of balancing money and wealth is simply that we can *and must* print enough money to match the real wealth we have and can create. The government has the pleasant duty to print this money—not your local bank, not the United Nations, not you and your BillyBucks. The easiest way for the government to get the money into circulation, where it needs to be, is to send it directly to the people, as we do now with Social Security, Aid to Families with Dependent Children (AFDC,) unemployment insurance, and the like. If they did no more than that, just printing and mailing more of it, they would at least help us keep and use the real wealth we are creating for ourselves, and they would be worth the salaries we are currently paying them.

But an even smarter government could actually *help us create more wealth*, for example, by spending more money on commercial attachés in Kazakhstan and less on self-serving and wealth-destroying bureaucrats in the Bureau of Silly Milk Rules. Now think hard. What on earth could we do to encourage our elected leaders to make smart decisions that create wealth for us all, instead of stupid decisions that enrich a few special interests at the expense of everyone else? My shocking proposal is to pay them the way we pay just about every high-level free-enterprise manager. I put it in italics above, and you still probably read over it without believing your eyes. Yes, I propose we give our leaders a *cut of the action*, paying them partially *on commission*, as it were.

## SYSTEMATIC POLITICAL BRIBERY

That's one way to put it. We bribe car salesmen to sell cars. We pay bonuses to middle-level managers who keep costs down in their departments. We pay million-dollar salaries plus stock options to hundreds of CEOs who manage to keep their companies afloat, and even more to those with good track records. We pay multimillion-dollar contingency fees to lawyers winning exorbitant pain-and-suffering cases that arguably destroy real wealth in this country. Our society continues to pump billions of dollars into bloodthirsty rings of illicit drug dealers. But do we have any concept of giving a leadership that *accomplishes peace* a reward of a penny more than we'd give a leadership that led us into a Yugoslavian catastrophe? Have we ever given a cent to a congressman for doing the right thing by his constituency and the nation, as opposed to selling out the people to those much-vilified "special interests"?

Of course not. No democracy or republic in the history of the world has paid its leaders according to how well those leaders governed. More the opposite. Overall, outright corruption might be the norm, and just plain stealing from the public till has probably enriched more politicians than has good, honest decision-making. At present, we scream that we want our congressmen to ignore the special interests, and we want to take the special interest money away from them. Vote the Department of Silly Price Supports ("DSPS") out of existence, we say—but the "DSPS" helps pay for the congressman's re-election. And what do we offer the congressman to be good instead? *Absolutely nothing.*

I say we pay our leaders more when they do their jobs well. How radical is that? Call it bribery or anything you want, but what are the alternatives? Right now we pay the government the same way the communists paid everybody—you get the same every year, or a small raise, no matter how stupid or smart you've been. What a system! We have absolutely no mechanism for raising our leaders' salaries for good behavior. Instead, we presume the charlatans are lucky to get anything at all from us, and scream bloody murder every time Congress tries to vote themselves any pay raise at all.

And our leaders are so grossly underpaid, it is a miracle all of them aren't robbing us blind purely out of spite. Somehow we have decided the people running the most powerful nation on earth, people with the power to make us and much of the rest of the world richer or incinerate the biosphere within a few hours, those leaders are worth about as much as your average ambulance chaser or Wal-Mart manager, and less than the average sawbones. *And not a cent more, dammit!* I say we not only get the government we deserve, we get the government we pay for. And if we don't want to pay, then we'll let the special interests pay for and get the kind of government that serves them well, while we bitch and moan on the sidelines.

A generation of political leadership did in fact avoid the nuclear holocaust. A generation did open up the world for free trade. A generation helped spread the concept and toys of democracy around the world so thoroughly, despite censorship and repression, that today even the communists have freed their citizenry. In recent years they have helped us rise out of the oil crisis and 14 percent inflation to a point of abundance and low inflation. So how do we show our appreciation? We pay them a fraction of what managers at their level are worth, and crucify them in public every time we get a chance. It's a miracle that so many decent people still throw themselves open to government service. We can't blame our political leaders for not following a better economic plan these last five years. When they asked the renowned gray-haired suits for advice, the old economists only gave them losing options to choose from.

## *EXACTLY* HOW MUCH COMMISSION SHOULD THEY GET?

Give me a break. I don't know. Who knows exactly how much we should pay a shoe salesman? Right now our government pay system has no relation to any benchmark, other than what everyone earned last year, the most thoughtless system of all. The old economics aspires and pretends to predict and analyze everything with exact equations, but fails utterly at being able to predict even the direction of interest rates, inflation, the stock market, or any other important variable. The new economics of cybernetic adjustment is based on what is happening in the real world, as opposed to the world of irrelevant equations. It offers us a lot of leeway insofar as the exact numbers are concerned, as long as we are generally heading in the right direction. You do not have to calculate ahead of time exactly how hard to press down on your car's gas pedal. You press first and, as long as you watch the speedometer, you will not go rocketing out of control.

The right direction for the money supply is to increase it at least until we approach matching the amount of real wealth we have already created. The right direction with our elected leaders is to increase their salaries when they are doing well, and decrease salaries when they have messed up. This simple concept of pay for performance, understood by everyone the first time they get a report card in first grade, is miles ahead of the absolute lack of a system we have now. We don't even have the grounds for a debate about the amount of pay our leaders should receive. If one of our leaders even broaches the topic of a pay increase, we vote him or her out of office.

I propose only that there be some grounds for debate, and the grounds should be, "How good a year have you had?" Remember the famous crack by Babe Ruth, when he was challenged to explain why he got paid more than the president? "Well, I had a better year than he had," was Babe's answer. We have never given our leaders the opportunity to challenge our current multimillion-dollar athletes, CEOs, or lawyers to a comparison of who indeed has done more for the society around them. I personally wouldn't know exactly whom to pay, and how much, for avoiding World War III, but the profits for that long-term decision leave a lot to be spread around. The point would

*We have never given our leaders the opportunity to challenge our current multimillion-dollar athletes, CEOs, or lawyers to a comparison of who indeed has done more for the society around them. I personally wouldn't know exactly whom to pay, and how much, for avoiding World War III, but the profits for that long-term decision leave a lot to be spread around.*

be to encourage our leaders, when one of those famous "waste" bureaucracies comes up for funding, to realize that, at the end of year, when the salary review comes around, they will be able to argue that they saved money on that one by voting "No." We should give them at least the hope that they will be rewarded, a hope they can balance against the certainty that the lobbying group for the Department of Silly Price Supports will contribute to the congressman's reelection campaign. Then, I am betting that more of them will do the right thing, enough more of them that the "DSPS" will finally get voted into richly deserved oblivion. Along with the carrot, they should fear the stick. They have never suffered a pay cut. But if they manage to destroy enough wealth (e.g., by inhibiting free trade) that we suffer inflation, reduced PPP, or a rise in the cost of living, their standard of living should suffer as much as ours does.

Of course, most actions are more ambiguous in regard to whether they contribute to the creation or destruction of our common wealth. Most legislative rewards and punishments should be collective, as opposed to individual—but the sponsor of a good bill might get more, and those with the worst attendance should get less. Making estimates of the exact value will always require guesstimating, and even the direction of value—that is, did this create or destroy wealth?—will often lead to heated and unresolved argument. For example, did invading Iraq create or destroy real wealth—and I don't mean only for the Kuwaitis, but for us (and how does the Kuwait wealth redound upon our own fortunes)? Those debates, even when unresolved, would not be a bad thing—in fact, I think they would be the best form of debate, forcing us to confront questions of value instead of pure politics with no external framework of reference. Remember, the value of real wealth is not just a dollar-and-cents measure of gold in Fort Knox. Value includes a clean environment, freedom, hope in the ghetto, security, health, and happiness, as discussed at length in the front half of this chapter. A debate on the wealth-creating aspects of our leaders' actions would elevate the discussion, not degrade it.

Many actions to create wealth are unambiguous, however, and clearly deserving of reward. As I have emphasized, ground zero for our legislators is to print the money and get it into circulation any way they can. Any way they can create more wealth without slowing up this process is an improvement from ground zero. Managing work programs at decent pay, building roads, pipelines, fiber optic networks, or cleaning up the environment are better than simply sending unemployed blue-collar workers checks on the condition they stay home and *not* do anything. A rejuvenated space program would better employ our unemployed scientists than would one more retraining program that only adds to their unused skills, or another résumé-writing workshop for jobs that don't exist. Put them to work exploring our universe, guarding us from the next asteroid like the one that wiped out the previous dominant species on "our" planet. Put the money into health care that will increase services and shorten waiting lines instead of the one just proposed, which is guaranteed to restrict choices, lengthen waits, make some advanced care so unprofitable it won't even be offered in this country (the Canadian model), and will inhibit job creation by foisting even more social expenses on the very businessmen we count on to create jobs.

Look at it this way. Say you have one Congress that gets us into a messy war, passes laws leading to inflation and unemployment, can't pass GATT or NAFTA, and cuts social services to the point we have rioting in our ghettos. Another Congress uses our military power to help distribute food in other people's crazy wars, leads the world into further free trade while consolidating the hope for democracy and free enterprise in the formerly communist countries, brings new hope and life to the poor, and controls inflation while funding massive reemployment of the nation's greatest resource: its people. Right now we do not have the concept, much less the mechanism, to reward the second group as compared with the first. That's crazy, folks.

The government does not build bridges, or space stations, clean the environment, or counsel the afflicted. American citizens, allied in groups we call "businesses," get the real work done, and ultimately create our real wealth. But the government can help as well as hurt. Our leaders will have the burden as well as the joy of spending the money we need to print. They can create even more "Departments of Silly Price Supports" or obstructive paper collectors (worst), or simply send out checks on condition people stay home and feel bad (stupid, but still gets the job done). Or they could do better, and should be encouraged to do so. Ideally, government jobs might gain the respect and normal incentives that would encourage some of the readers of this book to undertake the immense responsibilities of running for and holding office themselves.

## INTERNATIONAL REPERCUSSIONS OF THE NEW ECONOMICS

If we let our deficit go and print more money, will international financial markets panic, sending the whole world into a tailspin and depression? Don't be silly! That argument is one of the deficit mongers' more feeble and desperate scare-fantasies. If we decrease our taxes and increase our spending 1 percent, nobody is likely to notice, much less panic. When Reagan lowered taxes by 10 percent and tripled our national debt, did Europe and Japan panic? Of course not; they made money hand over fist. How do the mongers dream up these fantasies?

On the contrary, what international markets most desperately need is a "Big Customer." Everybody is lean and mean, full of manufacturing and service capacity, but no one thinks his nation can afford to buy. As I described in chapter 6, the world followed our stumble-footed lead into higher interest rates, deficit reduction, and recession in 1988-1991. The Western money supply has been squeezed to the point that the whole world suffers the illusion it can't afford to buy its own wealth—call it *the illusion of poverty*. We need one brave nation to get the ball rolling again—someone to buy enough to get foreign factories back up to speed, foreign workers back on the job, foreign consumers buying everyone's products (including our own).

This century it has been our turn to lead, and we should do so again. Our first step will be to work with any GATT agreement we can get, and *of course* we will get the short end, as we have gotten in every round since 1946. (And *of course* no nation has benefited more from freer trade since then than we have, either.) Second, we should not only sign NAFTA but encourage its extension to other interested southern nations like Argentina and Columbia. Third, we need to dissolve all trade barriers with the formerly communist countries and start buying whatever trash they have which we can fit in our basements, if that's the best they can make at this stage in their renaissance. (Remember, if we don't buy their exports, they might never reach the next stage in their evolution from communism. Then we can start building more nuclear bomb silos and bomb shelters in our basements again.)

The whole Western world is suffering a self-induced liquidity crisis or cash flow problem. If Europe and Japan had more brains than we have, they wouldn't have followed our "soft landing" lead, or would have cranked up the printing presses themselves by now. But they haven't. Fortunately for international markets in a global age, one sound *and sufficient* currency is as good as another, so it might as well be ours. Let them supply us with the manufactured commodities of the old industrial age, while we increase our own U.S. wealth in ways that only we can. We can move on into the future, at their expense, until they catch on and follow our lead—again.

## REVIEW

The "New Economics." What a pretentious, self-aggrandizing title, don't you think? I am ashamed to use it, given the modest nature of the contributions to economic science proposed here. After all, the simple message of this chapter is merely to recognize what real wealth is, match wealth with the money supply, get the money into the economy so as to create even more wealth, and base our leaders' pay partially on performance. Frankly, everything proposed except for the last has already been done, numerous times here and around the world. All I offer is an explanation for why it works, so that we discontinue the destructive practices proposed by the deficit mongers and return to the right actions we did in the past without knowing why.

Of course, I know how apoplectic these modest proposals will make the old economists in the audience. I have given this talk enough times in the last two years to recognize a conniption fit when I see one. This chapter presses every panic button they knew they had and one they just discovered. "Print money" to them is like "Eat meat" to an anorexic. "Start it in the hands of the poor" to them sounds like "Tax me to death," no matter how much I rail against taxation. "Gold is *not* real wealth" is simple blasphemy and they stop their ears with wax. "Spend money on foreign goods" means "Sell our country to aliens," according to their interpreter. And the concept of the *government* adding wealth, and earning a big pay raise, is the new, inconceivable heresy, the one that sets them foaming at the mouth. When they regain their composure, they will dismiss this chapter as a "Fairy Tale" which is "not worth discussing," as they have dismissed far more modest exposes of deficit-think.

These old thinkers will never change their minds. Facts don't matter to them. The harm they have caused they will never admit, even to themselves. They have devoted their lives and souls to a wrong, harmful course of action, and it is simply not in the nature of professional wise men to say, "You know, I never thought of it that way! Golly! That means I have been *wrong all my life*. Thanks for setting me straight, kid."

Therefore, I have not written *to* them. I have written *against* them. Because they have categorically dismissed any new ideas since they got their Ph.D.'s, they will not have to read this book to know they disagree with it, and they won't read it. But they will try to dissuade the open-minded readers, the voters of this country, the voters who will have to decide between the discredited and bankrupt economics of the deficit mongers on the one hand, and the new economics proposed in this book on the other. The deficit mongers will avoid confronting my ideas, preferring shrill excoriation unadorned by reason, or dragging out the disproven arguments already demolished in chapter 6. They will not fight fair, and they will portray these ideas as more dangerous than I have portrayed their own.

So think back. Is what I say radical, or is it simple common sense? Real wealth is not paper or gold; it is the house, car, or safety you spend money to get. Wealth came first, and money was invented later as a bookkeeping device. Money should match our real wealth. When we have more real wealth, we need more money. And we *do* have more wealth, because of peace, free trade, and hard work. Thus, we need more money. We should increase the amount slowly, by reducing taxes and increasing spending 1 percent, so as to keep the currency sound. Due to higher productivity, we need fewer people to do the jobs invented just twenty years ago. We have to keep our people going until we invent new jobs. Our government can help create real wealth with those new jobs, and we should encourage our political representatives to do the right thing.

I beg you to go through the simple, straightforward ideas presented in this chapter to find a single proposition that is wrong, a single statement that flies in the face of common sense. Piece by piece, the new economics is so simple that I would be ashamed to spend so many pages explaining it, except for three reasons. First, look at the material on money in any of the texts or articles by the old economists. They brush by what money stands for in a quick, uncomprehending paragraph, rushing on to what they find interesting—money for the sake of money, questions of the "demand for money" and "price levels." Their analysis makes for nice figures and equations, but completely fails to address the important questions of macroeconomics: What is causing the recession? Why are people unemployed? What are the full effects of free trade? How can we buy the things we make?

Second, there is no shame in writing in a simple, comprehensible style with no math. Look at the old economics. Piece by piece, their ideas are as simple as those presented here—the problem is that most of theirs are irrelevant or wrong. They owe their professional lives to making simple ideas *sound* complicated and mathematical, or why else would anyone hire them? But I challenge them to show how one single truth of macroeconomics was discovered by mathematical analysis. Math in economics exists because it is fun and macho for the economists, who use it only to rephrase what has already been recognized in a statement of words.[4] The textbook version restates this chapter in the language of propositional mathematics, with a few computer simulations of the effects of increased productivity and the concentration of income thrown in. But the math adds nothing. I'm writing it only to get a version of these ideas adopted by a few sympathetic economics professors who need to have the math in order to maintain their own credibility with their peers. But the book you're holding, this simple and vivid verbal story of our economy, is the necessary statement. As simple as it is, it goes well beyond the irrelevant and disproven assertions of the deficit mongers who are presently dragging us through this endless recession.

Third, simple ideas would have saved millions of lives in World War I and throughout the history of bloodletting. Don't march the young men into the machine guns. Don't send your daughter to be bled to death. The solutions to tragedies even worse than our recession were as simple as my advice to "Print more money." Sadly, no one wrote down those simple ideas and explained them to the people who mattered—the people volunteering to charge the machine guns, the patients putting their veins beneath the knife. Perhaps the people with common-sense insights were too humble, perhaps they felt sure their great military generals and physicians *must* know what they're doing. Of course, the generals and physicians themselves said they knew exactly what they were doing, insisting to the end that even more charges into machine guns, even more "heroic" bloodletting was needed, calling upon even more sacrifice from their trusting victims.

Re-read this chapter if you still can't believe that wealth is more important than money, if you still can't believe that the solution is as easy as "spend more and tax less." Listen to the arguments of the old economists to see if their criticisms make any sense. Compare the two approaches. Theirs means more of the same that has caused the Great Depression of the thirties and the Great Recession of the nineties. Their prescription is higher taxes, lower spending, wealth destruction, and unemployment, all in the service of their Golden Idol of deficit reduction. Ask them to show you one single person on earth who has benefited from deficit reduction. I show how to create wealth through good jobs, using money as a tool instead of enslaving ourselves to it. Read carefully, because if you can't find anything wrong with this book, and begin to doubt your faith in the deficit mongers and their Golden Idol, you might have to change your thinking.

I know from my public talks that most of the people I present these ideas to are in fact persuaded that the old economics is deeply flawed and these new ideas make a lot of sense. This book was not written to interest and amuse. This book was written to change the system, so people will be back to work at good jobs, able to earn the abundant wealth we have already created and is ours to claim. The next chapter shows what must be done to convert these ideas into action.

# PART IV

## The Future and How to Get There

# 12

# Practical Political Action: Here's What I Want You to Do...

Okay, let's roll up the sleeves and turn the ideas discussed so far into action. This chapter attempts to *provoke*, not just *invite,* action. It then discusses *whom* we need to change (you and your political representatives), *what* to change (ideas and votes), and *how* to accomplish these changes.

It is time for this nation to substitute good ideas for the bad ideas that have caused our pointless Great Recession. Being right isn't enough, and you can't just phone the president. The debate with the deficit mongers is not arguing for the sake of arguing, nor meant merely to interest and amuse you. The point is to change your thinking and your actions. "You" are the voters of this country—the ones who are ultimately in charge. The political leadership won't change their thinking and actions until you do. There's no sense hollering at them—or at the Japanese, NAFTA, drug dealers, or our schools—until you can tell Congress what you want them to do.

All you want them to change is their minds and their votes—which isn't easy, but it's not like demanding an instant cure for AIDS. You change their minds and votes by changing your own and your friends'—with discussion, calls to talk shows, letters to the editorial page and Washington, political donations, and perhaps by running for office yourself. The point is to act, not just suffer and complain.

## GEE: YOU SHOULD WRITE THE PRESIDENT

I've changed a fair number of minds with my presentation of these ideas, and I wish I had a dollar for every time someone has been kind enough to suggest I talk to the powers that be. I say, "Thank you" for the gesture of support, but that's not how to change things. *Having* a good idea, *getting* the right answer to a very tough problem is only the first step in a very long road to hoe. It is the most necessary step, because if you don't head off in the right direction, every other step might only lead you farther from your destination.

But step two is *not* getting the king to do it all your way starting tomorrow. We as a nation suffer as much as every other nation from the collective illusion that "The Boss is in Charge"—whether the boss is the quarterback, CEO, or president of the U.S. We tend to give him or her too much credit when things go well and too much blame when things go wrong, either because of luck or the actions of the rest of the players. People seem to have an emotional faith in and anger towards the presidency that reminds me of an adolescent's attitude toward his father. Dad actually does have the keys to the car and lots of money. So we're really ticked off when he won't give us what we want.

The president is not Dad. He's not even king of the U.S. He is as much trapped by bad ideas as the rest of us are. He has less power and influence on the U.S. than the quarterback does on his team or the CEO on her company. I have tried to find an example of a sitting president receiving an idea from someone outside of his inner circle, acting on that idea, and accomplishing anything with those actions. Folks, it has never happened once.

In fact, few presidents give a toot for ideas anyway. Reagan had a strong ideology and some sharp phrasings of what he believed in, but what would you call an "idea"? Carter had one unimpeachably clear and indisputably noble idea—that the U.S. should promote human rights and less torture around the world. He was roasted by his own state department for it, and ignored by the citizens, so he failed to accomplish his goals.

The cliché "idea" of streamlining the bureaucracy never gets anywhere. Bush relied on personal relationships. He trusted his advisers and was ill-advised. Insiders admitted the utter dearth of ideas driving any part of his reelection campaign, especially regarding the economy.[1] They decided to sack the entire economic team near the end, but had no alternative plan, and by then it was too late. Ross Perot is a hard-core deficit monger, with no more ideas than "Spend less and tax more!" Read his book if you can stay awake through its empty pages. He hasn't accepted a new idea from anyone in his adult life—he disregarded his best friends' advice whenever they deviated an iota from his plans.[2] Clinton already sympathizes with this book's major premise, that the deficit doesn't count[3]—but he is savvy enough to know that it would be political suicide, not only for himself but for the Democratic party, were he to state or act on that belief. He couldn't even pass a measly $16 billion spending stimulus package, and was forced to support a tax increase, due to the *citizenry's* national hysteria over the deficit bogeyman.

Believing that an idea will carry the day merely because it is correct is touching but naive. Believing that the big guy, whoever he is, will do the work of forcing change upon a deluded citizenry is foolish. That's not how the system works. It might be fun and convenient to rail against our president and representatives over dinner, but it misses the point. Change is accomplished by the people. Change will only occur if I can convince *you* that the deficit mongers are wrong and *you*, the reader, have to do something about it.

## Why So Many Rude and Vicious Attacks on the Poor Deficit Mongers?

I admit I've been a bit hard on the likes of Alan Greenspan, Wayne Angell, Warren Rudman, Paul Tsongas, Henry Figgie, Paul Simon, and the editorial staff of the *Economist*. Whenever I've neglected to twist the knife in their sorry hides for more than three or four pages in a row, I've gone back and inserted a few more barbs. I know this offends not only the mongers themselves, but all the genteel academics and even many of the kinder-hearted voters I hope to persuade with my arguments.

But the pointless suffering, the needless disaster described in chapter 2, is too widespread and urgent for us to waste more time on academic thought-pieces. Innocent Americans and citizens of democracies around the world are paying a terrible price for the errors of their economic leadership. If you have forgotten what is at stake, look at page 3 of any *Wall Street Journal*, where they report how many thousands are getting laid off today. The deficit mongers are as responsible for our recession as the British generals and bloodletting physicians were responsible for the carnage they commanded. When I hear Ross Perot calling upon *other people* to "sacrifice" even *more* by paying higher taxes while cutting more spending, I see General Haig calling for more thousands of men from the reserves to sacrifice to the German machine guns, on top of the half-million young men already thrown away under his command.

Nations have been ruined because their citizens respectfully followed leaders with bad ideas. At least a hundred million slaughtered innocents would have lived if Hitler, Stalin, Mao, Idi Amin, Pol Pot, and Saddam Hussein had been driven from power by people high enough to understand the horror and be able to do what needed to be done. Remember Montezuma and Cortez? It is morally remiss to treat these people with deference and kid gloves. The most renowned Italian physician wrote in 1800 against the evils of bloodletting—in a polite tract to his fellow professionals. He was ignored for over a century. The communists never allowed into print books like this; anyone pointing out the carnage their leaders had wrought was summarily executed. Thus, their victims are more sadly blameless than we are. We must not impose a fatal censorship upon ourselves, keeping our discussion of the economy in refined journals, following Emily Post rules of etiquette designed to keep anyone's feelings from being hurt. We make ourselves victims by being so polite we flinch from branding *anyone's* ideas *wrong*, no matter how fatal those ideas are.

The economists never repented their errors of the Great Depression. Today's mongers have learned nothing from the lessons of the past, ignoring them with an infuriating smugness. They will continue to ravage our economy without entertaining a scintilla of doubt, never troubling their minds to read the "Fairy Tales" of "Dr. Feelgoods" who are "beyond discussing things with." What is stranger is the respect accorded them by their victims. People who send money to Ross Perot are like people about to be beheaded who press a gold coin into their executioner's hand. Perhaps they think Ross's folksy wit will make the blow that destroys their own job more sudden and painless.

## POKE 'EM TILL THEY HOLLER

We cannot continue to allow the deficit mongers to ignore the arguments against them as cavalierly as they ignore the suffering they caused in the Great Depression and are causing now. They all, like Michael Kinsley, prefer to dismiss the arguments against themselves with a wave of the hand: "There's no point in arguing with those who believe the deficit is not a serious problem."[4] The mongers have gotten away with ducking and running, without ever once explaining why the deficit *is* such a serious problem, because *we have let them* get away with it. Recently, *Firing Line* featured a "debate" on the deficit. The people supposedly *against* deficit hysteria included Lester Thurow, who is regularly in print saying the deficit *is* a huge problem. In two hours, no one asked the critical question that humiliated George Bush: "How have you personally been hurt by the deficit?"

The deficit mongers cannot answer the arguments made here. Read the reviews and critiques of this book if you don't believe me, and judge for yourself. Better yet, watch or listen to open debate between me and the mongers, presuming any have the guts to try to uphold their bankrupt ideology once they know what they are up against. Right now, I cannot get anyone to stand up to me in the talks I give. The organizers ask around for an old economist to argue with me, and at first one or two will be interested, when all they know is that some guy is going to say the deficit is a myth. But then they get ahold of a copy of chapter 1, which I have been passing out for some time. Suddenly they find a schedule conflict which unfortunately prevents them from taking part—and being made a fool of.

Try it yourself, if you can tie one down long enough. Just three questions will get them sidling out the door, in my experience:

- What is scarce besides money and jobs—so what good is the old science of "the allocation of scarce resources"?
- Why shouldn't we print enough money to match the real wealth we already have, as long as it doesn't cause inflation?
- Exactly how have you or anybody you know ever been hurt by either the bogeyman or the deficit—compared to the hurt caused by taxes and unemployment?

They won't come on stage if they think they can protect their honor by hiding. They would greatly prefer to bluster authoritatively to their own kind, assuming their own conclusions about the deficit. Remember, senior professionals in any field never change their minds based merely upon facts and common sense. Thus, they have no reason to consider, much less debate, *anyone's* new ideas, including these. The only reason they will come out is to protect their wounded vanity, *if* it can be wounded deeply enough. That is the second reason I have done my darndest to insult them up one side and down the other. Not only do they deserve it for the great harm they cause, but they will only take the field if they are publicly slapped in the face. For them to refuse to argue is an admission of intellectual guilt or of cowardice. You decide which.

## OH, NO! A NEW IDEA!

Everybody *says* they want new ideas, but whenever a new idea comes up, everyone's first instinct is to presume it is nonsense. I'm not complaining. It's a fact of life, like gravity—and despite gravity, we still have airplanes and Michael Jordan. The instinctive reaction of absolutely everyone to whom I have presented these ideas over the last two years, including my wife, has been disbelief. And if people had only two seconds to decide whether to spend the next half hour figuring out what "the myth of the deficit" is all about or watching "Roseanne," I wouldn't get many takers. In a sense, normal inertia puts everybody on the side of the deficit mongers at first, because we all keep our old ideas until we are forced to muster up the energy to consider changing them.

By sharply criticizing the old ideas and the deficit mongers who preach them, I am only doing what is absolutely necessary. Any new idea starts off swimming upstream against a tremendous flow of indifference, inertia, and intellectual laziness. As common sense and obvious as many of these ideas are, they are in fact new to the present debate, and I don't want you lumping them in with the old wisdom. Whether or not you end up persuaded by these arguments, I want you to see that I am *widening the range* of the debate. The best answer to any problem is found by searching among the widest range of possible answers, and I am broadening the range as much as I can. If I could be any more extreme, if I could purposely go beyond what I think is absolutely true in order to make my point, I would. In fact, I will do so, in the next chapter. After long thought, reading, analysis, and debate, I am convinced that everything I have written is dead-on accurate. In chapter 13, I go outside of any expertise I have in order, as I say there, to provoke the people with real expertise (e.g., in the environment or child care) to plan how to improve the post-deficit world.

I want you to understand that I am not saying that what you used to believe about the deficit is fundamentally all right, and this book will fine-tune the details. *No*. The old economics is *wrong*. The new economics I propose is different. It is a science focused on the nation, not a science of the household budget—which is what "economics" means ("household science"). Call it national economics, or nationomics, for short. You will have to get it from this book. While many of the new ideas agree with some other people's work, the following ideas in particular are different: balancing money and real wealth; cybernetic economics; econo-rexia; the nature of real wealth; and the destructive power of bad ideas.

*The new economics I propose is different. It is a science focused on the nation, not a science of the household budget—which is what "economics" means ("household science"). Call it national economics, or nationomics, for short.*

## What an Entertaining Show!

For Tom Clancy or a stand-up comic, entertaining you with words is an end in itself. This book has attempted to be engaging, even amusing at times—but only as a means to an end. If you fall asleep or your mind wanders while reading, it doesn't matter how accurate the ideas are. They will stay on the page, where they don't do anybody any good. Every stylistic choice has been made to further the goal of bringing the ideas from the page into your head, where they might do the economy some good. To that end, I have put more thought into using vivid examples like BillyBucks or images like the Golden Idol than does any other economics writer. If you passively read *every* book the way you read a mystery, starting at word one and never skipping a word till the end, and then fail to get past chapter 2 because it is too depressing, or chapter 6 because parts are too technical, I fear you would not have been the kind of reader I am counting on. I have written for the man or woman of action. Anyone who will take the initiative to discuss these ideas, write to his representatives, or work for change in the other ways outlined in this chapter will also, I presume, possess the initiative to tackle this book on his own terms.

Thus, I have written too much, rather than too little, trusting that the kind of readers I am trying to reach will do their own editing, because each of them will edit the book in his or her own way. You're right—some of the examples are repeated or redundant. That's intentional; an idea will sink in for one person one way and another person in another, so I've included two versions. One main charge against economists is that they are not specific enough—for example, ask the mongers exactly where the new jobs are coming from. I've given you the specifics. When you've had enough, I trust you have skipped on ahead.

The specifics I have edited out have been the math and the jargon of academically respectable, sterile analysis. I studied calculus at MIT, taught statistics at Berkeley, and proposed a mathematically complex approach to subjective probability in my Ph.D. dissertation (the effect of "skew second-order distributions"). I assure you, I am not ducking the math. I can write in as much math-ese as anyone would like. Also, I spent the requisite five years writing the high jargon necessary for academic publications and tenure. Not this time. You should have learned in college that the more complex and hard-to-read the writing, the tinier the idea. Those who have nothing to say want to at least *sound* intelligent while saying it. I have aimed at having real substance that sounds simple rather than vacuous nonsense puffed up to sound important.

Back to the deficit mongers. I must confess to a tinge of shame over my shock-radio, Rush Limbaugh treatment of those folks. The most difficult strategic choice in the writing of this book and for the tenor of the public presentations has been how confrontational and adversarial a stance to take. I feared I was being inconsistent with my own idea of cooperative, win-win approaches to solving the problems of our economy. After all, if national economics proposes that liberals and conservatives, Democrats and Republicans, rich and poor, young and old, etc., are *not* at odds over dividing up our great pie of abundance, if we must not distract ourselves by arguing over who gets what at the expense of the other—then why can't I bring the old deficit mongers into the happy family of common interests? They too are patriotic human beings and kindly to their grandchildren.

Hitler, Mao, and Pol Pot were tremendous patriots and kindly to their grandchildren as well (Stalin was a bastard to everyone). I am not criticizing the mongers' kindness at home or in church. I am criticizing their destroying our economy and ruining the lives of millions of Americans. Such wanton cruelty as they have inflicted, and would inflict in even greater measure if not stopped, cannot be given kid-gloves treatment.

Listen at any party or talk show. People are comfortable with the notion that there are good guys and bad guys as far as the economy is concerned. I have not invented the concept of *the enemy* for the first time in this book. In fact, many people *need* an enemy, need to know explicitly who the bad guys are, in order to be motivated to work for a good cause. Half of the votes in a democracy might be directed *against* one candidate more than for the other. People are already angry, and people already envision economic enemies at every turn. (Later in this chapter I will defend the innocents who are being wrongly excoriated.) For that substantial proportion of the citizenry who are motivated to act by knowing who their enemies are, I have given them their enemies list. What is shocking is that this list does not contain the usual suspects—the prez, Congress, foreigners, fat cats, unions, etc. Rather, the list contains a bunch of old fogies generally thought to be the upright consciences of sound economic policy. The identity of the culprits is only surprising because these gray advisers had seemed mere obedient mind-servants of the real bosses; but should you be so surprised that, in effect, the butler did it?

## BAH HUMBUG! I AIN'T BUYING ANY OF THIS CLAPTRAP!

If I had to rely on a jury of twelve of my peers to convict me of being right about the deficit, I would have quit before I began. Jury selection demands its members be free of preconceptions about the guilt and innocence of the accused, but no one is free of preconceptions about the economy. And too many people are proud of the fact that, once they have an opinion, any opinion, they never change their mind. You know the type. They have never changed an opinion, much less admitted they were wrong, in their entire lives.

So I know that virtually *no* hard-core deficit mongers will change their minds *one bit*. They wouldn't change their minds if God spoke to them from a burning bush while attended by the Archangels, so they won't change their minds for me. Few of them will buy the book, because in general they only buy books that support their preconceptions—check out their bookshelves if you don't believe me.

A sure tip-off on who the hard-core, tight-money fanatics are is their response to the Parable of the Cancer Cure. The parable has been carefully constructed so that the key to solving the dilemma is simply to *print more coupons*. You may try to argue that the parable does not apply to the U.S. economy (you'll still lose), but there is no arguing that thirty-seven hundred people die without the cancer medicine, *only* because too few coupons have been printed. So I am constantly amazed and amused at how some people cannot force their mouths to utter nor their minds to conceive the words "Print more coupons." Perhaps they see what's coming, and don't want to get trapped into agreeing to print more *money*, which is against their religion. Or they don't like doing "more" of anything. At any rate, they are so dogmatically rigid that, even after the right answer has been explained, they cannot repeat it. Everyone else will understand the parable and will be interested in moving on to judge the point I am making, but the econo-rexics sit frozen, saying nothing or gaping like fish out of water. Some have tried to sidestep the obvious by jumping to secondary issues, such as how to increase production next year—which will also expire unused on the shelves if too few coupons are printed. One came up with the novel solution of printing *no* coupons at all and dumping all of the medicine! Tight money is the answer to *all* problems, in the minds of true-blue, anti-government old economists.

But we're not giving up on them. The point of this book, and of your discussions with them (*arguments*, I hope) will not be to persuade them of anything, because that cause is futile. Rather, the point is to *shut them up*, or at least stifle their enthusiasm for further deficit mongering in public. Right now they are pretty full of themselves. As one of them notes, "Deficit reduction may never be this trendy again."[5] We need to buck the trend.

I have found that you cannot turn a bully into a nice person, but you can scare him into not pushing the decent folk around. The deficit bullies can be left behind on the scrap heap of history. There is no need to save their economic souls. I want this book to give them pause when they are tempted to rant against the deficit in public. I want them to remember that the last time they started lecturing (outside the family dinner table), they ran into this one disagreeable person (you) who had some damnably aggravating arguments about the *real* deficit between money and wealth. The old monger knew you must be wrong, and tried to bluster and bully you, but knew he wasn't answering your arguments at all. Worse, he realized the other people at the bar or on the train *knew* he was merely blustering, and that his answers were missing the point.

Not all of the mongers will be smart enough to shut up when they see what they are up against. The biggest fools among their number will be our greatest allies. As one philosopher observed, "The best way to argue *for* an idea is to argue *against* it—*badly*." In some debates you might see me in, I will let a monger go on a bit long, and you may wonder why I'm not cutting him off and objecting to some egregiously silly point he is making. I'll let him ramble in order to hang himself with his own words, interjecting only to encourage him to elaborate on the foolish position he is trying to take. When I'm most disciplined, I'll let him pontificate aimlessly until his fellow audience members interrupt him: "Get on with it! Either make a point, ask a question, or shut up." This has already happened.

Ideally, the most well-spoken mongers will be the ones smart and chastened enough to curb their tongues, protecting their honor by deserting the field of battle. Only the most stubborn, hell-for-leather, I-don't-give-a-damn-what-anyone-thinks mongers will slog through the swamp of their own devise, attacking against all odds my position on the high ground. I shall welcome their brave offense.

## VOTING AND LOBBYING

Not many full-blown deficit mongers attend my talks, and some of those who do are there by mistake—they misread the title of the lecture ("The National Debt: Fact or Farce?") and think I am going to attack the *deficit*, not the deficit *hysteria*. By definition, the people who voluntarily leave their television, compact disks, and good books to pay to hear some guy they never heard of talk about (yawn) the national economy—these people are more than intellectually alive, well educated, and clearly on the smart end of the spectrum. These people are also open-minded enough to at least entertain the possibility of a new analysis of the economy, to give that guy they never heard of a chance to tell them something they haven't heard before. They are the fairest audience someone with new ideas could hope for. As I tell these audiences, democracy exists because of people like them. If I can't persuade people who have voluntarily come to hear something new, who by virtue of their own self-selection tend to be intelligent and open-minded, maybe these ideas aren't worth listening to, and a new national economics doesn't have a chance.

In fact, the best part of my life is seeing how many people *are* persuaded. People pay close attention, ask relevant and challenging questions, and—this is the litmus—they change their minds. Many have been already suspicious of the prevailing idiocy of high taxes and low spending, and my analysis gives them the specific answers they have been wanting to hear. In an hour or two of discussion, even before they had this completed book to read, people's votes were changed. They would not be tempted to vote for higher taxes and the closing of the police department, against all self-interest and common sense, in the Golden-Idol cause of deficit reduction. Some go further than I propose here—"Why only 1 percent?" they ask. These people I encourage to go beyond me, to improve upon and challenge the boundaries of the economics outlined here. The best ones ask what they can do to bring these ideas to others.

If people leave this book or a presentation convinced, but don't *do* anything about it, my efforts have failed. People in this country are suffering only because of errors in our political economy. The economy can only be changed politically. Changed minds must result in changed votes, and changed votes must bring us new political leadership. The president alone is not enough. We must change the minds—or the members themselves—of both houses of Congress.

## WE'RE SUPPOSED TO CHANGE *WHOM*?

Who's the most important person to change? The president? Your senator? Or li'l ol' *you*? The answer is—*you*, the readers of this book, the voters comprising our democracy. Our leaders won't change until you do. If you read this book, agree with every word, and then stay home November 2, vote a straight party ticket, or focus on a single issue like abortion rights, gun control, or the candidate's race, then you *deserve* to pay higher taxes and lose your job. I hope for your sake that you are so consoled by your filial duty to the family political party or your special interest that you don't mind writing out that extra big check to the IRS, or standing in line at the unemployment office until your benefits run out. I have already confessed to all of the tricks I have used to activate you to change and act, beyond just a dry recital of the economic facts. If you read this and say, "Gee! He's right—that deficit baloney really is all wrong," but then you don't change your behavior, nothing will have been accomplished.

Some cynics cop out. "What we the people do doesn't matter," they say. "The people on top don't give a damn about the little man, and the whole world is in the grip of you name it—capitalist pigs, the international Zionist conspiracy, the Trilateral commission, the liberal Eastern establishment, etc." *Hogwash*. People who declaim the impotence of the American voter lie in the face of the facts. Their fatalism is appropriate for some ancient religion, for times when cruel kings and pestilence ravaged helpless humanity at will. But now their fatalism only serves their laziness. Look at them—their cynicism, their pessimism may depress *you* when you have to listen to them, but it is plain that they are not depressed. By blaming every problem upon a vague group of big guys, they take themselves off the hook, they give themselves an excuse to stay home watching TV on voting day, just one more excuse to blame everything wrong with their lives on somebody else. You know this type as well.

The fact is that our leaders do respond to their constituents, almost to a fault. What is the one group in American society that cannot be crossed in any congressional vote? A group that a century ago was entirely powerless, and often destitute. But now our senior citizens—don't call them "old folks"—have earned an ever-growing stock of money and power. And they've earned it through AARP—the American Association of Retired People, the strongest lobbying organization in the history of democracy.[6] How did they get their power—by sympathy, as with the disabled? No. More through the simple but absolute power of the ballot box. As a candidate, if you talk about cutting Social Security, you just might as well resign from the race. Our senior citizens take the time to read what's going on and go to the polls to vote. Surprise—they get what they want. And they'll get their benefits cut if they let the mongers weaken their resolve.

Just listen to our candidates and elected officials stumbling all over themselves trying to say and do everything they can to pander to their constituencies. We frequently poke fun at them for doing so, criticizing them for saying one thing to one group of voters and another thing to another, in an attempt to remain in everyone's good graces. But the same cynics who will complain the loudest one minute about our leaders' lack of integrity will complain the next about how hopeless it is to get anything done to help this country. What sense does that make? If, as is plain, our leaders jump at the voters' whim, whose fault is it if they jump in the wrong direction or don't jump at all? We have to tell them where to go, and telling them all to go to hell will only result in sending ourselves there after them.

Listen to the awful things we say about our political leaders. The jokes are so continuous and vicious you cannot say people are merely "making fun" of our leaders. Again, the rhetoric of president-bashing reminds me of nasty adolescents complaining about their parents. Ask the jokesters what they would do differently, and you get no more sensible answer than "Give me everything I want and damn the consequences!" Worse, you get the answer proposed by Bob Dole—no answer at all. So you hated Bush—what would you have had him do differently about the economy, before you read this book? So you hate Clinton—what do you propose he do, presuming that the deficit reduction god must be fed? It might make you feel superior, like a big shot, to vilify our leaders, but it accomplishes nothing else. One of the first things Clinton tried to do after the election was pass a measly $16 billion spending package. It foundered miserably on the shoals of Deficit Reduction. Did you write our president in support? Will you vote against the senators who voted for spending cuts that cost us thousands of good jobs? Did you even talk to your friends about how we needed those jobs for the good of this country? Our political economy won't change until our voters change their ideas about the political economy. You're a voter. The ball is in your court, and it will stay there until you take a whack at it.

## DON'T BLAME THE INNOCENT

How foolishly off the point it is to treat our president and Congress like enemies of the people, when they are scrambling to do whatever they can to satisfy the whims of us, their constituents. Another reason I have been so hard on the deficit mongers is that I want you to put the blame where the blame is due. Real enemies do exist, and they, ironically, have survived not only without the blame they deserve but with widespread respect, just as the British General Douglas Haig did during and long after World War I was over, even though his butchery was apparent for all to see. Instead, many blame their politicians. Others blame themselves. The millions who lose their jobs in a deficit-reduction recession have done nothing wrong. Think of the defense industry engineer or assembly line worker laid off as his share of the Peace Dividend. He is no more guilty than was an old-time warrior who ran the Huns so far out of the country that his tribe decided they didn't need defenders anymore—and who then fired the warrior without giving him any other job to do. Don't blame our unemployed, especially if you're one of them yourself.

*At least blaming the president or ourselves is relatively harmless. After running off one more one-term president, we'll get another—it's not as though we'll have no president at all. The next one, if he's stuck with the cause of deficit reduction, will fare no better, but on average we won't be any worse off.*

At least blaming the president or ourselves is relatively harmless. After running off one more one-term president, we'll get another—it's not as though we'll have no president at all. The next one, if he's stuck with the cause of deficit reduction, will fare no better, but on average we won't be any worse off. Some people who blame themselves feel so bad they commit suicide (as did Gino, one of my unhired MBA graduates), but others might be motivated to change things, and they will help this country get going again (especially after reading this book, I hope). Human misery increases for those who inaccurately blame themselves, but their misery might not harm the rest of us too directly.

But hating the Japanese, NAFTA, or our hard-working fellow Americans for imaginary evils can cause permanent and dangerous harm. Just as in the Depression, American economic leaders squeeze the money supply until we suffer an American recession, and then try to blame the rest of the world for it. In the 1930s we passed the Smoot-Hawley Trade Act, raising tariffs and international tension to the point where world war was a natural consequence. Now we want to blame the Japanese and Mexicans for stealing our jobs. Look around you and think again about the source of your problems. The Japanese made your VCR, built the car factory nearby, and buy more stuff from us per capita than we buy from them. The Mexicans want the opportunity to make things for us cheaply, so they can buy expensive things from us with the money they earn. They have added to the wealth of this country. On the other hand, how have the deficit mongers added a cent of value to our public storehouse? By squeezing the money supply, they have caused our wealth to rot in the storehouse, to gather dust on the shelves. We wrongly blame our international friends who help produce our common wealth and ignore the wrong-headed money engineers who cause that wealth to go to waste.

Yes, we have enemies, but we have to know who they are—Alan Greenspan, Wayne Angell, Ross Perot, Warren Rudman, Paul Simon, Phil Gramm, et al. They are *not* the Japanese or Germans—those guys were our enemies when they were shooting bullets at our soldiers, not when they are sending us cars and televisions. Our enemies list should also *not* include our hard-working fellow Americans. Union members are fighting a losing battle to retain the spending power the whole country needs. Our managers are blamed for downsizings they know are hurting their beloved companies, body and soul. But with their potential customers unemployed and penniless, everyone has to downsize just to survive. Many of our government workers are already grossly overworked—just check your parole officers or the local office of the INS—but have to listen every day to demands for cuts in evil government spending. To listen to people talk about our national educational system, it is a wonder any of us can read, much less access our spreadsheets. At the same time, highly educated people of all stripes are fired, some even told they are overqualified for the miserable jobs they would lower themselves to take. Not a single industry cries for a lack of qualified workers. We have all the education we need, which makes some graduates feel all the worse because they don't have a job to use all that talent and training on. Don't blame our schools for the recession, whatever else you may blame them for.

Several books written in the last few years try to place the blame for America's ills in several directions. All are remarkably off the point. I would be glad to critique them one by one at your request, but they make so many errors that a full critique would take a book as long as this one. Be my guest to do so yourself, based on what you've learned form this book. The most common theme worth debunking is Lester Thurow's (and others') castigation of our industry for poor international "competitiveness." Their general gripe is that this country cannot make things well enough for other countries to want to buy them. What a load of bunk. They pick on a very narrow range of high-tech manufactured products, items from previous stage of the industrial age, like cars and electronics. All our ills were due to the Japanese and Germans being able to make this stuff better than we can, they say.

Wrong on every level. Although manufacturing is important, it represents a shrinking portion of economic activity, just as farming devolved to secondary status a generation ago. We lead in medicine, entertainment, education, scientific research, and the world's currently leading industry—tourism. Manufacturing will always be important, yes, just as farming is—but it is increasingly within the range of ability of every small and formerly backward country to do it themselves, so there will be less and less money in it.

And anyway, it turns out we *do* manufacture as well as anybody. The ink is barely dry in the poor-competitiveness books as we find American cars taking the value lead not only here, but overseas as well. Our labor productivity has become the highest. The vaunted Japanese competitiveness initiative in HDTV cost tens of billions and came up empty in the face of our free-market approach. According to the competitiveness guys, we should be swimming in dough by now, because we did exactly what they said we needed to do. But what good does it do to make great cars, if no country on earth has the money to buy them?

Blaming us for not making good enough cars when, first, our cars are great, and, second, the world has a wonderful abundance of cars no one can afford to buy, is worse than a waste of time. It's like blaming a man for not working hard enough, if he were working eighty hours a week and earning more money than he could spend—and in the meanwhile, his family was falling apart due to his absence. There is no point blaming the producers of the world when our problem is insufficient consumption. There is no point making enemies of nations that want to help us produce more wealth, when the problem is letting ourselves use and enjoy the wealth we have already produced. Don't vent your energy on the innocent when the real enemies are laughing at you from beyond the next hedgerow, ready to fire another round into you while you are looking in the wrong direction. Give credit where credit is due—to your fellow hardworking citizens and the people around the world who have bought into the dream we gave them of Western free enterprise, all of whom have filled the shelves with remarkable wealth. Put blame where blame is due—on the monetarily bloodletting econo-rexics who tax away our ability to buy that wealth and who fire the people who only want to help make and buy more. Blame Alan Greenspan and Warren Rudman, not your fellow victims.

## YOU WANT ME TO CHANGE MY *MIND*? I'D RATHER CHANGE MY *GENDER*

It's not easy to change minds, but it's not as impossible as it would be to fix many other kinds of problems. For example, it's not like demanding a cure for AIDS. The well-organized victims of this horrible disease have done everything in their power to mobilize popular and governmental support for their humane cause—a medical cure for an unexpected plague. They have succeeded to a remarkable degree in gaining both the sympathy and financial support of non-victims, a degree of support rare in human history. Since the mid-1980s, more money has been spent on AIDS research than on any other disease, more than on diseases such as cancer that threaten and kill even greater numbers of people than AIDS does. But what is the result? Everyone who gets infected still dies, slowly and in terrible pain. Due to AZT and other amelioratives, many live longer before dying. Many more have saved themselves through widespread and strict behavioral changes. But the medical breakthrough everyone desired simply hasn't occurred, and may never be found. Society at large might benefit more from AIDS research than the AIDS victims themselves will, due to what we're learning about viruses in general. All the king's horses and all the king's medicines haven't saved a single life, as far as I know.

Changing minds is also a lot easier than recovering from a nuclear war or giant meteorite. Say we found out tomorrow that an asteroid was headed this way, about as large as the one that wiped out the dinosaurs. It would land in a month. Now *that* would be a problem. We all might end up dead. The same with a nuclear holocaust. If Abdel-Rahman's followers wanted to improve on the job they did at the World Trade Center, and they got ahold of a modest-size nuclear bomb, all they would have to do is detonate it in Moscow. Moscow has a Dr. Strangelove-type fail-safe system which would automatically launch a retaliatory strike against guess whom. We, of course, would have to retaliate or preempt their incorrect "retaliation," and before you can say "cinder," the biosphere has a pollution problem you wouldn't believe. Again, *that* would be a real problem. (Of course, if we were not enslaved by deficit-think, both threats could be eliminated. See chapter 13. But first things first. The point of this book is to eliminate deficit-think.)

Fortunately, the economy is not threatened by problems as intractable as those presented by AIDS, an asteroid, or nuclear holocaust. We have an abundance of wealth. Our problem is of our own making, like bloodletting and the carnage of World War I. All it takes to liberate our wealth is a good idea, an insight, the correction of a complete misunderstanding.

## WHY WOULD A POLITICIAN CHANGE FOR THE *BETTER*?

This one's easy. Asking politicians to vote for lowering your taxes and increasing spending should be like convincing water to flow downhill. Why are our political leaders threatening to commit the unnatural act of stealing your money with both hands, by raising your taxes while reducing spending and services? Because they're afraid of *you*. Because they think *you want* them to take away your money. Because they read polls in which *you* say the number one problem facing this nation is the National Debt. Remember, these people really are our slaves. Watch them kissing babies and remembering everyone's name twelve hours a day. They would vote to spend a trillion dollars to chase the bogeyman if the polls said you thought it was our number one problem, a bunch of gray-haired experts agreed—and no one objected (hint: similar to what's happening with the deficit hysteria).

Right now they are terrified of what *you* will say if they do the right thing, if they lower taxes and keep needed services. All they need is a reason to do the right thing, all they need to know is that there is an economic and moral case to be made for doing the right thing. All they need to see are a few letters in their mailbag asking them to care about what really matters and stop wallowing in the deficit hysteria. The existence of this book and the support of its readers by itself can have a substantial effect on the current leadership, if you make your support clear to them. At present, they have no answer to the deficit mongers when the mongers demand another pint, another charge at the machine guns, another tax hike, another thousand workers fired. Our leaders need two kinds of answers. The first kind is the ideas themselves, here in the book. The second answer is the poll results and the letters from constituents—letters from people like *you*.

We are not asking them to change their religion, sex, or political party. The most important change is in their attitude, a change measurable in their votes on specific issues. The attitude change required is valuing the wealth of this country and its people above that of the current Golden Idol, the "federal deficit." Even if they don't understand or agree with this book completely, they should at least entertain doubts about the general faith in the deficit bogeyman. These doubts should help push them over the line to vote correctly on tax and spending issues. Politicians have to believe with all their heart that they absolutely *must* increase your taxes or cut your services before they dare to cast such unnatural votes. Undercut that heartfelt belief, and watch their votes change.

■

*Asking politicians to vote for lowering your taxes and increasing spending should be like convincing water to flow downhill. Why are our political leaders threatening to commit the unnatural act of stealing your money with both hands, by raising your taxes while reducing spending and services? Because they're afraid of you. Because they think you want them to take away your money.*

■

The votes will change all the faster if they know that waiting in the wings is a challenger for the next election who definitely *will* vote for lower taxes and better services. Of course, most challengers say they'll do the right thing when they're on the hustings, but fall prey to the prevailing deficit hysteria once they've won our confidence and the election. But a challenger with solid reasons to cut taxes and raise spending, with a number of letter-writing supporters—*that* will get the attention of your faithful representative in Washington. The fact is, they stand to lose the office they have striven all their lives to attain. It happens every election. Special-interest money and the incumbency are powerful supports, but a challenger with a vision greater than their own, with a clear-cut plan to lower taxes and bring more federal money back home.... Count on it. They will sit up and take notice.

## I SLEPT THROUGH CIVICS. TELL ME AGAIN—HOW DOES THE SYSTEM WORK?

Even if you stayed awake, the class may have skipped over the most important ideas. What they taught you about state versus federal systems, the separation of powers, the judiciary, etc., was important, yes. But most important is *what the people do* in a democracy. Democracy depends on an educated and involved citizenry. That's part of the reason you had to go to school—in monarchies and dictatorships, for example, the leaders prefer a largely illiterate populace. The fact that you are reading this book proves that the system worked in this regard, at least for you. You are interested in the ideas guiding your country, and you are willing to pay money to spend hours reading, possibly changing your minds and your votes.

You are the democratic elite, the opinion leaders in your immediate society. (Admit it, don't be modest.) What you say—or don't say—matters, even if only a little bit. When you talk to your family and friends, they are listening. Don't think they have to raise their hand and say, "Gee. I never thought of it that way before. You've completely changed my mind" to prove you have had an effect. With good ideas as well as bad, a little bit goes a long way, even if you don't see the effects immediately. So the first thing you have to do is what many of my readers have already done—simply keep discussing the economy, throwing in a few ideas from here that people haven't heard before, being the reasonable and well-informed friend you always have been.

Just because you are in fact an elite, don't sell any of your friends and family short. Economics is not like nuclear physics, beyond the ken of everyone but specialists. Anybody who can read—heck, anyone who can talk and who possesses a modicum of common sense—is able to see through the deficit hype after even a brief introduction to a new point of view. The barrier is not IQ level or years of schooling, but rather a history of having ever listened to a new idea or not. Anyone who actually listens to you when you're talking—as opposed to those who are only waiting for you to stop so that they can start in again—is a likely prospect for economic conversion. This includes most young people. Remember, just because they don't *say* they've changed their minds does not mean they've ignored you. And even if they don't change their minds one iota, you have accomplished a major end if you can shut them up a little bit when they would otherwise be inclined to pontificate about the demon deficit themselves. Quieting the propounders of bad ideas is almost as important as spreading new ones.

This is the day of the media and the talk show. You've probably heard these ideas debated on one already. Don't passively let everyone else do the talking. Phone in yourself. You will enjoy being the one the others can't answer sensibly. If you attend a talk by a deficit monger, be sure to stand up and ask him the kind of questions that make him squirm, meaning anything from chapter 6. You won't be able to make your own case from Part III unless you're on the stage with him, but you want to let members of the audience know the monger can't answer some straightforward questions. Don't expect to change his mind a bit. He will bluster on the louder and more forcefully the more you draw blood with your points. Just ask, sit back, and let the rest of the audience draw their own conclusions.

What if you have no local programs to attend? Try to organize one yourself. This may be as easy as a call to the local college. They often have a speaker series and are eager for new ideas about whom to invite. Call the radio station and ask when they schedule the economy and deficit as topics on their talk shows. If I'm in town, I'll show up for free, but don't wait for me—get someone to debate a local deficit monger, or try it yourself. Honest, once you've tried upholding these ideas in open debate against the bankrupt philosophy of the old economics, your friends probably won't be able to drag you off the stage.

Check the opinion columns of your local newspaper. Every week or so a columnist will discuss some aspect of the economy. Write back to the paper and set them straight. Or write directly to a local columnist with a sharp idea or two. Even if he disagrees, even if he himself criticizes or scorns every new idea he hears, you will have accomplished something important by widening the public debate.

You have a local public access cable television station. They are hungry and eager for interesting programming. Either become part of an existing program on the economy, or propose your own economic discussion as part of a series they undoubtedly have on current issues.

## I Think Better than I Talk or Write. What Can I Do?

Okay, maybe I am indulging in a bit of wishful thinking in the above section. I see and talk with so many well-spoken citizens in the course of my presentations that I've got the impression a lot of people could do the job I'm doing as well or better than I'm doing it myself. Some indeed will. If you, however, never talk to a single friend about this book, much less go on TV, you can accomplish the most important effect entirely on your own: *vote*. For whom? For the candidates who will tax less and spend more. Vote *against* anyone making a cause of deficit reduction, who has signed "the pledge to reduce the deficit" or who supports Paul Simon's balanced budget amendment.

And write to those you intend to vote against. Yes, I know you just said you can't write well. You don't have to write more than a few words to catch your representative's attention. Copy this down:

> "I won't vote for you if you vote to [version 1] raise my taxes by supporting [a tax-raising issue] or [version 2]

> cut spending on [a vital local service]. Sincerely, [your name]. The address is simple: Senator [or Representative] Doe, Washington D.C. 20515."
> Or, phone (202) 224-3121 (Senate) and (202) 225-3121 (House).

That's all it takes. The vital words are "I won't vote for you." That gets right to the point. Whatever else you say doesn't matter a tenth as much as that. You are a voter. You have power. Use it.

## HOW RELENTLESSLY NEGATIVE! *WHOM* CAN I SUPPORT?

I like you. You may not believe it after the roasting I keep giving the deficit mongers, but I usually follow the adage, "If you don't have something nice to say, don't say anything at all." Unfortunately, it is immoral to stay politely silent in the face of Hitler, the British generals, bloodletting—or the economic savages ruining our economy, when you can explain why they are wrong. But the hard-core mongers are a minority, and the majority of our legislators are relatively innocent and tractable running dogs, chasing the trendy bandwagon of deficit bashing. Most of our legislators' votes do support lower taxes and higher spending most of the time.

So write them and say "Thanks" when they do. Even when you intend to voice a criticism in a letter, it's a good idea to start the letter with some positive support for whatever your representative has done right this term. Being too negative will portray you as a constituent irretrievably against him or her, and thus not worth trying to accommodate. If, on the other hand, you are perceived as relatively sympathetic, the legislator will be more anxious to keep your vote.

Also, if you start off nicely, there's more of a chance your representative or an aide will actually read enough of your argument, objection, or request to begin to think about the substance of what you're saying. Piece by piece, letter by letter, you the constituents may help educate your political leaders, even if they don't have time to read entire books like this one. Over time the general theme may sink in. And being nice encourages this sort of learning. A second adage I struggle to apply is, "You catch more flies with honey than with vinegar."

The best honey, if you can afford it, is a political contribution to the representatives who deserve it. Give them ideas, votes, and money. If the one you have doesn't deserve all three, look for another. Someone out there wants to run. Sound them out and encourage them. If you really can't find a single soul who will help us rise our of the deficit mongers' morass, then . . .

## RUN FOR OFFICE YOURSELF

Yes, you. Where do you think politicians come from, another planet? Try out these ideas on people in addition to your friends. Gauge their response. Then ask them to defend the actions of the people already holding office from your district. Admit it: there's a good chance they would vote for you based on your economic position—the most important issue in any non-wartime election. By the time you read this, I intend to have a political action committee able to supply you with moral, tactical, and even financial support. Also, I would be happy to speak on your behalf at my expense about your economic philosophy when I'm in your area. You won't be alone.

The main plea of this chapter is for you to *act*, not just sit and complain. Just as I wish I had a dollar for everyone who says I should write the president, I also wish I had a dollar for everyone who says, "This may very well all be correct, but what's the point? The system will never change." This kind of world-weary, cynical pessimism not only flies in the face of the facts, but is a lazy cop-out, an excuse to do nothing but feel superior and above the fray. Such people use widespread criticism as a substitute for, not a goad to action. People too often vent their best energy in spirited criticism and confrontation. You can have the wit and the vitriol of a Rush Limbaugh, but if you don't have a program of change and action, you're just another entertainer, or an audience member paying twenty dollars to laugh and jeer away the hours.

Life is short. The country needs help. You can do something that matters.

# 13

# Creative Spending in a Secure World

The new economics, unlike the old, offers a clear and positive vision of the future. Once we are freed from the bondage of deficit-think, the people of this nation can begin to create a better future, employing our human and natural resources to improve our world, instead of sitting on our hands watching things fall apart. Three related visions are offered. The first is a smorgasbord of ways for the nation to spend money to create wealth for all. The second is the alternative: the continuing decline and international disasters we will suffer if we remain hostage to the myth of the deficit. The next chapter describes another way to use and distribute our national wealth: the national dividend, akin to the dividends that successful companies pay their stockholders.

***Creative spending programs.*** We can fund national programs for the common good ranging from the obvious to the blue-sky speculative. We can begin to choose how to accomplish obvious social goods like cleaning up the environment and improving our infrastructure, instead of squabbling over which we will let deteriorate most. Instead of making additional painful cuts in spending and entitlements, we instead will have the challenge of figuring out how best to start money flowing through the system, allowing free enterprise demand to guide growth.

***The cost of failure.*** Alternatively, history shows us the tragic costs we will have to pay if we allow our economic anorexics to continue leading us to ruin. The costs of a failure of economic vision are vivid in history. Our tight-money policies in the late 1920s and early 1930s led directly to trade wars. Trade wars distracted us from the cooperation the West needed to nip Tojo and Hitler in the bud. Being cheap led to depression and world war. Massive deficit spending was essential to winning the war. And the third World War was won purely by spending, without firing a shot. We can lose the fourth by following tight money policies, or we can save New York by creating the new security we need to stop terrorism.

## HOW TO SPEND THE MONEY WE NEED TO CREATE

Many of you will be outraged by the spending programs proposed here. Good. Thus far this book has offered sound logical and historical analysis. I will now step out of my area of expertise to speculate in fields in which I have only a layman's knowledge. Some of these speculations are likely to be unrealistic to the point an "expert" may find them humorous. But the point is to get you involved in a higher level of debate, a debate beyond the grim Hobson's choice of which necessary spending program to cut next or which tax to raise.

Right now we are paralyzed by the myth of the deficit. The national economic and social debate ranges only from A to B, rehashing painful dilemmas and leading us nowhere but further into danger. Acting on unfounded fears of the deficit requires some harmful combination of spending cuts and tax increases. In either case, the cure is worse than the disease. And the impotence of the old economic theory is truly bipartisan: both of the political parties are half wrong and half right. I recommend lowering taxes and increasing spending. The Democrats want to increase spending, but they also want to raise taxes. The Republicans want to reduce taxes, but they also want to decrease spending. Ross Perot gets it all wrong: he wants to raise taxes and lower spending. He'd also like a trade war with Japan and a dead NAFTA, making him the Herbert Hoover of the 1990s.[1]

In the debate over which tax to increase, whose entitlement to cut, and how many trade wars to start, there are no experts, and there are no winners. But in the post-deficit age of abundance there are many experts, and it is only a question of which plan wins more. I would hope to provoke you to think, in your own areas of special knowledge, how you could come up with better programs than the ones I propose here.

Even with a great deal more money, it is not easy to create real wealth in the best way. Employing a post-deficit economics of abundance does not mean an automatic end to all of our problems. Life always presents problems; the trick is getting the right class of problems. Having cancer or a dead child is the wrong class of problem; being called to give too many talks or getting sore from too much tennis is the right class of problem. Thus, also for our national economic debate in the future. A family with a lot of money has in general a better class of problems than a family with too little, but they have interesting and challenging problems nonetheless. In that spirit, the following shows you the better class of problem we will have in the post-deficit age of abundance.

The main problem of spending the money we need to create is getting it out of the government's hands and into circulation. There are two general ways to transfer money from the government to the people. First is direct transfer payments, such as Social Security. I will discuss expanding this method via the "National Dividend" at the conclusion of this chapter. The more complicated way is direct government spending on projects, as opposed to giving it to people.

## THE GOVERNMENT PAYS FOR, BUT DOES NOT DO THE WORK

Despite all the respect I showed for our government in chapter 11, I severely doubt its ability to run any normal business well. Government businesses rapidly become entrenched bureaucracies whose main goal is self-preservation. I see government instead in the role of the "big consumer," *purchasing* public goods with the funds it creates. However, we must not let the government actually *do* any of the work itself. The job of the citizenry is to debate what we want to buy for our common good through government spending. The government should serve to create the standards for the goods and services we decide on, and then fairly choose the private enterprises which will contract to do the real work. The model would be road building and defense contracts, not the post office and public schools. Therefore, for all of the following projects I discuss, private business would be expected to compete for contracts to do the real work. The government's job is to *pay and get out of the way.*

## A RENEWED AND IMPROVED INFRASTRUCTURE

The most non-controversial programs would renew our infrastructure, but there will still be plenty of room for debate. My layman's experience with road building, for example, leads me to believe that many projects are dragged out, others are too big for the small repairs that are needed, and still more employ suboptimal materials that wear out faster than other materials on the market.[2] We cannot blame the industry, which reasonably enough wants as much work as it can get. But with all the work that we can get done during post-deficit economics, we will need to upgrade the standards of the construction industry to those of our internationally competitive businesses. Remember, the construction industry has been almost entirely shielded from international competition. Any business shielded from competition is categorically likely to be slack and, thus, relatively easy to improve.

Questions for the infrastructure would include the following: Where do we build roads? Where do we instead repair them? Where, in fact, should we remove them (e.g., in downtown malls or wildlife parks)? Extra initial expense should be allocated towards using longer-lasting concrete and improving the esthetics of the highways. That is, sealing off road noise and danger from neighborhoods as well as putting some greenery on the rights of way themselves. Extra money allocated for safety and beauty (if you can conceive of any road being beautiful) is an investment that pays off as long as the road is used.

The 1993 floods in the Midwest raise a number of problematic issues regarding permanent infrastructure improvements. The same government-subsidized levees that helped protect private farmland served to inundate nearby towns; without the open flood lands to absorb much of the river's flow, downstream cities suffered a higher flood level, which caused the river to overflow their own levees. Also, the wider question remains as to the public good of subsidizing, repeatedly rebuilding, and insuring private ownership and building in coastal or river flood areas.

We should seek more creative solutions to the standard natural disasters. *Every year* some area of the U.S. will be flooded and another will suffer a drought. How pointless is this, given the fact that the Mesopotamians and Romans were building aqueducts thousands of years ago, and today the Israelis have a network of waterways making them the Middle Eastern desert country with the best agriculture. What would be the costs versus benefits of a national water grid, modeled on our power grids? When one area needs extra electricity, for example, due to air conditioning demands in a heat wave, power can be brought from another area that has more moderate temperatures. A water grid would work the same way. As high rainfall began to accumulate in one area of the country and low rainfall in another, we would begin to pipe the excess from where it was a threat to where it was salvation.[3]

As simple and straightforward as this idea sounds, it might be entirely unrealistic for a number of reasons. The size of the pipes might need to be monstrous to be effective, for example, or rights of way may be impossible to obtain. But looking at the extent of our highway system, or noting that Iraq took only two years to rebuild most of its infrastructure after our 1991 bombing, I think that something like a water grid could at least be considered. As I write this, Missouri and Iowa have been slowly inundated for months while the Carolinas are drying up. The disaster has not been a sudden development. Watching the water inch up to the top of the levees has been slow torture to the residents of proud farming families watching their land and homes be destroyed. It certainly could not have hurt, and might have offered crucial help, to have been siphoning off excess Missouri River water and sending it east these last few months.

Of course I am only speculating here. But the point of this chapter is to show the next levels of the national debate we can engage in once we get beyond the blank wall of "deficit" thinking. If not a water grid, we should be considering which forms of long-term, value-added investing we should be undertaking. Even if a water grid cost $100 billion, it might save us the billion or ten we seem to spend every year on a very predictable problem. Following the example of BillyBucks, it would be as though the owner put drainage ditches around the foundation of his building instead of repairing the water damage every year. The spending adds value to the property, as well as saving money by spending money.

A simpler alternative would be digging channels and repositories for excess water. An additional deep channel alongside the major flood rivers is an obvious possibility. More cost-effective would be the denomination of some lowland areas as flood plains. More futuristic would be using underground caverns, some of which are as large as lakes, to receive excess water. It is to our shame that we are still *filling sandbags* as our main defense, and spending our billions to shovel overflow sewage off the streets of Davenport, Iowa.

## A CLEANER ENVIRONMENT

Similarly, a clean environment for our country is as important and valuable as a clean environment for your home. Tolerating a poisoned lawn or a junked auto in front of the house would hurt both your quality of life as well as the market value of what you own. Environmental spending has two main goals: fixing or cleaning up what has already been harmed, and keeping whole what is still all right. In the future we might even aspire to improve that with which we have been blessed.

I am far from expert on environmental issues, and I would look to others to carry out this debate more accurately. I offer only one guiding principle in particular that is open to some controversy. In the age of deficit-dominated thinking, we have tried to charge individuals and businesses for the costs of maintaining and cleaning up our environment. In some cases that is entirely appropriate—criminals should be fined, and manufacturers of dangerous chemicals ought properly to incorporate safety costs into their prices. But the long arm of aggressive laws seeking scapegoats and deep pockets has led to both injustice and inefficiency. Legitimate old-line businesses which had a small amount of their waste hauled by an unscrupulous disposal company to an unapproved site now find themselves put out of business by deep-pockets, retroactive laws repeatedly suing them for twenty-five-year-old violations.[4] At the same time, other cleanup does not get done because no deep pockets can be found.

Thus, the guiding principle I propose is this: because a clean national environment is a classic public good, it should generally be paid for out of public funds. Environmental impact statements should be done at government expense—perhaps even in some cases by government bureaucrats, if it is efficient to keep a cadre in permanent employ. Polluted sites should be first cleaned up at government expense; let the courts decide afterwards if penalties and fees should be assigned to directly guilty parties. Get down to business, and stop wasting seven dollars on overhead for every dollar spent on cleanup.[5]

Perhaps the greatest general threat to the cleanliness of the environment is the creation of energy. The oldest ways are the worst. Wood-burning stoves were a threat to Aspen. Coal brings acid rain as well as black lung and mining accidents. Oil and gas pollution has been somewhat tamed by catalytic converters and the like, but still result in smog alerts in large cities around the world. And nuclear power, while safest on average, has a potential for large-scale disaster which we may never be able to completely defend ourselves against.

But I do not think we need to cut back at all on our use of energy. In fact, we could multiply our use as people climb out of third-world poverty around the globe. And with technology we already possess, we can make all of the energy we want with virtually no pollution. Hydroelectric power is already a mainstay, creating electricity and lakes at the expense of rivers. I don't know that we can build too many more dams, and ultimately may want to remove some of those already in existence. Why? Because there is no theoretical or practical reason not to provide all of our power through wind, sun, geothermal, and renewable resources like grain alcohol. We already have wind farms. Solar cells and panels have merely to be built and improved upon. In ten years we could run all of our automobiles on alcohol or fuel cells, not to mention batteries. The success of the California wind farms demonstrates that the government does not even have to fund these projects—merely giving the industry tax breaks (since rescinded) helped it take off.

Also on the prevention side, government funds could be used to buy special lands in order to preserve, for example, old growth forests, instead of restraining private owners' actions on those lands. Urban lands freed from military use could be, in effect, traded for especially valuable or irreplaceable timber and wetlands.

Beyond preservation is the radical idea that human beings might work to improve the environment they were born with. I know, from living in California and befriending a number of radical environmentalists, that the idea that humans can do anything but destroy the earth constitutes blasphemy. But we can see that the sea and rivers mold the land, that the land overtakes the sea, that the winds blow the soil about, that mountain ranges block the clouds, and warm seas fill the air with moisture. Every part of the environment works to give us life and destroy us with the thousand natural calamities the earth is heir to. Thus, I would say it is in keeping with the natural order that we work to create nature preserves in Africa, future old-growth forests in the Northwest, variable lakes near the Mississippi, and freshwater trout streams where no water has run before. To spend money to create wealth in this fashion makes as much sense as landscaping your own backyard. It adds to the value of your life as it adds to the value of your property.

## Space and the Weather

The environment, like the infrastructure, might best be conceived of as a national security issue in a post-nuclear age. At present, despite all our science, we consider catastrophes like earthquakes and floods to be inevitable. We feel we either have to repair the damage, or abandon whole states (California) or flood plains (within ten miles of the Mississippi, or near any coastline). I expect that two hundred years from now we will move catastrophe theory out of the mathematics departments and make some use of it. Small changes can have massive ultimate effects on world climate, we know. Why not try to change or avert some of those effects, instead of just passively noting them? Perhaps El Nino, the giant current in the South Pacific that affects weather across our continent, could be moved off of its most threatening swirls by the buildup of a single undersea ridge near El Nino's point of origin. Or perhaps simply blasting a canyon through an existing ridge would serve the same purpose more easily.

In two hundred years we should have discovered how to bring rain clouds to the deserts. We already know that if we seed hurricanes we can diminish their landfall force to a fraction, but we don't do it.[6] Why can't meteorology advance from mere passive understanding to a more proactive science? Space stations might develop a practical use: large reflectors might be able to focus the sun's heat into otherwise cold-air banks with the effect that jet streams move, and clouds form over the Sahara. If global warming becomes a problem, we could solve it the same way nature has used to bring the ice ages—with dust in the atmosphere that deflects the sun's rays.[7] I can understand respecting the environment, but letting it destroy us and other species due to a lack of imagination is not the kind of respect it desires or deserves.

*The ultimate security for not only our nation but humankind is to have enough people living outside the earth that even if we blow ourselves up, we as a species will survive. We already have the technology to place a self-sustaining colony on a space station or the moon.*

We are as ready for an asteroid as the dinosaurs were. If we wanted to give NASA something to do, in thirty years we could be ready to blast one off course—if we started today.[8] The ultimate security for not only our nation but humankind is to have enough people living outside the earth that even if we blow ourselves up, we as a species will survive. We already have the technology to place a self-sustaining colony on a space station or the moon. At this point they could not sustain themselves through the generations necessary for the earth to become non-radioactive after a full-scale holocaust. But it would simply be a matter of normal science to expand our exploration of space to the scale necessary for the creation of a permanent small society out of harm's way. It has been a quarter-century since we landed on the moon. Since then, we have convinced ourselves that further exploration is beyond our means. But we have the science and technology, we have the people, and we have the metal ships waiting to be built. If Queen Isabella had had a monetarist advisor, Columbus would have stayed in Spain.

## World Peace

As I already discussed, the source of much of our new real wealth is the peace resulting from the demise of Soviet communism. The value of avoiding war is immense. The main value is the buildings and people *not* destroyed by a war. The secondary value is the resources that do not have to be deployed to avoid a war threatened by a fatally powerful adversary.

We have, half by luck and half by design, accomplished the hardest part of peace: the defusing of our nuclear standoff with the USSR, accurately called Mutually Assured Destruction. To now maintain this peace is, by comparison, so easy that it would be criminal to squander this opportunity to give our grandchildren a world safe from holocaust. Deficit-think threatens to lead us back to war, as I will emphasize later. Here I want only to point out how the printing and spending of U.S. dollars can add continuing real wealth to our country by avoiding the normal human disaster of war while reducing the expense of maintaining our defenses.

The main threat to stability in Russia is not Stalinism or nationalism but their economy. We are currently spending less than 1 percent to help them of what we formerly spent to defend ourselves against them. Spending money to help them means something other than widespread charity. The worst form of help is large grants from our government to theirs. What doesn't get stolen by ex-Soviet bureaucrats just ends up subsidizing the continuation of old central-planning blunders. But we can spend money fruitfully by supporting the private business enterprises that sprout like weeds anywhere in the world where they are allowed to. We can buy goods from new Russian enterprises which follow Western models. We can insure, through our OPIC (the Overseas Private Investment Corporation), the many American businesses willing and eager to brave the disappointments of working with the ex-communists.

The point is that a modest amount of money now could save us the catastrophic costs of waging or defending against a nuclear war later.

A graver threat to our own security than the ex-Soviets is now Islamic fundamentalist terrorism. The bombers might have put a small nuclear device under the World Trade Center if they could have, and within a decade they probably will be able to. Unless we stop them before then. They are honest enemies. They make plain they regard us as "The Great Satan," an "enemy of God," and a central tenet of their religion is that such enemies must be sent to hell, even at the sure cost of their own lives.[9] Even Hitler was not as open and straightforward about his designs against his enemies as the Islamic fundamentalist terrorists are against us, and we must respect their forthright proclamations.[10] To protect ourselves against them will require a vastly different national security effort than that we employed against the Soviets. But that effort, whatever form it takes, will require resources—resources which we must pay for.

The most noble form of that effort would be to build up a store of what business calls "goodwill"—and for which a business pays handsomely when purchasing a rival company. Right now in Somalia and Bosnia we have a challenge which we failed in the 1940s, when we sat idly by as the Germans gassed millions of Jews. We have advanced to the point where we now agonize about what to do. And in Somalia we even accomplished a notable humanitarian act by getting the food out to the innocents during a time of war.

However, that relatively easy triumph of compassion and politics has fizzled, and many in our country preach against it and similar ventures. Why? Because our natural inclination is to follow now the policies that helped save the world during World War I and World War II. That is, we do almost nothing until we then jump in with guns blazing in every direction until all the bad guys are dead. Such a strategy was admirable and effective enough in its day. And halfway measures have indeed caused problems. The failure in Vietnam of the policy of "escalating commitment," as well as the mocking visage of Saddam Hussein on TV after Bush let him off the hook, has reinforced the all-or-nothing approach.

Thus, we look with horror at real genocide in Bosnia while fearing to do anything at all, because of the impossibility of going over and killing all the bad guys. But we have the perfect model for action in what has already happened in Somalia. The United Nations (UN) has made up a better name for it than we did: "Safe Havens." They simply want to create zones in which non-combatants (mostly women and children) will be safe from atrocity and starvation. Creating a Safe Haven does not mean imposing peace or reforming the murderous warriors. It aims only to save the lives of non-combatants. It is what we did in Somalia.

But the UN is impotent to accomplish this good idea. The UN has proven time and time again that some kinds of hard actions are beyond its capabilities, and fielding an effective combat force is one of them. Therefore, I propose we create the Safe Havens ourselves. Although Safe Haven is a better name, we might consider my alternative—"the American Zone"—as a crass marketing ploy to purchase more of the "goodwill" I mentioned earlier. Remember, I am still regarding the money we would be spending in even this most merciful and altruistic of ventures as an investment in our own country's future welfare and strength.

An "American Zone" would be a safe haven for innocent non-combatants in a time of war. It would have one clear-cut objective: saving the lives of innocent people. *That* objective can be accomplished. Objectives would *not* include the following impossible tasks: imposing peace; punishing the bad guys; teaching the nation democratic ideas; setting up free enterprise capitalism; etc. As noble as these further objectives are, they could not be accomplished short of full-scale war, and we showed in Vietnam that they might not be accomplished even then.

Our great success in Somalia began to wither the first day a gung-ho Marine following his new orders shot a sixteen-year-old Somalian boy who appeared to be carrying a gun. The "gun" turned out to be a stick.[11] Since then, the additional, non-protective war measures undertaken by the UN (following our example) have resulted in mobs killing Western journalists after the UN troops attacked the main bad guy in Mogadishu. And the death of a troop of Marines in another ill-fated attempt to capture him.

I propose we restrict our actions to the most pure and unobjectionable: saving innocent lives. We let the country sort out its civil wars on its own as it will, even if that means going communist or choosing a corrupt strongman. Imposing our standards of democracy and free enterprise will not be the point. Look at it from the perspective of the people whose goodwill we want to earn: coming in as an imperialistic hegemon saving people, only in order to convert them to our ways, is *not* a selfless act. It differs little from being taken over by foreigners. They are right to be sensitive to our presence in that case, even if we are saving lives. But a power coming in with a single, unobjectionable goal, to save defenseless women and children's lives, cannot but earn a begrudging respect that could endure for generations. My hope would be that one of these future generations might then develop a version of our democracy. But that would be a hope, not a precondition or goal of our support.

Creating the "American Zone" would seem to be expensive and dangerous, though not so much so as in Somalia. We would have to take and control enough land within the warring country to attract and house all of the innocents who could get there, as well as help them get in. How? I suggest an all-volunteer force consisting of three distinct kinds of American service people.

First would be the military contingent, trained specifically in defensive strategy and attitudes. Most military training implicitly aims at attack, later if not sooner. But the military forces in an American Zone would have to face an entire tour without a single search-and-destroy mission, and without the catharsis that comes from shooting a bad guy. Success would be defined as enforcing the safe zone so effectively, so vigilantly, that the warring combatants would not dare to attack it.

The second kind of American service people would be the Peace Corps. They would work with the noncombatant residents as Peace Corps volunteers have always done: helping to dig wells, administer food aid, build shelters, grow crops, educate the young, and in general tend to the human needs of the noncombatants. They would help humanize our military forces as well, by working in conjunction with them—perhaps even socializing with them. Military volunteers and Peace Corps types would probably do each other both some good by interacting with and ameliorating each other's extremes in a mutual enterprise of humanitarian relief.

The third type of participant might not be necessary. If the warring combatants in the focal country did present a continuing physical threat to the existence and safety of the American Zone, those physical aspects of the threat would have to be defused. By "physical," I mean actual enemy armaments and platoons, as opposed to big talkers and persuasive ideologies. Should the warmakers set up large-bore cannon aimed at the American Zone, we should not wait until the shells strike. When they present a large enough and clearly threatening target, we would use our best military might to take them out. Knowing they could expect such a strike, they ought not to mount one in the first place.

The job of the UN would be twofold. First, we would welcome and encourage them to set monitors to keep us on our toes not to commit any atrocities as we did in Vietnam. If we're not going to be the good guys, there is no point in our being there. If we are acting as we ought, we have nothing to fear, not even unfair reporting. Second, the American Zone hopefully will not have to last forever. The test of our being able to go will be when the people we are protecting no longer want us. Whenever the majority of inhabitants of a zone vote for us to leave, we will. The UN can administer the vote, and we will let them tell us the vote is valid and we must leave. Their desire to get rid of us will itself show our help was a success.

Few nations would want us around forever. I am not proposing we transform the Zones into little Monacos in which the noncombatants have never had it so good in all their lives. Giving them life and safety is all we would aspire to do, unless we actually do want to create a parasite class addicted to American welfare. But the question might nonetheless be asked as to how long and at what cost our occupation would last. The length and cost would depend on the number of countries in crisis and the duration of their wars. But look at what we have been doing for fifty years. We still have large forces in friendly nations like South Korea and Germany, accomplishing essentially nothing. ("Nothing" was sometimes good, in that no one attacked who might otherwise have started a war against our allies.) I challenge any military leader who calls this proposal unrealistic to give me a fraction of the forces we have spread around the globe since 1946 and let me show what we could do with them in Bosnia.

People now laugh at the presumptuous phrase, "New World Order." But the old world order was the mortal embrace of Mutually Assured Destruction. Its fallout was the bipolar tension that supported, with arms and ideology, bloody surrogate conflicts around the globe. These have already begun to decline. I do not advocate having the world's only remaining superpower undertake to enforce order by shooting all of the bad guys. Yes, bad guys are out there—genocidal thugs in the Hitler, Tse-tung, Stalin, Pol Pot, Idi Amin, and Saddam Hussein mold. They will always exist. We could not eliminate them all, even if we tried. I advocate not killing all the bad guys, but rather saving as many of the innocents as we can. We do this not to propagate our own world view, we do this regardless of whether our Western world view is "better" than theirs or not—we save innocent lives for the simple reason that we have the ability to save them. To have such power and nonetheless do nothing is wrong.

Before you think we would have trouble staffing these zones, have your local twenty-year-olds read this and ask them what they would think of being a designated good guy for six months to a year, helping save lives and coming back a modest hero. I and most of my friends would have loved to do something like this when we were that age, risks and hardships and all. Instead, we got Vietnam.

The terrorists who bombed the World Trade Center have a substantial constituency. Hundreds of millions of people hate the U.S., and not without cause. We have indeed taken sides against

Islam in the Middle East, and ignored Moslem distress in Bosnia. Buying their oil is not enough, and empty threats will only make them more dangerous. The main point: Spending money now to do the right thing can prevent a terrorist nuclear bomb from ever going off. Yielding to deficit-think means we will instead pay to rebuild New York and Washington, D.C., after our honest and forthright enemies accomplish their brave intentions.

## HEALTH CARE FOR ALL

How preposterous it is to have convinced ourselves we have a health-care "crisis" when we have an abundance of all of the health care we could use! We have been closing hospitals for a decade due to overcapacity, and we still have more bed space than we need. The fanciest, most modern equipment—magnetic resonance machines and *PET* scanners—is everywhere. Doctors complain that even their incomes are declining. The only reason we have any kind of nursing shortage is our misuse of nurses; many leave the profession due to overwork and disrespect, and the remainder spend much of their time filling out forms, doing paperwork better done by clerical aids. Even hospitals are laying off workers, and the stock prices of health-maintenance organizations (HMOs) and drug companies have fallen.

*If we allow health-care resources to go unused, dying on the shelves like unbought cars and computers, it is not the fault of our health-care system—it is the fault of an economic idea that deifies currency and tight monetary policy above the real wealth that money is supposed to represent.*

Why? The fallacy of deficit-think has convinced us we cannot afford to use the hospitals, machines, and people who already exist and want to serve. Remember again, the real wealth is the health care itself, not the money used to buy it. If we allow health-care resources to go unused, dying on the shelves like unbought cars and computers, it is not the fault of our health-care system—it is the fault of an economic idea that deifies currency and tight monetary policy above the real wealth that money is supposed to represent.

We could, today, subsidize the health-care industry at a basic level that would allow uninsured individuals access to not only the basics, but the optional dental and surgical procedures that our real economy can supply in abundance. Of course, by definition, not everyone in the world can get the "best" doctor, whatever that means. Private insurance and personal decisions will guide those who can afford it and wish to spend much more to get the service they prefer at a substantial premium.

We already let everyone have emergency room service at public hospitals regardless of ability to pay. As inefficient a service this often is—some use it to treat the flu—it is far better than even the best health care available in the non-Western world. We do as much for law. Right now three-quarters of the defendants in our nation's courts are represented by public defenders. While the non-public defenders are probably as a group "better" (whatever that means) than their public counterparts, they have both received largely the same education, and the public defenders might even be better practiced due to their substantial caseloads. The legal system has provided for itself, and no one has seen it lead to the degradation of its service. Blunders are made by private as well as public defenders, of course.

It is not the place of this book to describe in a few paragraphs or pages the outlines of who should be provided what care at public expense. The point is to realize that what we require for health care we already have: the *people*, *hospitals*, and *technology*. Only if we let our obsession with the deficit stop us from using the resources we already command will we create an artificial health-care "crisis" for ourselves.

In fact, the only shortage that does exist in health care—organ donors—could be instantly and easily resolved. Thirty thousand people are presently waiting for organs, and every year twenty-five hundred die before they can get one.[12] The solution:

People needing organs should get first priority based on how long they themselves have been registered as a donor. At first blush you might regard this as heartless—what if a sixty-five-year-old with low chances of survival were to get a vital heart ahead of a twenty-two-year old who had not had time to be a donor as long as the older person? Here's the everyone's-a-winner trick: Few people need organs. The problem now is that even fewer than necessary become donors, because they are offered exactly zero incentives to do so. Given a cost-free but valuable incentive, enough people will then sign up in order to get a higher priority for an organ which only one in a hundred will ever need. So many will sign up, in fact, that there will be more than enough organs to serve even those people who have *not* signed up as donors. It would be that easy.

The health of our people will also be served in the future by our treatment of the very young and very old. As we live to ever-greater ages, we spend more of our later years in a state of dependency. And as more women either want or need to work, our very young people need day care. Our retired people these days command more wealth on average than do our infants, so their challenge to improve nursing home care is perhaps not properly the province of the public sector.

But the care of our nation's children is. Right now the day-care industry is impoverished. The future of an increasing proportion of our nation's children lies in the hands of people paid near minimum wage without benefits.[13] I would not want the federal government to take over the job of day care; but extra money could be used to help. One major issue is the safety of the children in day care. A second-order issue is the safety of day-care workers from false accusations of unbelievable and never-proven "satanic rituals." Both children and workers could be helped by the improvement of the service to include multiple caregivers at all times, as well as the construction of facilities with no closed rooms. Alternatively, we could use the same permanent video cameras (presently recording us at the bank money machine and most check-out lines) to keep both the workers and their accusers honest.[14]

I envision the ideal day-care center as being built in the middle of a retirement community. The senior citizens living there would be more entertained than irritated (I hope) by the sight of the children visible through the windows. Day care as an enhanced version of a day in the park as opposed to daily warehousing would be the aim. A clear federal function could be to certify day-care workers and then take financial and legal responsibility for the one in a thousand or ten thousand who is guilty of bad actions towards the children.

## Rehabilitate the Addicted

Perhaps the most destructive waste of our national wealth, especially human, is the addiction of so many people to drink, drugs, and compulsive activities such as gambling. With the high employment we now take for granted, we don't notice the loss of these people's labor as much as we notice the theft and destruction resulting from the endless drug war. I expect us to come to the same conclusion about the drug war as we did about prohibition: the war on booze (or drugs) leads to greater harms than the booze or drugs themselves. When drugs are decriminalized, related murder and theft will virtually cease. Who murders now for alcohol or cigarettes? The innocent will stop paying the high price we all pay now.

But when drugs are decriminalized, just as gambling has been effectively decriminalized by the proliferation of state lotteries, the number of people who may succumb to the temptations of the vice will rise. But the existence of the temptation does not mean we must give up and accept that people will succumb. We do not have laws against overeating, although we know it is bad for people. But the great majority of people do resist the temptation to overeat or even drink too much without legal sanctions against them.

And we can help millions more fight against the natural human temptations ever at hand. Right now the waiting lists for drug-treatment programs are so oversubscribed that some drug addicts commit visible crimes for which they are easily caught because that is their only way to get treatment before they destroy themselves. (This trick doesn't work in California anymore, because prison drug-treatment programs have been closed in order to balance their budget deficit.) While drug treatment is no more an exact science than is crime prevention, nutrition, or almost anything else, we have learned a lot in the last few decades. People made fun of "Just Say No," but the attitudes of our schoolchildren towards drugs have measurably changed as a result of the campaign. We have developed nicotine substitutes, anti-alcohol drugs, and a fairly effective drug-testing program.

More controversial are the results of expensive detoxification programs. Many people go in only to end up back on drugs. But when the enemy is addiction, any success at all is remarkable. In addition to chemical relief such as methadone, the spiritual self-help approach of the twelve-step industry is noteworthy. The cost/benefit effect of (1) detox, (2) a continuing twelve-step type program, and (3) three-quarter-way houses before returning to the unprotected environment would be, I propose, far higher than the billions of dollars we spend making the Colombian warlords rich with our present "War on Drugs." Read what the British and other European states have done with their addicts. We can do at least as well. And we have plenty of people who want to try. Religious groups can treat people directly, instead of pressuring the government to do their work for them with punitive laws. Psychology majors, now going back for MBAs they don't want, would love to be employed in the restructuring of destroyed lives. And we will need those lives to be back in the work force to accomplish the many tasks of a post-deficit America.

## Hope in Our Ghettos

Our present economic system has given up on millions of people in our ghettos. We imprison the exact product we can expect to come out of a system which offers no hope except crime to those raised in its despair. I am in favor of imprisoning or, if need be, executing the ruined individuals who would remorselessly shoot the people I love in order to steal their watches, but post-deficit America can instead offer hope and new life to the human beings living in our inner cities. The old economics is utterly impotent before the challenge of the ghetto. They would counsel our ghetto citizens to study hard and learn computers. What a joke. First of all, anyone taken as a child from his lily-white suburb and raised in the projects would be lucky to stand a one-in-ten chance of coming out of that environment with any kind of degree. Second, even those heroic individuals who do make it through college and out of the projects find themselves in the same unemployment lines as their suburban cohort—and just as unable to help their communities as if they were uneducated.

There are so many ways to help, it is criminal we do so little. Small investments can bring huge rewards, compared to the costs of warehousing millions in prisons, which is all we do now. California spends twenty-five thousand dollars a year on its prisoners, more than on its college students. They pay their guards sixty thousand dollars a year, more than their teachers and professors. The main problem I see in the ghetto, having lived in two of the worst, is the lack of role models for the boys there. It is bad enough not to have an honest, respectable job. It is an unimaginably sad state of reality that children growing up see *no one* with a respectable, honest job. I am talking more of the young boys than the girls, because the girls can see their mothers as honest, overworked parents. But try to put yourself in the place of an eager, energetic young boy who sees that the only guys in the neighborhood with any respect and income are the pimps and drug dealers. How can we expect him to grow up any differently?

The sharpest way I can imagine to invest one dollar to create two dollars' worth of goods is to hire neighborhood father figures. These would be men between the ages of, roughly, thirty and fifty who would live in the same neighborhoods—mainly the projects—as the young boys whom they would help. Their simple job would be to do dad-like things with their charges while visibly having the respect and status that these boys would like to see and emulate in a honest man. Yes, one in a hundred would abuse their trust, but the effects would be sure on balance to be far better than leaving these poor boys to their own devices in a hell we have, with our current welfare policies, helped to create.

Two other approaches utilize excellent social structures already in place in our ghettos. The first is the church. I hope that even those of my readers who are not religious can appreciate the healthy do-goodism that comes from the active faith of the people in the ghetto. They have worked for the treatment of addicts and to clean up their neighborhoods of crack houses and prostitution. These people are already good and decent, somehow having survived and even thrived despite their environment. They might benefit merely from our funding some of what they already do, so that they can do more of it (and, remember, so that they can spend money which will work its way throughout society and eventually into the hands of, yes, the rich). Helping churches develop and run their own nursing homes—paying in particular for the recently retired (or unemployed)—to take care of their oldest seniors would be a use of federal funding that would be bound to help without harming.

The second existing institution is sports, for example, basketball programs run by the local YMCA and YWCA. Society can afford billions of dollars to entertain well-off (mostly white) spectators. We televise the exploits of the one-in-a-hundred-thousand elite. For a tiny fraction of that cost we could create local, untelevised teams in our ghettos. For example, the coach of a project basketball team would earn about twenty thousand dollars. The young players would earn about ten to fifteen thousand dollars and would enjoy the prestige of making the team. They would probably have the time and desire to make additional honest money on the side. Who cares if anyone came to watch them play (though I bet the crowds would be better than you think).[15]

If sports for the passive viewing of the well-off is worth billions to society, it is worth a few percent of that amount to gainfully and respectfully employ the energies of talented, energetic, aggressive young people who might otherwise use their vigor to cause harm. Until we offer them thirty-thousand-dollar jobs to build roads or clean the environment, we should follow the sports model. Entertainment and recreation are indeed a kind of "wealth." When we can combine them with making our society healthier and safer, their utility is magnified.

## THE OPPORTUNITY COSTS OF FAILURE

The above offers so many do-gooder projects that you may at this point be overwhelmed by what I described as "the right class of problems." An excess of good programs (which I am sure you can improve upon) might have put you in a hypercritical state of mind that makes you stop to ponder instead of taking action. This book is *not* written as an idle exercise for utopian thinkers who just want to sit around and debate programs. Thus, I want to remind you of the alternative vision of the future that the old economists offer us with their deficit-reduction plans.

After the stock market crash of 1929, the federal government caused a depression by squeezing the money supply. With the depression in full swing in 1932, both political parties advocated a balanced budget as the key to economic recovery. They passed the largest tax increase in the nation's history. In an economic conference of forty-six prominent Americans before the U.S. finance committee, most said the depression was the natural result of economic law, punishing the "extravagances" of the 1920s. Fortunately, the people voted Hoover out and FDR in, and followed the philosophy of Eccles and Keynes rather than the tight-money men who themselves had caused the unnatural depression.

As I write this, our legislators, both Republican and Democrat, have voted down a modest spending package and instead have voted to increase taxes. The only threat to the tax increase was that the deficit mongers said it was not high enough!

At the same time they criticize the president's proposal for costing us jobs and halting economic recovery, they say the main fault is that the plan only reduces, but does not eliminate, the deficit. And since the only way to eliminate the deficit is to raise taxes even higher, and cut even more spending, they (especially Perot) are advocating even more job losses and a further deepening of the recession. At the same time, Greenspan says that despite our low inflation, he intends to raise the discount rate anyway, because he just knows inflation is a threat no matter what the facts are. This is exactly the same kind of crazy thinking that turned the stock market crash of 1929 into the depression. Thank God the stock market crash of 1987 occurred before the principals who gave us the "soft landing" gained control.

The best conservative economic thinking in 1929 led in four years to the following: Half of the banks failed, and the rest suffered heavy losses. In the cities, between 21 percent and 62 percent of home mortgages were in default. In the country, 45 percent of farm mortgages were delinquent. Virtually all business lost money, and losses of small corporations equaled 33 percent of their value. Twelve percent of the largest cities, as well as three entire states, defaulted on their obligations. Unemployment was over 30 percent. Output plunged 30 percent.[16]

At the same time, we decided national defense was too expensive, and we let Hitler and Tojo run unheeded through their parts of the world. Ultimately, at a massive cost, we won World War II. The opportunity loss of wealth converted into bombs instead of cars and houses was far secondary to the lives lost. Today we keep hoping Saddam Hussein will go away of his own or his people's accord, and we watch the UN observers play games with him regarding their taking a look at his atom bomb facilities, and those in North Korea.

In the 1930s, the depressed Western nations tried to blame their economic problems on each other. We led the way with our highest tariffs ever. The Smoot-Hawley laws were countered in kind overseas, leading to rates over 50 percent and a constant trade war that virtually stopped commerce between formerly friendly nations. But the depression was not our overseas partners' fault. *Excess production by any means is never the cause of poverty*—only when we do not let ourselves use that production are we poor. Thus the trade war only made things worse for everyone. In fact, relations among the allies became so bad due to trade friction that the resulting lack of communication stopped us from working together against Hitler while he could still have been stopped.

Try to explain to me what jobs your children are going to hold. As in the depression, everyone is squeezed, even those who keep their jobs. Kenichi Ohmae predicts an unemployment rate of 30 percent in the Western nations, including Japan, if we continue current policies.[17] Meanwhile, our unemployed sit at home as our roads and sewers fall apart. Non-polluting energy sources stay ever in the future. Scientific research grinds to a halt, too "expensive" for the government or a necessarily lean and mean private sector.[18] A generation of scientists who could explore space in person sit in front of their telescopes. Millions can't see a doctor while hospitals and doctors sit waiting. Families fall apart in despair. Riots may not be far behind.

Ask young people in their twenties now what they think of their prospects. We are creating a new Lost Generation, or "generation X," as they describe themselves. The Bureau of Labor Statistics predicts that almost one in three of this decade's college graduates will take jobs that don't require a degree—serving fast food, selling clothes, or faxing and photocopying. What do you say to a young lady like Barbara Andaman, who graduated with degrees in communication and business and a 3.8 grade-point average, while holding three jobs—and now struggles with three part-time jobs, including being a nanny, to support herself barely above the official poverty level? In college, she says, she was a "carefree, perky ball of energy." Now she cries a lot. "I feel old and defeated, like there's nothing left. I miss the old me a great deal."[19]

Though of course many of her peers do have good jobs, Barbara is *not* a strange exception. Imagine what it means in underused human potential. Young people who have worked hard all their lives to do the right thing—graduating from high school, getting through four or more years of college, staying the course while most of their peers drop out along the way—only to find that one-third, literally millions of the *successful* students, the graduates, end up flipping burgers? As they say, "'Career track' is not a popular term around here." What is the morality of breaking our implicit pact with our children by leaving them hanging this way?

We should be ashamed of ourselves. We are passing up the opportunity to give as much to future generations as we have had given to us—namely, the chance to work hard and earn a decent living. People retiring now did not get fired during the depression—that was their parents' generation. People retiring now had to work hard and save money to raise their children, yes—but they did so in an economy which not only provided them with jobs, but provided them jobs with benefits and jobs with a future. We've gone backwards. Now a decent job seems to be a privilege for an elite few, and benefits are sliding back to pre-depression levels. Security, confidence, and even hope are being drained from two generations.

Finally, we risk allowing the deficit hysteria to lead us into a pointless war, whether of weapons or of trade.[20] That would be truly criminal, given the alternative economics outlined in this book. We have the choice, and we have the ability, to do the right thing by the next generation. All we need to do is claim what we have earned for our nation and our children. You must understand that our fear of the deficit is leading us to imitate the actions that caused the depression and World War II. We need to imitate the actions that led us out of the depression and helped us avert World War III.

# 14

# The National Dividend: Your Share of America, Inc.

One final speculation about a future possibility of post-deficit economics is sure to raise the hackles of many—perhaps most—of the readers of this book. But this book has not been written like a political speech, bowing and scraping in every direction, anxious to please and careful not to offend. Here is just one more idea in a book full of them. Take it as you wish.

After about ten years of reducing taxes and increasing spending, after ten years of increasing employment, keeping low inflation, attaining a higher standard of living, and accomplishing some of the programs outlined in this chapter, I hope people will understand and trust the new economics enough to go even further. The main way to earn money is to work for it, yes. But another time-honored way to earn money, under both socialist and capitalist regimes, is to receive checks regularly, substantial checks, not for *doing* anything, but simply for *being* who you are. Examples are Social Security and corporate dividend checks.

## THE EXAMPLE OF SOCIAL SECURITY

One blessing to arise out of the ashes of the 1930s was Social Security. The "National Dividend" would simply extend that blessing to American society at large. In the 1930s, we decided that one class of people would get paid modestly whether or not they worked. There were two reasons these people would get money: First, they were old and, presumably, less fit to work. Second, they had already worked and had contributed, involuntarily, a proportion of their wages, making their Social Security income in effect a pay-back of their own money. Thus Social Security is a lie on two counts, while the great truth underlying its success is never spoken aloud.

***Social Security Lie No. 1:***
***"You're washed up at age sixty-five."***

First, people do not automatically become invalids at age sixty-five or sixty-two, or even at seventy-eight, for that matter. In the old days, perhaps, farming and other physical work may have become too wearying, but we know that putting hard-working sixty-five-year-olds out to pasture is far more likely to kill them than keeping them on the job is. And in a skills-driven, information society, we end up firing people who are close to their peak in performance skills. If anything is "wrong" with mature people, it is that they might be set in their ways and unwilling to change. But change is not always necessary, and if change *is* necessary, then the ability to learn new skills should be the criterion for selecting employees, not their age.

***Social Security Lie No. 2:***
***"Here's your money back, which was invested for you."***

People do *not* get their own money back. They pay money to the government. The government spends it immediately on anything it wants. When people retire, they know the government will print more money, if need be, to give them their retirement checks, or else pillage the income of whatever elite proportion of the population still has taxable jobs. The retired recipients' own contributions are long gone, with nary a consideration as to how much it was, or whether it was well invested or frittered away at embassy dress balls. The *present* generation is doing quite well on their forced Social Security investments, thank you. They paid in at a low rate, but are now expected to live long enough that, on average, they can expect to collect triple what they would have collected if they had invested in a basket of stocks and bonds over their working lifetimes. Right now, we are paying in so much that we will get far less than we would if we invested the money ourselves.

## SOCIAL SECURITY: THE GREAT TRUTH

But a great and wonderful truth underlies Social Security, and we can learn from it now. The truth is that we have enough real wealth as a nation that we can distribute and share it among ourselves, like Social Security, on the grounds of our mere citizenship rather than as a reward for continuing labor. We, the people, own this country. The investments of sweat, blood, and lives have paid off, and all we have to do is cash the checks. What checks? Any corporation that had survived for centuries and become an acknowledged world leader would be paying substantial dividends to its shareholders, not dunning them for more contributions. Successful and even barely surviving, money-losing corporations send out quarterly dividend checks to their shareholders, for which checks the shareholders simply sit at home and watch the mail.

We are all shareholders in America. Our country has created more wealth than we know what to do with—and I mean this literally, in the sense that our failed monetary policies cause our wealth to sit on the shelves, and cause even greater potential wealth never to be created. Not to distribute its wealth to its shareholders would be criminal for a corporation, and is immoral for a nation.

## THE EXAMPLE OF CORPORATE DIVIDENDS

We commonly talk about corporations earning (or losing) money: "Exxon made $400 million last year"; "GM lost a record $2 billion last quarter." Why does it sound absurd to say, "The U.S. made half a trillion bucks last year"? Nobody ever even thinks, much less talks, in terms of the country having a "good year" or a "bad year." The closest we come to evaluating ourselves this way is to call a bad year one in which many public figures are assassinated or a few natural disasters occur, as though those were in any way our fault as a polity. *But overall, we do not have a clue as to what constitutes good or bad actions as a nation—so it is impossible to evaluate the results.*

For corporations, life is deceptively easy. They can look at a hard-core, objective, numerical bottom line and exhibit that to the outside world. They know the bottom line can be misleading, of course—a dying corporation such as Lockheed can rake in huge "profits" by dismembering and selling its cold war relics. A thriving corporation can "lose" a fortune by taking a write-off that strengthens its business for the next twenty years. But among the forest of ambiguous corporate goals, one tree stands out clearly: making money. For a nation that prints its own money, it may seem impossible to use any version of that criterion. After all, "making money" has an entirely different meaning when you control the printing presses.

The concept of wealth creation, however, is the same for nations, corporations, and individuals. I'm referring to chapter 9's concept of *real wealth,* as opposed to mere money. In general, people or businesses make money in proportion to their creation of some form of real wealth. Say you work for and partially own a corporation—that is, you are an employee who owns some stock. You work and you own. The company makes money. You earn a salary based on your work and dividends based on your ownership. Nobody complains. They would complain, however, if the company refused to pay dividends to its owners. And it should be the same for the nation. We should get paid for our specific work *and* for our general ownership or "equity" in the country which we the people own.

Our "work" for the U.S. should properly be understood in the most general terms, comprising all of the forms of wealth enumerated in chapters 9 and 10 . But to help explain the concept, here's one overly specific example. Say you do some volunteer work in your spare time on a township community board that develops a park in your neighborhood. You get "paid" for your work every time you use the park. The "dividend" you would earn on your share of ownership in the nation would depend, pursuant to this work, on how the park affected the real wealth of the nation as a whole. Again to make the point, take an absurdly extreme example: say the only existing U.S. laboratory that made the miracle cancer cure had to be destroyed to make the park. Well, hooray for the park. But the real wealth of the nation would actually decline based on the "work" you did on the community committee that made such a fatal decision.

The point is that work can, on balance, destroy as well as create real wealth. A corporation can try New Coke. A person can work like a dog, but end up losing his life's savings by opening a restaurant that goes bankrupt. A nation can decide to subsidize a steel mill which pollutes its homeland in order to badly manufacture a commodity already in great oversupply. On the other hand, a person may spend a few extra hours calling on a long-shot prospective customer who ends up not only buying immediately, but serving as a source of commissions for years to come. A company can decide to do the hard and boring work of writing the operating software for IBM microcomputers for relatively little money up front—but for a long-term share of the profits (Microsoft).

And a country can decide to avoid war, engage in free trade, protect the environment, allow free enterprise to thrive, etc. This nation has already earned its real wealth, far more than it has already paid its citizens. Yes, most of our profits should be reinvested in programs such as those previously described. The people who work in those programs will all be paid their salaries directly. But all of us, as equity holders in our country, can share in the wealth, just as shareholders in a smart and thriving company share in their corporation's profits. We have, as a nation, earned the mountain of real wealth we are sitting on, so much of it unused. In that way we're like a corporation which had windfall profits it refused either to reinvest or pay out to the shareholders. Instead, it kept the money, unused, under the corporate mattress, not even earning interest. Worse, our own real wealth is being wasted every day that an educated person sits home without a job, every day that thousands of airline seats fly empty. The wealth is there. You see it with your own eyes, all about us. All we have to do is claim it.

## But Some Lazy Bums Haven't Earned It!

Neither have most of the owners of a company's shares. Dividends are paid based on the merit of the company, not of the shareholding recipients. Many have inherited it. Most have done nothing more meritorious than bought into a mutual fund. Only a few percent even bother to vote their shares—far less than the number of ghetto residents who vote in elections. Are they in any respect responsible for the failure or success of the company? But nobody, least of all they themselves, questions whether they have earned their dividends as they cash their checks.

*Electricity, water, roads, inventions like the flush toilet—most of the essentials and conveniences we rely on every day were here waiting for us, gifts from previous generations.*

It should be the same with the dividend checks we'd receive as shareholders in America, Inc. Most of our real wealth we have inherited, you know. The hard work was already done before we waltzed onto a pretty cushy scene. We did not have to do the dirty, immoral job of killing and running off the original inhabitants. We did not have to fight to break away from our European landlords in England, France, and Spain. We did not have to build cities out of forests, farms out of deserted plains. Do you even know how your city's sewage system works—where it *is*, for that matter? Electricity, water, roads, inventions like the flush toilet—most of the essentials and conveniences we rely on every day were here waiting for us, gifts from previous generations. We did not have to employ or *be* the slaves on whose backs much of the nation's early wealth was accumulated. We did not write the seminal documents, the Constitution and Bill of Rights, upon which so much of our real wealth is based.

Yes, the old guys cut down all the trees back East and messed up many of the country's rivers. We're replanting the forests and cleaning up the water. But we have received far more, I believe, than we're adding. But none of us seems ashamed to use the tremendous gifts of the past without so much as a thank-you, except maybe in late November.

I'm not trying to guilt-trip you. Rather the opposite. I want you to recognize the huge amount of real wealth we already have, which we already use—so you can understand we have immensely *more* real wealth which we are failing to use. Just as corporate dividends and the national dividends of the past are partialed out without regard to how much anyone has worked to deserve them, so can shares of the huge abundance—what we call excess capacity or surplus production—be shared with us, the owners of the tremendously productive nation that has created the wealth.

## How "Funny Money" Makes Us Seriously Richer

Many of you have been so thoroughly indoctrinated with the anorexic gospel of the inflation fanatics that you cannot help but cringe at the thought of printing more money. Even when all your logical objections have been countered, you will still, like an anorexic fearing food, push away a feast and choose starvation. So let me hammer away again with the reason we can get away with what so many regard as a dangerous indulgence. Remember the example of the miracle cancer cure? The real wealth was the medicine itself. The ration coupons were only a device invented to represent the real wealth. Having too few coupons allowed the real wealth to go to waste. The national divided checks would not give away real wealth that wasn't there. Rather, the checks would attempt to remedy the shortfall in the number of "coupons" (that is, money) compared to the amount of "medicine" they were supposed to match (this country's real wealth, sitting unused on the shelves).

The essential lesson of the principle of money/wealth equivalence is that we must print enough money to match our real wealth. By this principle, the wealth-creating projects proposed in chapter 13 have one surprising flaw. I mentioned earlier that printing one dollar to create two dollars' worth of goods is not only not *in*flationary, but is actually *de*flationary. Similarly, projects that spend money to create a great deal of real wealth could be deflationary. We may need to print more money than we spend on these projects just in order to retain the critical balance between real wealth and the money supply.

And why do we need to keep enough money flowing through the economy? Using up the "medicine" or real wealth is only half the story. People spending their National Dividend checks would not only avail themselves of the wealth we have already created, but they would give millions of other citizens something as treasured as goods—their *jobs*. People who buy create jobs for the people who work. Remember that even if benevolent aliens from outer space landed and decided tomorrow to provide us with all of our goods and services absolutely free, we would still want jobs to keep ourselves busy. Thus, the creation of good jobs is an end in itself.

## THE END OF THE WELFARE STATE

Some of you are saying, "This 'National Dividend' sounds like some sort of giant welfare program, if you ask me." It's like welfare only if you consider Social Security and corporate dividends to be like welfare. And they're not, in important ways. Our current welfare or public assistance programs have three flaws which the "National Dividend" does not. First, welfare destroys real wealth by perversely requiring that recipients *not work* in order to receive it. Idiotic. Don't let me get started on how ridiculous this provision is. Second, it requires the breakup of families. Again, keep me speechless. A more Stalinistic program of negative social engineering is hard to imagine. Do we *want* to keep the recipients on the bottom, or what? Third, the label "Welfare recipient" is a badge of shame attached to a stigmatized few percent of the population. People are humiliated, and their spirits can be broken.

The National Dividend avoids all three problems by being given to *all qualified citizens*, not just the poor without jobs who agree to kick Dad out of the house and suffer the scorn of their middle-class neighbors. The fairest way to distribute the Dividend would be to make it the base disbursement everyone would receive from the government every month. If you already received a government pension, veteran's disability check (as I do), or Social Security in excess of the Dividend, well, that's your good luck, but you won't get any more. The dividend would essentially be a no-strings floor grant from the government.[1] Yes, rich people would get it, too. Remember, the model is two programs that work extremely well—and rich people collect Social Security *and* corporate dividend checks.

We already give huge payments in addition to welfare grants to rich and poor alike—for example, milk price subsidies. These programs are almost as perverse as the welfare system. The goal of the subsidies is to help small farmers earn enough money to keep their farms and feed their families. To accomplish this goal we screw up the normal price system for milk with a Byzantine system of price supports more crazily bureaucratic than anything the Soviets were able to construct in seventy years of Communism. And most of the money ends up going to well-off corporate farms. The supports not only make an ugly sham of our ostensibly free-enterprise system, but they are also inflationary—the *point* is to keep milk prices *high*. Finally, they lead to ugly trade wars. French farmers, addicted to a panoply of supports for generations, are happy to bring down GATT worldwide as well as break up their European Community.

## PAY PEOPLE, NOT PRODUCTS

The goal of price supports and subsidies is to get money to the farmers. The perverse process of getting the money in their hands creates a giant bureaucracy, high prices, and international tensions. I propose we eliminate these three diseased middlemen. We should pay people directly, not using products as a tool to do so. After all, we don't *need* the products we subsidize—if we needed them, private enterprise would take care of paying for their production. The products sit in silos, or worse, serve to create international tensions and undercut free trade in goods we *do* need.

Perversely, the French farmers don't want to be paid just for being worthy citizens. They have been offered a handout, but they refuse it. They want their giant, nationally destructive handout to be disguised as "just payment" for their honest labors—labors making more overpriced food than the world wants to eat. But I should stop picking on them and their American counterparts. Their pride in their ancient calling has been instilled from birth by society, and it is only their admirable drive to want to *work* to *earn* a living that causes trouble. That same society has instilled in them a scorn for welfare recipients, who by common definition are shiftless bums. Rather than become members of that detested tribe, they would happily cause a trade war to keep filling silos full of unneeded grain and cheese.

Good people hate receiving welfare. But I have never seen anyone ashamed to accept a corporate dividend check or Social Security payment. By sharing our common wealth with our citizens in this fashion, we do not destroy the very images of themselves as productive hard workers which we want them to retain. The "National Dividend" supports people without tearing them down. Better yet, they have the same stake in their nation that corporate shareholders have in their company. They know that when their country does well, it's good for them as well. A pride based on mutual well-being is far healthier, I think, than either an adversarial, I-hate-my-country attitude or a nationalism based on the traditional hatred of outside groups.

## NOW I CAN WORK AT MCDONALD'S!

Paying people to do nothing will get more of them working at low-paying jobs. Yes, I have already asked you to believe ten impossible things before breakfast, and you might be feeling like Alice lost in Wonderland. But let me talk to you about what the academic economists call people's "personal utility functions." Basically, the concept recognizes that a dollar is not worth the same to everybody—*and*, not every dollar is worth the same to you. That is, the difference between your earning nothing or $50,000 one year is a lot more important to you than the difference between earning $300,000 and $350,000. In the first, the $50,000 is the difference between starvation and a comfortable life. In the second case, the same amount of money, $50,000, is the difference only between two levels of luxury. Yes, you can tell me some guy fights harder to go from one million up to two than anybody else fights for his first chicken—but you didn't see how hard he fought to get up to his first million.

But the story isn't as simple as having each higher dollar worth less to you than the previous dollars. At the very low, rock-bottom of the scale, an individual dollar is worth less than it is partway up the scale. Think of it. If you have no money at all, how important would it be for you to earn one hundred dollars a year in America? You would merely move from destitution to destitution. If you had a brain in your head you would gamble losing your entire one hundred dollars for even a small chance at earning enough to live on. If too little to live on is choice number one, than you are rational to try choice number two, no matter how long the odds are.

And no matter if choice number two is on the far side of the law. Some people deal drugs for the fun of it. Some people sleep in and watch soap operas all day because they are born lazy. But many others go wrong in our society because they are as smart and hard-working as you and I are, but the options they have are between certain poverty and something else, anything else—and a lot of those "anything else's" result in their breaking the law and ruining their own lives even more than they harm ours. Many want to work. Even inner-city criminals put to work on the Iowa levees managed to greatly impress the farmers whose land they were saving.[2]

The point is, a family with a guaranteed minimum income from their shares of the National Dividend will find it rationally worthwhile to make a career out of a minimum-wage, dead-end job. Let's be realistic. Such jobs constitute a large and growing proportion of jobs available. If we try to make them pay better, all we do is put the company out of business or force them to automate. But it is completely fair, even under the most strict interpretations of GATT, to quasi-subsidize the competitiveness of American industry by making the minimum wage, in effect, a living wage. Right now, people trying to support a family on a wage a dollar an hour above the minimum can't afford a telephone.[3] No telephones! In 1990s' America! A base income will allow both families and businesses to thrive which are presently working desperately against both poverty and imminent bankruptcy.

## DOWN WITH MEDICAID AND FOOD STAMPS!

An ultimate aim will be to replace a score of bloated federal bureaucracies with a single giant check-writing machine. Yes, people need money for basic medical care and food, housing, etc. Under the current system, however, about half of the money gets eaten up in overhead. Also, the current system exerts a constant Big-Brother paternalism dictating the choices people get to make about how to live their lives and spend their money. Folks living off of the dividends of the stocks they inherited seem to do pretty well without the government forcing them to spend a certain amount on food, so much on medical, etc. But we seem to take it for granted that most Americans need the government to decide that a portion of our income will be taken out of our hands, before we ever see it, and spent on insurance for medical care designed to keep us alive for years after we're brain dead or otherwise miserable. Either as mandated deductions by your employer or as specific allocations through programs like Medicaid for those who don't have employers, money for a beer and an aspirin a day is taken and spent on making sure you have a personal dialysis machine or as many CAT scans as the CEO of IBM gets. Maybe some of you like that enforced discipline because you don't trust your own judgment. I find it insulting.

And the conditions we attach to aid are worse than humiliating and meddlesome. We make current aid an effective reward for conduct which neither the recipients nor the polity like. Explain to me again exactly why we reward people for staying out of work and for kicking Dad out of the home—that is, we take the medical, food, and general aid they absolutely need to raise a family out of their hands when they get a bad job or marry a guy making minimum wage. Downright crazy. We presently pay thousands of dedicated social workers—who have better things to do, and hate the assignment—to snoop around their fellow citizens' homes to see if a man's shoes are under the bed.

If we are going to put conditions on people's receiving the "National Dividend," those conditions should encourage actions which both we and the recipients agree is worthwhile. As a jumping-off place for debate, I suggest three conditions:

- citizenship,
- graduation from high school, and
- no felony convictions in the last three years.

Non-citizens would remain eligible for other aid, as they are now. Making them ineligible for the "National Dividend" would be done only to avoid dangling one more giant carrot in front of them, when they are already swimming across oceans and seas to get here. The other two would give a large and concrete motivation for our youngsters to take their educations seriously. Ask any public school teacher what effect it would have on the attention spans and work habits of their students if graduation meant an earned share of America's profits for life. Ask any cop what he or she believes it would mean if the army of young hooligans demolishing our urban neighborhoods actually had a positive stake in this country, a stake which they could lose. Ask any social worker what effect it would have on family values in the ghettos if Dad not only could live with the family, but he brought with him a guaranteed income he had earned by graduating and keeping his nose clean. Again, these suggestions are designed, like those in chapter 13, to provoke debate by those more qualified than I in various specific fields. But you don't need a Ph.D. in social policy to see our present system wastes time, energy, and money to enforce perversely counter-productive incentives at the cost of human dignity.

## MAKE 'EM WORK FOR FREE

The National Dividend would not exactly *make* people work for free, but it would allow them to do so, which is effectively the same thing. Many of the people supported by the dividends they earn on Great-grandad's stock do wonderful work for a variety of upper-crust do-gooder causes, from the opera guild to the Episcopal Church. They enjoy the luxury of using their time and energy where it does the most good, without submitting to impersonal market forces and wages to dictate the course of their working lives. Yes, markets and wages do a

*Yes, markets and wages do a generally fine job of employing humanity in productive activities, far better than communism or monarchies have ever done. But markets and wages are not perfect, and we can afford to have a certain proportion of work done in this country that does not, strictly speaking, make money.*

generally fine job of employing humanity in productive activities, far better than communism or monarchies have ever done. But markets and wages are not perfect, and we can afford to have a certain proportion of work done in this country that does not, strictly speaking, make money.

The fact that many jobs, like being a brownie leader or Big Sister, do not make money is more the fault of the system than of the job. A pure old-style economist will argue that the fact he or his neighbor the lawyer get paid to write long tracts which bore to tears even their like-minded brethren *proves* that such work is worth more than charitable activities. Nonsense. Present free market salaries are far more influenced by institutional factors than by the free interplay of value and production. Lawyers and economists get paid what they do because they run the system that decides what economists and lawyers get paid, whereas people who run the church's Thanksgiving Dinner outreach program do not influence the financial system.

This disparity does *not* mean we should pay our lawyers or economists less. And we certainly cannot afford to pay all of our charity do-gooders as much as we pay our institutionalized professionals. Nor do many charity workers want or need a wage. Thus, I am not suggesting we pay someone for doing anything which they love doing so much they presently do it for free. I only want them to be able to make the personal choice to undertake such tasks, just as the trust-fund babies get to choose their life's activities irrespective of the income those activities afford. People willing to take the demanding responsibility of running a scout troop should not have to say "No" because they need the extra bucks a minimum wage job pays in order to buy Christmas gifts this year.

The American not-for-profit, but non-governmental "third sector" has already become, as a collective, the nation's largest employer.[4] The third sector includes, for example, the Red Cross, Salvation Army, community chests, Meals on Wheels, health-care groups such as the American Heart, Lung, and Mental Health associations, and many cultural and educational institutions. Some of them already pay some of their workers, but at salaries far below those in the for-profit or governmental sectors. One of every two adults already works in such jobs, usually in addition to their for-pay work in for-profit organizations. They already put in "the equivalent of 7.5 million *full-time* work years, unpaid time worth $150 billion per year," according to Peter Drucker. Just because work is not paid does not mean it is not important. It creates a tremendous amount of our real wealth. The "National Dividend" would free up even more people's time to do work that maximizes their personal talents more than the market-and-jobs system can do on its own.

## BEYOND WEALTH AND MONEY

Wealth is great. Money is a powerful motivator. This entire book has been devoted to the relation between money and wealth. And the definition of wealth has been broadened to include intangibles like "peace" and "freedom" which the old economics failed to comprehend. Thus, you may find it ingenuous of me to conclude by saying that wealth is not the be-all and end-all of our existence. But, of course, it isn't. Money and wealth are merely means to larger ends.

It is a necessary means, however. I am sick and tired of the elitist, hyper-liberal scorn of mere business, which was indoctrinated into me as a liberal-arts major at Berkeley. Students and professors whose every comfort and essential, from apartments and cars to movies and cappuccino, were provided by the system of raw profit and free enterprise—these people would presume to look down their noses at it all. They indulged as fully as anybody else in the creature and political comforts of the system, while not deigning to offer anything back to it but their supercilious condemnation. And I am not talking about radical Berkeley communists alone. I'm talking about many of the people who run our country and its major institutions. These are the kind of people who drive their cars to zoning conferences that ban new roads and close open roads to traffic. These are people who presume to tell the poor, whom the do-gooders ostensibly love, that the poor need free and unlimited health care more than they need a job and money for a beer. These are the people I mentioned before, who would decide on behalf of the poor that the poor would not want to receive free money if that free money would make America's rich and powerful even more rich and more powerful. They have one eye and would prefer to blind the world.

Many of them are my friends. God knows, I was one of them myself. Many cherish an abstract "freedom" for themselves and others, cherish it above all material wealth. But they forget that wealth is not all chains. Bound by poverty and the constant threat of unemployment, human souls cannot rise. The abundance we already have, the jobs and income I propose we unleash, do not entail an enslavement of poor-but-noble characters behind bars of wealth. Secure employment in a decent job at a living wage should be the foundation for further growth. How hypocritical for the voices which scorn mere wage earning to already enjoy secure employment themselves. They are the equivalent of the generals in the rear sending others to death at the machine guns, the moral counterparts of the Rudmans and Simons who would fire millions of less-fortunate Americans at no risk to their own jobs. This kind of hyper-liberal, business-hating moralizer forgets Virginia Woolf's cry for a "room of one's own," a minimum of time and substance, as a precursor for personal and professional growth in her writing and life.

One may write. Or read others' writings. One may commune with God. Others may choose to watch more TV. You may choose to play more tennis with friends or toss a softball to your little boy. The wealth this country already has earned would allow every mother in the nation to spend all day with her children, if she so desired. While scientists and blue-collar workers keep their days busy building the Mars spaceship or whatever, others will be debating the great social and cultural issues beyond the scope of this book: abortion, gene research, species preservation, the new or future World Order, the nature of God and humanity, and the ends of time. Generations already dead have done 99 percent of the practical hard work to give us the fundamental, sewers-and-potatoes wherewithal to consolidate what they have earned, and extend those benefits to all. To keep what we have and move forward into a richer material, cultural, and spiritual world, we will need the contributions of time, energy, and talent of every human being on the planet. The greatest steps have already been taken. As banal as it may sound, all we need do to step out into an unbelievable new world is for our government to create a sound but *sufficient* currency, encouraging the full employment of our human and natural resources towards the creation of real wealth. I trust people to take it from there themselves.

# Footnotes

*A note on the sources:*

Primary references are *The Wall Street Journal (WSJ), the Economist,* and *Business Week* for three reasons: First, you can easily find all three on microfilm in any library in the country. Second, all of their editors **vehemently disagree** with my theses. The most conclusive rebuttal uses your opponent's own words to hang him. Third, they are five years more current than academic articles and offer more substance. After all, their staff are better paid than professors, and have actually learned how to *write*.

**Chapter 2**

1. Alan Murray, "Improbable Growth. Deficits and Droughts Fail to Deter Economy From Its Record Rise. A 67-Month Expansion Shows No Signs of Slowing Up As Joblessness Falls to 5.3 percent." *WSJ* (July 11, 1988), A1. In June, 346,000 jobs had been created. One economist said, "It's stunning. These are gains one would expect to see when an expansion is in its very early stages, not when it is more than five years old."

2. Bartley, *The Seven Fat Years,* 4-5.

3. Alan Greenspan began surreptitiously raising interest rates in the summer of 1988, in order not to spook Bush's election. The Fed regards jobs, growth, and exports as *problems* which they must cure by purposely raising interest rates until we have a recession. See my forthcoming book, *You're Fired! The Fed's War on Jobs, 1988-2002.*

4. Lucinda Harper, "Jobless Total Greatly Exceeds Prior Estimates," *WSJ* (November 17, 1993), A2.

5. Tom Smith, University of Chicago, National Opinion Research Center. Quoted in "It All May Have Been Worse Than It Seemed," *WSJ* (October 19, 1993), B1.

6. Name withheld by request. Letter to *Physics Today*, October 1990, 121. G. Pascal Zachary, "Black Hole Opens in Scientist Job Rolls," *WSJ* (April 14, 1993), B1.

7. George Anders, "Required Surgery. Health Plans Force Even Elite Hospitals to Cut Costs Sharply," *WSJ* (March 8, 1994), A1. "Health Care Industry Is Now Restructuring; With It Comes Pain. After the Fat Is Cut, Efforts to Save Are Apt to Mean Closures and Fewer Jobs," *WSJ (*June 16, 1993), A1. Tim Ferguson, "Hospitals' Charts Take a Turn for the Worse," *WSJ* (August 10, 1993), A16.

8. David Frum, "A Nervous Upturn," *Forbes* (September 27, 1993), 64. Junda Woo, "Jobless New Lawyers Seek Other Venues," *WSJ* (January 22, 1993), B1.

9. Trudy Bell, "Jobs at Risk," *IEEE Spectrum* (August 1993), 20.

10. Tony Horwitz, "Not Home Alone. Jobless Male Managers Proliferate in Suburbs, Causing Subtle Malaise. Quietly Desperate, They Seek Work, Go to Libraries, Upset Family Members. Experiencing 'A Sort of Death,'" *WSJ* (September 20, 1993), A1.

11. Leslie Scism, "Finance Staffs Are Targets of Cost Cuts. Restructurings Are Reaching Up to Top Executives," *WSJ* (May 25, 1993), A4.

12. Julie Lopez, "College Class of '93 Learns Hard Lesson: Career Prospects Are Worst in Decades," *WSJ* (March 20, 1993), B1.

13. Joan Rigdon, "Glut of Graduates Lets Recruiters Pick Only the Best," *WSJ* (March 20,1993), B1.

14. Aaron Bernstein, "The Young and the Jobless. Prospects for Youth Are Even Grimmer Than in Past Recoveries," *Business Week* (August 16, 1993), 107.

15. "Alumni Flood Campuses for Career Counseling in the Stagnant Job Market," *WSJ* (April 27, 1993), A1.

16. Julie Lopez, "Out in the Cold. Many Early Retirees Find the Good Deals Not So Good After All. Buyout Plans Grow Skimpier, and New Jobs Are Scarce. From Money Man to 'Santa,'" *WSJ* (October 25, 1993), A1.

17. "Midlife Americans Glum About Prospects," *AARP Bulletin* (September 1993), 4.

18. Neal Templin, "Some GM Workers Go to Great Lengths to Hold Steady Jobs. Auto-Making Gypsies Bounce From Factory to Factory; Mike Raper, Weekend Dad," *WSJ* (November 5, 1993), A1.

19. Lucinda Harper, "Economy is Already Feeling the Impact of Federal Government's Spending Cuts," *WSJ* (August 18, 1993), A2.

20. Al Ehrbar, "Price of Progress. 'Re-Engineering' Gives Firms New Efficiency, Workers the Pink Slip. One Company After Another Redesigns Tasks to Curb Its Need for Employment," *WSJ* (March 16, 1993), A1.

21. Michael Allen, "Explain this: Economy Grows, But Loans Shrink," *WSJ* (September 15, 1993), T1.

22. Trudy Bell, "Jobs at Risk. [Part 3:] Automation and Layoffs," *IEEE Spectrum* (August 1993), 27.

23. Joan Rigdon, "Retooling Lives. Technological Gains Are Cutting Costs, and Jobs, in Services. Employment Starts to Plunge as Productivity Increases," *WSJ* (February 24, 1994), A1.

24. "Up and Up Until It Popped," *Economist (*August 14, 1993), 73. "America's aging baby-boomers are saving more, and putting their money into fast-growing mutual funds. How much cash can the securities markets absorb?"

25. "Retrograde Taxation," *WSJ* (March 23, 1994), A14. Paul Craig Roberts, "The Unbearable Costs of Clintonomics," *Business Week* (June 7, 1993), 18.

26. Alecia Sweasy, "'Exclusive' Town Panics as Plunging Home Prices Smash Social Barriers." *WSJ (*November 22, 1993), B1. "Falling Household Worth Could Prolong the Downturn. . ." *Business Week* (February 11, 1991), 16. "Poor Baby Boomers. They're Stuck with Real Estate. Attitudes on Mobility Change as the Investment of the '80s Becomes the Home of the '90s," *WSJ* (July 10, 1990), A1.

27. *Figure*. "Housing Starts," *WSJ* (August 17, 1989), A1, reporting Commerce Dept. data. Related story by David Wessel, "Housing Starts Edged Up; Figures Help to Dispel Fears About Recession," A2. Second *Figure*, based on Commerce Department data.

28. K. Dominguez, R. Fair, and M. Shapiro, "Forecasting the Depression: Harvard Versus Yale," *The American Economic Review,* 78, 4 (1988), 595-612.

29. Paul Magnusson, "That Was No Recession, That Was a 'Contained Depression'—And We're Still In It," *Business Week*

(November 8, 1993), 24. Quoting Jerome Levy.

30. "Ready to Take On the World," *Economist* (January 15, 1994), 65. Quotes "Manufacturing Productivity," by the McKinsey Global Institute (October 1993).

31. Henry Rosovsky, "Highest Education. Our Universities Are the World's Best," *The New Republic* (July 13 and 20, 1987), 13.

32. "O Brave New World. The Delegates Who Gather in Detroit for Clinton's Job Summit Will Tell One Another That Better Training Can Solve the Rich World's Jobs Deficit. The Evidence Is More Ambivalent," *Economist* (March 12, 1994), 19.

33. George Gilder, "America's Best Infrastructure Program," *WSJ* (March 2, 1993), A16.

34. "Examiners Crunch Credit," *WSJ* (March 1, 1993), A16. Fred Bleakley, "Loan Demand Will Remain Sluggish Even If Economy Improves, Surveys Say," *WSJ* (October 20, 1993), A8.

35. Michael Kinsley's lead editorial in *The New Republic* (February 27, 1994).

36. Douglas Harbrecht, "'Cross My Heart and Hope To Die, I'll Cut the Deficit.' A Pair of Political Unknowns Ask Candidates to Take a Pledge," *Business Week* (September 28, 1992), 102.

37. "Experts Blame Hard Times, Social Woes for Surge of Child Abuse," *L.A. Times* article in *Fort Worth Star-Telegram* (October 31, 1993), A17. Rochelle Sharpe, "Latchkey Kids in '91 Exceeded 1.6 Million, Census Bureau Finds," *WSJ* (May 20, 1994), A7D.

38. "Social Security Critics, Allies Clash at Entitlement Summit." *AARP Bulletin* (January 1994), 3.

## Chapter 3

1. James Dale Davidson, *The Plague of the Black Debt*. Baltimore: Agora (1993), 5. A widely-distributed marketing device for his newsletter and large book, *The Great Reckoning*.

2. See, e.g., Pilzer, *Unlimited Wealth*.

3. Owen Ullmann, "The Global Greenback. 'Dollarization' Is Bucking Up Economies Worldwide," *Business Week* (August 9, 1993), 44. "The new world economic order is upon us—and it's awash in greenbacks. Never before have so many foreigners used dollars for so many purposes, from stabilizing economies to selling soap."

4. "Big MacCurrencies. Our Big Mac Index Confirms That the Dollar Is Undervalued Against Other Main Currencies," *Economist*, (April 9, 1994), 88. "Using far more sophisticated techniques, Goldman Sachs...estimates the dollar's PPP [purchasing power parity] to be 179 yen, compared with our 170 [and an official exchange rate of only 104 yen]. This suggests that the dollar is even more undervalued than the Big Mac [index] suggests."

5. Eisner, *The Misunderstood Economy*, 10.

## Chapter 4

1. Sources, in order, are Alan Greenspan, Ronald Reagan, Warren Rudman, woman on PBS, Rob Norton in *Fortune*, *Business Week* editorial, David Calleo (*The Bankrupting of America*, New York: Morrow, 1992), and William Shaffer (letter to *WSJ*, July 1, 1992).

2. Russell Chandler, *Doomsday*. Ann Arbor: Servant (1993), p. 98.

3. Paul Gigot, "The Bad News is the U.S. Economy Keeps Humming." *WSJ* (July 14, 1989), A10, quoting Stephen Marris of the Institute for International Economics.

4. Milton Friedman, "A Monetary and Fiscal Framework for Economic Stability," *Amer. Econ. Review,* 38, 3 (June 1948), 245-264. Note 10, dealing with outstanding bonds held by banks: "...Use the monetization of the debt as a means of providing a secular increase in the quantity of money....the government would commit itself to retiring, through the issuance of new money, a predetermined amount of the public debt annually."

5. Milton Friedman, "Why the Twin Deficits Are a Blessing," *WSJ* (December 14, 1988), A14.

**Chapter 5**

1. Milton Friedman, *A Program for Monetary Stability*. New York: Fordham U. Press (1960). Milton remains as adamant as ever. In a letter to the *WSJ* on February 12, 1993, he says that, to explain inflation, "...one word would suffice: money."

2. Is Milton Friedman backing off? He has subtly changed his famous dictum to read, "*Substantial* inflation is always and everywhere a monetary phenomenon" (*Money Mischief*, p. 193). But "substantial" inflation is certainly not an affliction of the West.

3. Paul Zane Pilzer, *Unlimited Wealth*. Or visit your local mall.

4. Benjamin M. Friedman, "Monetary Policy Without Quantity Variables." *Amer. Econ. Rev.*, 78, 2, 440-445 (May 1988).

5. Alan Murray, "Improbable Growth. Deficits and Droughts Fail to Deter Economy from its Record Rise. A 67-month Expansion Shows No Signs of Slowing Up as Joblessness Falls to 5.3 percent. Still, Pessimists Predominate." *WSJ* (July 11, 1988), A1-12.

6. Milton Friedman, *Money Mischief*, 213.

7. "Supermarket Chains Chop Prices to Keep Rivals from Cutting into Their Business." *WSJ* (March 25, 1993), B1-6. Discusses reasons for "the difference between consumer perception and the reality at the checkout." Micheal Mandel, "Fear of Flying Prices," *Business Week* (August 17, 1992), 26. "There it is: a yawning gulf between perceptions and actual inflationary pressures...Strange thing is, the gulf persists despite mounting evidence."

8. See, e.g., "What Happened to Inflation?" *Economist* (October 30, 1993), 19; Neela Banerjee, "Economists Say Inflation Fears Fueled by Purchasing Index Are Overblown," *WSJ* (March 11, 1994), A5A; and "Divided on Inflation. Some Economists Scoff, But, Surprisingly, a Number Say Something Is Out There." *WSJ* (July 7, 1993), C1-2. "No wage pressures, no scarcity. But anxiety rises...In fact, chronic overcapacity plagues businesses ranging from airlines to publishing to telecommunications. And even where American companies are beginning to fill their order books, foreign competition generally deters them from raising prices."

9. "Bond Prices Fall Sharply on [Favorable] Data." *WSJ* (April 29, 1994), C1.

10. "Of Bonds, Bulls and Bears." *Economist* (April 9, 1994), 81-82, following their earlier, confidently wrong predictions in "Much Ado about Nothing," (March 26, 1994), 94-96.

11. Figgie, *Bankruptcy 1995*, 2.

12. Three from *The American Economic Review* are: Michael Darby, "The Price of Oil and World Inflation and Recession," (September 1982) , 738-751; Robert Gordon, "Supply Shocks and Monetary Policy Revisited," (May 1984), 38-43; and Richard Roll, "Orange Juice and Weather," (December 1984), 861-880. The rigid position is held by the Editor of the *WSJ*, Robert Bartley: "The Great International Growth Slowdown." *WSJ* (July 10,

1990), A16. "The oil shocks were…only an artifact of the underlying money disorders."

13. Paul Barrett, "Justices Reject Cigarette Firm's Antitrust Appeal. Ruling Makes it Tougher to Win Suits Contesting Rival's Deep Price Cuts," *WSJ* (June 22, 1993), A3-5. "…Justice Kennedy amplified the already considerable skepticism in legal circles about suits attacking deep discounting, which, in the short run at least, benefits consumers…There may be a situation in which industry giants tacitly cooperate, first to reduce prices to discipline discounters, and then to raise them to recoup their losses…But…this sort of scheme is so 'implausible' that juries generally shouldn't be allowed to rule for plaintiffs who rely on it….First, predatory-pricing schemes aren't likely to work… Second, price reductions…benefit customers, even if they hurt smaller companies. The purpose of the antitrust laws, Justice Kennedy stressed, is to promote consumer welfare, not protect small competitors."

14. "Greenspan Takes the Gold," *WSJ* (February 28, 1994), A14.

**Chapter 6**

1. John Wilke, "State of Siege. New Hampshire Firms Struggle as Bank Crisis Dries Up Their Credit. All 5 of the Biggest Lenders Are Ailing, and Businesses Can't Finance Expansion. Soaring Unemployment Rate," *WSJ* (February 21, 1991), A1.

2. Daniel J. Mitchell, "Budget Deficits Have Little Impact on Interest Rates," *WSJ* (February 25, 1993), A16. Paul Evans, "Do Large Deficits Produce High Interest Rates? [No,]" *Amer. Econ. Rev.* (March 1985), 68-87.

3. "Why Cutting the Deficit May Not Boost Investment," *Business Week* (December 27, 1993). In a study by Steven Fazzari of 5,000 manufacturing companies, "the impact of lower interest rates on capital investment is highly exaggerated…Far

more potent determinants...were the prospects of rising demand and the strength of the internal cash flow...[D]eficit reduction...is more likely to inhibit business investment by slowing economic growth and hurting cash flow than to stimulate it via lower interest rates."

4. "Reducing Debt is Top Priority at Small Firms," *WSJ* (September 8, 1993), B1-2. "As bank loans are the lowest in two decades, one might expect to see small businesses rushing out to borrow, borrow, borrow. But the reverse seems to be true: Many small companies are rushing to pay off debt. Numerous small business owners fear that the current tepid economic recovery won't last. Then, as profits decline, even low-cost debt would shackle them with interest payments...restrictions...and threats to their personal assets required as collateral."

5. Juliet Schor, *The Overworked American*, 2: "...We could now produce our 1948 standard of living...in less than half the time it took in that year."

6. Anita Raghavan and Michael Sesit, "Financing Boom. Foreign Firms Raise More and More Money in the U.S. Markets," *WSJ* (October 5, 1993), A1-8.

7. L. Dwight Israelsen, "Marriner S. Eccles, Chairman of the Federal Reserve Board," *Amer. Econ. Assoc. Papers and Proceedings* (May 1985), 357-362.

8. Robert Kuttner, "Why Europe Didn't Take the Last Step Toward Union," *Business Week* (August 23, 1993), 10.

9. John Rossant and Julia Flynn, "The Yanks Are Buying. Exports Are Booming for Currency Slashers Britain, Sweden, and Italy," *Business Week* (October 11, 1993), 51.

10. Damon Darlin and Masayoshi Kanabayashi, "Buying Binge. Japan's Consumers Go on a Spending Spree and Economy Booms," *WSJ* (January 5, 1988), A1.

11. George Melloan, "Japan's Economic Machine Needs an Overhaul," *WSJ* (March 13, 1993), A21. "Stock prices tripled from 1986 to 1989. At that point central bank governor Yasushi Mieno felt it was time to begin a controlled deflation of the bubble before it burst and the economy crashed...But once Mr. Mieno got the bubble shrinking, it didn't want to stop. Stocks last year hit a low...Bank balance sheets are loaded with sharply devalued real estate. Consumers, instead of spending, began saving more...so Japanese companies are having to deal with stagnant demand and sharply reduced earnings..."

12. Michael Williams and Jacob Schlesinger, "Clouded Sun. Japan, Economically and Politically Ailing, Is Sinking into Gloom. Euphoria of '80s Boom Ends as People Cut Spending Amid Worries Over Jobs," *WSJ* (December 29, 1993), A1.

13. Dick Nanto and Shinji Takagi, "Korekiyo Takahashi and Japan's Recovery from the Great Depression," *Amer. Econ. Rev.* (May 1985), 369-374.

**Chapter 7**

1. John Laffin, *British Butchers and Bunglers of World War I*. Gloucester: A. Sutton (1988). John Ellis, *Eye-deep in Hell. Trench Warfare in World War I*. Baltimore: Johns Hopkins (1976).

2. Louis N. Magner, *A History of Medicine*. New York: Mark Dekker (1992), 206.

3. James T. Flexner, *Washington, The Indispensable Man*. Boston: Little, Brown (1969), 399-400.

4. "Big Giver," *WSJ* (April 27, 1994), A1.

**Chapter 8**

1. Charles Morris, "It's Not the Economy, Stupid," *Atlantic* (July 1993), 49-62.

2. Paul Krugman, *Peddling Prosperity*.

3. Hilary Stout, "Key Economic Statistic Comes Under Fire. Some Call Capacity Utilization Figures Outmoded," *WSJ* (December 13, 1988), A2. Howard Gleckman, "A Tonic for the Business Cycle. Just-In-Time Delivery May Be the Remedy for Wild Inventory Swing," *Business Week* (April 4, 1994), 57.

4. Milton Friedman, *Money Mischief*, p. 20.

5. Milton Friedman, "A Monetary and Fiscal Framework for Economic Stability," 250.

6. Paul Krugman, *Peddling Prosperity*, 52.

7. Morris, *op cit.*

8. "Disgusted of MIT. The Winner of the Nobel Prize for Economics in 2024." Review of Paul Krugman's *Peddling Prosperity* in the *Economist* (April 30, 1994), 99.

9. Krugman, *op cit.*

**Chapter 9**

1. Robert Eisner, *The Total Incomes System of Accounts,* 8-10.

2. "Grossly Distorted Picture. Despite Big Improvements in National-Income Accounting, Statisticians Still Hold up a Distorting Mirror to the World's Economies," *Economist* (February 5, 1994), 71.

3. George Jaszi, "An Economic Accountant's Audit," *American Econ. Assoc. Proceedings* (May 1986), 411-417. He replaces Kuznets' "net total of desirable events enjoyed by individuals" with his own "goods and services bought." Why? Jaszi is staggered by the prospect of measuring anything that does not already have numbers attached to it: "I perceived that, equipped

with [Kuznets'] definition, no one could possibly measure it. It dawned on me [to] bring Kuznets' definition down to earth."

4. Fred Hirsch, *The Social Limits to Growth*, Harvard (1976).

5. Leslie Helm and Charles Gaffney, "The High Price Japanese Pay for Success. Alcoholism, Emotional Breakdowns, and Even Suicide Are Increasing," *Business Week* (April 7, 1994), 52. Barbara Buell, Neil Gross, and Gharles Gaffney. "The Myth of the Japanese Middle Class. What's Life Like in the 'Economic Miracle'? Drabber than You Think," *Business Week* (September 12, 1988), 49.

6. Neil Behrmann, "Bullion Proves to be Poor Security for Mideastern Investors, Dealers Say," *WSJ* (August 13, 1990), A5. "The invading Iraqi army looted Kuwaiti banks, houses, and bazaars, stealing large quantities of gold…'the young Middle Eastern generation isn't as gold-minded as their elders'…they are educated abroad and understand sophisticated currency and bond and equity investments."

7. One could construct an entire library of books describing the ills of contemporary economics. Two accessible articles are "The Poverty of Economics" by Robert Kuttner in the *Atlantic* (February 1985), 74, and "Washington's Misleading Maps of the Economy; Policymakers Can't Rely on the Government's Inadequate Statistics," *Business Week* (June 3, 1991), 112.

**Chapter 10**

1. "The Consumer Price Index: 1987 Revision," U.S. Department of Labor, Bureau of Labor Statistics (January 1987). Report 736.

2. Gene Koretz, "Inflationary Fears: Vastly Inflated?" *Business Week* (February 1, 1993), 20. Quoting Robert Gordon of Northwestern University.

3. Pamela Sebastian, "No Sale. Visions of Prices Past Haunt Home Sellers Caught in a Soft Market. A Unique House in Rye, N.Y., Not Bringing What It 'Should,' Sits for 2 Years," *WSJ* (July 25, 1990), A1.

4. "Poor Baby Boomers: They're Stuck with Real Estate. Attitudes on Mobility Change as the Investment of the '80s Becomes the Home of the '90s," *WSJ* (July 10, 1990), A1.

5. Glenn Yago, "Junk Bonds Are Food for Growth." *WSJ* (July 28, 1988), 24. Sobel, Robert, *Dangerous Dreamers*, New York: Wiley (1993).

6. Schor, *The Overworked American*, 21.

7. Brent Bowers, "Safety First. How a Device to Aid in Breast Self-Exams Is Kept off the Market. Other Nations Approved It, but U.S. Demands Proof Simple Pad Isn't Risky. Nine-Year Battle with the FDA," *WSJ* (April 12, 1994), A1.

8. Cynthia Owens, "Thai Disaster at Hotel Brings Safety Promises. Officials Vow to Enforce Codes After Collapse Vividly Points to Lapses," *WSJ* (August 16, 1993), A5.

9. Mitchell Pacelle, "Japanese Investors in U.S. Real Estate Finally Take Big Losses on Soured Assets," *WSJ* (April 19, 1994), A2. "Their losses will probably be closer to 50 percent..."

10. Eamonn Fingleton, "Air Control. Japan's Principal International Airport is a Traveler's Nightmare—and Destined to Stay That Way." *Atlantic* (July 1990), 32-38.

11. *Harper's Index* (April 1993), 13.

12. Henry Rosovsky, "Highest Education. Our Universities Are the World's Best," *The New Republic* (July 13 and 20, 1987), 13.

13. "Just How Welcome is the Job Market for College Grads?"

*Business Week* (November 9, 1992), citing studies by two Labor Department economists.

14. "The Entertainment Economy. America's Growth Engines: Theme Parks, Casinos, Sports, Interactive TV," *Business Week* (March 14, 1994), 61.

15. Mokyr, *The Lever of Riches*, 197-200.

16. Ibid., 224 and 189.

17. Robert Reich actually tested a version of this destructive choice, reported in "Do We Want the U.S. to be Rich or Japan Poor?" *WSJ* (June 18, 1990), A10. He offered groups choice A (By the year 2000, we grow 25 percent, but Japan grows 100 percent) versus choice B (We grow 10 percent, Japan grows 10.3 percent). A class of Harvard grad students, a conference of executives of large American corporations, a gathering of senior State Department bureaucrats, and a meeting of several hundred citizens of Belmont, Massachusetts all chose B. Only a group of economists chose A.

**Chapter 11**

1. Mokyr, *The Lever of Riches,* 179.

2. James Bovard, "The Sacred Cows That Keep Milk Prices High," *WSJ* (May 9, 1989), A22.

3. William Echikson, "The Price of Pâté," *World Monitor* (March 1992), 19. "One suggestion is to pay farmers to take care of the land instead of for producing more and more overpriced, unneeded meat...but it's not a popular idea in the countryside. ...it's very difficult to accept morally. We are here to live, to be productive.'"

4. Krugman, *Peddling Prosperity*, 8: "You don't progress as an economics professor by solving problems of the real economy...Instead, you progress by convincing your colleagues you are

clever...thus the most popular economic theories among the professors tend to be those that best allow for ingenious elaboration without fundamental innovation—ways to show that you are smart by putting old wine in new bottles, usually with fancier mathematical labels." This sounds like a hatchet-job expose of the folly of ivory-tower economics. But Krugman irrationally concludes that such professors are to be respected above what he calls the mere "policy entrepreneurs" and supply-side "cranks" who actually do solve the problems of the real economy. As you might guess, Krugman is a failed "policy entrepreneur" who has been very successful at "putting old wine in new bottles."

**Chapter 12**

1. Ruth Shalit, "What I Saw at the Devolution," *Reason* (March 1993), 27.

2. Carolyn Barta, *Perot and His People*. Summit: Fort Worth, 1993. S.C. Gwynne, "Who's In Charge Here?" *Time* (October 12, 1992), 43. "Dallas lawyer Thomas W. Luce III, Perot's confidant and loyal spear carrier for 20 years—the man Perot reportedly blamed for his earlier troubles—has returned to corporate law."

3. Casey Bukro, "Economist Sees Truth Deficit in Discussions of U.S. Debt," *Chicago Tribune* (July 6, 1993), 3-2. "Eisner [who says deficits don't matter] quoted the president as saying: 'I've been reading your stuff on budgets and agree with you, even if nobody else does.'"

4. Michael Kinsley, "Pete's Plan." *The New Republic* (October 25, 1993), p. 6.

5. "Supercuts," *The New Republic* (October 4, 1993), 7.

6. Lindley Clark, Jr., "How the Biggest Lobby Grew," *WSJ* (January 27, 1994), A12.

## Chapter 13

1. Robert Bartley, "Perot's Secret Plan Looks Familiar: Ask Bush, Hoover," *WSJ* (July 20, 1992), A14.

2. Ralph Nader, "Big Consumer. It's Time to Tap Government's Buying Clout," *Mother Jones* (November/December 1990), 37. "For example, consider 20 years of opposition to a clearly superior highway technology—a kind of pavement that can last three times longer."

3. "Time Hasn't Tamed Wally Hickel," *Business Week* (April 13, 1992), 68. "Southern California thirsts for water. Alaska is awash in it. So why not build a 2,000 mile undersea pipeline as flexible as a garden hose, and let Alaska turn on the spigot? At $100 billion...Hickel still likes it. 'The Romans did it,' he says, matter-of-factly. 'People have been moving water from where they have it to where they need it for years.'"

4. "Another Victim of Superfund," *WSJ* (February 23, 1993), A16.

5. Richard Stroup, "Newly Vulnerable to Superfund's Claws," *WSJ* (January 4, 1994), A18, quoting a study done in the late 1980s by the Institute for Civil Justice.

6. R. Howard, J. Matheson, and D. North, "The Decision to Seed Hurricanes," *Science* (June 16, 1972), 1191-1202.

7. "Changing the world," *Economist* (February 26, 1994), 85. Reporting on sessions at the American Association for the Advancement of Science's annual meeting. "Geo-engineering: deliberately modifying the climate so as to counteract inadvertent (and undesirable) changes that have already been made...[e.g.,] $CO_2$ could be pumped direct from power stations into the ocean depths...Mirrors in space or dust high in the atmosphere could block out some sunlight...A thin layer of dust could be put into the stratosphere relatively easily and cheaply by battleship guns

pointing straight up. There is evidence that this can successfully shield the earth from the sun. The eruption of Mount Pinatubo in 1991 threw 20m tonnes or so of muck into the atmosphere. That pall around the world...appears to have cooled the surface roughly as computer models would have predicted...enriching sunsets." "People who live in terror of waves of extinction and disaster seem unwilling even to contemplate doing something positive to avert them."

8. "The Threat From Space," *Economist* (September 11, 1993), 13.

9. Bernard Lewis, "The Roots of Muslim Rage," *Atlantic* (September 1990), 49.

10. "Egypt: Staying Away," *Economist (*February 19, 1994), 45. "Last week the Gamaa al-Islamiya, or Islamic Group, issued another in a series of warnings to foreign investors and tourists to get out of Egypt. It apologized in advance—to God, not the putative victims—for the spilling of blood. The new message was much more explicit than previous threats, and it equates foreign tourists with the [secular, non-fundamentalist] Egyptian regime. 'Anyone who helps a regime that is opposing Islam,' the group said in its faxed message, 'should receive the same punishment as the oppressors.'"

11. Joshua Hammer, "Mogadishu Postcard. Lone Rangers," *The New Republic* (November 22, 1993), 9-11. "Knight's platoon ...has been in Mogadishu...long enough to develop an abiding hatred for the Somalis they ostensibly came here to protect...Knight has a variety of phrases for what he'd like to do to them, including 'smoke 'em,' 'waste 'em' and 'wax 'em...I've returned fire on kids 10, 11, 12 years old. I've got no fucking choice'...you can't help getting the feeling that some [members of the platoon] are still spoiling for a fight."

12. Preena Khanna, "Scarcity of Organs for Transplant Sparks a Move to Legalize Financial Incentives," *WSJ* (September 8, 1992), B1.

13. "Child's Play," *WSJ* (July 27, 1993), A1. "Paltry pay sends turnover soaring among day-care professionals…'Parents can't afford to pay, teachers can't afford to stay, and the children are in jeopardy because of it.'"

14. Ruth Coxeter, "One Way to Limit Adventures in Baby-sitting," *Business Week* (August 2, 1993), 73. "A camouflaged video-surveillance system called Babywatch" is already being marketed.

15. Stephanie Forest, "Terry Murphy's Wonderful Wannabe Road Show. 'Street Basketball' is scoring as an effective, low-cost promotion," *Business Week* (November 22, 1993), 88.

16. Ben Bernanke, "Nonmonetary Effects of the Financial Crisis in the Propagation of the Great Depression," *Amer. Econ. Rev.* 73:3 (June 1983), 257-276.

17. Kenichi Ohmae, "The Vampire Summit," *WSJ* (July 7, 1993), A20.

18. John Carey, "Could America Afford the Transistor Today?" *Business Week* (March 7, 1994), 80.

19. Christina Duff, "Poor Prospects. In a Portland Hot Tub, Young Grads' Anxiety Bubbles to the Surface. Twentysomethings Find Life Bleak As They Sort Mail, Fret About Their Poverty," *WSJ* (July 28, 1993), A1.

20. Douglas Harbrecht and Owen Ullman, "Tough Talk. Are the U.S. and Japan Headed for a Trade War?" *Business Week* (February 28, 1994), 26.

**Chapter 14**

1. Two very conservative writers agree. In a symposium entitled "Working on Welfare" in *Reason* (April 1994), 22, Charles

Murray says: "I think we ought to put on the table Milton Friedman's old idea of the negative income tax...The negative income tax kicks in at the age of 18 whether or not you have a child. This means you have 16-year-old girls looking at their 18-year-old sisters and people in school and what do they see? They see some of these girls hitting 18 with no encumbrances in the form of babies, and, as endearing as those babies are, the 16-year-olds see that if they don't have any children they can spend this minimum income on all sorts of fun things. They see other women who are hitting 18 and who are spending their income on diapers and baby food."

Also, Friedman, in "A Monetary and Fiscal Framework For Economic Stability," 248, proposes: "A predetermined program of transfer expenditures...Such a program is exemplified by the present system of social security under which rules exist for the payment of old-age and unemployment insurance. Absolute outlays...will vary automatically over the cycle. They will tend to be high when unemployment is high and low when unemployment is low. Note 6: It may be hoped that the present complex structure of transfer payments will be integrated into a single scheme co-ordinated with the income tax and designed to provide a universal floor to personal incomes."

2. James Stuart, "Battle on the SNY. Coached by a Farmer Known as Peanuts, the People Came Out to Fight the Mississippi as it Threatened to Breach a Levee That Had Stood Firm for More Than a Century," *The New Yorker* (August 9, 1993), 35.

3. Tony Horwitz, "The Working Poor. Minimum Wage Jobs Give Many Americans Only a Miserable Life," *WSJ* (November 12, 1993), A1.

4. Peter F. Drucker, *The New Realities*. New York: Harper and Row (1989), 197.

# Bibliography

Bartley, Robert L. 1992. *The Seven Fat Years: And How to Do It Again.* The Free Press: New York.

Batra, Ravi. 1987. *The Great Depression of 1990.* New York: Simon & Schuster.

Bell, Trudy. "Jobs at Risk." *IEEE Spectrum*, August 1993, 18-35.

Bernstein, Peter. 1990. *The debt and the deficit: False alarms, real possibilities.* New York: Norton.

Brockway, George. 1991. *The End of Economic Man.* New York: HarperCollins.

Davidson, James Dale and Lord William Rees-Mog. 1994. *The Great Reckoning: Protect Yourself in the Coming Depression.* New York: Simon and Schuster.

Congdon, Tim. 1988. *The Debt Threat: The Dangers of High Real Interest Rates for the World Economy.* New York: Basil Blackwell.

Crittenden, Ann. 1993. *Killing the Sacred Cows: Bold Ideas for a New Economy.* New York: Penguin.

Dent, Harry S. Jr. 1993. *The Great Boom Ahead: Your Comprehensive Guide to Personal and business profit in the new era of prosperity.* New York: Hyperion.

Drucker, Peter F. 1990. *The New Realities.* New York: Harper and Row.

Eisner, Robert. 1986. *How Real is the Federal Deficit?* New York: The Free Press.

*The Total Incomes System of Accounts.* 1989. U. of Chicago.

*The Misunderstood Economy: What counts and how to count it.* 1994. Cambridge: Harvard Business School: Cambridge.

Ellis, John. 1976. *Eye-deep in Hell: Trench Warfare in World War I.* Baltimore: Johns Hopkins.

Figgie, Henry F. Jr. with Gerald J. Swanson, Ph.D. 1993. *Bankruptcy 1995: The Coming Collapse of America and How to Stop It*. Boston: Little, Brown.

Friedman, Benjamin M. 1988. *Day of Reckoning: The Consequences of American Economic Policy.* New York: Vintage.

Friedman, Milton. 1992. *Money Mischief.* San Diego: Harcourt Brace.

"A Monetary and Fiscal Framework for Economic Stability," *Amer. Econ. Rev.*, 38, 3, June 1948, 245-264.

Harrison, Bennett & Barry Bluestone. 1988, 1990. *The Great U-turn: Corporate Restructuring and the Polarizing of America.* USA: Basic Books.

Heilbroner, Robert. April 1993. "Anti-Depression Economics." *Atlantic.*

*21st Century Ccapitalism.* 1993. New York: Norton.

Hirsch, Fred. 1976. *The Social Limits to Growth*. Cambridge: Harvard U.

Jaikaran, Jacques S. 1992. *Debt Virus: A Compelling Solution to the World's Debt problems.* Lakewood, Colorado: Glenbridge.

Kennedy, Paul. 1993. *Preparing for the twenty-first century.* New York: Random House.

Krugman, Paul. 1994. *Peddling Prosperity*. New York: Norton.

Kuhn, Thomas S. 1970. *The Structure of Scientific Revolutions.* Second Ed. University of Chicago Press.

Luttwak, Edward N. 1993. *The Endangered American Dream: How to Stop the United States from Becoming a Third-World Country and How to Win the Geo-economic Struggle for Industrial Supremecy.* New York: Simon & Schuster.

Malabre, Alfred L., Jr. 1994. *Lost Prophets.* Boston: Harvard.

Mokyr, Joel. 1990. *The Lever of Riches: Technological Creativity and Economic Progress.* New York: Oxford U.

Morris, Charles R. 1990. *The Coming Global Boom: How to Benefit Now from Tomorrow's Dynamic World Economy.* New York: Bantam.

Peterson. Peter G. 1993. *Facing Up: How to Rescue the Economy from Crushing Debt and Restore the American Dream.* New York: Simon & Schuster.

Peterson, Wallace C. 1993. *Silent Depression: The Fate of the American Dream.* New York: Norton.

Pilzer, Paul Zane. 1990. *Unlimited wealth: The theory and practice of economic alchemy.* New York: Crown.

Ritter, Lawrence S. & William L. Silber. 1984. *Money.* Fifth and revised Ed. New York: Basic Books.

Schor, Juliet B. 1992. *The Overworked American: The Unexpected Decline of Leisure.* Basic: NY.

Schwarz, John E. and Thomas J. Volgy. 1992. *The Forgotten Americans: Thirty Million Working Poor in the Land of Oppotunity.* New York: Norton.

Thurow, Lester C. 1981. *The Zero-Sum Society: Distribution and the Possibilities for Economic Change.* New York: Penguin.

Vedder, Richard K. & Lowell E. Gallaway. 1993. *Out of work: Unemployment and Government in Twentieth-Century America.* New York: Holems & Meier.

Vilar, Pierre. 1991. *A History of Gold and Money* 1450-1920. New York: Verso.

# Appendix

## A Critical Review of Other Books on the Economy

The following books were on the shelves of your better local bookstores or libraries in early 1994. They fall into six categories:

***Read 'em and weep.*** The doomsayers. All is lost, it's our own damn fault, and there's nothing to be done but bar the door and load your AK-47.

***Hooray! We're all gonna be rich!*** Written before the Miracle of the Soft Landing, they noted that the West had indeed earned a huge abundance of real wealth, and the world economy should be booming. They have no clue as to why the wealth is sitting wasted on the shelves, and their books are disappearing.

***Soak the rich.*** Vanquish the deficit by raising taxes on corporations, the "rich," and middle-class social security recipients. Guess who? Liberal Democrats.

***Screw the poor.*** Vanquish the deficit by cutting welfare and social security and firing everyone in the government. Guess who? Conservative Republicans.

***Screw everyone.*** Vanquish the deficit by raising taxes <u>and</u> cutting spending. Written by the deficit mongers, who greatly prefer recessions to prosperity.

***Excuse me, but the deficit isn't quite as bad as it's made it out to be.*** The calm (zzzzz. . .) voices of reason who note certain flaws in the way the deficit is measured.

## READ 'EM AND WEEP.

James Dale Davidson & Lord William Rees-Mog. *The Great Reckoning: Protect Yourself in the Coming Depression.* 1994. New York: Simon & Schuster. Jim says that tight money is causing a Depression, so we'll have to balance the budget and tighten up even further. [Huh?] You can cover your own rear end by installing bullet-proof glass in your car and subscribing to one of his three newsletters.

Ravi Batra. *The Great Depression of 1990.* 1987. New York: Simon & Schuster. Following his kind of advice—raise taxes, cut spending—is what *gave* us the Great Recession.

Benjamin M. Friedman. *Day of Reckoning: The Consequences of American Economic Policy.* 1988. New York: Vintage. In effect, "It's 1988. I don't care if taxes and unemployment are down while wages and profits are up. We need to raise everyone's taxes immediately or we're sure to go to hell." As if Harvard needed another embarrassing professor. Benjamin should go on tour with his colleague who claims the million Americans who've been kidnapped and molested by spacemen need more sympathy and understanding.

Paul Kennedy. *Preparing for the Twenty-First Century.* 1993. New York: Random House. His advice: Don't bother—it's hopeless. He updates the guys in the 1970s who predicted we'd run out of everything by 1990. Paul says not only that we'll run out of food and starve, but that there's no solution—even a great new food technology wouldn't help, because technology is always bad.

## HOORAY! WE'RE ALL GONNA BE RICH!

Harry S. Dent, Jr. *The Great Boom Ahead: Your Comprehensive Guide to Personal and Business Profit in the New Era of Prosperity.* 1993. New York: Hyperion. The "Great Boom" will come because everyone is reaching their prime earning years, no one will get fired, everyone gets raises, and no one loses benefits—just like in the '60s-'80s. Someone should buy this guy a newspaper.

Charles R. Morris. *The Coming Global Boom: How to Benefit Now from Tomorrow's Dynamic World Economy.* 1990. New York: Bantam. While he realized that "bogeyman" deficits were OK and low interest rates were good, he literally did not conceive that attempts to kill the bogeyman while raising interest rates could be bad. Charles was so embarrassed by his timing on this one that he now says it is impossible for anyone to forecast or affect the national economy.

Paul Zane Pilzer. *Unlimited Wealth: The Theory and Practice of Economic Alchemy.* 1990. New York: Crown. Correct: Technology *can* make us rich. Wrong: Technology all by itself *will* make us rich.

Robert L. Bartley. *The seven fat years: And how to do it again.* 1992. The Free Press: New York. The economy got it right in the '80s—until the Grand Poobahs started following advice like Bartley's. He conveniently forgets all his on-the-record pronouncements in *The Wall Street Journal*, which he edits, advocating the money-supply squeezing that caused the recession.

## SOAK THE RICH.

John Kenneth Galbraith. *The Culture of Contentment.* 1992. Boston: Houghton Mifflin. The complacent white-collar class is the problem. The solution is a revolt by the underclass or stiff taxes: "Nothing so contributes to social tranquillity as some screams of anguish from the very affluent." And let's regulate the moneymen.

Robert Heilbroner. *21st Century Capitalism.* 1993. New York: Norton. The deficit is only an accounting problem. We need to utilize the public sector to provide adequate growth, raise taxes, and control wages.

Wallace C. Peterson. *Silent Depression: The Fate of the American.* 1993. New York: Norton. The problem is that middle-class jobs are disappearing or getting worse. The solution is more government jobs, better education, universal health care, and taxing the rich. Favors a Keynesian vs. austerity approach to the deficit.

Lester C. Thurow. *The Zero-Sum Society: Distribution and the Possibilities for Economic Change.* 1981. New York: Penguin. Tax the rich to provide guaranteed government jobs for all.

John E. Schwarz and Thomas J. Volgy. *The Forgotten Americans: Thirty Million Working Poor in the Land of Opportunity.* 1992. New York: Norton. The problem is people who work who remain poor. The solution is a higher minimum wage, higher earned income credit, and education support. Money comes from increased government revenues. Nothing in it for the rich.

## SCREW THE POOR.

Henry Figgie, Jr., with Gerald Swanson. *Bankruptcy 1995. The Coming Collapse of America and How to Stop It.* 1993. Boston: Little, Brown. See pages 48 and 77. I don't want to pick on poor Figgie anymore. He got wiped out and lost his company because it expanded into a cash-poor economy—*exactly the kind of economy his book advocates.* As ye sow, so shall ye reap, Henry.

Bennett Harrison & Barry Bluestone. *The Great U-turn: Corporate Restructuring and the Polarizing of America.* 1988, 1990. USA: Basic Books. The problem is corporate mergers. The solution is high-tech education and technological competitiveness. The new problem: their solution didn't work.

Richard K. Vedder & Lowell E. Gallaway. *Out of Work: Unemployment and Government in Twentieth-Century America.*

1993. New York: Holems & Meier. All government intervention in employment, monetary, and fiscal policy is bad. Return to pre-Keynesian, pre-1930 laissez faire. Invisible hand is all we need. Ignores deficit, debt, and taxes.

## SCREW EVERYONE.

Peter G. Peterson. *Facing Up: How to Rescue the Economy from Crushing Debt and Restore the American Dream.* 1993. New York: Simon & Schuster. Our sin is "profligacy." His solution is fiscal bloodletting: a balanced budget, sacrifice, reducing home interest deductions, raising the retirement age to 68, increasing sin taxes, capping business health-care deductions, imposing a gas tax of 50 cents a gallon, and cutting benefits for people with money.

Ann Crittenden. *Killing the Sacred Cows: Bold Ideas for a New Economy.* 1993. New York: Penguin. Solve everything by taxing corporations and the rich and using means testing for benefits. Cap domestic spending and cut military spending in half. Confuses "bold" with "mean."

Edward N. Luttwak. *The Endangered American Dream: How to Stop the United States from Becoming a Third-World Country and How to Win the Geo-Economic Struggle for Industrial Supremacy.* 1993. New York: Simon & Schuster. Problem is lawyers, under-educated workers, and our inner cities. Solution is trade wars, better education, federal VAT, and more government control over business decisions.

## EXCUSE ME, BUT THE DEFICIT ISN'T QUITE AS BAD AS IT'S MADE OUT TO BE.

Robert Eisner. *The Misunderstood Economy: What Counts and How to Count It.* 1994. Boston: Harvard Business School Press.

Accurate and to the point, as far as it goes. If you're going to buy one book by a mainstream economist, this is it.

Robert L. Heilbroner & Peter Bernstein. 1990. *The Debt and the Deficit: False Alarms, Real Possibilities.*

Tim Congdon. *The Debt Threat: The Dangers of High Real Interest Rates for the World Economy.* 1988. New York: Basil Blackwell. Debt causes high interest. Solution is fiscal reflation (but only by countries with low deficits) and lower interest rates.

## AND ONE INCOHERENT BOOK THAT GET'S IT RIGHT FOR THE WRONG REASON

Jacques S. Jaikaran. *Debt Virus: A Compelling Solution to the World's Debt Problems.* 1992. Lakewood, Colorado: Glenbridge. Issue "debt-free" money, because interest is usury and always bad.

# Acknowledgments

This book would not have been conceived, much less written, without a foundation we all take for granted—an American heritage of intellectual and political freedom that allows anyone who wants to stand up and holler. Throughout world history and even today, people presuming to criticize the power structure as I do here put their lives at risk. The worst I have to fear is criticism or disagreement. My education was largely funded by government grants and loans, an education remarkably richer than anyone born to my social stratum could have imagined fifty years ago. One of my universities, Berkeley, actually *encouraged* original thinking, an extraordinary position rarely encountered in any educational institution at any time or any place. The alumni office at my most recent university, TCU, has helped me develop my presentation by sending me to speak to TCU alumni groups around the country. I have given these audiences the credit they earned in chapter 12.

Before those formal talks, my friends and family had to put up with impassioned economic challenges over dinner and at other supposedly social get-togethers for two years. My fellow academics take these kinds of discussions as part of their job, but I fear my loved ones got more than they bargained for out of having a professor in the family. Talking with a range of people from blue-collar unemployed to retired diplomats helped me overcome the narrow range of expression and jargon often developed by those writing for academic journals.

At home, my wife, Mike, deserves even more of the credit that normally goes to a writer's spouse. She married a man with one of the most secure and institutionalized jobs in the world who then decided to forego tenure at a very well-to-do university in order to write provocative economics books. She is quite aware of not only the lack of benefits for writers, but the certainty of my making less than a fraction of the money a business professor makes. I guess she's happy enough to have a guy who jumps out of bed at seven every day eager to get readin' and writin' again. Such unconditional and devoted support, like that from my parents, is responsible for all of the chances I have taken in my life.

Early support from two editors at Harcourt Brace, Tom and Emily Thompson, was critical in my deciding to move these ideas from the discussion to career stage. From then on, the list of people includes the following: Janet Hildebrand, Jennifer and Paul Halpern, Larry Peters, John Harvey, Mike Butler, Ranga Ramasesh, Bob Boatler, Jean Walker, Devonna Finney, David Nelson, Melissa Allen, Bronson Davis, Sue Winter, Andy Kesling, David Van Meter, John Ohendalski, Cinda Cheney, Gene Gregory, John Clement, Al and Kay Meredith, Walter and Margaret Creamer, Dave McKendrick, David and Marja Meharry, Delores Nelson, Robert Skipper, Nestor Andriouk, Walter Fisk, and my TCU business students. At Berkeley and Stanford, I'm grateful to Phil Tetlock, Barry Staw, Charles O'Reilly, Jim March, and Bill Barnett. For the support they have given my research at various stages, I also thank the Hauss-Schmidlapp Trust, The Charles Tandy American Enterprise Center, The Fulbright Committee, and the MacArthur Foundation.

Finally, thanks to The Summit Group, the first publishers I presented this manuscript to. Mike Towle got back to me within two hours, and the enthusiasm they showed, and the rapid action he and company president Len Oszustowicz were able to take, have been gratifying. Now I can get on to my book on the other half of the national economy, the monetary as opposed to fiscal: *You're Fired! The Fed's War on Jobs, 1988-2002.*

# Index


## A

AARP, 49
 strongest lobbying organization, 291
Abundance, economics of, 161-163
Action, needed by constituents, 304
Addictions, need rehabilitation for, 326
Agencies, Federal Regulatory, 225
Aid to Families with Dependent Children (AFDC), 262
Alaska Airlines
 best airlines still lost money, 34, 206
Allocation of scarce resources, 16, xiii
Allocation of scarce resources, old science of, 282
American Association of Retired People, See AARP
American Economic Association, 77
American Heart Association, 349
American Lung Association, 349
American Mental Health Association, 349
American Zone, safe haven during wars, 319-320, 321
Angell, Wayne, 91, 131, 193, 280, 294
 responsible for recession, 152
Anorexics, compared to economic anorexics, 92
Anti-trust, hurt businesses, 169
Apple (Computers), 169
Arts, as wealth, 236-237
Assets, of United States greater than debts, 124

## B

Balance, of money and supply, 163, 164
Bankruptcy
not possible if assets greater than debts, 124

not prevented by productivity, 254
Bill of Rights, much of real wealth based on, 341
Blame, put where it is due, 293
Bond market, 96, 121
Brown, Jerry, 155
Buchanan, James, 131, 144
Budget
balanced, xii
government's lack of principles in setting, 257
Bundesbank (Germany), 19, 91
recession of, 132-134
Bureau of Alcohol, Tobacco, and Firearms (ATF), 226
Bureau of Labor Statistics, predicts fewer jobs requiring degree, 332
Bush, George, 10, 25, 44, 117, 279, 281, 292

## C

Cancer cure
parable of, 12, 17, 54-55, 59, 81, 287, 339, 342
parable of, x, 3-6
Capitalism, 171
central law of, 256
Carter, Jimmy, 155, 279
CDs, 35, 256
Certificates of Deposit, See CDs
Change
difficulty of, 247
is possible, 155
Children, safety for, 325
Civil Aviation Commission, and deregulation, 225
Class prejudice, 150-151
Clinton, Bill, 10, 44, 130, 172, 173, 279, 292
Clinton Health Plan, 27
will keep money supply tight, 238
Coca Cola, 112
College graduates, hard to find jobs for, 29
Communists, capitalists' economic competitors, 170
Compensation, unemployment, 255
Competitiveness, myth of poor U.S., 295-296
Congressmen, good among should be paid more, 263-268
Constitution, United States, worth a fortune, 189
Constitution, much of real wealth based on, 341
Consumer, psychology, 24
Consumer Price Index (CPI), 94, 95, 113, 204, 205, 206
measures effects of prices, 110
Contracts, government, 225
Corporate dividends, 338
money for doing nothing, 335
Cost of Living Index (COL), 204, 210
Council of Economic Advisors, 131
Crime
freedom from as wealth, 188
growing out of control, 241
prevention cheaper than punishment, 241-242
Criminal class, ever-widening, 241
Crowding out
theory of, 16, 118

*Currency*
*backed up by real wealth, 62*
*insufficient amount, 67*
*monetary system not likened to personal checking account, 13, 53*
*must be sound, 62*
*must retain value, 63*
*needs to be sound and sufficient, 94, 178, 202*
*sound, 163*
*what backs it up, 79-80*
*See also, Money*
*Customers, lack of, 32-33*
*Cybernetics, 254, 284, xiii*
*Cybernetics, defined, 209-211*

# D

*Darman, Roger, 25*
*Davidson, James, 154*
*responsible for recession, 152*
*Day-care, need for, 325-326*
*DeBeers, 198*
*hoards diamonds to keep prices up, 194*
*Debt, National, 76, 298, ix*
*an accounting error, 78*
*Congress' request to increase, 166*
*irrelevant as economic indicator, 56*
*many books written on the evils of, 145*
*too small, 68*
*Debt*
*dollar amount of United States, 67*
*monetizing of, 16, 70, 119*
*Defense*
*inflationary nature of, 103*
*layoffs in industry, 21*
*Deficit, false, 24, 59, 61, xii*
*has helped country, 66*
*misplaced fear of, 71*
*Deficit, National*
*ignores much of important wealth, 81*
*irrelevant as economic indicator, 56*
*is a myth, ix*
*is bogus, 7*
*no one hurt by, 10*
*not like personal checkbook, 79*
*not real deficit, 3*
*Deficit, real, 57*
*a shortfall in our money supply, 79*
*corrected by spending more and taxing less, 53*
*defined, 6*
*Deficit, trade, 186*
*Deficit-think, need to eliminate, 297*
*Deficit-to-GNP, ratio of, 20*
*Deficit*
*attack on hysteria caused by, 289*
*calculations are wrong, 83*
*lesser lies about, 117-137*
*myth of is harmful, 75*
*no one really hurt by, 43*
*no real hurts caused by, 282*
*not cause of inflation, 85*
*often confused with recession, 9*
*real, 288*
*reduction of, xiv*
*spending leads to prosperity, 19*
*what it measures, 57*
*Deficit mongers*
*and real wealth, 195*

criticism against, 286-290
defined, 153
Deficit reduction
destruction of real wealth by, 242-243
illness not cure, 128-129
Deflation, 95, 205-206
Demand, increased does not always raise prices, 167
Democracy, depends on educated and involved citizenry, 300
Depression
caused by money being printed too slow, 178
See also, Great Depression
Deregulation, 225, 225
Deutschemarks, 19, 102
Diamonds, 194, 198
Disasters, natural, 315
creative solutions to needed, 311-312
economic costs of, 311
inflationary nature of, 104
Disinflation, 16
Dole, Bob, 292
Dollar, still world standard, 68
Drucker, Peter, 350
Drugs, illicit, 326
Drug treatment centers, 327

E

Eccles, Marriner, 129-130, 330
Economy, should work fluidly, 254
Economics, old
needed in Eastern Bloc and Africa, 174
successful to an extent, 174
Economics
anti-deficit, 42
defined, 284
mathematical analysis of, 272
new, 10
new, xiii
no new theoretical developments in, 170
not keeping up with the times, 170-172
old, 10
old, xiii
supply-side, 16, 168
Western, abundance of goods and services in, 100
Economists, old, guide public policy, 39
Economists, not specific enough, 285
Education, neglected during deficit reduction, 234-237
Eisner, Robert, 77
Employment, encouraging as a means of increasing wealth, 221
Enemies, of sound economic policies, 286
Energy, solar, 314
Energy, creation of as greatest environmental threat, 314
Entertainment, as wealth, 236-237
Environment
costs of cleaning up, 313
preservation of, 314
regulations concerning, 225
Environmental Impact Statements (EIS), 313

# F


*Failures, costs of economic, 308*
*FDR, 130, 330*
*Fed, the*
  *See Federal Reserve Bank*
  *See Federal Reserve Board*
*Federal deficit*
  *See Deficit*
  *See Deficit, National*
*Federal Deposit Insurance, 35, 49*
*Federal Mutual Fund Insurance, no such thing as, 35*
*Federal purchasing, declined, 32*
*Federal Reserve Bank, 16, 96, 166*
*Federal Reserve Board, 25, 130-132*
  *caused recession by raising interest rates, 122*
  *soft landing fiasco, xi*
*Figgie, Henry F., 154, 280*
  *one of today's deficit mongers, 77*
  *predicts economic doom and gloom, 48*
  *responsible for recession, 152*
*Fisher, Irving, 40*
*Foreign trade, 107, 227, 228, 229, 261, 268-269*
  *efforts to block, 260*
*Free-Enterprise system, 343*
*Freedom*
  *is wealth, 350*
  *value of, 180, 184, 185*
*Free enterprise, 108, 215*
*Free trade, 43, 107, 226, 230*
*Friedman, Milton, 77, 164, 165, 166*
  *Nobel Prize winner, 101*


# G


*GATT, 33, 136, 267, 269, 344, 346*
*General Agreement on Tariffs and Trade,See GATT*
*General Motors, firing of workers, 250*
*Germany, too little money like United States, 214*
*Ghettos*
  *need for help in, 327-330*
  *using existing social structures in, 329*
*GNP, 20, 59*
*Goedel's Theorem, 172*
*Goedel, Kurt, 172*
*Gold, 199*
  *history of, 193-193*
  *idol of many, 115, 116*
  *no scarcity of, 162*
  *not real wealth, 192*
*Gold standard, 12, 158*
*Goods, need balance of money and, 97*
*Government*
  *duty to print money, 262*
  *economic goals of, 257-259*
  *function as money-maker, 222*
  *function as tragedy preventor, 223*
  *job to print sound currency, xi*
  *task is to create sound and sufficient currency, 178*
*Gramm, Phil, 294*
  *responsible for recession, 152*
*Great Depression, 9, 17, 18, 40, 129, 273, 294, 330*
  *economists' errors in, 281*

*Great Recession, 9, 26, 40, 42, 65, 210-211, 213, 220, 273, 277, x, 3, 6*
*caused only by deficit in our money supply, 53*
*scapegoats blamed for, 43*
*soft landing prescribed, 8*
*solution to spend more and tax less, 51-53*
*will not end quickly and painlessly, 47-48*
*Greenspan, Alan, 15, 25, 91, 132, 144, 156, 280, 294, 296, 331*
*caused soft landing, 131*
*chairman of the Federal Reserve Board, 25*
*dishonor's Eccles's memory, 130*
*knowingly caused recession, 131*
*leader of old economists, 45*
*responsible for recession, 152*
*will not change, 137*
*Gross Domestic Product, 242*
*Gross National Product, see GNP*

## H

*Happiness, value of, 180*
*Health*
*as wealth, 190*
*value of, 180*
*Health care, 237-239*
*crisis, 190, 191, 323-325*
*the Canadian model, 267*
*Health Maintenance Organizations, See HMOs*
*Heilbroner, Robert, 77*
*HMOs, 323*
*Hoover, Herbert, 309, 330*
*Housing starts, as an economic indicator, 38*
*Human welfare, as wealth, 191*
*Hyperinflation, 101, 113, 201*

## I

*IBM, 109, 169, 339*
*Ideas*
*bad, power of, 139-158*
*new, battle against, 283*
*Incomes*
*current disparities in, 349*
*proposed base in National Dividend plan, 346*
*Indexing, price, 112-113*
*Index of Leading Indicators, 39*
*Inflation, 341*
*caused by money being printed too fast, 178*
*defined, 214*
*fallacies about, 86-102*
*feared by old economists, 212*
*no relation to deficits, xii*
*not caused by deficit, 85*
*panic, 115*
*real causes of, 103-116*
*Infrastructure*
*improving, 232-234, 307, 310, 311*
*Innovators, struggles of, 240*
*Interest, on debt, 119*
*Interest rates, 34, 120-122*
*increased not caused by deficit, 85*
*supposed high not caused by deficit, 33*

*Internal Revenue Service, See IRS*
*International Business Machines, see IBM*
*International trade, 122-123*
*See also Foreign trade*
*Investing, value-added, 312*
*IRS, and financial reporting laws, 226*

## J

*Japan*
*bubble economy in, 134*
*recession in, 134*
*too little money like United States, 214*
*Jobs*
*creative destruction of, 246*
*loss of, 26-27, 32-33*
*See also Layoffs*
*See also Unemployment*
*scarcity of, 167, 332-333*
*Junk bonds, 42, 69*
*Just-in-Time*
*management technique, 126, 171*
*manufacturing technique from Japan, 218*

## K

*Kennedy, John F.*
*Kennedy, Paul, 104*
*Keynes, John Maynard, 143, 165, 330*
*stimulus approach, 14*
*Kinsley, Michael, 281*
*Krugman, Paul, 161, 172*
*Kuhn, Thomas, study of change, 155-156*

## L

*Labor, high productivity of, 296*
*Land, as wealth, 183*
*Laws*
*financial reporting, 226*
*some encourage crime, 226*
*See also Regulations*
*Layoffs, 21, 25*
*See also*
*Jobs> loss of*
*Unemployment*
*Letters*
*to Congress*
*address for, 303*
*from constituents is important, 299*
*Leveraged buyout, 18*
*Life, as wealth, 183*
*Love, as wealth, 188-189*

## M

*Macroeconomics, 14*
*important questions of, 271-272*
*Management, slovenly, as inflation causer, 111*
*Marxist economy, 157*
*Massachusetts Institute of Technology (MIT), study of physical resources, 162*
*McCracken, Paul, 131*
*Meals on Wheels, 349*
*Medicare*
*expenditures are transfer payments, 156*
*falsely considered as main cause of deficit, 49*
*Mergers-and-acquisitions raiders, 68*

*Microsoft, 339*
*Mieno, Yasushi, Japan's Paul Volcker, 134-135*
*Military, U.S., 320-321*
*Milliken, Michael, 42*
*Mitchell, George, 25*
*Mitchell-Dorman Tax Hike, 213*
*Monetarism*
*golden idol of, 143*
*main contemporary economic theory, 60*
*Monetizing*
*of government debt, 16, 70, 119*
*Money*
*decline in supply caused recession, 60*
*more must be printed, 200-201*
*more to life than, 350-352*
*must be balanced with wealth, 200*
*need balance of goods and, 97*
*need to print more, ix*
*not enough of it, 163-166*
*not real wealth, 208*
*thought of printing more often causes fear, 342*
*value of to individuals varies, 345*
*Western supply of, 268*
*what backs it up, 79-80*
*what makes it valuable, 198*
*See also, Currency*
*Moral problems, lies concerning, 125-128*
*Morris, Charles, 161, 172, 173*
*Multigenerational centers, suggested, 326*
*Mutual funds, 256*
*Mutually Assured Destruction, 216, 317, 322*
*threat of, 135*

# N

*NAFTA, 226, 227, 231, 232, 260, 267, 269, 277, 294, 309*
*NASA, 316*
*National Aeronautics and Space Administration, See NASA*
*National Debt, 298, ix*
*National Debt, Congress' request to increase, 166*
*National Dividend, xv, 342, 343*
*guaranteed minimum income proposed, 346*
*monetary lessons to America at large, 336*
*not like public assistance, 343*
*requirements for recipients, 347*
*supports people, 344*
*to replace Medicaid and food stamps, 346*
*will allow people to work for free, 348*
*National Income and Product Account (NIPA), 69*
*Natural resources, as wealth, 180-183*
*North American Free Trade Agreement, See NAFTA*

# O

*OPEC, 106, 115, 162*
*Organization of Petroleum Exporting Countries, See OPEC*

*Ostmarks, became deutschemarks, 102*
*Overseas Private Investment Corporation (OPIC), 317*

# P

*Payments, transfer, 56*
*Peace*
*economic value of, 215-216*
*is wealth, 350*
*value of, 179-180*
*world, 317, 318, 319*
*Peace Corps, 320*
*Perestroika, inhibited by envy, 151*
*Perot, Ross, 15, 43, 44, 45, 46, 117, 227, 279, 280, 281, 294, 309, 331*
*Personal utility functions, 345*
*Political Action Committee, 304*
*Politicians, need to change economic attitudes, 299*
*Poverty, illusion of by whole world, 268*
*Preservation, environmental, 314*
*President, writing to, 278*
*Price indexing, 112-113*
*Prices*
*not always raised by increased demand, 167*
*selling, 206-207*
*Productivity, 217-220*
*defined, 217*
*paradox of, 245-248*
*rapid increase in, 249*
*Progress, efforts to halt throughout history, 248*
*Prosperity, achieved by spending more and taxing less, 50*
*Protectionism, 106-107*
*Psychology, consumer, 24*
*Psychology, panic, 115*
*Purchasing power, 249*
*Purchasing Power Parity (PPP), 88, 203,204, 210*

# R

*Reagan, Ronald, 12, 67, 278*
*lowered taxes, 268*
*tripled deficit but brought prosperity, 76*
*tripled National Debt, 131*
*Reaganomics, 25*
*Real estate*
*commercial properties have lost value, 95*
*houses not selling, 37*
*prices decline in, 37*
*Recession, 99*
*caused by decline in money supply, 60*
*caused by Federal Reserve Board raising interest rates, 122*
*caused by forced raising of interest rates, 46*
*caused by money being printed too slow, 178*
*caused by shortage of money, xi*
*Greenspan's, 130*
*list of those responsible for, 152*
*not caused by deficit, ix*
*often confused with deficit, 9*
*rightful blame placed on old economists, 41*
*See also Great Recession*

*Recreation, as type of wealth, 330*
*Red Cross, 349*
*Regulations*
  *danger of, 223, 224*
  *environmental, 225, 313*
  *good ones are difficult to write, 223*
  *governmental, 221-226*
*Retirement, 252-253*
  *reasons for, 253*
*Rich, effects of printing more money on, 255*
*Riksbank (Sweden), 134*
*Ritter, Lawrence, 164, 165*
*Roberts, Paul Craig, 77*
*Roosevelt, Franklin Delano, See FDR*
*Rubles, 203*
*Rudman, Warren, 46, 130*
*Rudman, Warren, 148-149, 153*
*Rudman, Warren, 294, 296, 351*
  *responsible for recession, 152*
*Rules, See Regulations*
*Russia, barter society under Communism, 197*

## S

*Sacrifices, innocent, 156*
*Safe Havens, 319*
*Salvation Army, 349*
*Say's Law, 167, xiii*
*Scarcity*
  *eliminated by old economics, 14*
  *false assumption of, 159*
  *in Eastern Bloc and African countries, 173*
  *old economics of, 160*
*Schlesinger, Helmut, 91*
  *Germany's Alan Greenspan, 133*
*Security, as wealth, 186-187*
*Silber, William L., 164, 165*
*Silver, not real wealth, 192*
*Simon, Paul, 46, 130, 280, 294, 351*
  *responsible for recession, 152*
*Smoot-Hawley Trade Act, 43, 294*
  *high tariffs of, 331*
*Social bonds, as wealth, 188-189*
*Social justice, 239*
*Social Security, 30, 35, 250-251, 253, 262, 343*
  *direct transfer payments in, 309*
  *expenditures are transfer payments, 56*
  *falsely accused as main cause of deficit, 49*
  *lies of, 336-337, 336-337*
  *recipients punished for working, 259*
  *senior citizens voted against cuts, 291*
  *truth of, 337*
*Social Security Act of 1935, 130*
*Soft landing, 213*
  *caused by Alan Greenspan, 131*
  *disastrous, 173*
*Solar energy, 314*
*Solow, Robert, 77*
*Space exploration, need for, 316*
*Special Interest Groups (SIGS), not ignored by Congressmen, 263*
*Spending*
  *creative, 307-308, 307-308*
  *recommended increased, 309*

*Sports*
*as wealth, 236-237*
*teams proposed for ghettos, 329*
*Star Wars, 67*
*spending on, 42*
*Stock Market Crash of 1929, 40, 129, 132 , 330, 331*
*Stock Market Crash of 1987, 132 , 331*
*Stock Market Crash of 1989, 132*
*Subsidies, farm, ridiculousness of, 251-252*
*Supercollider, and loss of jobs, 28*
*Supply-side economics, 16, 168*
*Supply*
*abundance of, 89*
*does not always create demand, 167*

# T

*Taber, John, 130*
*Takahashi, Korekiyo, finance minister of Japan, 135*
*Taxes, 110-111*
*go higher and higher, 36*
*need less, 202, 257*
*need less, x*
*not inevitable, 20*
*one source of income for the government, 82*
*recommended lowering of, 308*
*Technology, 316*
*Third-party payers, 114*
*Third sector, not-for-profit employers, 349*
*Thurow, Lester, 281*
*debunking his myth of poor U.S. competitiveness, 295*
*Time and Motion, studies of, 218*
*Tobin, James, 77*
*Total Quality Management (TQM), 171*
*Trade, foreign, 227, 228, 229*
*Trade deficits, 186*
*Trade wars, 33, 332*
*Tsongas, Paul, 46, 49, 149, 280*
*responsible for recession, 152*

# U

*UN, See United Nations*
*Unemployment, 27-33*
*compensation, 255*
*of highly educated, 27-28*
*permanent through retirement, 252-253*
*Unions, 111*
*United Nations, 319*
*United States, financial system best in the world, 219*

# V

*Value, placed on intangibles, 180*
*Verbal warfare, needed against deficit mongers, 301*
*Versailles Treaty, 229*
*Volcker, Paul, 134*
*recession of, 25*
*Voting*
*necessary to change economy, 290-292, 302*

## W


Wages
  frozen for years, 31
  See also Incomes
Wal-Mart
  one out of fourteen jobs created there, 235
  Sears competitor, 169
Walt Disney, 112
War
  avoidance of as wealth, 187
  inflationary nature of, 103
  safety zones from, 319
War on Drugs, 326, 327
Washington, George, was bled to death, 146
Wealth, real, 7, 11, 57, 62 , 227, 242, 338
  abundance of, 7
  creating, 214
  defined, 177, 179
  exemplified, 177-195
  is not money, 208
  most inherited, 340
  must be matched by amount of money in circulation, 177
Wealth
  abundance of in U.S., ix
  added by the government, 270-271
  allocation of, 245
  distribution of our national, 307
  dollar value of United States, 67
  includes intangibles like peace and freedom, 350
  more to life than, 350-352
  no shortage of, 63-64
  unused, 340
  varies among individuals, 194
  varies among nations, 194
Weather, effects of, 315
Weimar Republic, 209
  not model of money supply, 201
  too much money in, 214
Welfare, recipients punished for working, 259
Wind farms, 314
Works Progress Administration (WPA), 18


## Y


Yen, 203


## Z


Zero-based budgeting, 258